Beyond 1848:

Readings in the Modern Chicano Historical Experience

Michael R. Ornelas
San Diego Mesa College

KENDALL/HUNT PUBLISHING COMPANY
2460 Kerper Boulevard P.O. Box 539 Dubuque, Iowa 52004-0539

CREDITS

for Mom

Contents

Contents

Preface

Not long ago during a serious discussion about non-static stereotypes one overly enthusiastic student offered a curious, and I thought humorous, definition for the class to consider. "Non-static stereotypes are images that don't cling," she said confidently. As I struggled to control myself and the rising banter that ensued among her classmates, I tried my best to assert that she was partly correct. Stereotypes change. They evolve as historical imperatives demand. My conviction, after nearly two decades of often fascinating discussions with students, is that stereotypes exist in part because they fill the void created by ignorance. In my estimation, there is an abundance of this affliction with regard to the circumstances and conditions of the Chicano presence in this country. As a result stereotypes persist in the vacuum.

I am hopeful that this collection is much more than an assault against stereotypes. Experience, contact and maturity usually erase these images among reasonable people. My hope is that readers and students of history will recognize the resiliency of a people scarcely known by American society in general. I am hopeful, too, that readers will come to some understanding of the complexity of the Chicano experience since the middle 19th century in order to elevate reason above fear and apprehension. Many students, many times, have admitted their "fear" of Chicanos.

The anthology is divided into two major sections. Section one includes historical themes and questions that are traceable to the middle 19th century. 1848 is our beginning primarily because this date marks a significant shift in Mexican and American relations. Of equal importance, in my view, is that the modern Chicano experience begins with an unprecedented dislocation from the nation of their birth through the forces of armed conflict and international treaty. The Americanization of the Southwest, accelerated by the imposition of United States sovereignty over the region, profoundly re-shaped the experience of the inhabitants of the region, the first Chicanos. Numerous historians, including Douglas Monroy, Richard Griswold del Castillo, and David Montejano, among others, have uncovered historic patterns of subordination and downward mobility during these early years. It can be convincingly argued that an almost total racial, economic and political subordination was firmly in place by the beginning of the 20th century. Each of the articles in this section support and expand upon the subordination process and resistance to it. For the most part this is the Chicano experience in the 19th century.

Some years ago Sociologist Rodolfo Alvarez proposed that native and immigrant Mexicans, similar to African Americans and Native Americans, lacked the freedom to negotiate a social position with American society. As a result of decades of erosion of the Chicano economic and political base during the 19th century, subsequent Mexican immigrants entered into a pre-defined subordinate socio-economic and political position. Their status was set before their arrival in the United States. Several of the selections in section two elaborate on the continuity of the subordination process into the 20th century. Others explore patterns of resistance, accommodationist strategies, and the evolution of the Chicano response to challenges of the later eras. What emerges is that Chicanos have demonstrated a remarkable resiliency to adapt, resist, challenge and endure in the face of disturbingly oppressive conditions at every turn. This is their legacy for the future and to humanity. American society, as it faces the next century and witnesses diversity emerge at every corner, may need to pay attention. How can the United States endure as a leader in a world of staggering cultural diversity if it fails to resolve its own political contradictions?

While I have assembled this collection I have incurred some debts that I would like to acknowledge. Richard Griswold del Castillo, friend, colleague and prolific historian, was always willing to answer my questions during my reading and research project during my recent sabbatical leave at San Diego State University. My conception of this project began under his guidance. My friend and colleague at Mesa College, Joel Pérez, deserves my genuine thanks for his able assistance on the technical end. Richard Lou, friend and colleague at Mesa College gave generously of his time and photographic skill. José E. Limón, Douglas Monroy, Thomas E. Sheridan and Ricardo Romo all gave generously of their fine work. This collection is a tribute to the work of all of the contributors as well. Macedonio Arteaga and Alicia Chávez are also owed my thanks for their generous giving of their time and efforts as they raise their new child, Iyari. And I would like to thank my wife, Eva. She is a model for our lovely children, Diego Armando and Bianca Maya, inheritors of the Chicano legacy presented in this collection.

Michael Raúl Ornelas
Chicano Studies Department
San Diego Mesa College

I

1848-1900

The following articles from the Treaty of Guadalupe Hidalgo are included here in order to indicate the degree to which the United States government attempted, at least ideally, the incorporation of Mexico's northern territories and its former citizens. These articles also indicate that those affected by its provisions were included with all the rights of citizens, an unprecedented incorporation of non-whites as full citizens.

The Treaty of Guadalupe Hidalgo
Selected Articles

Mexico: February 2, 1848

Treaty of Guadalupe Hidalgo. Treaty of Peace, Friendship, Limits, and Settlement (with additional and secret article which was not ratified), with Map of the United Mexican States and with Plan of the Port of San Diego, signed at Guadalupe Hidalgo February 2, 1848. Originals of the treaty and additional secret article in English and Spanish.

Treaty and additional and secret article submitted to the Senate February 23, 1848. Ratified by the United States March 16, 1848. Ratified by Mexico May 30, 1848. Ratifications exchanged at Querétaro May 30, 1848. Proclaimed July 4, 1848.

Article V.

The Boundary line between the two Republics shall commence in the Gulf of Mexico, three leagues from land, opposite the mouth of the Rio Grande, otherwise called Rio Bravo del Norte, or opposite the mouth of its deepest branch, if it should have more than one branch emptying directly into the sea; from thence, up the middle of that river, following the deepest channel, where it has more than one, to the point where it strikes the southern boundary of New Mexico; thence, westwardly, along the whole southern boundary of New Mexico (which runs north of the town called *Paso*) to its western termination; thence, northward, along the western line of New Mexico, until it intersects the first branch of the River Gila; (or if it should not intersect any branch of that river, then, to the point on the said line nearest to such branch, and thence in a direct line to the same) thence down the middle of the said branch and of the said river, until it empties into the Rio Colorado, following the division line between Upper and Lower California, to the Pacific Ocean.

The southern and western limits of New Mexico, mentioned in this Article, are those laid down in the Map, entitled *"Map of the United Mexican States, as organized and defined by various acts of the Congress of said Republic, and constructed according to the best authorities. Revised Edition. Published at New York in 1847 by J. Disturnell:"* of which Map a Copy is added to this Treaty, bearing the signatures and seals of the Undersigned Plenipotentiaries. And, in order to preclude all difficulty in tracing upon the ground the limit separating Upper from Lower California, it is agreed that the said limit shall consist of a straight line, drawn from the middle of the Rio Gila, where it unites with the Colorado, to a point on the coast of the Pacific Ocean, distant one marine league due south of the southernmost point of the Port of San Diego, according to the plan of said port, made in the 1782, by Don Juan Pantoja, second-sailing master of the Spanish fleet, and published at Madrid in the year 1802, in the Atlas to the voyage of the schooners *Sutil* and *Mexicana*: of which plan a copy is hereunto added, signed and sealed by the respective plenipotentiaries.

In order to designate the Boundary line with due precision, upon authoritative maps, and to establish upon the ground landmarks which shall show the limits of both Republics, as described in the present Article, the two Governments shall each appoint a Commissioner and a Surveyor, who, before the expiration of one year from the date of the exchange of ratifications of this treaty, shall meet at the Port of San Diego, and proceed to run and mark the said boundary in its whole course, to the mouth of the Rio Bravo del Norte. They shall keep journals and make out plans of their operations; and the result, agreed upon by them, shall be deemed a part of this Treaty, and shall have the same force as if it were inserted therein. The two Governments will amicably agree regarding what may be necessary to these persons, and also as to their respective escorts, should such be necessary.

The Boundary line established by this Article shall be religiously respected by each of the two Republics, and no change shall ever be made therein, except by the express and free content of both nations, lawfully given by the General Government of each, in conformity with its own constitution.

ARTICLE VIII.

Mexicans now established in territories previously belonging to Mexico, and which remain for the future within the limits of the United States, as defined by the present treaty, shall be free to continue where they now reside, or to remove at any time to the Mexican Republic, retaining the property which they possess in the said territories, or disposing thereof, and removing the proceeds wherever they please; without their being subjected, on this account, to any contribution, tax or charge whatever.

Those who shall prefer to remain in said territories, may either retain the title and rights of Mexican citizens, or acquire those of citizens of the United States. But they shall be under the obligation to make their election within one year from the date of the exchange of ratifications of this treaty: and those who shall remain in the said territories, after the expiration of that year, without having declared their intention to retain the character of Mexicans, shall be considered to have elected to become citizens of the United States.

In the said territories, property of every kind, now belonging to Mexicans, not established there, shall be inviolably respected. The present owners, the heirs of these, and all Mexicans who may hereafter acquire said property by contract, shall enjoy with respect to it, guaranties equally ample as if the same belonged to citizens of the United States.

ARTICLE IX.

The Mexicans who, in the territories aforesaid, shall not preserve the character of the citizens of the Mexican Republic, conformably with what is stipulated in the preceding article, shall be incorporated into the Union of the United States and be admitted, at the proper time (to be judged of by the Congress of the United States) to the enjoyment of all the rights of citizens of the United States according to the principles of the Constitution; and in the mean time shall be maintained and protected in the free enjoyment of their liberty and property, and secured in the free exercise of their religion without restriction.

ARTICLE X.
(prior to its omission by the United States Senate)

All grants of land made by the Mexican Government or by the competent authorities, in territories previously appertaining to Mexico, and remaining for the future within the limits of the United States, shall be respected as valid, to the same extent that the same grants would be valid, if the said territories had remained within the limits of Mexico. But the grantees of land in Texas, put in possession thereof, who, by the reason of circumstances of the country since the beginning of the troubles between Texas and the Mexican Government, may have been prevented from fulfilling all the conditions of their grants, shall be under the obligation to fulfill the said conditions within the periods limited in the same respectively; such periods to be now counted from the date of the exchange of ratifications of this treaty: in the default of which the said grants shall not be obligatory upon the State of Texas, in virtue of the stipulations contained in this Article.

The foregoing stipulation in regard to grantees of land in Texas, is extended to all grantees of land in the territories aforesaid, elsewhere than in Texas, put in possession under such grants; and, in default of the fulfillment of the conditions of any such grant, within the new period, which, as is above stipulated, begins with the day of the exchange of ratifications of this treaty, the same shall be null and void.

The Mexican Government declares that no grant whatever of lands in Texas has been made since the second day of March one thousand eight hundred and thirty six; and that no grant whatever of lands in any of the territories aforesaid has been made since the thirteenth day of May one thousand eight hundred and forty-six.

After United States Senate ratification of the Treaty of Guadalupe Hidalgo Mexican and American commissioners met to discuss and explain changes and omissions to the treaty. Of particular interest to Mexican officials was the alteration of Article IX and the omission of Article X. The Protocol of Querétaro, originally an oral explanation, was subsequently placed into written form and submitted to Mexican commissioners. Apparently satisfied that these changes would not result in subsequent denials of the intent of the articles, the Mexican commissioners accepted what came to be known as the Protocol of Querétaro.

The Protocol of Querétaro
May 26, 1848

PROTOCOL

In the city of Querétaro on the twenty sixth of the month of May eighteen hundred and forty-eight at a conference between Their Excellencies Nathan Clifford and Ambrose H. Sevier Commissioners of the United States of America, with full powers from their Government to make to the Mexican Republic suitable explanations in regard to the amendments which the Senate and the Government of the said United States have made in the treaty of peace, friendship, limits and definitive settlement between the two Republics, signed in Guadalupe Hidalgo, on the second day of February of the present year, and His Excellency Don Luis de la Rosa, Minister of Foreign Affairs of the Republic of Mexico, it was agreed, after adequate conversation respecting the changes alluded to, to record in the present protocol the following explanations which Their aforesaid Excellencies the Commissioners gave in the name of their Government and in fulfillment of the Commission conferred upon them near the Mexican Republic.

FIRST.

The American Government by suppressing the IXth article of the Treaty of Guadalupe and substituting the III. article of the Treaty of Louisiana did not intend to diminish in any way what was agreed upon by the aforesaid article IXth in favor of the inhabitants of the territories ceded by Mexico. Its understanding that all of that agreement is contained in the IIId article of the Treaty of Louisiana. In consequence, all the privileges and guarantees, civil, political, and religious, which would have been possessed by the inhabitants of the ceded territories, if the IXth article of the Treaty had been retained, will be enjoyed by them without any difference under the article which had been substituted.

7

SECOND.

The American Government by suppressing the Xth article of the Treaty of Guadalupe did not in any way intend to annul the grants of lands made by Mexico in the ceded territories. These grants. notwithstanding the suppression of the article of the Treaty, preserve the legal value which they may possess; and the grantees may cause their legitimate titles to be acknowledged before the American tribunals.

Conformably to the law of the United States, legitimate titles to every description of the property personal and real, existing in the ceded territories, are those which were legitimate titles under the Mexican law in California and New Mexico up to the 13th of May 1.846, and in Texas up to the 2d March 1.836.

THIRD.

The Government of the United States by suppressing the concluding paragraph of the article XIIth of the Treaty, did not intend to deprive the Mexican Republic of the free and unrestrained faculty of ceding, conveying or transferring at any time (as it may judge best) the sum of twelve millions of dollars which the same Government of the United States is to deliver in the places designated by the amended article.

And these explanations having been accepted by the minister of Foreign Affairs of the Mexican Republic, he declared in name of his Government that with the understanding conveyed by them, the same Government would proceed to ratify the Treaty of Guadalupe as modified by the Senate and Government of the United States. In testimony of which their Excellencies the aforesaid Commissioners and the Minister have signed and sealed in quintuplicate the present protocol.

Richard Griswold del Castillo's article discusses the ways in which the federal and state courts have interpreted provisions of the Treaty of Guadalupe Hidalgo since 1848. As Griswold reveals, most of the decisions handed down by the courts resulted in the erosion of rights originally guaranteed through this international treaty. Of particular importance is how Griswold links changes in interpretations with changes in United States political history.

The U.S. Courts and the Treaty
Richard Griswold del Castillo

If the treaty was violated by this general statute enacted for the purpose of ascertaining the validity of claims derived from the Mexican government, it was a matter of international concern, which the two states must determine by treaty or by other such means.
Barker v. Harvey (1901)

Conquest gives a title which the courts of the conqueror cannot deny, whatever the private or speculative opinion of individual may be.
Chief Justice Marshall
United States v. Alcea Band of Tillamoks(1946)

When it was promulgated by President James K. Polk on July 4, 1848, the Treaty of Guadalupe Hidalgo achieved the status of a law of the United States. Since its ratification more than two hundred federal, state, and district court decisions have interpreted the treaty, expanding and changing the meaning of the original treaty.

A review of selected U.S. court cases shows that Anglo American land corporations and the state and federal governments were the primary beneficiaries of the legal system's interpretation of the Treaty of Guadalupe Hidalgo.[1] Although some Indians and Hispanics lodged lawsuits citing the treaty guarantees, the vast majority of them were unsuccessful in their efforts.

The U.S. courts' interpretation of the treaty roughly paralleled the political history of the United States. The Civil War and Reconstruction period was one of great expansion in civil and political rights in American jurisprudence with the ratification of the 13th, 14th, and 15th amendments, abolishing slavery, defining citizenship, and expanding the electoral franchise. The period after Reconstruction until the early 1930s was largely one of conservative politics, with the exception of a progressive reform movement in the first two decades of the twentieth century. Juridical settlements mirrored a society caught up in a struggle for wealth and preoccupied with the supremacy of the white race. Examples of this conservative trend include *Plessy v. Ferguson*, which affirmed segregation in public facilities; *In re Debs*, which undercut labor unions; and *United States v. E. C. Knight Co.*, which vitiated anti-trust legislation. Since 1930, there has been periodic resurgence and decline of liberal and conservative political philosophies. During this period the U.S. Supreme Court lost its liberal majority and became more balanced politically, and neither political party has enjoyed a monopoly of both the legislature and the presidency.

The U.S. Supreme Court decided almost half the major cases interpreting the Treaty of Guadalupe Hidalgo. The political evolution of the Court influenced how the justices regarded the treaty. Prior to the Civil War, the Supreme Court had been concerned primarily with the nation-state relationship and the preservation of the union. During the tenure of Chief Justice Taney, the Court sought ways to avoid a civil war over the issue of slavery and sectionalism. The sanctity of property was foremost in their reasoning. For example, when they rendered their famous *Dred Scott* opinion in 1857, they stated that Congress had no power to exclude slaves as property from the territories.

After the Civil War the Court turned to the relationship between government and private business and tended to favor the latter. Many Supreme Court decisions opposed the government's attempts to regulate or restrain the excesses of capitalism. Not surprisingly, in the decades following Reconstruction, the Court opposed interpretations of the Treaty of Guadalupe Hidalgo that might hinder the growth of the American economy in the Southwest.

The Supreme Court changed its views in 1937 when it abandoned its opposition to government programs that challenged private business. Increasingly thereafter the Court adopted a more balanced opinion of the role of government in the economy.[2] After World War II the Court was more inclined to concentrate on the relationship of the individual to the government, and specifically on civil rights.

The court cases decided by district, territorial, and state supreme courts usually reflected the pressures of regional interests and local concerns. Most cases came from courts in California and dealt with the issue of property rights, a concern emerging out of that state's growing population pressures on natural resources. Court cases coming from Arizona and New Mexico focused on Indian- and tribal-rights questions as well as challenges to Hispano community grants. Cases decided in Texas reflected a recognition of the Mexican common-law traditions in that state but only those that did not conflict with Anglo-American rule.

1848-1889

In the first period of juridical interpretation, federal and state courts issued judgments that tended to interpret the treaty liberally. Generally the courts bolstered the status of the treaty as a document confirming and protecting rights. On the subject of property rights, the courts sought to clarify the meaning of the language in Article VIII and the Protocol of Querétaro. In 1850 the California Supreme Court ruled that an inchoate title (i.e., not clearly a legal Mexican title) was protected by the treaty and that its legitimacy could be affected or questioned only by the federal government. This construction went far beyond the implied guarantees in the stricken Article X and the Protocol of Querétaro. Even landholders lacking clear titles would be protected until the grants could be examined by the U.S. courts.[3] Sixteen years later, in *Mintern v. Bower et al.*, the California court further expanded this concept to include perfected land grants. In that case the court decided "that perfect titles to lands which existed at the date of the treaty of Guadalupe Hidalgo in Mexicans then established in California, were guaranteed and secured to such persons not only by the law of nations, but also by the stipulations of that treaty."[4] This meant that those individuals who held perfect titles need not submit them before the Board Of Land Commissioners established in 1851 to validate titles. This position, which recognized the primacy of federal treaty obligation over congressional legislation, guided California until it was overturned in the federal case of *Botiller v. Dominguez* in 1889.

Other court findings also interpreted the Treaty of Guadalupe Hidalgo liberally. In *United States v. Reading* (1855) the Supreme Court ruled that the treaty protected the property rights of a Mexican citizen who had fought in the U.S. Army against Mexico at the very time his land grant was pending certification by the Mexican government. Because of the treaty's protection, the Court ruled that his military action did not result in a forfeit of land rights. In *Palmer v. United States* (1857), the Court argued that the dates given in the Protocol of Querétaro were not limiting and that in New Mexico and California legitimate titles might have been made by Mexican officials after May 13, 1846. In *Townsend et al. v. Greeley* (1866) the Court held that town or community grants as well as private ones were protected by the treaty.

In other rulings the Court interpreted the treaty to legitimize the transfer of Mexican law to the conquered Southwest. In *United States v. Moreno* (1863), the Supreme Court affirmed that the treaty protected land grants that were legitimate under Mexican law; in 1884 the Court ruled that treaty stipulations did not invalidate the powers of local officials, acting under Mexican law, to make legitimate land grants prior to the implementation of American laws, and in *Philips v. Mound City* the Court advanced the position that the treaty also protected partitions and divisions of land made under Mexican law prior to July 4, 1848.[6]

In this period the implications of the treaty for the civil rights of former Mexican citizens were also a concern of the courts. In the 1870 *De la Guerra* case, the California court interpreted the treaty as confirming U.S. citizenship for Mexicans. In New Mexico the presence of a large group of Hispanicized Pueblo Indians complicated the issue of citizenship. The territorial government in New Mexico did not give Indians citizenship, but in 1869 the New Mexico Supreme Court ruled that by virtue of the treaty, the Pueblo Indians were citizens of the territory and of the United States. In *United States v. Lucero* the justices analyzed the treaty extensively to support this view. After reviewing Article

9, Justice Watts, writing for the court, stated: "This court, under this section of the treaty of Guadalupe Hidalgo, does not consider it proper to assent to the withdrawal of eight thousand citizens of New Mexico from the operation of the law, made to secure and maintain them in their liberty and property, and consign their liberty and property to a system of laws and trade made for wandering savages."[7] The justices thus proposed that the Pueblo Indians were not tribal Indians subject to laws administered by the Department of Indian Affairs. This interpretation regarding the treaty status of the Pueblo Indians was reaffirmed by the New Mexico Supreme Court in 1874 but reversed in 1940.[8]

A narrower view of the meaning of the treaty in this period was largely limited to the question of the application of the treaty to Texas. In 1856 the Supreme Court heard a case involving a land-grant claim in Texas that sought remedy under the treaty. In *McKinney v. Saviego* the Court decided that the treaty did not apply to Texas lands. Justice Campbell, writing for the Court, summarized Article VIII in the treaty and asked: "To what territories did the high contracting parties refer to in this article? We think it clear that they did not refer to any portion of the acknowledged limits of Texas." The Court argued that Texas had been recognized by the U. S. government as an independent country and had been annexed as a state prior to the Mexican War. Therefore, the Treaty of Guadalupe applied only to those territories annexed by the United States in 1848. This interpretation was sustained by several subsequent decisions, and it stands as law today.[9]

1889-1930

A liberal view of the meaning of the Treaty of Guadalupe Hidalgo prevailed in the period prior to the landmark judgment of *Botiller v. Dominguez* in 1889. This case inaugurated a decidedly conservative attitude regarding the extent to which the treaty was important in protecting the property of the former Mexican citizens. The most far-reaching impact of the *Botiller* case was summarized in the statement written by Justice Miller for the Court.

> If the treaty was violated by this general statute (the Land Law of 1851), enacted for the purpose of ascertaining the validity of claims derived from the Mexican government, it was a matter of international concern, which the two states must determine by treaty or by such other means as enables one state to enforce upon another the obligations of a treaty. This court, in cases like the present, has no power to set itself up as the instrumentality for enforcing the provisions of a treaty with a foreign nation which the government of the United States, as a sovereign power, chooses to disregard.[10]

In *Botiller v. Dominguez* the Supreme Court held that the sovereign laws of the United States took precedence over international treaties. This appeared to be in direct contradiction of the Constitution, which (in Article VI, Section 2 and Article III, Section 2, Clause I) gave treaties the same status as the Constitution. The Supreme Court's decision, some argued, sanctioned the confiscation of property and violated the due process provision of the Constitution. Nevertheless the case became an important precedent guiding the Court in its future interpretation of conflicts between treaty obligations and domestic laws.[11] The judgment in *Botiller* declared that the American courts had no responsibility to hear cases involving violations of the Treaty of Guadalupe Hidalgo. To resolve conflicts arising over the treaty there was no recourse but to international diplomatic negotiation.

Eventually the *Botiller* case was cited as a basis for denying lands to the California Mission Indians, who had legal title to their ancestral lands under Mexican law but had not filed their title before the Land Commission as stipulated in the 1851 law. For the Court the right of the government to provide "reasonable means for determining the validity of all titles within the ceded territory" superseded the inhabitant's treaty rights.[12]

Just as the *Botiller* decree became a rule of law in subsequent years, the courts continually reconfirmed the right of Congress and the courts to implement the treaty through laws "to ascertain the legitimacy of title." If these implementing laws ran counter to the protections of the treaty, the congressional laws would take precedence. This principle was affirmed in *California Powderworks v. Davis* (1894), in *United States v. Sandoval et al.* (1897), and in *Arisa v. New Mexico and Arizona Railroad* (1899).[13]

The courts also interpreted the treaty so that it would be more restrictive as to the land rights claimed by former Mexican citizens and those who had acquired their lands. The Supreme Court determined that the treaty "did not increase rights" and that "no duty rests on this government to recognize the validity of a grant to any area of greater extent than was recognized by the government of Mexico."[14] This in itself might have been a reasonable assertion but it hinged on the government's view of the scope of legitimate Mexican laws, and increasingly the courts took a narrow view. One question that arose was whether Mexican landholders would be protected from squatters and speculators during the time it took for the U.S. courts to determine the validity of their Mexican titles. In 1901, in *Lockhart v. Johnson*, the Supreme Court ruled that neither Articles VIII or IX gave such protection. In this case a portion of the Cañada de Cochiti land-grant in New Mexico had been purchased from the U.S. government by a mining company while the grant was pending action by the Surveyor General's Office. An American who had purchased the original grant argued that the mining company's occupancy had violated the Treaty of Guadalupe Hidalgo. Justice Peckham stated for the Supreme Court: "(T)here are no words in the treaty with Mexico expressly withdrawing from sale all lands within claimed limits of a Mexican grant, and we do not think there is any language in the treaty which implies a reservation of any kind."[15]

This 1901 doctrine, that the treaty did not protect land claims from public sale, differed from the long-standing policy of the General Land Office, which had interpreted the treaty to mean that "all lands embraced within the Mexican and Spanish grants were placed in a state of reservation for the ascertainment of rights claimed under said grant."[16] In California the courts also ruled that the treaty would not provide special protection for Mexicans who owned property. In 1913 the California State Supreme Court argued that "the treaty of Guadalupe Hidalgo requires only that the rights of Mexican grantees in their property shall be equal to that of citizens of the United States." And in 1930 it ruled that the treaty did not bind the government to follow the Spanish or Mexican statute of limitations with regard to land or water rights.[17]

Article X in the original treaty, which was stricken out by the U.S. Senate, was not part of the official document proclaimed as law in 1848. Among other things Article X had specified that "all grants of land made by the Mexican government . . . shall be respected as valid, to the same extent that the same grants would be valid, if the said territories had remained within the limits of Mexico." The striking of this article emerged as a point of law for the courts and became a basis for rejecting land claims.

In *Interstate Land Co. v. Maxwell Land Co.* (1891) the U.S. Supreme Court rejected the assertion that a grant was invalid because it had been declared so by a Mexican law prior to 1848. After analyzing the circumstances surrounding the removal of Article X by the Senate, including President Polk's message to Congress, the Court stated that "this claim was one of the class which was expressly refused to be recognized by the treaty" (more accurately by the absence of Article X).[18] In another case, *Cessna v. United States et al.* in 1898, the Supreme Court interpreted the absence of Article X to rule against a New Mexican land claimant whose grant had been rejected by the Court of Private Land Claims. Accordingly, "when the U.S. received this territory under the Treaty of Guadalupe Hidalgo, they refused to recognize as still valid and enforceable all grants which had been assumed to be made prior thereto by the Mexican authorities. Article X, as proposed by the commissioners, was rejected by this government."[19]

Thus the absence of Article X, with its specific guarantees of due process after 1848 under Mexican law provided a basis for the courts to restrict further the meaning of the treaty. The Protocol of Querétaro, which had been drafted to assure the Mexican government that the spirit of Article X would be retained, was not a matter for future juridical consideration.

The final area of conservative interpretation of the treaty in the period 1889-1930 was in Indian affairs. Three cases illustrate the trend. In 1897 the Supreme Court construed the treaty so as to benefit the government and undercut historic understandings between Mexican and Indian communities in New Mexico. The pueblo of Zia claimed proprietory and grazing rights in northern New Mexico by virtue of their use of land with the agreement of the Mexican settlers. The Court, however, ruled that, by ceding Mexican lands to the public domain the treaty provided the basis for revoking these prior concessions as well as for denying any claims of land ownership on the part of the Indians.

The Court also moved to question any extension of citizenship rights to Indians. In an 1869 judgment the New Mexican territorial court ruled that the treaty conferred U.S. citizenship on Pueblo Indians. In a 1913 case the Supreme Court stated that "it remains an open question whether they have become citizens of the U.S." Also, "we need not determine it now, because citizenship is not in itself an obstacle to the exercise by Congress of its power to enact laws for the benefit and protection of tribal Indians as dependent peoples."[20] The next year the Court ruled that the California Indians had not been given citizenship by the Treaty of Guadalupe Hidalgo. Chief Justice White attacked the argument that the California Indians were entitled to citizenship by virtue of the treaty as "so devoid of merit as not in any real sense to involve the construction of the treaty." A later court arrived at similar conclusions regarding the status of the Pueblo Indians in New Mexico.[21]

Although the bulk of court constructions of the treaty from 1880 to 1930 were based on a conservative reading of the document, there were a few cases in which the courts expanded its meaning. Despite earlier indications by the U.S. Supreme Court, in *McKinney v. Saviego*, that the treaty would not apply to Texas, the Texas Supreme Court made a series of rulings that validated the treaty as applying to certain regions of the state. In *Texas Mexican Railroad v. Locke*, the Texas Supreme Court ruled that Mexicans holding valid titles on March 2, 1836, and continuing to hold them until July 4, 1848, "were protected in them by Article 8 of the Treaty of Guadalupe Hidalgo." In a 1914 verdict the same court ruled that the treaty had the "force of law in Texas," and this same principle was affirmed by at least two other Texas rulings.[22] In these decisions the Texas Supreme Court asserted the right of the state to incorporate the treaty into its local laws even though the U.S. Supreme Court refused to do so with respect to the national law. One basis for this difference of interpretation was that in Texas the treaty was being invoked to preserve the rights of property owners who had purchased the lands of former Mexican title holders.

In a similar vein the treaty became the weapon in a struggle between the state and the federal government over the use of the Rio Grande. In 1897 commercial interests in New Mexico sought to construct a dam near Las Cruces to divert water for irrigation projects. The federal government sued the private company, charging that, among other things, the dam would violate Article VII of the Treaty of Guadalupe Hidalgo, which had stated that "the navigation of the Gila and of the Bravo [Rio Grande] . . . shall be free and common to the vessels and citizens of both countries, and neither shall, without the consent of the other, construct any work that may impede or interrupt, in whole or in part, the exercise of this right." Although it did not address the international question directly, the Supreme Court did find that "if the proposed dam and appropriation of the waters of the Rio Grande constitute a breach of treaty obligations or of international duty to Mexico, they also constitute an equal injury and wrong to the people of the United States."[23] The U.S. government was concerned for the rights of the people of the El Paso region to the water and was using the treaty to buttress their position. The result was that the Supreme Court found in favor of the U.S. government and the project was halted. A subsequent lawsuit, in 1902, reconfirmed this opinion. Finally, in 1914, after securing an agreement with Mexico through an international treaty, the federal government undertook the project, constructing the Elephant Butte Dam.[24]

1930 TO THE PRESENT

The Great Depression, which began in 1929, marked the beginning of a liberal political response that lasted well into the 1960s. Conservative reaction to the social and economic policies of the Democrats occurred during the 1950s, 1970s, and 1980s. Thus the political environment surrounding the juridical interpretation of the treaty became more polarized. Neither strict nor liberal interpretations predominated. Increasingly the treaty became a tool for advancing the interests of various interest groups. Various governmental agencies used the treaty with mixed success to enlarge their powers. Corporate interests sought to interpret the treaty to bolster their positions. Native Americans, mobilized by the New Deal and Vietnam War eras, sought redress for past injustices. Mexican Americans began to use the treaty as a weapon to reclaim lands and rights.

The treaty became part of the struggle between the federal government and the western states. As early as 1922 the states of the Colorado River basin had agreed to a division of the waters of that great river system, and in the early 1930s the federal government neared completion of the Hoover Dam project. In 1931 the federal government successfully asserted its control of the nonnavigable sections of the Colorado River in *United States v. Utah*, citing the Treaty of Guadalupe Hidalgo as a basis for its claim against the rights of the states. The treaty provided the legal basis for federal control of dam projects on the river. Similarly, in this same period, the federal government used the treaty to justify its rights to the California tidelands.[25] In the 1960s the federal government sued the gulf states of Louisiana, Alabama, Florida, and Texas in an attempt to control oil-rich lands beyond the three-mile limit. The states of Texas and Florida cited the treaties that had settled their international boundaries to successfully retain control of lands beyond three miles off shore. The state of Texas cited Article V of the treaty, which stipulated that the Texas-Mexico boundary would begin "three leagues from land opposite the mouth of the Rio Grande." The Florida treaty with Spain contained similar language. Since a league was approximately two miles, both states could claim a six-mile limit. Using this same wording in the treaty, the Mexican government had, since 1936, asserted a three-league offshore limit on its gulf coast. Consequently the Supreme Court found in favor of Texas and Florida but against the other states citing the Treaty of Guadalupe Hidalgo as a major basis for its decision.[26]

Corporate interests have also had some success in using the treaty to their benefit. In 1940 in *Chadwick et al. v. Campbell* the Circuit Court of Appeals for New Mexico gave a lengthy interpretation of the treaty in deciding a corporate struggle over land containing valuable oil and gas leases. Campbell, representing one group of investors, successfully sued Chadwick and the trustees of the Sevilleta de la Joya grant, who controlled 215,000 acres in Socorro County. The trustees had lost title to the lands following nonpayment of taxes. Chadwick argued that the treaty guaranteed protection of Mexican land grants. The court ruled that the treaty did not exempt Mexican landholders from taxes but that "under the Treaty of Guadalupe Hidalgo, private rights of property within the ceded territory were unaffected by the change in sovereignty.[27] In *Summa Corporation v. California* (1984.) an investment corporation successfully challenged an attempt by the State of California to declare their lands part of the public domain. The corporation persuaded the court that the treaty had been legitimately implemented in the actions of the California Land Commission. The court ruled that the corporation's land rights derived from Congress's interpretation of the treaty in law.[28] This was the same argument employed by the federal government in earlier periods to justify its appropriation of the public domain.

During this period (1930 to the present), Native Americans seeking redress for the loss of their tribal lands and liberties used the treaty as one of many treaties that courts might consider. On the whole their efforts were frustrated. Most judicial decisions were against the Indians' rights and in favor of a limited interpretation of the treaty.

In *Tenorio v. Tenorio* (1940) the New Mexico Supreme Court echoed an earlier suggestion of the federal court that the Treaty of Guadalupe Hidalgo did not embrace Pueblo Indians. This judgment reversed an earlier territorial court position in the *Lucero* case, which had applied the treaty to the Pueblo peoples. In 1945 the Supreme Court also ruled that the treaty could not be used to give support to the land claims of the Shoshonean Indians, many of whom had lived within the Mexican Cession in Utah, Nevada, and California. The courts also rejected California Indian claims, refusing to agree that the treaty was a substantive basis for a fiduciary duty towards these people. In *Pitt River Tribe et al. v. United States* (1973) two members of this California tribe sued the government to recover the true value of lands that had been settled in a financial agreement in 1964. The court rejected their appeal, which had been based largely on the treaty.[29]

Two of the most significant interpretations of the Treaty of Guadalupe Hidalgo as it affected American Indians were made in April and May of 1986. They represented both a victory and a defeat for Indian rights.

On January 4, 1985, an officer of the Department of the Interior charged José Abeyta, an Isleta Pueblo Indian, with violating the Bald Eagle Protection Act because he had killed one of these birds to use its feathers in religious ceremonies. Abeyta defended himself before the U.S. District Court in New Mexico, asserting that Indians were protected in the exercise of their religion by Article IX of the Treaty of Guadalupe Hidalgo, which had promised that all Mexican nationals would be "secured in the free exercise of their religion without restriction." The District Court again overruled the 1945 *Tenorio* ruling that the Pueblo Indians were not protected by the Treaty of Guadalupe Hidalgo. Judge Burciaga ruled for the court: "Because the Treaty of Guadalupe Hidalgo afforded protections to the Pueblos, however, it is in this dimension more than a settlement between two hostile nations: it is a living Indian treaty.[30] The court then moved to dismiss the charges against Abeyta based entirely upon the protections of religious liberty contained in the Ist Amendment and the Treaty of Guadalupe Hidalgo. This was a significant finding in that, for the first time, the language of the treaty itself was the primary basis for a legal decision.

One month later, on May 5, 1986, the U.S. Court of Appeals in California decided another case involving Indian rights, specifically the claim of the members of the Chumash tribe to the Santa Barbara, Santa Cruz, and Santa Rosa islands. The Chumash peoples claimed that they had occupied the islands since "time immemorial" and that the Treaty of Guadalupe Hidalgo, by failing to mention the islands as part of the ceded territories, left the tribe in legal possession. The court, in a footnote, issued its opinion of this argument: "While the court generally must assume the factual allegations to be true, it need not assume the truth of the legal conclusions cast in the form of factual allegations."[31] The Indians further argued that if the treaty did apply to them, then "the aboriginal title of the Chumash Indians to the islands came to be recognized by Article VIII and IX of the 1848 Treaty of Guadalupe Hidalgo." The court responded that this argument was "novel and creative but does not appear to have any merit." In rejecting the tribal claims, Judge Fletcher maintained (1) that Indian title to land "derives from their presence on land before the arrival of white settlers" and (2) that the treaty did not convert Indians' claims into recognized titles, because only the Land Commission could do this, and the Chumash had failed to present their claim within the stipulated time limits.

Since the 1930s the treaty has been an instrument most widely used by plaintiffs of non-Mexican origin seeking a variety of remedies. Only a few court cases have been initiated by those whom the treaty was intended to protect. In this period, six court cases citing the treaty directly impinged on the fate of the Mexican-American population. In the 1940s the state of Texas and the Balli family engaged in a series of legal battles over ownership of Padre Island. Alberto Balli had inherited what he thought was a legal Mexican land grant from his family. In 1943 the state of Texas sued the Balli family to recover the land grant, arguing that it had not fulfilled the technical requirements of Mexican statutes. The District Court in Texas found that the Balli family had met most of the requirements of the law and that their rights were protected under the Treaty of Guadalupe Hidalgo. In a series of rulings, the court resoundingly supported Balli against the state. The Texas Supreme Court later affirmed this verdict on appeal. This was a major land-grant victory for Tejanos, and it was based squarely on an interpretation of the treaty. It also was an indication that, notwithstanding previous court decisions exempting Texas from application of the treaty, it was still possible to interpret the document as applying to land-grant cases in that state.[32]

A few years later the courts faced this issue again but ruled in the opposite direction, to divest a Mexican family of its land. In 1946 Amos Amaya and his family, all citizens of Mexico, sued the Texas-based Stanolind Oil and Gas Company to recover lands allegedly taken illegally under the Treaty of Guadalupe Hidalgo. Circuit Court Judge Waller, in his ruling, cited Article VIII of the treaty, specifically that portion requiring the title of Mexican citizens to be inviolably respected: "We regard the phrase as a covenant on the part of the United States to respect from thenceforth any title that Mexicans had, or might thereafter acquire, to property with the region, but not that it would guarantee that those Mexicans would never lose title to persons by foreclosure, sales under execution, trespass, adverse possession, and other non-government acts."[33] Because the Amaya family failed to follow the timetable for land recovery under Texas statutes, the judge sustained the lower court's ruling against recovery of their lands. As he put it, "The provisions of the treaty do not save the Appellants from the fatal effect of the passage of time under the statutes of limitations in the State of Texas."[34]

The issue of the property rights of Mexican citizens reemerged in 1954 during the height of a nationwide campaign to deport or repatriate Mexican immigrants. Robert Galván, a legal Mexican immigrant accused of being a communist, was brought for deportation hearings before the U.S. District Court in Southern California. He in turn filed for a writ of habeas corpus, arguing that his deportation would violate the Treaty of Guadalupe Hidalgo provision protecting the property of Mexican citizens. The court responded that although the treaty was entitled to "juridical obeisance," it did not specify that Mexicans were entitled to remain in the United States to manage their property.[35]

Another Mexican-American land-rights issue came before the court in a series of cases launched by Reies Tijerina and the Alianza Federal de Mercedes Libres in New Mexico. In the 1960s a group of Hispano land-grant claimants led by the charismatic Reies López Tijerina sought to regain their lost community grants. Concurrent with their court battles, the organization sponsored a series of meetings and rallies that eventually erupted in violent confrontations, a take-over of Tierra Amarilla courthouse, shootings, and a statewide manhunt for the leaders of the Alianza. In 1969, with the land-grant struggle still fresh, Tijerina launched another campaign to change the public-school system in New Mexico by forcing reapportionment on local school boards of education and by requiring the teaching of all subjects in both Spanish and English. As in the land-grant wars, Tijerina relied heavily on the legal and moral force of the Treaty of Guadalupe Hidalgo. In a class-action lawsuit on behalf of the "IndioHispano" poor people of New Mexico, Tijerina sued the State Board of Education. On December 4, 1969, the District Court dismissed the suit for a variety of causes, including the court opinion that Tijerina had misinterpreted the scope of the treaty. Tijerina had based his suit for bilingual education on Articles VIII and IX of the treaty, but the court found that the treaty "does not contemplate in any way the administration of public schools. In addition we are not of the opinion that the treaty confers any proprietary right to have the Spanish language and culture preserved and continued in the public schools at public expense."[36] Addressing Tijerina's contention that the rights of poor people were being violated, the court ruled, "This is an unsound position as that treaty has nothing to do with any rights that 'poor' people may have."

Tijerina appealed the District Court ruling to the Supreme Court, and on May 25, 1970, that court also dismissed the appeal. Justice Douglas wrote a dissenting opinion, arguing that although the treaty was not a sound basis for the case, it could be argued on civil rights under the 14th and 15th amendments.[37]

Another land-rights case occurred in 1984, when the Texas Mexican property holders who were members of the Asociación de Reclamantes brought a case before the federal courts. They sought reimbursement for lands taken from them in violation of the treaty. As a result of counterbalancing international claims, the Mexican government had become liable to compensate the heirs of Tejano landholders for their losses. In the 1984 case the Asociación members outlined the damages they sought from the Mexican government. The U.S. Court of Appeals, however, declined to hear the case on the basis that the violation had not occurred within the United States. Of significance, however, was the statement of the judge recognizing that the Tejano landholders had rights that "were explicitly protected by the Treaty of Guadalupe Hidalgo." This suggested a reversal of the *McKinney v. Saviego* (1856) opinion in which the treaty was interpreted as not being applicable to Texas. U.S. acceptance that the 1941 treaty with Mexico settled the outstanding claims against Mexico appeared to be an admission of the validity of the Tejano land claims under the treaty.[38] This point has not, however, been explicitly tested in the courts.

CONCLUSION

It is difficult to characterize in a few words the direction the American courts have taken in interpreting the Treaty of Guadalupe Hidalgo. The courts have changed their opinions several times on a number of issues, most notably regarding the applicability of the treaty to Texas and the Pueblo Indians. About half of the cases entailing a major interpretation of the treaty have involved Mexican American or Indian litigants. In these cases, defeats outnumbered victories by about two to one. The treaty has been more important in legitimizing the status quo, particularly in justifying federal, state, and corporate ownership of former Spanish and Mexican land grants. About three-fourths of the cases decided since 1848 have been about land-ownership rights, and only a small percentage have been about civil rights under the treaty.[39]

The Treaty of Guadalupe Hidalgo has remained a viable part of the U.S. system of laws, having been interpreted again and again by the federal and state courts. Unfortunately, the treaty has not effectively protected and enlarged the civil and property rights of Mexican Americans. This apparently unfulfilled promise of the treaty fueled a Mexican-American political movement in the 1960s and 1970s that sought to achieve a justice denied them by the American courts.

Notes

1. The procedure followed to analyze United States court cases dealing with the Treaty of Guadalupe Hidalgo was to utilize the on-line computerized reference system called LexisNexis. This system enables a user to access all court cases mentioning a specific treaty or law and to generate paragraphs where the treaty was referenced in the court conclusions. Shephard's Citations were also used to access references to the treaty that did not appear in the Lexis-Nexis system. In this way more than 200 court cases were singled out, along with some detail on the treaty interpretation given by the court. My study was focused on how the court interpreted the treaty, not on how defendants and plaintiffs argued using the treaty. Only direct references to the treaty were the subject of this study, not the hundreds of cases flowing from land-grant litigation where the treaty was not a substantive concern. Of the 200 cases sampled, only 64 were found to be substantial interpretations of the treaty. My judgment as to what constituted an important interpretation depended both on the length to which the court went in discussing the treaty as well as the importance ascribed to the treaty by the court. Most references to the treaty were minor, where the document was used as a point of reference to make some larger legal argument.

2. Robert McCloskey, *The American Supreme Court* (Chicago and London: University of Chicago Press, 1960), pp. 103-105.

3. *Reynolds v. West* I Cal. 322 (1850).

4. *Mintern v. Bowers et al.* 24 Cal. 644 (1864) at 672.

5. *United States v. Reading* 59 U.S. I (1855); *Palmer v. United States* 65 U.S. 125 (1857); *Townsend et al. v. Greeley* 72 U.S. 326 (1866).

6. *United States v. Moreno* 68 U.S. 400 (1863), *City and County of San Francisco v. Scott* III U.S. 768 (1884); *Phillips v. Mound City* 124 U.S. 605 (1888).

7. *United States v. Lucero* I N.M. 422 (1869) at 441. For California's interpretation see *People v. de la Guerra* 40 CAL 311 (1870).

8. *Tenorio y. Tenorio* 44 N.M. 89 (1940) reversed the *Lucero* decision and ruled that the treaty had not made the Pueblo Indians citizens of the United States and that they were not entitled to the protections of Article VIII and IX.

9. *McKinney v. Saviego* 59 U.S. 365 (1856) at 263. This decision was affirmed at the state level in *The State of Texas v. Gallardo* 135 S.W. 644 (1911).

10. *Botiller v. Dominguez* U.S. 238 (1889).

11. *Horner v. United States* 143 U.S. 570 (1892; *Grant v. Jaramillo* 6 N.M; 313 (1892); 54 S.W. 366 (1898).

12. *Baker et al. v. Harvey* 181 U.S. 481 (1901); *United States v. Title Insurance Co. et al.* 265 U.S. 472 (1924).

13. *California Powderworks v. Davis* 151 US 389 (1894); *United States v. Sandoval et al.* 167 US 278 (1897); *Arisa v. New Mexico and Arizona Railroad* 175 US 76 (1899).

14. *United States v. Greely et al.* 185 US 256 (1901).

15. *Lockhart v. Johnson* 181 US 516 (1901) at 528.

16. Ibid. at 523.

17. *City of Los Angeles v Venice Peninsula Properties et al.* 31 Cal. 3d 288 (1913); *City of San Diego v. Cuyamaca Water Co.* 209 Cal. 105 (1930).

18. *Interstate Land Company v. Maxwell Land Co.* 80 US 460 (1891) at 588.

19. *Cessna v. United States et al.* 169 US 165 (1898) at 186.

20. *Pueblo of Zia v. United States et al.* 168 US 198 (1897); *United States v. Lucero* 1 NM 422 (1869); *United States v. Sandoval* 231 US 28 (1913) at 39, 48.

21. *Apapos et al. v. United States* 233 US 587 (1914); *Tenorio v. Tenorio* 44 NM 89 (1940).

22. *McKinney v. Saviego* 59 US 365 (1856); *Texas Mexican Rail Road v. Locke* 74 Tex. 370 (1889); *State of Texas v. Gallardo et al.* 106 Tex. 274 (1914); *State of Texas v. Sais* 47 Tex. 307 and *Clark v. Hills* 67 Tex. 141.

23. *United States y. Rio Grande Dam and Irrigation Co. et al.* 175 US 690 (1899), at 699, 700.

24. *United States v. Rio Grande Dam and Irrigation Co. et al.* 184 US 416 (1901).

25. *United States v. State of Utah* 238 U.S. 64 (1931); *United States v. O'Donnell* 303 U.S. 501 (1938).

26. *United States v. States of Louisiana et al.* 363 U.S. 1 (1960); For a discussion of the diplomacy surrounding the negotiation of Mexico's off shore limit see 99 *Cong. Rec.* 3623-3624, June 3, 1936.

27. *Chadwick et al. v Campbell* 115 F. 2d 401 (1940).

28. *Summa Corporation v. State of California ex rel. State Lands Commission et al.* 104 S.Ct. 1751 (1984), at 1754.

29. *Tenorio v. Tenorio* 44 N.M. 89 (1940); *Pitt River Tribe et al. v. United States* 485 F. 2d 660 (1973).

30. *United States v. Abeyta* 632 F. Supp. 1301 (1986); at 1301.

31. *United States ex rel. Chunie v. Ringrose* 788 F. 2d 638 (1986).

32. *State of Texas v. Balli* 173 S.W.2d 522 (1943).

33. *Amaya et al. v. Stanolind Oil and Gas Co. et al.* 158.2d 554 (1946).

34. Ibid., at 559.

35. *Application of Robert Galvan for Writ of Habeus Corpus* 127 F. Supp. 392 (1954).

36. *López Tijerina v. Henry* 48 F.R.D. 274 (1969).

37. *Tijerina et al. v. United States* 398 U.S. 922 (1970).

38. See *Treaty on Final Settlement of Certain Claims, United States and Mexico*, 56 Stat.

1347, T.S. No. 980 (Nov. 19, 1941).

39. *Asociacíon de Reclamantes et al. v. United Mexican States* 735 F.2d 1517 (1984); See *Treaty on Final Settlement of Certain Claims, United States and Mexico,* 56 Stat. 1347, T.S. No. 980 (Nov. 19, 1941).

In this selection John R. Chávez explores the erosion of the Chicano land base and the subsequent loss of social position. As a result of population pressures, untimely and unfair legislation and immigrants imbued with anti-Mexican hatred, the first generation of Chicanos experienced an unprecedented downward mobility. Chávez also explores early Chicano resistance as the first generation struggled against the erosion of their economic and political position. Despite these efforts Americanization of the economic and political base of the Southwest was virtually complete by 1900.

The Lost Land
John R. Chávez

We can date to 1848 the modern Chicano image of the Southwest as a lost land. The conquest of the present Southwest severed the region from the control of Mexico City and the local Mexican elites. In some places the Anglo Americans seized complete political power almost immediately after the military conquest, but in other areas, notably New Mexico, the native leadership managed to maintain some influence after the occupation. Command of military power, of course, determined that Anglos would hold the major positions everywhere in the Southwest, but the factor that decisively undermined Mexican political strength was the enormous growth of the Anglo population. We have already seen that the increase of that population in eastern Texas destroyed local Mexican dominance even before the revolution of 1836. *Nuevomexicanos* were more fortunate because they remained a majority in New Mexico well into the twentieth century. In northern California, on the other hand, where the Gold Rush of 1849 resulted in a huge influx of Anglos, *californios* were left powerless almost immediately. Once having lost control of the government, Mexicans soon found themselves losing their economic base to the newcomers. Owing to the quagmire of litigation created by the requirement that Spanish and Mexican land grants be verified, Mexican elites in many parts of the Southwest lost their lands and with them they lost the social position that helped sustain the prestige of Mexican culture in the region.[1] Finding their culture steadily declining with the increasing influence of Anglo society, Mexicans began to see themselves as *"foreigners in their own land,"*[2] a self-image that appeared repeatedly in their writings and that affected their relations with the dominant group for much of the nineteenth century. One result of that alienation was the appearance, in both legend and reality, of the often well-born native hero who, victimized by Anglo society, rebelled against it.[3] Yet, though Mexicans felt themselves increasingly alienated from the Southwest, they continued to see it as their homeland. The fact that Mexico had once embraced the region

25

was still too recent for Southwest Mexicans to have forgotten; not yet separated from their history in the borderlands, they still recalled their dispossession.

A week before the signing of the Treaty of Guadalupe Hidalgo, gold was discovered in northern California, a discovery that was to cause unprecedented immigration to the area. Although a Mexican ranchman had found gold in southern California in 1842, his find had been too small to attract people from far outside the locality. The discovery of 1842, however, increased the overall population of California from under 10,000 before the North American occupation to over 90,000 by 1850. The U.S. Census of 1850, which excluded Indians, listed 91,635 people in the state, of which approximately 7,500 were native "white" Spanish-speaking Californians. In addition to these *californios* there were about 6,500 other Mexicans who had recently arrived in the gold fields from areas south of the new international boundary.[4] Furthermore, in the first year of the Gold Rush 5,000 South Americans came to California, bringing the total Spanish-speaking population up to roughly 20,000. Despite this increase and the arrival of many foreigners who spoke neither Spanish nor English, by 1850 Anglo-Americans outnumbered the Spanish-speaking three to one. In two years the Latin Americans went from a large majority to a minority.

The *californios* were, needless to say, amazed at the numbers of new arrivals and felt threatened. Mariano Vallejo, a Californio who had long supported annexation to the United States, left a largely unfavorable description of the newcomers, a description which incidentally revealed his own ethnocentric and even racist sentiments:

> Australia sent us a swarm of bandits . . . The Mormons, lascivious but very industrious people, sent the ship *Brooklyn* . . . Mexico inundated us with a wave of gamblers . . . Italy sent us musicians . . . (who) lost no time in fraternizing with the keepers of gambling houses . . .

Although Vallejo emphasized the negative, he did praise those he considered good workers, such as the Mormons and Italian gardeners who became small farmers. He had nothing but praise for the Germans, and he held the Chileans in high regard: "Chile sent us many laborers who were very useful and contributed not a little to the development of the resources of the country." On the other hand, reflecting the extreme prejudice against Asians in nineteenth century California, Vallejo wrote, "I believe that the great Chinese immigration which invaded California in '50, '51, and '52 was very harmful to the moral and material development of the country, . . . the Chinese women,. . . it seems had made it a duty to keep the hospitals always filled with syphilitics." Though this racial slur was vicious, Vallejo saved his most bitter remarks for the non-Mormon, Anglo majority from the rest of the United States:

> But all these evils became negligible in comparison with the swollen torrent of shysters who came from Missouri and other states of the Union. No sooner had they

arrived than they assumed the title of attorney and began to seek means of depriving the Californians of their farms and other properties.[6]

At first the population increase was confined to the mining region in the interior of northern California, which permitted *californios* to retain some political control along the coast, especially south of Monterey. Because of this political strength, eight Mexicans participated in the constitutional convention that in 1849 formed the first state government of California; their experience at the convention reflected their people's position in relation to the Anglo American majority. Since the proceedings were conducted in English, the *californio* delegates, finding it necessary to use interpreters in their native country, felt like foreigners; at one point one of the Mexicans became angry when he sensed that an Anglo representative had called him a foreigner. Even though they declined to vote as a block on all matters, in general the *californio* delegates did promote the interests of their people. Realizing that Mexicans were now a minority, the Spanish-speaking representatives engaged in many maneuvers to make the Mexican position under the new regime more secure, but their success was limited.[7]

Since *californios* continued to own most of the land in the proposed state, they feared that the highest taxes would be placed on them. Their representatives gained a concession on this matter when it was decided that assessors would be elected locally, thus permitting Mexicans, in counties where they were numerous, some control over their own taxation. The *californio* delegates also succeeded in having the new constitution require that all laws be translated into Spanish. With regard to the franchise, they confronted the serious threat of racial discrimination when the question of Indian voting rights arose; since some of the Mexican delegates were mestizos, and one was an Indian, they strongly opposed the effort to deny Indians the vote. Despite this resistance, the convention decided that only certain Indians would be allowed to vote and only by direct action of the legislature. Given the large white majority at the convention, this has to regarded as a small victory for the *californios*.[8]

Though the Mexican delegation managed these few successes, the five southern California members failed to achieve perhaps their most important objective, that of separating their area from the north. By creating a territory in the south where they were the majority (and would be until the 1870s),[9] the *californios* of that area hoped to escape domination by the Anglo majority that had settled in the north. To achieve this the *californio* delegates from the south engaged in several complex maneuvers. One was to push for territorial status rather than statehood for all of California, thus keeping the boundaries less rigid and permitting future division. Another was to include within the state, if such it was to be, as much as possible of the land considered at one time or another part of California by Mexico, in other words all of present California and Nevada, and fractions of other present states. By creating such a large state, Mexicans from the southern counties hoped it would eventually become unwieldy and subsequently be divided, possibly leaving the Spanish-speaking in control of southern California. Though these machinations met with no success and were carried out by the Mexican delegation from the south, they revealed the desire all *californios* had for a land where they might retain a measure of independence. This desire did not disappear with the Constitutional Convention of 1849; movements for the division of the state continued for years.[10]

One of the most articulate agitators for such a division, and for other actions beneficial for California's Mexicans, was Francisco Ramírez, editor of *El clamor público*, the Spanish-language newspaper of Los Angeles during the 1850s. Ramírez was a progressive who hoped for full participation of his people in the brilliant future he predicted for California. Despite the unrest caused by the Gold Rush and the threat that the mines might be exhausted, in June of 1855 Ramírez optimistically wrote:

> As great as California's mineral resources are, its livestock and the invaluable products of its agriculture are no less notable . . . Adding to these great elements of prosperity, a clear and glossy sky and a healthy climate, it can be said that California is the paradise of America. In regard to natural beauty, the sublime picturesque scenes of lovely Italy and Switzerland do not equal it.

With an increase in the number of respectable citizens, the improvement of highways, and the building of railroads, Ramírez saw California becoming the center for commerce with the Orient, trade which would result in the riches necessary to raise great cities. In this picture we find elements of earlier images of the Southwest: the natural paradise of the Aztecs, the early Spanish land of gold, and the Mexican land of promise. Interestingly, we also find an Anglo vision of prosperous cities built by commerce, especially commerce by rail.[11]

Ramírez drew this optimistic sketch of California in an early issue of his newspaper (published from 1855 through 1859). Though he never doubted the state would reach greatness, he always suspected Mexicans would have little share in the prosperity. By August 1856 he bitterly commented that "the faith that {*californios*} had in the new government that had just established itself on the shores of the Pacific has vanished forever." And he added, "All are convinced that *California is lost to all Spanish-Americans* . . ." The more he dealt editorially with issues directly affecting his people, the more publicly pessimistic he became. His early public optimism may be attributed to the knowledge that many of his first subscribers were Anglos, whom he was hesitant to offend; certainly he was privately aware of the abuses Mexicans and other Latin Americans had suffered in California since 1848. In fact Ramírez complained in August 1856, "Despotism, (and) crime have existed here since that day of the discovery of gold. . . . Brute force is the only law that is observed." Unfortunately for Latin Americans much of that brutality and despotism was directed at them.[12]

Because of their proximity to the mines, *californios* were some of the first to reach the gold fields. They were followed by other Mexicans, collectively called Sonorans, who trekked from northern Mexico, across the southern California deserts to the coast, then north to the mines. Chileans and Peruvians found it relatively easy to reach the state by ship directly up the Pacific coast. Because these people arrived early and possessed the rich mining tradition of Spanish America, they were more successful in the gold fields than were the Anglos who were forced to learn from them. As a result, animosity between Anglos and these "foreigners" developed to such a point that the legislature passed the Foreign Miners' Tax Law of 1850, a law whose "avowed purpose," as Josiah Royce sarcastically remarked, "was as far as possible to exclude foreigners from these mines, the God-given property of the American people." When officials attempted to collect the exorbitant tax in Mexican mining settlements, they encountered resistance. Before long, rioting between Anglo and Latin American miners broke out; eventually the Latin Americans were expelled, with many of the Mexicans fleeing to Southern California. The violence of the gold fields, which often amounted to race war, soon spread throughout California; and some Mexicans, chased from their claims, became bandits as a way of getting revenge. Before long almost any crime was blamed on Mexicans, and the lynching of Mexicans became common through much of the third quarter of the nineteenth century.

Interestingly, much of the so-called banditry took on the character of a guerrilla resistance movement. Among the bandits and those who gave them aid were Latin Americans of all types, peons and aristocrats, native *californios* and newcomers. Of the native poor, historian James Miller Guinn commented:

> a strange metamorphosis took place in the character of the lower classes of the native Californians . . . Before the conquest by the Americans . . . There were no organized bands of outlaws among them . . . The Americans not only took possession of their country and its government, but in many cases despoiled them of their ancestral acres and their personal property. Injustice rankles, and they were often treated by the rougher American elements as aliens and intruders, who had no right in the land of their birth.[14]

Of the disinherited native elite, Josiah Royce wrote, "those numerous degraded Spanish or half-breed outlaws, the creatures of our injustice, the sons sometimes . . . of the great landowners whom we had robbed, if one remembers how they infested country roads . . . , one sees at length in full how our injustice avenged itself upon us . . ."[15] While many of the California bandits were simply criminals who preyed on all ethnic groups, at least two gained reputations as resistance fighters; these two were the legendary Joaquín Murrieta and Tiburcio Vásquez.

The facts of Joaquín Murrieta's life are obscure; he so successfully concealed his identity from the authorities that they were never quite sure who he was even after they claimed to have killed him in 1853. According to one version of his life, he was a

Mexican miner whose claim was jumped by a group of Anglos who had already killed his brother; they knocked him unconscious, raped his wife, then murdered her. Murrieta became an outlaw, swearing to avenge himself on all Anglos.[16] He became a legend during his own life: soon crimes all over California were attributed to his efforts, and other bandits were mistaken for him. Though Anglos regarded him as a curse, Mexicans and other Latin Americans saw him as a hero; long after his exploits, corridos, popular ballads, were sung in praise of him. In one of these, sung in the first person, we find a clear statement of the Mexican's view of himself in relation to the conquered Southwest of the 1850s:

> I came from Hermosillo (Sonora)
> In search of gold and riches;
> With fierceness I defended
> The noble and simple Indian.
> ....
> Now I go out on the roads
> Americans to kill,
> You (who) were the cause
> Of the death of my brother.
> ....
> I am neither gringo nor stranger
> In this land where I walk;
> California is Mexico's
> Because God wished it so;
> And in my serape . . . I carry
> My certificate of baptism.[17]

Clearly the anonymous balladeer, and many of those who repeated the song, refused to acknowledge the presence of the new boundary. This ballad suggests that Mexicans, even those born south of the new border, continued, in opposition to the Anglo conquerors, to identify with the land of the Southwest, and to some extent with the native Indians.

Though Murrieta was a half-mythic character, the motives that supposedly drove him to crime are similar to those of the very real Tiburcio Vásquez, captured in 1876. While Murrieta seems to have been a Sonoran miner, Vásquez belonged to a relatively well-off *californio* family. He became an outlaw because of the repeated insults he and other *californios* suffered when courting their own women in competition with Anglo men; as he put it, "A spirit of hatred and revenge took possession of me. I had numerous fights in defense of what I believed to be my rights and those of my countrymen." Apparently he felt this spirit was widespread because he once claimed he could revolutionize southern California if he had $60,000 to buy arms and recruit men. Indeed the condition of the

Spanish-speaking in California was such that many prominent *californio* families were represented among the bandit rebels who roamed the highways in the third quarter of the nineteenth century.[18]

One reason for rebellion of some of the younger members of the elite was the Land Law of 1851. Although, as *El clamor público* noted, "The first occupants of this soil were of Spanish descent (sic)"[19] and were entitled to their property by the Treaty of Guadalupe Hidalgo, the Land Law of 1851 required them to prove ownership of their estates. Anglo squatters, believing in a "right of conquest," had challenged the validity of Spanish and Mexican land grants. Since the boundaries of the original grants were often loosely drawn, the *californios* were soon caught in what seemed endless difficulties: an unfamiliar judicial system conducted in English, unscrupulous lawyers who demanded exorbitant fees often payable only in land, squatters who refused to pay rent until grants were validated, raising money through profitable sales or low-interest loans while claims were being processed, and making land productive without sufficient cash. The Land Law of 1851 together with the *californios'* unfamiliarity with the competitive Anglo economic system eventually led to the loss of their property. (Because the population there was smaller, the process was slower in southern than northern California.)[20]

In the articles of *El clamor público* protesting the land losses and other injustices inflicted on Latin Americans, Francisco Ramírez proposed a variety of possible solutions to these problems. Besides advocating division of the state, which would free southern California from a legislature heavily influenced by squatters, *El clamor público* suggested even more extreme measures. At one point Ramírez helped promote an unsuccessful plan to settle *californios* and other Mexicans in Sonora where they might escape Anglo domination. (He himself left Los Angeles and lived in Sonora between 1860 and 1862.) In one issue an article was published arguing that California be made a protectorate of the European and Latin American nations whose citizens had settled in the state. This was argued on the grounds that California had been "grabbed from Mexico," "that the Hispanic-American and European population, spread throughout the territory, . . . (had) established unchangeable customs," and finally that the United States threatened to "infest" the Pacific region of the world that was the heritage of Latin Americans "emanating originally from the Inca." In a tone of surrender, *El clamor público* once also commented:

> We are now under the American flag, be it through our own choice or by force, and it is probable that we will remain thus always. We should then accept the events and vicissitudes of our age and familiarize ourselves with the new language, habits, and customs; thus we will not be dominated but equal in everything. This is best for us and our posterity.

Surely, however, Ramírez never truly agreed with this statement since his more extreme ideas were published after he had written it.[21]

In order to participate fully, especially economically, in California's brilliant future, Ramírez feared Mexicans would have to assimilate, cutting completely their ties with Mexico, the nation which "to insure its independence, and (to insure) that its name did not disappear forever . . . was forced to part with a great portion of its territory," and was forced to leave its northern citizens "strangers in our own country."[22] Though Ramírez and other *californio* progressives fervently believed in economic development, they did not wish to renounce Mexican culture, a renunciation that U.S. society demanded before it would allow them to feel at home in their native country. Even Mariano Vallejo, who had desired annexation to the United States, feeling it would bring prosperity to California, did not give up all ties to Mexico. In 1877 when he went to Mexico City to lobby for a railroad between that capital and his state, he commented,

> I am an American because the treaty of Guadalupe placed me on the other side of the line dividing the two nations, but I was born a Mexican, my ancestors were Mexicans. . . . I have both Mexican and American children and I desire for my native land all the prosperity and progress enjoyed by the country of some of my children and mine by adoption. The day that Mexico has a railroad which devouring distance unites it with California, commerce and industry will progress.[23]

Even as Vallejo sought closer ties with Mexico, however, a railroad was being planned from the East to southern California, a railroad that would destroy Mexican dominance in its last major bastion in the state. The boom of the 1880s would bring thousands of Easterners to Los Angeles.

Though they often admired the political ideals and the material advances of the United States, Mexicans throughout the Southwest were at the very least uncomfortable with Anglo civilization because, like Ramírez and Vallejo of California, they saw the damage this civilization was inflicting on their people and their culture. Even those like Vallejo who favored North American rule felt that their property, their way of life, and even their lives were too often threatened. Despite these threats, most Mexicans tried to make the best of their difficult situation. Even in Texas, where relations between Anglos and Mexicans had been hostile since before the Texas Revolution, a San Antonio newspaper, *El bejareño*, found positive things to say about *tejano* life in 1855:

> As a consequence of one of those changes that are daily observed in the destiny of nations, Texas was violently separated from the Mexican nation. . . . Did this change result in good or evil for the country? The liberty that we enjoy, the wealth and general prosperity, the moderation and fairness of our laws on one side, on the other, the military despotism, the poverty, the edicts, the political convulsions that prevail in Mexico . . . peremptorily answer the question for any intelligent and rational man.[24]

Yet we do find that at least one thing disturbed *El bejareño*: "The majority (of *tejanos*), we must confess, lacks education, and they frequently pay for this deficiency, finding themselves strangers in the land of their birth . . ." The newspaper clearly saw education, especially education that would teach the ways of the Anglo, as a means toward greater acceptance and participation in the society that had taken possession of Texas. From this we may infer that *El bajereño* saw the retention of Mexican culture as an impediment to success in the new society, as excess clothing merely serving to alienate *tejanos* from the United States. But such was not the case. The newspaper wanted *tejanos* to be able to function comfortably in the new society, but not to abandon the "old ways." We find this attitude clearly evident in a brief description of the schools *El bejareño* desired: "We will always persist in promoting the foundation and stimulation of the *Public Schools* in which, without losing the language of Cervantes, Mexican-Texan children will acquire the national language . . ."[25] Thus, as early as 1855, Southwest Mexicans were calling for an educational system that would teach them English , and by extension other Anglo ways, without depriving them of their own language and culture.

Even though *El bejareño* claimed that life was much better in Texas than in Mexico, many *tejanos* disagreed. Juan Nepomuceno Seguín, one of the *tejanos* whom José Enrique de la Peña had labeled traitors for their support of the Texas Republic, later found life in Texas so difficult that he left and lived in Mexico for several years. Although he had been a cavalry officer during the Texas Revolution and had served as mayor of San Antonio under the Texas Republic, he was accused by certain envious Anglos of disloyalty. A general in the Mexican Army, in a deliberate attempt to discredit him, had announced that Seguín was actually a loyal citizen of Mexico; using this statement against him, Seguín's Anglo rivals succeeded in destroying him politically. Fearing for his life, Seguín left Texas in 1842 and did not return until 1848, by which time he was no longer a serious threat to his rivals, who by then controlled San Antonio. In his memoirs in 1858, Seguín described his decision to flee Texas: "A victim to the wickedness of a few men, whose imposture was favored by their origin, and recent domination over the country; a foreigner in my native land . . . Crushed by sorrow . . ., I sought for a shelter amongst those against whom I had fought . . ." Though Seguín clearly felt no loyalty to Mexico, he found that being a "Mexican" in Texas was far from comfortable; so true was this that even in 1858 he was writing his memoirs to counter the attacks that were still leveled against him.[26]

Many *tejanos* went to Mexico after the Anglo occupation because, for decades after San Jacinto and Guadalupe Hidalgo, it was simply unsafe in Texas. Bandits from both the United States and Mexico roamed South Texas, making harmonious ethnic relations difficult. Several times, "wars" between Anglos and *tejanos* broke out across the state. Between San Antonio and the Gulf, commercial rivalry between teamsters of the two groups became open conflict in 1857. In 1877 months of interracial violence over rights to salt beds near El Paso ended with the flight of many *tejano* families into Mexico. The Civil War, which found *tejanos* generally opposed to the slave-holding Confederacy, also led to much racial warfare. But the most important episode was the revolt of the Texas equivalent to California's Murrieta and Vásquez--Juan N. Cortina. Cortina was born in the lower Rio Grande Valley into a wealthy Mexican family. In 1859, when a marshal arrested and mistreated a former employee of the family, Cortina shot the officer, declaring war against those Anglos who were persecuting *tejanos*.[27] Cortina sought redress for the ills inflicted on his people and called for armed rebellion against the oppressors: "Mexicans! My part is taken; the voice of revelation whispers to me that to me is entrusted the work of breaking the chains of your slavery . . ."[28]

Indeed Cortina had done his part; for before making this statement he had occupied Brownsville and punished a certain group of Anglos he considered especially cruel. In late 1859 his forces gained much support in the area between Rio Grande City and Brownsville, a distance of a hundred miles. Though he carried the Mexican flag, Cortina attempted neither to regain South Texas for Mexico nor to establish an independent state, but to improve the conditions of his people by threatening Anglos with violence if they failed to respect Mexican rights. During this Texas rebellion from September to December of 1859, Cortina failed to liberate *tejanos*, but he did win several victories over forces sent against him by the governments of both Mexico and Texas. However, he was defeated by U.S. troops at Rio Grande City in December 1859 and fled to Mexico. In 1861 he made one more raid into Texas to avenge several Mexicans who had been killed by Confederates, but was again forced across the border.[29]

After his intrepid but unsuccessful Texas revolt, Cortina spent the rest of his life involved in the maelstrom of Mexico's politics, where he acted as daringly as he had in Texas.[30] Significantly, Cortina had carried on his anti-Anglo activities in the old, Mexican-settled sections of Texas, sections that remained extensions of Mexico. Since these areas contained Mexican majorities, Anglo dominance seemed especially unjust; consequently resistance was stronger and more successful. Like Seguín, Cortina was forced into Mexico after experiencing the problems of being a "Mexican" in Texas, but unlike Seguín, he resisted before he left and briefly continued his fight from Mexico paying little attention to a boundary that to him, as to most Mexicans, was unjust and artificial.

By the 1880s, because of better enforcement on the part of U.S. and Mexican authorities, open conflict along the border had temporarily lessened, yet the life of *tejanos* continued to be difficult. Since they had long been outnumbered, their political power in the state was minimal; even in their enclaves in South and West Texas, the constant pattern of violence and intimidation that had driven many to Mexico prevented those who remained from being sufficiently assertive. Land grant difficulties of the sort experienced in California had occurred in Texas after the revolution, and later *tejanos* lost other property when they were unable to compete effectively in the aggressive Anglo economy. With their political and economic base undermined, *tejanos* made little progress even in such areas as education.[31]

In 1879 we find *El horizonte*, a Corpus Christi newspaper, still asking for the public schools that *El bejareño* had requested in 1855:

> Mexican children in Corpus Christi are not even foreigners . . . (and yet) innumerable are the Mexican heads of family with their children who have been turned away from the door of the school covered with shame, turned away from where they were going to demand the completion of the faultless obligation (*sic*) to which they have a right as citizens.

This lack of education made *tejanos* a "disinherited class" subject to harassment by Anglos merely because "the former (the Mexican) is the son of Guatimoc (*sic*, last emperor of the Aztecs) and the latter are sons of Washington." To remedy this situation *El horizonte*, going beyond the earlier position of *El bejareño*, argued not only that public education be extended to Mexicans but that it be bilingual. Otherwise it would be completely ineffective: "It would be convenient to appoint a professor who speaks English and is Mexican, because otherwise, that is to say, to appoint a teacher who does not know Spanish perfectly, we believe no result would be obtained at all, and the children would do nothing more than waste precious time." *El horizonte* realized that if *tejanos* were ever to live comfortably in Texas, they had to learn the language and ways of the dominant group, but the newspaper did not believe this could be done by ignoring Mexican culture.[32]

While Mexicans in Texas and California by 1850 found themselves and their civilization inundated by Anglo immigrants, the situation in New Mexico, which then included most of Arizona and part of Colorado, was at first different. New Mexico attracted few Anglo immigrants soon after 1848 because it had little gold, less arable land than neighboring areas, problems with the Apaches, and a native Mexican population about ten times that of either Texas or California. In fact, because U.S. troops provided a market for local goods, the initial North American occupation of New Mexico brought a measure of prosperity to the province. This prosperity and the promise of improved defense for the territory even permitted *nuevomexicanos* to expand their areas of settlement so that in the early 1850s the Spanish-speaking were able to found their first permanent towns in present-day southeastern Colorado, an area formerly belonging to but never really occupied by Spain and Mexico. Present day Arizona north of the Gila, also left unsettled by Spain or Mexico, was made part of the U.S. territory of New Mexico after Guadalupe Hidalgo. With the Gadsden Purchase of 1854, a sliver of land, including Tucson and the Mesilla Valley, was added to the territory. The United States thus incorporated another though smaller group of Mexicans within its boundaries; these new residents, especially those in the Tucson area, also benefitted initially from the Anglo-American occupation.[33]

The relationship that Anglos and Mexicans saw between themselves and the geographical space they occupied strongly affected events in the territory of New Mexico from 1848 until statehood was achieved by Arizona and New Mexico in 1912. The division of the huge territory of 1854 into the present day states, the location of the various state capitals, the promotion of public schools, the building of railroads, as well as the writing of constitutions, the adjudication of land claims, and the perpetration of interracial violence were all heavily influenced by the Anglo desire to minimize Mexican control of the area. As Anglos moved into the territory, the problems that were experienced in California and Texas eventually occurred in New Mexico also, becoming severe in the 1880s. By this time, with the Apaches subjected by the military, *nuevomexicanos* had pushed out of their Rio Grande enclaves east into the Texas Panhandle, and also southeast and southwest within present-day New Mexico. However, this expansion ceased when confronted by the movement of Anglo Texans in roughly the opposite directions. The traditional animosity between Texans and Mexicans together with the competition for space led to widespread violence. In the Panhandle a Mexican folk hero of French-Mexican descent, Sostenes l'Archeveque, avenged the murder of his father by killing more than twenty Anglos. Unfortunately, these killings resulted in wholesale retaliations against Mexicans who were forced to retreat into New Mexico, but this retreat did them little good since throughout the territory Mexican sheep herders and Anglo cattlemen constantly fought each other. For example, in southern New Mexico the entrance of Texans caused violent competition for pasture land. As a result, many Mexican families, fleeing Texan terrorism, abandoned their homes and ranches in the Socorro and Doña Ana areas and went to Mexico.[34]

The movement of Anglo cattlemen into New Mexico was followed by a wave of farmers in the mid-1880s, increasing the struggle for land, the best acres of which were usually the legal property of *nuevomexicanos,* the first settlers. As in California, Mexicans gradually lost their property through unfamiliarity with the new legal and economic system so that by the turn of the century four-fifths of the early Spanish and Mexican grants were in Anglo hands. Outraged by their deteriorating situation, *nuevomexicanos* in the 1880s organized several groups of nightriders who vandalized the property of those they held responsible for native losses. In New Mexico an additional factor depriving Mexicans of land rights was a congressional act of 1891 setting aside large tracts as national forest, tracts that had formerly been considered land held in common by ranchers and villagers for grazing purposes. As a result of this act, *nuevomexicanos* were forced to reduce their flocks of sheep, thus cutting the production of wool and causing a depression in the industry. (To this day grazing rights in the national forests are an important issue to Chicanos in New Mexico.) Yet in spite of the loss of land and the dwindling of their economic base, *neuvomexicanos* were able to maintain and have contin-ed to maintain some political power in New Mexico because they have always formed a large percentage of the population. Also, the delay in the arrival of significant numbers of Anglos permitted *nuevomexicanos* to gain some political and economic expertise before the major conflict of the 1880s. Finally, a small number of the elite, who were able to hold on to their economic position, kept a measure of political power and prevented their people from losing all social prestige.[35]

New Mexico then is the one place where Southwest Mexicans succeeded in keeping a modicum of permanent control over their homeland. In fact, partly because Mexicans seemed to have too much power in the northern Rio Grande Valley, Anglos in other parts of the territory constantly tried to escape the rule of Santa Fe by proposing divisions of the huge territory of 1854. (As we have seen, Mexicans had unsuccessfully tried a similar scheme in California, but in that case to escape Anglo dominance.) From as early as 1854, attempts were made to create a territory of Arizona with a boundary running east-west from Texas to California, thus including present southern New Mexico and excluding present northern Arizona. In 1861-62 an invading Southern army actually established such a territory under the Confederacy. Many Mexicans actively opposed the short-lived new government because it derived from Texas, legalized slavery, and specified that English would be the language of the legislature, thus severely limiting Mexican participation.[36]

In 1863, after the Confederate withdrawal, the federal government organized the Arizona territory that would eventually become the state. This new territory was formed and controlled by Anglo businessmen who hoped to build railroads and develop the mineral resources of the area without interference from Santa Fe. Although Mexicans were more numerous than Anglos, and Indians heavily outnumber all the settlers, Anglos were able to make immediate control because of their connections with big business in the East. The small Mexican elite, nominal owners of much land that was often in Indian hands, had some influence but not nearly as much as their counterparts in New Mexico.[37] The separation of the Mexicans in Arizona from their compatriots in New Mexico deprived the former of the protection of Santa Fe; yet since they were still a majority of the settlers in the new territory, they could at least hope to yield more power in the future. This was not true of the many Mexicans who were separated from Santa Fe when they were included within the boundaries of Colorado Territory in 1861.

Unlike the isolated group in and near Tucson, Mexicans in southeastern Colorado lived close to Santa Fe: their separation from that capital by an unnatural boundary weakened them by making them a minority in Colorado rather than part of the majority in New Mexico. The division of the Mexican population in this way permitted Anglos to gain more leverage in Santa Fe by increasing their own percentage of the voters in New Mexico, Though the usual reasons given by Anglos for the new boundary involved slavery and land speculation,[38] this division of the Spanish-speaking at the very least revealed a disregard for, if not a deliberate denial of, the Mexicans' desire to govern themselves in the areas where they lived. Indeed fear of undue Mexican political strength in the Southwest also influenced the placing of capitals in Anglo towns rather than Mexican settlements. Tucson was passed over in favor of Phoenix, and an attempt was made to replace Santa Fe with Albuquerque, where Anglos had settled in large numbers. This followed the pattern set in Texas and California, where Austin had replaced San Antonio, and Sacramento had replaced Monterey and Los Angeles.

In spite of such geopolitical maneuvers and the support of the military, Anglo-Americans in New Mexico Territory could not completely exclude *nuevomexicanos* from government, simply because the latter made up a vast majority, especially in the first years after the conquest. Consequently, from the beginning the U.S. officials appointed Mexicans, even those who had not cooperated in the conquest, to important positions in the government. Interestingly, one of the results of this policy was to further the cleavage between those *nuevomexicanos* who favored Anglo-American rule and those who opposed it.[39] As time passed, this cleavage developed into one between those who favored "Americanization" and those who wished to retain Mexican culture--a cleavage that persists.

Two of the more noteworthy supporters of Americanization were Miguel Antonio Otero I, New Mexico's delegate to Congress from 1855 to 1861, and his son, Miguel A. Otero II, who served as territorial governor form 1897 to 1906. Though born in New Mexico, the senior Otero attended college in Missouri and New York, entering the legal profession in 1852. His family's business ties with merchants in Missouri oriented him toward acceptance of the customs and political rule of the United States. He married a woman from a prominent Southern family and was a successful businessman, becoming vice president of the Atchison, Topeka & Santa Fe Railroad. According to his son, politically Otero "represented the progressive American element in the Territory. The Otero, Chaves and Armijo families were all for the American Party as against the Mexican Party . . . a powerful anti-American priest-ridden party." The Oteros sided wholeheartedly with the forces of economic development and thus supported the coming of the railroad, which they must have realized would undermine Mexican culture.[40]

In 1882, at the opening of the Montezuma Hotel in Las Vegas, New Mexico, the senior Otero praised the railroad as a civilizer. His rhetoric curiously mingled symbols from the Indian, Mexican, and Anglo traditions of the territory:

> The Pecos Indians . . . implicitly believed that their mighty but ill-fated emperor, the glorious Montezuma, disappeared from view amid the clouds of their native mountains, that he promised to return . . . that he would come in glory from the east . . . The last remnant of the faithful old tribe has disappeared . . ., but we who will fill their places, have lived to see the return of the mighty chieftain (the train from Chicago later named the *Chief* and the *Super Chief*. With power and majesty he comes, with the ancient sun-god from the east, and tonight we hail his coming in the new and splendid halls of the Montezuma!)[41]

In this speech Otero alluded to a southwestern Indian legend, incorporated from the Spaniards and Mexicans who thought the Aztecs had originated in New Mexico a legend that paralleled the Aztec myth of the beneficent god, Quetzalcóatl, who was to return gloriously from exile in the east to rule Mexico City. In 1519 the Aztec emperor Montezuma (confused with Quetzalcóatl in the Southwest) mistook Cortes for the returning god and allowed the Spaniards to seize his palace unopposed. Ironically, Otero was similarly welcoming a conquering god from the east, the beneficent railroad that would help New Mexico.

That other *nuevomexicanos* disagreed is evident from a statement made in 1872 by Francisco Perea, who once ran for office on a platform opposing the building of railroads. "We don't want you damned Yankees in the country," he said, realizing that the trains would bring immigrants from the East; "We can't compete" with you, you will drive us all out, and we shall have no home left us." In 1880 at Cow Creek Hill, railroad construction workers and local Mexicans actually fought a pitched battle because the natives feared the trains would bring invasion of their lands.[42]

During his terms in Congress, Miguel A. Otero I tried to have New Mexico admitted as a state but failed. From the time of the conquest until 1872, both traditional and progressive Mexicans hoped for statehood, the former because it would bring them home rule, the latter because it would mean full acceptance in the Union. Early movements were frustrated not only by the national struggle between the free and slave states but also by the eastern view of New Mexico as a foreign land. The Civil War ended the slavery issue, but the prejudice against "foreign" New Mexico persisted. In 1872 traditional *nuevomexicanos* made a final effort to gain home rule through statehood; they were opposed, according to historian Howard Roberts Lamar, by Anglos in the southern counties who thought New Mexico should wait "until enough Americans were there to balance the Spanish influence effectively."[43] Later, because the Anglo population greatly increased in the late 1870s and the 1880s, *nuevomexicanos* lost interest in statehood. Territorial status then had the advantage of preventing the growing local Anglo population from gaining more political power. In 1889, in an important referendum in which education was a major issue, *nuevomexicanos* as a whole voted against statehood because it seemed untimely to progressives and a definite threat to traditionalists. Progressives, including the younger Otero, thought, because few nonsectarian public schools teaching English and modern democratic (Anglo) ideals existed, that *nuevomexicanos* were unprepared for statehood. Traditionalists, knowing that such schools would be promoted under a new government, voted against statehood because they wanted, at best, schools supported but not administered by the state.[44]

Although the Catholic Church vehemently opposed secular public school education, the issue, as far as Mexicans were concerned, was not simply religious. In 1889 the Archbishop of Santa Fe proposed a system of state supported church schools like that of Quebec, a system that permitted French Canadians to preserve their language and customs as well as religion.[45] In 1884 Archbishop Jean Baptiste Lamy had condemned those Catholics who refused to send their children to Catholic schools (which composed the majority of schools in the territory) because English was not used to the exclusion of Spanish. He had argued that though English was the language of commerce, "we cannot but recommend that they (the schools) neglect not to perfect the children in the knowledge and use of their beautiful native castilian (sic) language, of which they should always show themselves proud . . ." Since the language and customs of *nuevomexicanos* reflected and reinforced their Catholicism, the church sought to preserve much of their culture. To most Mexicans, religion, language, and ethnic identity were inseparable. In 1873, *El clarín mejicano*, a Santa Fe newspaper, had argued that it was practically the sacred duty of Mexicans to subscribe to the paper because it was in Spanish: "Little can be said in favor of the Spanish people of this country . . . who do not wish to support a newspaper written in the language of their parents who gave them birth and taught them the Holy Faith, which . . . is so . . . respected by *nuevomexicanos*." Mexicans saw secular public schools as a threat not only to their religion but to their culture.[46]

By the turn of the century *neuovomexicano* opposition to statehood lessened primarily because the number of Anglos increased to the point where they could draft a constitution and have the territory admitted with a minimum of Mexican help. If *nuevomexicanos* hoped to have any influence on the educational and other policies of the new state, they would have to participate in the statehood movement. The administration of the younger Miguel A. Otero as governor from 1897 to 1906 was instrumental in winning *nuevomexicanos* support for statehood. Otero was born in St. Louis of a Mexican father and an Anglo mother, educated in the East, and raised in close contact with Anglo businessmen and politicians. It is not surprising that on his appointment one Chicago newspaper praised Otero as "thoroughly American in every way."[47]

Although he spoke Spanish, Otero considered his Mexican culture of minor importance. From his lengthy memoirs, we can infer that he saw assimilation of Mexicans into the larger society as an inevitable consequence of progress. To him, the decline of Mexican culture was unimportant as long as *nuevomexicanos* advanced economically and politically with the rest of society. In fact, in his memoirs he regarded antagonism between Anglo and Mexican interests as a thing of the past. He claimed that with increased (Anglo) immigration, new railroads, new industries, and Americanized cities, New Mexico in 1881 "became one of the great territories of the Union" and that "even such old prejudices as the racial discrimination between Americans and Mexicans were gradually wearing off . . ."[48] Nevertheless, being the first *nuevomexicano* appointed governor, Otero was very popular among Mexicans, and having become an advocate of statehood, he soon had their support by paying special attention to local disputes and by pardoning criminals liberally, two policies that were especially appreciated because they made the Governor appear accessible to the "little man" in the way governors had been during Spanish and Mexican rule. Otero also gained Mexican support by keeping the capital at Santa Fe and by opposing the admission of New Mexico and Arizona as a single state.[49]

Much of the opposition in Congress, and in the East, to New Mexico statehood resulted from the belief that the Spanish-speaking were too powerful in the territory. Consequently, in 1906 an attempt was made to join predominantly Anglo Arizona to New Mexico, thus making Anglos the majority in the new state. This plan, Lamar has commented, appealed to Anglos in New Mexico and progressive *nuevomexicanos*, but most

> Spanish-Americans in New Mexico did not care to become a minority in a giant state when they could be a majority in a smaller one. Using the same reasoning, the Anglo-American citizens of Arizona were opposed to an increase in the portion of their own Spanish-American minority.[50]

Although Anglos and progressive Mexicans had enough votes to pass "jointure" in New Mexico, Anglo-Arizonans overwhelmingly rejected the idea in the referendum held in their territory. Even though Otero had opposed jointure, fearing his political machine would lose control in a larger state, his position also served the interest of traditional *nuevomexicanos*. Because jointure was defeated, in 1912 New Mexico was admitted separately to the Union with a constitution heavily influenced by the Spanish-Speaking. Since Mexicans still made up much of the population within the boundaries of the new state, they were able to safeguard their culture, at least in writing, in a number of ways. Among the numerous guarantees were the recognition of Spanish as an official language and the promise of bilingual education.[58]

Although Otero had indirectly helped preserve Mexican culture in the Southwest, the real credit belonged to those who intentionally sought that end. Casimiro Barela, leader of the Spanish-speaking in Colorado for decades, definitely earned such credit. Like his counterparts in New Mexico's legislature and constitutional convention, Barela consciously advanced the interests of his group; he once stated: "When it comes to my people, especially if it concerns discrimination, I abandon my political ideas and dedicate myself to their defense at any time or place." In 1847 Barela was born into a wealthy New Mexico family; in 1867 he migrated to southern Colorado at the head of a Spanish-speaking colony. Although this area had not been permanently settled by Spain or Mexico, Barela still regarded it as his native land, constantly reminding Anglos: "Mexicans were the legitimate owners of this country which came to them through their inheritance from their ancestors." In defending the rights of his people, he repeatedly based his arguments on the Treaty of Guadalupe Hidalgo, a treaty in which he believed Mexico had desperately sought to protect "her own children, who in their own land, in their own country were to be left like strangers . . . . "[52]

Barela served continuously in Colorado's territorial and state legislatures for over forty years after his first election in 1871, and was also a delegate to the Constitutional Convention in 1875-76. At that convention the major social cleavage was between the

Protestant, English-speaking, northern counties. An attempt by Mexicans to have the state support Catholic and other private schools failed miserably; however, Barela succeeded in having laws published in Spanish for at least twenty-five years, and also prevented a knowledge of English from being required of all voters. Barela spent his long career facing the problems that confronted Mexicans throughout the Southwest: land grant disputes, prejudiced courts, gerrymandering, discriminatory election laws, and interracial violence. His success and that of others like him was limited, but because of them Mexican culture in the Southwest lived to be rejuvenated in the twentieth century.[53]

Next to the heavy invasion of Anglo settlers, the most serious attack on Mexican culture in the Southwest during the nineteenth century was the assault on native landowners, an attack that almost uprooted Mexicans from the region. Though the loss of an exploitive elite's huge estates may seem deserved, the loss was also experienced by the common man because the native upper class was replaced by an even more oppressive foreign elite, more oppressive because it had little respect for the culture of the ordinary Mexican who would continue to do much of the heavy labor throughout the Southwest. Outside of New Mexico and Colorado, the loss of land destroyed the native leadership, leaving the average Mexican without representatives in the prestigious positions of society. Without such representation he gradually became alienated from the Southwest and increasingly looked south of the border for cultural reinforcement. Constant and easy communication across the artificial border made thoroughly "Mexican" Mexico seem more of a homeland even to the native whose family had been in the Southwest for generations. The common Mexican began to forget his history, to forget that he was indigenous to the Southwest as well as Mexico, For a time during the twentieth century, this loss of historical memory would obscure the Chicano's image of the Southwest as lost, and of himself as dispossessed.

Notes

1. See Robert J. Rosenbaum, *Mexicano Resistance in the Southwest: "The Sacred Right of Self-Preservation,"* The Dan Danciger Publication Series (Austin: University of Texas Press, 1981), pp. 25-35.

2. Pablo de la Guerra, Speech to the California Senate, 1856, quoted in David J.Weber, ed., *Foreigners in Their Native Land: Historical Roots of the Mexican Americans*, with a Foreword by Ramón Eduardo Ruiz (Albuquerque: University of New Mexico Press, 1973), p. vi.

3. Pedro Castillo and Albert Camarillo, eds., *Furia y Muerte: Los Bandidos Chicanos*, Aztlán Publications, Monograph no.4 (Los Angeles: Chicano Studies Center, University of California, 1973), pp. 1-11.

4. *Seventh Census of the United States: 1850*, pp. xxxvii, 972,976, xxxviii, quoted in Richard Lee Nostrand, "The Hispanic-American Borderland: A Regional, Historical

Geography" (Ph.D. dissertation, University of California, Los Angeles, 1968), pp. 147-48.

5. Jay Monaghan, *Chile, Peru, and the California Gold Rush of 1849* (Berkeley and Los Angeles: University of California Press, 1973), p. 250; for higher estimates of the Spanish-speaking population, see Arthur F. Corwin, "Early Mexican Labor Migration; A Frontier Sketch, 1848-1900," in *Immigrants--and Immigrants: Perspectives on Mexican Labor Migration to the United States,* ed. Arthur F. Corwin, Contributions in Economics and Economic History, no. 17 (Westport, Conn.: Greenwood Press, 1978), p. 25; and Juan Gómez-Quiñones,*Development of the Mexican Working Class North of the Rio Bravo: Work and Culture among Laborers and Artisans, 1600-1900,* Popular Series, no.2 (Los Angeles: Chicano Studies Research Center Publications, University of California, 1982), p.16.

6. Mariano Guadalupe Vallejo, "What the Gold Rush Brought to California," quoted in Myrtle M. McKittrick, *Vallejo: Son of California* (Portland, Ore. : Binfords & Mort, 1944), pp. 286-87.

7. Donald E. Hargis, "Native Californians in the Constitutional Convention of 1849," *Historical Society of Southern California Quarterly* 36 (March 1954):5, 9-10.

8. Ibid., pp. 6-8.

9. Matt S. Meier and Feliciano Rivera, *The Chicanos: A History of Mexican Americans,* American Century Series (New York: Farrar, Straus & Giroux, Hill & Wang, 1972), p.82.

10.Hargis, pp. 7-9.

11. *El clamor público* (Los Angeles), 19 June 1855; all translation from this newspaper are my own.

12. Ibid., pp. 6-8.

13. Leonard Pitt, *The Decline of the Californios: A Social History of Spanish-Speaking Californians, 1846-1890* (Berkely and Los Angeles: University of California Press, 1966), pp. 48-68 passim; Josiah Royce, *California: From the Conquest in 1846 to the Second Vigilance Committee in San Francisco, a Study of American Character,* with an Introduction by Robert Glass Cleland (New York: Alfred A. Knopf, Borzoi Books, 1948), pp. 282-85; and Rosenbaum, pp. 58-59.

14. Quoted in Carey McWilliams, *North from Mexico: The Spanish-Speaking People of the United States* (Philadelphia: J. B. Lippincott co., 1949; reprint ed., New York: Greenwood Press, 1968), pp. 129-30.

15. Royce, pp. 385-86.

16. *Joaquín Murieta, the Brigand Chief of California: A Complete History of His Life from the Age of Sixteen to the Time of His Capture and Death in 1853,* with Supplementary Notes by Raymund F. Wood, Americana Reprints, no 1 (San Francisco: Grabhorn Press, 1932; reprint ed., Fresno, Calif.: Valley Publishers, 1969), pp. 4-5.

17. "Corrido de Joaquín Murrieta," *in Literatura Chicana: Texto y Contexto/Chicano Literature: Text and Context,* ed. Antonia Castañeda Shular, Tomas Ybarra-Frausto, and Joseph Sommers (Englewood Cliffs, N.J.: Prentice-Hall, 1972), p. 66, my translation.

18. "Tiburcio Vasquez: An Interview with the Noted Bandit," in *Foreigners*, Weber, p. 227; Rodolfo Acuña, *Occupied America: A History of Chicanos*, 2nd ed. (New York; Harper & Row, 1981), pp. 113-14; and Pitt, p. 257.

19. *El clamor*, 2 August 1856.

20. Mario Barrera, *Race and Class in the Southwest: A Theory of Racial Inequality* (Notre Dame, Ind.: University of Notre Dame Press, 1979), pp. 21-22; and W(illiam) W(ilcox) Robinson, *Land in California: The Story of Mission Lands, Ranchos, Squatters, Mining Claims, Railroad Grants, Land Scrip, Homesteads,* Chronicles of California (Berkeley and Los Angeles: University of California Press, 1948), pp. 99-109 passim.

21. *El clamor*, 19 June 1855; 16 October, 24 July 1858; and 9 February 1856; for further discussion of the repatriation movement, see Richard Griswold del Castillo *The Los Angeles Barrio, 1850-1890: A Social History* (Berkeley and Los Angeles: University of California Press, 1979), pp. 119-24.

22. *El clamor*, 26 June 1855.

23. *Monitor republicano* (Mexico City), 27 June 1877, quoted in McKittrick, p. 347.

24. *El bejareño* (San Antonio), 7 February 1855, my translation.

25. Ibid.

26. Juan Nepomuceno Seguín, "Personal Memoirs of John N. Seguín . . . ," in *Northern Mexico on the Eve of the United States Invasion: Rare Imprints Concerning California, Arizona, New Mexico and Texas, 1821-1846*, ed. with an Introduction by David J. Weber, The Chicano Heritage (New York Times, Arno Press, 1976), pp. iv, 5-32 passim (of imprint no. 3; pages of each imprint in this volume are numbered separately).

27. Meier and Rivera, pp. 88-93; C[harles] L[eland] Sonnichsen, *The El Paso Salt War [1877]* (El Paso: Carl Hertzog and the Texas Western Press, 1961), pp. 58-59; and Arnoldo de León, *They Called Them Greasers: Anglo Attitudes toward Mexicans in Texas, 1821-1900* (Austin: University of Texas Press, 1983), pp. 82-83, 55-56.

28. Juan Nepomuceno Cortina, "Suffer the Death of Martyrs . . . ," in *Aztlan: An Anthology of Mexican American Literature*, ed. Luis Valdez and Stan Steiner, Marc Corporation Books (New York: Alfred A. Knopf, 1972), p. 115.

29. Charles W. Goldfinch, "Juan N. Cortina 1824-1892: A Re-appraisal," in *Juan N. Cortina: Two Interpretations*, The Mexican American (New York: New York Times, Arno Press, 1974), pp. 42-50 (of Goldfinch article; articles in this volume are numbered separately).

30. Ibid., pp. 51-63.

31. Meir and Rivera, p. 93; and Arnoldo de León, *The Tejano Community, 1836-1900*, with a Contribution by Kenneth L. Stewart (Albuquerque: University of New Mexico Press, 1982), pp. 48-49, 14, 17, 62, 188-89.

32. *El horizonte* (Corpus Christi), 8, 19 November 1879, my translation.

33. Meir and Rivera, p. 97; Richard L. Nostrand, "The Hispano Homeland in 1900," *Annals of the Association of American Geographers* 70 (September 1980): 382; and

Howard Roberts Lamar, *The Far Southwest, 1846-1912: A Territorial History*, Yale Western Americana Series, 12 (New Haven: Yale University Press, 1966), pp. 82, 420-22.

34. McWilliams, pp. 119-21; and Rosenbaum, pp. 95, 97.

35. Meier and Rivera, pp. 104-7; and Rosenbaum, pp. 25-26.

36. Robert W. Larson, *New Mexico's Quest for Statehood, 1846-1912* (Albuquerque: University of New Mexico Press, 1968), pp. 83-86.

37. Lamar, pp. 433-35, 421.

38. Ibid., pp. 219-21.

39. Ibid., pp. 85-86.

40. Miguel Antonio Otero, *My Life on the Frontier*, vol. 1: *1864-1882, Incidents and Characters of the Period When Kansas, Colorado, and New Mexico Were Passing through the Last of Their Wild and Romantic Years* (New Mexico: Press of Pioneers, 1935), pp. 280-86.

41. Ibid., pp. 275-76.

42. McWilliams, p. 119; and Lamar, p. 166.

43. Ibid.

44. Ibid., pp. 186-90; and Miguel Antonio Otero, *My Life on the Frontier*, vol. 2: *1882-1897, Death Knell of a Territory and Birth of a State*, with a Foreword by George P. Hammond (Albuquerque: University of New Mexico Press, 1939), p. 223.

45. *La crónica de Mora* (N. Mex.), 12 September 1889.

46. Archishop Jean Baptiste Lamy, Pastoral Letter, 20 February 1884, MSR12044, quoted by permission of the Henry E. Huntington Library, San Marino, Calif.; and *el clarín mexicano* (Santa Fe), 10 August 1873, my translation.

47. Lamar, pp. 198-99; and *Chicago Times Herald*, 11 June 1897, quoted in Larson, p. 195.

48. Otero, 1882-1897, pp. 1-2.

49. Lamar, pp. 199; and Miguel Antonio Otero, *My Nine Years as Governor of the Territory of New Mexico, 1897-1906*, with a Foreword by Marion Dargan (Albuquerque: University of New Mexico Press, 1940), p. 218.

50. Lamar, pp. 493-94.

51. Ibid., pp. 495-96; and Meier and Rivera, p. 113.

52. José Emilio Fernández, *Cuarenta años de legislador, o biografía del senador Casimiro Barela* (Trinidad, Colo.: n.p., 1911; reprint ed., The Chicano Heritage, New York: New York Times, Arno press, 1976), n. pag., my translation.

53. Ibid.: and Lamar, pp. 292-93.

In this selection David Montejano explores the pattern of incorporation, or Americanization, of the Texas region during the middle and late 19th century. During this time significant shifts in the economic and political order occurred necessitating a re-definition of the social order where whites held power. The new "race situation" confined Chicanos, through mechanisms of separation and control, to the lowest level of society by the 20th century. Montejano's analysis of racial and economic factors which played a role in Chicano subordination are similar to those uncovered by Thomas E. Sheridan, also in this section.

Race, Labor and the Frontier
David Montejano

This chapter examines the process of nation building, or "incorporation," that took place in the annexed territories. We return, in other words, to the point raised by Ashbel Smith--that a greater task and challenge than war was the substituting of American institutions for Mexican ones. In brief, "incorporation," a complex phenomenon with political, economic, and social elements, refers to the assertion of national authority, the penetration of a national market, and, finally, the establishment of the national culture and settlement of citizens from the national core. In this context, the term "frontier" refers to the territorial fringe or periphery of an expanding nation-state or political entity; it is an area that has not been fully incorporated within the nation.

The incorporation of the annexed territories followed two general sequences. One sequence was the road of accommodation generally followed beyond the Nueces. The previous chapters have described the peace structure that obtained among the Rio Grande settlements and the systematic market displacement of landed Mexicans. Another question that figured prominently in the experience of annexation concerned the organization of work. For ranch labor, the Anglo landowners simply adopted the style of the Mexican dons and maintained the *patrón-peón* relations characteristic of the region. Beyond the ranch, however, the pioneer entrepreneurs found that there was a scarcity of labor. Or, to state it more concisely, few Mexicans were willing to work for "day wages."

The second sequence followed in Texas was the more traumatic and sweeping experience of completely uprooting the old order and transplanting a new one--of expelling Mexicans above the Nueces and removing Indians from the "great plains" north of San Antonio. In this context, the organization of the cattle industry on the Indian frontier offers an instructive contrast to that of the Texas border region. Beyond the Rio Grande settlements, there was free land "free" once the Apaches and Comanches were finally removed in the 1870s. Nor was there a significant Mexican presence on the Llano Estacado (the "Staked Plains"), except for three hundred or so *comanchero* traders and sheepmen from the New Mexico settlements.[1] Thus, there was no race issue that could immediately stratify the frontier order. In fact, at an early point in its history, the range life appeared to hold the promise of an egalitarian society. What emerged, however, on the free soil of the Panhandle were some of the biggest "cattle kings" of Texas. As was the case for the Rio Grande settlements, the development of the frontier basically entailed the claiming of the livestock, land, and water of the open range, an experience that created social divisions based on property and privilege. This assertion of property claims on all land and livestock, moreover, signaled the demise of the open range and the cowboy era.

Toward the late nineteenth century, two signs indicated that the new territories had become incorporated. One was evidence of an end to the problem of securing wage labor. On both the Mexican and Indian frontiers, the earlier forms of work arrangements--characterized by the paternalism of the border ranches and the egalitarianism of the Panhandle ranches--gradually gave way to formal wage-labor contracts. The second sign concerned the migration and formation of Anglo-American communities. Facilitated by an expanding railroad network, the new settlements basically Americanized the old Spanish-Mexican towns of the region: Spanish was displaced as the common language, intermarriages declined, and separate neighborhoods were formed.

Within this framework, then, this chapter will address three related questions about the incorporation of the frontier territories: (a) the questions of labor and race in the annexed Mexican settlements, (b) the development of the cattle business on the Indian frontier, an example of a different type of incorporation; and (c) the final phase of incorporation or what is often referred to as the "closing of the frontier."

On the Mexican Frontier

For several decades after annexation, life along the border continued in much the same way as before. Even as the American mercantile elite displaced Mexican *rancheros* and money-poor landed elite from their land, the life of the landless Mexicans, the *peónes* and the *vaqueros,* remained generally unaffected. The cattle *hacienda* remained the dominant social and economic institution of the border region, and the work relations that linked Anglo *patrón* and Mexican worker remained paternalistic and patriarchal. The development of a cattle industry required no fundamental changes in traditional labor relations. The longevity of the *hacienda* as a social institution was due to its resiliency: finding a market, it would respond and produce; lacking one, it would turn inward and become self-sustaining.[2]

Beyond the ranch economy, however, Anglo and European pioneers who wished to experiment with such money crops as cotton or cane were severely limited by the scarcity of day laborers. Mexican workers were viewed as unreliable because many still owned small tracts of land and worked only to supplement their meager incomes. Mexican *rancheros* devoted themselves to cultivating corn, the most important subsistence crop in their diet. Once subsistence needs were met, Mexican *rancheros* turned to raising cattle, which was more profitable than farming. The Abbé Domenech never could understand how a *ranchero* of the lower border lived, "for he labours little or none; the very shadow of labor overpowers him, and he comprehends not activity, save in pleasures." The wonderment was largely rhetorical, however, for the *abbé* provided the answer to his own question. The *ranchero's* work in tending to "herds of oxen, horses, goats, and sheep" required very little labor, "and therefore does he like it so much."[3] Thus, few Mexicans were willing to pick cotton or cut cane.

On the other hand, the masterless, *ex-peón* population present in Texas may have refused to have anything to do with plantation labor. These *ex-peónes* were not just those left behind by the refugee elite of Texas, but comprised also those who fled peonage in northern Mexico. Escape to Texas at times reached such critical proportions that cotton cultivation in the neighboring state of Tamaulipas was threatened. The possibility of escape weakened debt peonage on the Mexican side, much as it had weakened American slavery on the American side. During the fifteen-year period (1845-1860) between the Mexican War and the American Civil War, the Texas-Mexican border was the boundary sought by both escaping Mexican *peónes* and black slaves. The boundary was also the working zone for slave and *peón* "catchers."[4]

Given these circumstances, far less cotton was cultivated in the Lower Rio Grande Valley in the decade after the Mexican War than in the preceding period under Mexican rule. American expansionist interests, as historian Graf noted, argued that the Mexican laborer was unreliable because he was "accustomed to compulsory labor in his own country if he did not have his own little piece of ground." Large scale planting was impossible because under the "free labor conditions of Texas" Mexicans worked only to satisfy their needs, which were few. According to this reasoning, there were two ways in which a permanent labor supply could be secured in the Lower Valley: (a) if the United States controlled both sides of the Rio Grande, black slave labor could be introduced with safety and large-scale plantations begun, or (b) if there was a "*peón law*" for western Texas, local authorities would have the power to compel the Mexicans to work and "thereby ensure the farmer a steady labor supply, as well as reduce vagrancy."[5] The Civil War, which followed shortly after these proposals were offered, made these questions moot.

Throughout much of the late nineteenth century, Mexican labor, according to employers' accounts, remained an unstable and unpredictable element. Two factors may be offered in explanation. One, Mexican laborers, ex-cowboys and *ex-peónes*, were being taught the discipline of commercial life. Perhaps the most common complaint by employers concerned the Mexicans' fondness of leisure time. One farmer who had moved to San Antonio from East Texas after the Civil War "had been accustomed to negro labor, but, as there were few negroes in the town, he was forced to employ Mexican laborers." Mexicans worked, until the 1880s, for fifty cents a day, and then for seventy-five cents.

Laborers were able to live on this wage because "they had few expenses, food was cheap, and clothing scant." Farmers understood that "to get a week's work out of a man it was necessary to hold his pay until Saturday. If you paid him Wednesday, you would not see him until Monday, and sometimes, he stayed away until need sent him to work again. At that time, no one ever thought of the farm hand buying ground or building more than a thatched hut on a squatter's site."[6] The early commercial enterprises of the border region had to make allowances for an incompletely trained wage labor force.

The second factor points to the lack of daily work, which may account for the much observed slow, listless work style of the Mexican laborer. Unattached *ex-peónes* had a difficult time surviving on wage labor in the late nineteenth century. In Mexico, for example, day laborers who were given work worked as slowly as possible for fear that there would not be any more work. As one observer put it, the day laborer is "suspicious if he is offered money, for that seems to mean that he is going to lose his job, which is far more of an insurance to him than such an uncertain and unproductive commodity as money." A debt that guaranteed a job was preferable to money. Available evidence suggests this situation may have obtained in the Texas border region, especially once the "open range" had been enclosed. During the severe drought and depression of the 1890s, for example, "with unemployment everywhere, day laborers in gangs sought jobs at the Santa Gertrudis and were put to work clearing brush."[7]

While Mexicans proved reluctant to perform farm labor, work on the ranches continued to be meditated by the old practice of debt peonage. Although peonage was formally illegal, most men and women on Texas ranches nonetheless looked to a *patrón* to provide them with the necessities of life, to give them work, to pay them wages, and, finally, to donate a *jacal* and provisions when they grew too old. In return, there was a loyalty to the ranch and its owners that acknowledged and repaid a *patrón's* sense of noblesse oblige.[8]

Peonage and Ranch Life

The country of the lower Rio Grande was characterized by large self-sufficient ranches. The Randado Ranch of the lower border was a typical large Mexican ranch--80,000 acres and 25,000 head of cattle, with a store, chapel, water tank, twenty or more adobe houses with thatched roofs, a little graveyard, a post office, and a school "where very pretty little Mexicans recited proudly in English words of four letters." The Anglo-owned ranches were similar but usually bigger. The Kenedy Ranch of "La Parra," 325,000 acres, had three hundred employees with a church and a school of 125 pupils. The King Ranch, atypical only because of its size, was a *hacienda* of 500,000 acres during Richard King's lifetime, with a commissary and store, stables, corrals, carriage and wagon sheds, blacksmith's shop, and houses for five hundred workers and their families.[9]

According to Jovita González, the "servant class" of the ranch was divided into two distinct groups: the "*peón* proper" and the cowboy. While the cowboy tended cattle and horses, the *peón* tended goats and sheep, worked the fields, and performed all the menial and personal labor around the ranch. The *peón* was "submissive to his master's desires, obeyed blindly, and had no will of his own." Debts for medical necessity, debts inherited from the father, food debts from the ranch commissary, and so on tied the *peón* securely to the ranch owner.[10]

In contrast, "the master had no control" over the *vaquero*, or cowboy, who was usually the son of a small landowner or sometimes a rancher himself. There were no regular paydays and years might pass before a cowhand would have a wage settlement with his employer. In the interim, clothing, ammunition, tobacco, and other necessities were purchased and sent to the cowboys by their employer. While generally more independent than the *peón*, *vaqueros* could also fall into debt for years. Catarino Lerma, in a 1928 interview with Paul Taylor, recalled how life was in the 1860s: "In the '60s the vaqueros got $10 a month and board. The pastores got $3 to $4 a month. They used to be in debt from $300 to $400. Ramirez, the Mexican rancher, wanted them in debt like slaves.[11] At these wages, a debt of three to four hundred dollars meant for a *vaquero* nearly three years of work owed, and for a *pastor* at least nine years owed. Pastores were especially vulnerable to indebtedness. In the late 1870s and early 1880s there was hardly a shepherd who was not in debt from one hundred to five hundred dollars. This did not signify that a *pastor* never changed employers. Debts were a "certificate of character," which new employers were expected to assume.[12]

In the absence of a "*peón* law," the character of peonage was expectedly inconsistent on the Texas Mexican frontier. Domenech believed that the *peónes* were "reduced to slavery by misery, idleness, or gambling" and that their condition was not hereditary and seldom lasted a lifetime." Sometimes peonage appeared to be the desire of the employer, sometimes that of the employee, and sometimes only the paternalistic shell of peonage remained in practice. This work tradition continued in force long after the mechanism of debt had been effectively discarded.

The Anglo pioneer ranchers, as noted previously, were Mexicanized to some degree. In the most extreme form, these ranchers acquired the traits of *hacendado*--a paternalistic bond with the vaqueros, an identification with the ranch, an obsession to expand one's land holdings. Ex-steamboat captain Richard King was an exemplary case of the new *hacendado*. In the words of Tom Lea, King with his Irish-accented Spanish was a curious blend of "pilothouse commander and hacienda patriarch."[14] A newspaper account published in Corpus Christi described Richard King as "eccentrically baronial," as one who fluctuated between fits of temperance (when he would "screw down his expenditures to the lowest cent") and the "wildest excesses of semi-barbaric hospitality." The article also noted that "as is King so is Kenedy, saving that he has always lacked hospitality, King's saving clause."[15]

Like the Spanish dons of the eighteenth century, King had solved his labor problem by leading an *entrada* (literally, "entrance") of settlers to his new Santa Gertrudis ranch. In 1854, after King had bought the herds of a drought-stricken Mexican village, he extended an offer to the village: he would resettle the entire community on his ranch where they could have homes and work. The village accepted the offer, and the resulting *entrada* consisted of more than a hundred men, women, and children with their belongings. The *vaqueros* and their families came to be known as Los Kineños, the people of the King Ranch. They became recognized for their skill and loyalty to the King family, providing the critical armed guard during the "troubled times" of the region. Among the Kinenos, it was common to find three generations of ranch hands--son, father, grandfather--working alongside one another.[16]

In less dramatic fashion, other Anglo ranchers obtained loyal, permanent workers by hiring the *vaqueros* of the grantees and *rancheros* they displaced. The core of Kenedy Ranch cowboys, for instance, consisted of the descendants of the families who had worked on La Atravesada before Kenedy purchased the grant in 1882.[17] Likewise, on the Mellon Creek Ranch of Texas pioneer Thomas O'Connor, the majority of hands were Mexicans, most of whom had been born and raised on the ranch. Included were descendants of the De la Garzas, who once owned a large ranch on the San Antonio River before the Texas Revolution. Many of the Mexican families had never left the ranch for any considerable length of time. They had "no idea of the value of money," noted the ranch biographer, "nor do they wish to have it. One of them refused a check for his wages saying that he did not want anymore of that paper because the rats always ate it up." Each of the O'Connor ranch divisions had several pensioners, for "every man who proves himself a faithful worker never need have any fears about his later years." Jesús Gonzales--"Old Casus"--had worked on the Mellon "for thirty-five years at least", he was kept as a pensioner with the nominal employment of chicken raising until his death. The bond of paternalism was strengthened by the Catholic religion shared by both ranch owners and workers. The chapel built for the Mexican colony by this Irish Catholic family was cared for by "Antonio Rodríguez, a faithful Mexican," whose son "inherited his father's charge, and jealously guards the little church and keeps it neat and clean."[18]

The general success of Anglo ranches along the Texas border rested on the ability of the owners to assimilate the ways of the *patrón*. In the smooth transition from Richard King to son-in-law Robert Kleberg, a critical factor was the latter's understanding that the necessary ingredients for labor relations at the Santa Gertrudis consisted of the "personal regard and responsibility of the *patrón* "and the "personal faith and loyalty of the *gente*." So effective were such paternalistic work arrangements that they survived as a feature of South Texas ranch life well into the twentieth century.

In places where peonage continued into the twentieth century, a certain evolution had taken place. Debt probably no longer constituted its underlying mechanism. Despite wages, perhaps the power of precedent, of sedimented tradition, was sufficient to keep the character of *patrón-peón* relations--essentially, labor relations circumscribed by paternalism, reciprocal obligations, and permanency--in place. The sense of belonging to a ranch was another important feature of this relationship.

The scarcity of work may also have been a major factor supporting the practice of peonage. Especially after the mid-1880s when the number of hands needed for ranching had declined, permanent ranch work under a benevolent pattern may have been a better situation than the alternative--migratory cotton picking. If the pattern fulfilled his obligations, there was little impulse on the part of the "free" *peón* to leave.

The chronic lawlessness of the region may have also reinforced the importance of the *patrón-peón* relationship. For the Anglo *patrón*, it was a question of being protected from the "treacherous" element of the Mexican population. For the *vaquero* and his family, it was a matter of being protected from the violence of Anglo lawmen, vigilantes, and outlaws. Both *hacendado* and *vaquero* required the services of the other. Several suggestive statements regarding this protective character of the *patrón-peón* relationship have come from the work of ranch folklorist J. Frank Dobie. Defending Mexicans from the charge of treachery, Dobie noted that the ranch Mexican "will take the side of his amo ("master"), if he likes him, against any Mexican that tries to do his amo an injustice." On another occasion, Dobie complimented the Mexican ranch hand as follows--"For uncomplaining loyalty, he is probably an equal to the 'befo de wah' darky and as trustworthy."[20]

The Matter of Race

Mexican-Anglo relations in the late nineteenth century were inconsistent and contradictory, but the general direction pointed to the formation of a "race situation," a situation where ethnic or national prejudice provided a basis for separation and control. The paternalism of the Anglo *patrónes* and the loyalty of their Mexican workers did not obscure the anti-Mexican and anti-Anglo sentiments and divisions of the ranch world.

In the late nineteenth century, these race sentiments, which drew heavily from the legacy of the Alamo and the Mexican War, were maintained and sharpened by market competition and property disputes. Every conflict provided an opportunity for a vicarious recreation of previous battles. The Mexican cattle "thieves" of the 1870s, for example, claimed they were only taking "Nana's cattle Grandma's cattle and that "the gringos" were merely raising cows for the Mexicans. Texas ranchman William Hale presented the other point of view: "Killing a Mexican was like killing an enemy in the independence war." Since this was a conflict "with historic scores to settle (Goliad and the Alamo) the killing carried a sort of immunity with it."[21] The English lady Mary Jaques, who spent two years on a Central Texas ranch in the late 1880s, noted in her journal that it was difficult to convince Texans that Mexicans were human. The Mexican "seems to be the Texan's natural enemy; he is treated like a dog, or, perhaps, not so well." What especially upset Lady Jaques, however, was the assimilation of such instincts by educated Englishmen who had settled in Texas. Describing the commotion over plans to lynch a Mexican, Jaques remarked: "It seems scarcely credible that even a fairly educated Englishman, holding a good position in Junction City, an influential member of the Episcopalian Church, should have become so imbued with these ideas that he . . . gleefully boasted that he had the promise of the rope on which the 'beast' swung, and also of his scalp as a trophy. 'I have one Mexican scalp already,' he exclaimed."[22] For both Anglos and Mexicans, the power of assimilation made actual participation in the Texas Revolution or Mexican War an irrelevant point. These shared memories simply provided a context for the ongoing conflict of the day.

The basic rules regarding Mexicans on many ranches called for a separation of Mexican and Anglo cowboys and a general authority structure in which Anglo stood over Mexican. As Jaques noted in 1889, the Texans ate in the ranch dining room and "would have declined to take their meals with the Mexicans." The Mexicans, for their part, "camped out with their herds" and cooked their weekly ration of flour, beans, and other groceries.[23] Likewise, underneath the much-discussed paternalism of the King Ranch and the loyalty of the *vaqueros* was a clear hierarchy of authority along race lines. Trail driver Jeff Connolly of Lockhart, Texas, recalled the days of herding King Ranch cattle to the Red River: "The only white men with the herd were Coleman and myself, the balance of the bunch being Mexicans. All the old-timers know how King handled the Mexicans--he had them do the work and let the white men do the bossing."[24] Nor were these bosses ordinary "white men." The ranch foremen and subordinate bosses were, as a rule, former Texas Rangers. An apparent exception to this pattern was Lauro Cavazos, descendant of the San Juan Carricitos grantees. Cavazos worked as foreman of the ranch's Norias Division, which comprised the old San Juan Carricitos grant.[25] Cavazos, however, was not actually an exception to the postwar authority structure, for there was no problem with Mexicans bossing other Mexicans.

This understanding about authority was carried well into the twentieth century. Again, J. Frank Dobie provides the clearest statement of the practice: on the smaller ranches and stock farms in the Lower Valley, the Mexicans were managed by Anglo owners or bosses, on the larger ranches, the *mayordomo* (overseer) was usually Anglo, but the *caporales* (straw bosses) were often Mexican. However, if "white hands" worked alongside Mexicans, then the *caporal* was "nearly always white."[26] Landed Mexicans represented the complicating factor in the Mexican-Anglo relations of the frontier period. Even during the worst times of Mexican banditry, the permanent Mexican residents who were landowners were seen as "good citizens" while the large "floating" population temporarily employed on ranches were seen as sympathizers of the raiders.[27] Similar distinctions were made in the less dramatic, daily encounters. For example, in her first trip to Corpus Christi in 1870, Mrs. Susan Miller of Louisiana stopped at the State Hotel and "was horrified to see Mexicans seated at the tables with Americans. I told my husband I had never eaten with Mexicans or negroes, and refused to do so. He said: 'Mexicans are different to negroes and are recognized as Americans. However, I will speak to the manager and see if he will not put a small table in one corner of the room for you.' He did so and we enjoyed our meal."[28] Evidence of inconsistent patterns at times comes from ironic sources. They indicate, nonetheless, that not all Mexicans were seen or treated as inferior. In fact, most pioneers, especially merchants and officials, were quite adept at drawing the distinction between the landed "Castilian" elite and the landless Mexican. Thus, L. E. Daniell, author of *Successful Men in Texas* (1890), described the physical appearance of prominent "Canary Islander" José María Rodríguez as "five feet nine inches in height, complexion dark, but not a drop of Indian blood in his veins." As if to emphasize this point, Daniell added that Rodríguez had "in his veins the blood of the most chivalric Knights that made the Olive of Spain respected wherever a Knightly name was known."[29]

The well-known aphorism about color and class explains the situation on the Mexican frontier--"money whitens." The only problem for upper-class Mexicans was that this principle offered neither consistent nor permanent security in the border region. Certainly it did not protect them from the racial opinion of many Anglos. One descendant of this upper class described their reaction as follows: "Now that a new country has been established south of the Rio Grande they call our people *Mexicans*. They are the same people who were called Spaniards only a short time ago. Some say the word in such a bitter way that it sounds as if it were a crime to be a *Mexican*. My master says he is one, and is proud to be one. That he is a member of the white race, whether he be called Mexican or not."[30]

On the Indian Frontier

An interpretation of the nineteenth-century Southwest can hardly ignore the notion of the "frontier," one of the most popular and ambiguous themes in American history and politics. One popular image is that the frontier was a country of free land and resources, a place where the most humble folk could stake a homestead and the young and ambitious had a chance to engage in trade. Another popular notion is that the western experience was basically democratic and egalitarian, a theme identified with historian Frederick Turner. Basically, Turner attributed the formation of American democracy to the frontier, where the hardy pioneer spirit of individualism dominated and overcame established tradition. Following Turner, Texas historians have emphasized the "fair play" and fundamental equality of frontier life."[31]

Western historians have often demonstrated the limited validity of these ideas. Despite the legendary fortunes of a few, the West was no "promised land," and many who went west left or died without bettering their condition. In similar fashion, the hardships of frontier survival and the necessities of frontier business--protection against Indians and Mexican bandits, the construction of irrigation systems, the annual cattle roundups, for example--were communal undertakings that imparted a basic sense of equality. But once law and order were established, the communal spirit and sense of equality among the American frontier communities tended to evaporate.[32]

The settlement of the Central and North Texas plains illustrates the manner of development on the open frontier. Settlement beyond the "tree line" of East and Central Texas followed the line of army forts and the removal of Indian tribes in 1870 to reservations in New Mexico and the Indian Territory. Unlike South and West Texas, there was no significant Mexican presence in the Staked Plains. The first Anglo settlers were cattlemen and the cowboys who worked for them. Initially there was no significant status difference between the two since every cowboy could theoretically become a cattleman. Range life between 1867 and 1880, as Walter Prescott Webb described it, was "idyllic"-- "the land had no value, the grass was free, the water belonged to the first comer." Mavericks, or unbranded cattle, presented an unparalleled opportunity to get into business, as another source put it, "without cash, capital, or scruple."[33]

Ten years of trail driving to northern markets, however, completely changed the situation. Success and failure, good and bad luck, the judicious investment and the foolish one combined to separate cowboys into two groups: those who owned cattle and fenced pastures and those who hired themselves out to tend the cattle and fences. The distinction became especially pronounced once the cattle boom attracted investors from "back East" and from London. English syndicates as well as American concerns made cattle and range investments representing millions of dollars. By the late 1880s British ranching interests controlled one of every four or five acres in the Panhandle.[34]

These investors had two ways of guarding their ranch interests. One was to buy out the ranch entirely at a handsome price and assign a manager to run the place. Thus, in the late nineteenth century, some of the largest Panhandle ranches were managed by British-accented administrators who reported to a home office in London or New York. The other safe avenue for investors who knew nothing about ranching (except from the exaggerated reports they read) was to work through cowboy partners in Texas, Such partnerships account for the making of the legendary "cattle kings." The accumulation of fortunes within a single lifetime came to those cowboys who were financed through the backing of English and American capitalists. Trail driver Henry Campbell, for example, had found financial backing with a Colonel Britton, a Chicago banker, and established the Matador Ranch, in which he had a one-fifth share. Charles Goodnight, hired cowboy, entered a partnership with the Englishman John Adair and organized the JA Ranch in the Panhandle. Shanghai Pierce, once a hired hand, amassed more than a million acres because of a profitable agreement with the Kountze Brothers' banking firm.[35] In brief, the entry of outside capital accelerated the differentiation of pioneers into "cattle kings" and "cow hands."

As the cattle industry came to represent huge investments of capital, the questions of water rights, grazing rights, and cattle ownership acquired a new significance. Ranches increased, herds became numerous, range rights became more precarious, and grass and water became scarcer. Cattlemen with land organized to assert their property rights as well as to extend their control over the public domain. They formed associations to control grazing and water rights, to organize roundups, to supervise branding, and to combat cattle diseases and thieves. In the process, they acted also to discourage the homesteader and the independent cowboy.[36]

Mavericking, once a common practice, became a dangerous activity in parts where established cattlemen desired to retain complete control of the range. Even the meaning of frontier terminology changed. "Rustler," for example, used to designate cowboys paid a commission for every maverick found and branded with the employer's brand. Once the big ranch owners agreed that no more maverick commissions would be paid, rustlers began to be looked on as thieves and outlaws, and in some places "rustler" was used as a derisive label for homesteader and small rancher.[37]

Partly as an effort to stop rustlers and homesteaders or "nesters," the large cattlemen began to enclose their ranges with wire fences. These enclosures set off a fence-cutting war across the range lands, from the Panhandle to South Texas. The fence cutters, according to a Ranger undercover agent, were "what I would call cowboys, or small cow men that own . . . from 15 head all the way up to perhaps 200 head of cattle and a few cow ponies, etc." Fence cutting to these cowboys, added the Ranger agent, was a communal activity endowed with a sense of righteousness. By 1884 the fence wars had become so serious that a special session of the legislature passed a law making it a penitentiary offense to cut an enclosure. It was a great loss for the cowboy. "They finally got it stopped," recalled an old-time Frio County fence cutter, "but it cost them lots of money."[38]

With the enclosed range, the cowboy witnessed the rapid disappearance of those features that had given him some personal satisfaction. The chances of becoming a rancher through mavericking and squatting on public land no longer existed. Whatever else the cowboy may have been, the cowboy was now a casual wage laborer. This was accompanied, moreover, by critical changes in personal relations between workers and owners. The boss who was both owner and cattleman, of humble origins, had vanished from the Panhandle country by the late 1870s. In marked contrast to the personal rule of these cattlemen was the formal rule of the big cattle companies who hired accountants and managers. A Panhandle county sheriff described the contrast: "They (the cattlemen) got right out with the boys on the trail; did just as much work as the boys, ate the same kind of food. Their cowboys would have died in the saddle rather than have complained. See what we have now; a bunch of organized companies. Some of them are foreign and have costly managers and bookkeepers who live on and drink the best stuff money can buy and call their help cow servants."[39] Specific cowboy grievances stemmed from the rigid control by the Panhandle Cattlemen's Association of the branding of mavericks, plus the association's opposition to cowboys owning small herds and taking up small parcels of public domain. In April 1883, led by the foremen of three large ranches, the cowboys of the Panhandle went on "strike" over the unsettled grievances. The Texas Rangers were brought in to break the strike, culminating in a pitched battle involving cowboys, small herd owners, and Rangers at Tascosa. This show of strength by the big landowners was all that was necessary to crush the strike, but resentment lingered for years. A few of the more embittered men formed the Get Even Cattle Company, which stole cattle from the different company ranches and drove them to New Mexico.[40]

Thus, the promise of the frontier civilization disappeared as old social divisions based on wealth and property resurfaced, although in distinctively western garb. Forty years after annexation, the appearance of rustic democracy and free land had largely evaporated. In sociological terms, the Panhandle frontier represented what might be called a social order with "open resources."[41] Because conditions were fluid and opportunities abundant, the social classes of the frontier society had not assumed a fixed character. Once the frontier was settled and its commercial opportunities monopolized by a distinct group, a society with closed resources and fixed, visible class lines appeared.

A Comparison with the Texas Border Region

In the late nineteenth century, the contrast between the cattle kingdoms of the Panhandle and those of the Texas border was a striking one. The Panhandle ranch was managed strictly as a business enterprise by corporate accountants or ranchmen turned businessmen. The wage contract, stripped of the camaraderie that once characterized the relationship between ranch owner and cowboys, mediated openly and formally the obligations and exchanges between owner and worker. Cowhands worked for wages, lived in bunkhouses, sometimes "struck" for better wages and working conditions, and were hired and let off according to the seasonal needs of the ranch. For the cowboy of the Panhandle, the contractual relations with the rancher made the class lines of the ranch world quite clear.

In contrast, the South Texas ranch, while a business, was operated by Mexican or Mexicanized Anglo *patrónes*, who maintained paternalistic relations with permanent *vaquero* workers. It was commonplace to find ranches with generations of workers on the ranch. Here the class distinctions between ranch owner and worker were clearly drawn, but these actors were bound to each other in a manner that tended to produce a sentiment of kinship. Such a bond tied the fate of the two classes and races together, making the ranch a self-sufficient and insular social world.

Despite the differences between the ranches of the Panhandle and of South Texas, the incorporation of these frontiers illustrates that a central element of the western experience concerned the monopolization of rights and privileges by big ranchers at the expense of the small cattlemen and independent cowboys. To put it another way, development entailed the elimination of the "unproductive" user of land (whether owner or nester), an experience characterized by market competition as well as by fraud and violence. Along the border this conflict assumed a racial character whereas in the Panhandle it had a nascent class character.

The basic regional differences can be summarized as follows. In the Panhandle area, the cattle and land stock companies of New York and London reorganized the open frontier and sharpened the class lines of the ranch world. Along the Texas border, the mercantile elite modernized the cattle *hacienda*, maintained old work arrangements, and eliminated the marginal ranchers.

End of the Frontier

The Catarino Garza affair of the early 1890s, a Texas-based rebellion against Mexican President Porfirio Diaz, briefly shifted national attention to the lower Rio Grande border. As was the general case with newcomers and passing travelers in the border region, the descriptions generated by the Garza incident were colored with a mixture of disbelief and jaundice. Journalist Jonathan Speed, writing for *Harper's Weekly,* described the Rio Grande frontier then as "an overlapping of Mexico into the United States, and the people, though they have been American citizens for more than forty years, are almost as much an alien race as the Chinese, and have shown no disposition to amalgamate with the other Americans." Soldier Richard Harding Davis, part of the troop assigned to track down Garza, wrote in his journal that the country was "America's only in its possession" and "Mexican in its people, its language, and its mode of life." Davis, describing the country as the "backyard of the world," recalled that General Sheridan once said "that we should go to war with Mexico again, and force her to take it back."[42]

By the time of Garza's aborted invasion of Mexico, the economic and social repercussions set off by the extension of railroads into South and West Texas and northern Mexico had been at work for fifteen years. In the late 1870s and 1880s, the railroads had opened the greater Texas-Mexican border region to more extensive American economic penetration and population shifts. Thus the Americanization of the cities and the railway-inspired economic boom went hand in hand. San Antonio in 1891 was symptomatic of the new era. The town was being "boomed," as Mary Jaques noted on a return visit, by "Eastern capitalists" who had faith in the future of Mexico. Moreover, the handsome residences of merchant millionaires, cattle kings, and "real estate princes" were replacing the old adobe houses and *jacales* with the Mexicans "being gradually driven out of the place."[43] In the rural areas, also, there were signs of an impending collapse of the old social order. The most telling of these signs was the appearance of wage laborers.

Securing Wage Labor

By the 1880s the work of the cowboy in Texas was increasingly irrelevant. One, the task of fencing was over and fewer men were needed to handle cattle, two, the railroad had brought shipping points much closer, rendering trail driving an inefficient way of shipping cattle to market. The number of cowboy laborers needed for ranching was reduced by a third, according to one estimate. The work of cowboys, moreover, was becoming specialized: on the large ranches, fencemending teams, construction teams, and roundup teams all handled their respective tasks. In general, cowboys had to devote less time to working with cattle and more time to mending fences and greasing windmills. As a result of such changes, Theodore J. McMinn of St. Louis, a cattle range expert, remarked on February 16, 1885, that the cowboy was becoming a "comparatively infrequent personage" in the ranch business: "Leasing, fencing, and the management of great herds by companies on strictly business principles have gradually eliminated the old-time cowboy." McMinn opined that, although fewer cowboys were needed, "a better class" of employees was the positive result.[44]

On the ranches with Anglo and Mexican hands, this meant the dismissal of the Anglo cowboys and the retention of the Mexicans, primarily because the latter received one-half to two-thirds the wages paid "any white man," as one report put it, a differential that remained fairly consistent from the 1880s through the 1920s. Thus, large ranches in West Texas favored the Mexican cowboy by a ratio of two to one over the Anglo hand. Likewise on the coastal plains in San Patricio County, the reorganization of the Coleman-Fulton Pasture Company to emphasize experiments in agriculture called for "replacing white cowboys with Mexicans, who would undoubtedly work for less, and for reducing the work year to nine months."[45]

The general result, however, was displacement from ranch work for both Anglo and Mexican cowboys. There were few alternatives for the ex-cowboy. Left to his own desires, the cowboy was not likely to leave the ranch and take up farm work. To advice that he give up herding one *vaquero* from Ysleta in West Texas recalled saying that "I was a woolly Texan from Spanish America and did not believe in doing any more work with plow or shovel than I could help." Nonetheless, in the latter quarter of the nineteenth century, *vaqueros* and *rancheros* from the Rio Grande settlements began to supplement their subsistence through seasonal agricultural labor, "which expanded or contracted as needed." In his own fashion, Dobie explained the predicament well when, in describing a Mexican ranch hand who had spent fifty years with one master, he noted that "had his *amo* not lost his fine ranch in the recent downfall of the cattle business, old Juan would yet be living on it with plenty of goat meat and *tortillas* as long as he could chew."[46]

For a period of time, the railroad provided work for the trail drivers it had displaced. Cowboys as well as former *peónes* extended the instrument of their final displacement throughout South and West Texas. One track camp, in J. L. Allhands' description, was in essence a "rolling village" composed of "about four hundred men, a most conglomerate and strange population, white, negro, and for a short while a few Greeks, with the slow plodding Mexican predominating."[47]

The railway network also provided an impetus for cotton production in the subhumid sections of the state, and this further accelerated the displacement of cowboys as ranchers turned their pastures into sharecropper plots.[48] In the 1870s Central Texas pastures were the first to be converted to cotton fields. Seasonal migrations from the Lower Valley to the cotton fields around San Marcos and Seguin began in earnest in the 1880s and before the end of the century had repopulated the area with significant Mexican settlement. Catarino Lerma recalled that "Mexicans used to walk to cotton picking or ride with burros" in the 1890s: "They went as far as Guadalupe and Austin and the Sabine River and never returned. The railroads here were all built by the Mexicans. Some Mexicans went to sugar cane in Louisiana, in the 1890s."[49]

In the Coastal Bend area of South Texas, the shift from cattle to cotton took place in the late 1880s. Newspaper editors, cotton farmers, and merchants discussed their views of the suitability of Mexican labor frankly, in public print. One such observation by S. G. Borden, who had been growing cotton for three years, suggested that the problem of securing trained wage laborers had been solved: "I have employed in cultivation almost entirely Mexican laborers, who I find work well, and readily learn to use our improved tools. Such labor is abundant along the Nueces River and can be secured at 75 cents a day, boarding themselves, and paying only for days of actual work. I have as yet had no difficulty getting cotton picked by the same labor, by contract at seventy five cents per hundred pounds, furnishing only sacks for picking."[50]

Americanizing the Cities

When the national rail system tied the old cities of the region--El Paso, San Antonio, Laredo--to the rest of the American union, all sorts of Americanizing influences began to be implanted immediately. The railroad prompted other changes, for it brought enough of the new American stock to enable them to form their own exclusive society. Intermarriages, which had been common from 1835 to 1880 throughout the region, gradually declined. Distinctions between Mexican and Anglo were drawn in sharp racial terms: the train's passenger car, according to one passenger, was "equally divided, 'For Whites' and 'For Negroes'--which in the south-west of Texas reads 'Mexicans.'"[51] As the Mexican elite declined as an important presence in the border region, the "peace structure" became irrelevant and was discarded.

San Antonio, the old capital of Texas, was the first city with a major Mexican community to experience the modernization introduced by the railroad. Speaking of his boyhood in San Antonio in the 1860s, William J. Knox remembered "about a rich and proud class of Mexicans who owned the center of town, living in the best houses, and also owning the hundreds of irrigated acres lying in this wellwatered valley." Rapid changes followed when the Southern Pacific Railroad reached San Antonio in 1875. The commercial lots around the plazas were sold by their Mexican proprietors, either because they had fallen into debt or because they thought it best to move. By the early 1880s almost all Mexicans had left Alamo Plaza and had moved across the San Antonio River to the areas west of Main and Military plazas. New businesses sprang up with new business methods, and banks appeared. Money could not be borrowed in long, loose loans. Mortgages were drawn with time limits, and "the Anglo-Saxon, by peaceful penetration gradually acquired the choice business sites and best farms." Concluded Knox: "Old San Antonio of brilliant court and docile peasant was no more."[52]

The pushing west of the Southern Pacific in 1878 from San Antonio to Eagle Pass and the building of the International and Great Northern in 1883 toward Laredo brought ruin to the freighters. In Knox's words: "The old 'freight trains' were manned, bossed, and in some cases, owned by Mexicans. Their place was taken by the iron horse managed by a different race." The fate of the Mexican teamsters was illustrated by the case of a Mexican teamster boss Knox knew by sight. In Knox's description, the Mexican boss rode a beautiful black stallion with the bearing of a Napoleon as he led his train out of the town amidst applause: "Years passed, changes came, and the discarded 'schooners' rotted away. The writer, years afterward, discovered the same old-time boss working for the city with pick and shovel; he still wore high-topped boots, and, as of old, retained the leather hat string beneath his chin."[53]

The technological changes affected everyone, Anglo and Mexican, in the frontier society. One Anglo freighter who did "runs" between San Antonio, Uvalde, Del Rio, and Eagle Pass, noted that "in 1881, with the coming of the Southern Pacific railroad, our trade went 'blooe.'" The freighter then became a ranch foreman.[54] But despite the color-blind nature of technological displacement, preliminary research suggests that Mexicans experienced a greater degree of "downward mobility." According to Allwyn Barr's study of nonmanual workers (or white-collar workers), in a thirty-year period from 1870 to 1900, "native whites" (meaning "Anglos") showed a 2 percent rate of downward mobility, European immigrants a 5 percent decline, Mexicans 14 percent, and blacks 17 percent.[55]

In May 1881, the Southern Pacific entered El Paso from San Diego, California. The following month the Atchison, Topeka, and Santa Fe had reached the town from the north. Two more railroads--the Texas and Pacific and the Galveston, Harrisburg, and San Antonio reached El Paso by January 1883. Until then the population of El Paso, in the words of historian William Holden, consisted of "only Mexicans, old Texans, and a few hardy adventurers from other states." Added Holden: "Within a short time El Paso began to throw off the lethargy of an isolated Mexican village and take on the aspect of a growing American town." The four railroads that converged on El Paso transformed the town into a major railroad, mining, ranching, and labor center. As important were the political changes associated with these developments. The railroads had attracted merchants and professionals, who in 1882 initiated a reform movement against the established political ring. By 1883, these reformers had won a special election transferring the county seat from Ysleta to El Paso, where Anglo businessmen and lawyers could better manage the political and economic affairs of the area.[56]

In Laredo, where the "peace structure" was in its best form, everything began to change with the arrival of the Texas-Mexican Railway from Corpus Christi in 1881 and the International and Great Northern from San Antonio in 1883. According to a promotional booklet, the railroads "infused new life into the old fashioned sleepy town." Buildings of modern American design were built and modern conveniences introduced. In 1882 the principal streets were graded and graveled and a handsome courthouse and city hall were built. In 1883 a water works company laid mains under streets and a telephone exchange was installed. The first English-language newspaper was established in 1884, and Laredo saloons began posting their prices in U.S. currency. In 1886 and 1887 smelting and sampling works were built by the Kansas City Ore Company and the Guadalupe Mining Company of Philadelphia. In 1888 the "Edison Incandescent system" was installed. In short, within a few years after the International had reached Laredo, the town had "blossomed" into modernity.[57]

Such modernity invariably signified important political shifts. In Laredo, electoral politics appeared to assume a distinct class character as two parties, one called *botas* (meaning boots) and the other *guaraches* (meaning sandals), organized the contending sides in 1885. The contest involved a class antagonism but not in the "rich versus poor" manner suggested by the party labels. Rather, the *bota* leadership represented the new merchants who had arrived with the railroad and the *guarache* leadership stood for the older aristocratic element of Laredo. Both sides had a loyal Texas Mexican following. In 1886 the botas won a clean sweep of city and county government, resulting in a riot between supporters of the two sides. The *guaraches* declined and thereafter the old Mexican elite settled for a minor role in a bipartisan coalition, formed at the turn of the century, called the Independent Club..[58]

In sum, the result of rapid growth after the arrival of the railroad was the formation of two societies, one Anglo and the other Mexican. San Pedro Creek, according to a visiting correspondent, had come to be "the dividing line between American San Antonio and Mexican San Antonio." "The aggressive, pushing" Anglo called "his San Antonio the San Antonio" and recognized "the Mexican San Antonio as only 'over the San Pedro.'" In Laredo the transition reduced the influence of the old guard but did not uproot the social order as in other places. According to Judge José María Rodríguez, there were several attempts by "land boomers to wreck that town and load it down with taxes." But Rodríguez had hope that the old families would "not sell out their land to the stranger and then rent from him."[59]

The Car of Progress

The Rio Grande region below Laredo was spared the trauma of railway-related modernization for another two decades. Brownsville, in fact, had declined since the boom days of the mid-nineteenth century. The "car of Progress," of which Brownsville entrepreneur Edward Dougherty had spoken so eloquently in 1867, had somewhere taken a wrong turn.

As single-minded as Dougherty and other merchants may have been about their commercial plans, economic development was not made of whole cloth, the result of a grand design agreed to by an export-oriented elite. Rather, it was an undetermined process influenced by various political and economic circumstances. One significant circumstance consisted of the competition that characterized the internal relations of the capital-based elite itself. The reward for "winners" was essentially the opportunity to implement a favored blueprint of development.

The mercantile elite, in other words, was by no means a unified class, a class filled with solidarity.[60] The same market forces--access to capital, control of technological innovations, skillful reinvestment of profits--that operated to the great disadvantage of the landed elite and the landless cowboys also exerted their influence within the mercantile community. The commercial fortunes of Brownsville in the late nineteenth century may serve as a case in point.

Within a few years after annexation, merchants had found themselves splitting up into strata with various degrees of status and privilege. Those who had moved quickly and gained control of some aspect of the Mexican trade found themselves becoming wealthier. The small merchants, on the other hand, were increasingly forced out of the northern Mexican trade for lack of sufficient capital. The small merchants resented the "monopolists," with much of their resentment centering on the high freight charges of the steamboat monopoly of Stillman, King, and Kenedy. The "antimonopolists" had plans to build a twenty-two-mile rail line from Port Isabel to Brownsville, but not much came of this talk until after the Civil War. In 1870 the Reconstruction state legislature, reminded of King's and Kenedy's "short loyalty" to the Union, granted the antimonopolists the required charter. By 1871 a narrow-gauge railroad was operating, and three years later King and Kenedy sold the steamboat company to Capt. William Kelly, a supporter of the antimonopolists. The twenty-year reign of the steamboat monopoly had been broken, one of the few times that King and Kenedy found themselves on the losing side. But this victory of the antimonopolists, complete as it seemed, was short-lived.[61]

In 1880 King and Kenedy joined with Corpus Christi merchant Uriah Lott to build a railroad from Corpus Christi to Laredo where it would connect with the Mexican National Railway to Monterrey. In the world of commerce, this was an unquestionable tour de force. King and Kenedy had outflanked their Brownsville rivals, for the cart and wagon trade between Brownsville and the Mexican interior could not compete with the railway route between Corpus Christi, Laredo, and Monterrey. By 1882 the new trade route had channeled the Mexican trade away from Matamoros-Brownsville to Laredo-Corpus Christi, two hundred miles north. Laredo grew from 3,521 in 1880 to 11,319 in 1890, a phenomenal increase. Meanwhile the Brownsville area receded into isolation, its population remaining roughly between 5,000 and 6,000 people for the last twenty years of the nineteenth century. The days of the big merchant had passed for the Brownsville area. The fleet of steamboats steadily dwindled until 1903 when the last riverboat stopped its runs. The King Ranch land books suggest that the financial collapse of Captain Kelly came earlier, in 1902, when he sold Henrietta King four thousand acres of land.[62]

Thus the Lower Valley, as Army Lt. W. H. Chatfield observed in a promotional booklet in the early 1890s, remained isolated from the great American population centers. This remoteness ("without the means of rapid transit"), together with its Mexican influence, had retarded its growth and the development of its natural advantages. "The sociology of this people," Chatfield added, was "particularly remarkable" and bordered on "the romantic," filled with a life of "pastoral ease," "urban success," intermarriages, and "freedom from crime." The subject was "a tempting one," but Chatfield's explicit mission was not sociological but commercial; he wished to advance "the awakening of this people from their long period of somnolence" through his description of business opportunities in the area.[63]

The politics of the Lower Valley retained a distinctive insular character. In Brownsville, the Anglos who had settled in the immediate postwar years had intermarried with each other and the elite Mexicans and for the next fifty years ran "the county, the city, and the Mexicans almost as a feudal family system." The first generation ruled until the 1870s and 1880s; the second generation offspring governed through the 1910s and 1920s. The tenure of this pioneer elite would not be broken until the early twentieth century with the immigration of Anglo farmers from the Midwest and the South, As one Valley resident noted: "The onrush of the new Americans, eager to make a fortune, anxious to accumulate wealth as soon as possible, changed the placid, easy-going life which had existed in the border counties."[64]

Notes

1. Terry G. Jordan, *Trails to Texas*, pp. 145-146; also J. Evetts Haley, *Charles Goodnight*, pp. 187-191.

2. Enrique Semo, *Historia del capitalismo en México: Los orígenes, 1521-1763*.

3. Domenech, *Missionary Adventures*, pp. 254-256; Robert Edgar Riegel, *The Story of the Western Railroads*, pp. 7-8, Graf, "Economic History," pp. 439-445.

4. Friedrich Katz, "Labor Conditions on Haciendas in Porfirian Mexico: Some Trends and Tendencies," *Hispanic American Historical Review* 54, no. 1 (February 1974): 32-33; Wilkinson, *Laredo*, p. 238, Mexico, Report: Cazneau, *Eagle Pass*, pp. 59, 80-81, 94-96; J.D. Thompson, *Vaqueros*.

5. Graf, "Economic History," pp. 449-450.

6. Knox, *Economic Status*, p. 3; also see M. García, *Desert Immigrants*, p. 72.

7. Wallace Thompson, *The Mexican Mind*, pp. 200-201, Lea, *King Ranch*, 2:501.

8. Wilkinson, *Laredo*, p. 237.

9. Richard Harding Davis,. *The West from a Car-Window*, p. 132; J. L. Allhands, *Gringo Builders*, p.21; Villarreal, "Mexican-American Vaqueros," p. 1O; Lea, King Ranch, I:148.

10. González, "Social Life," pp. 49-50.

11. Taylor Collection, no. 139-728.

12. P. S. Taylor, *American-Mexican Frontier*, pp. 116-117; González, "Social Life," pp. 49-50," James H. Cook and Howard R. Driggs, Longhorn Cowboy, p. 74.

13. Domenech, *Missionary Adventures,* pp. 308-309.

14. Lea, *King Ranch*, I:347-351

15. *The World* (Corpus Christi), May 23, 1878, cited in Goldfinch, *Juan N. Cortina*, pp. 33-34; also Lea, *King Ranch*, I:350-351, 355.

16. Bass, "Kleverg County,"p. 101; also Lea, *King Ranch*, I:123-124, 146; Allhands, *Gringo Builders*, p. 21.

17. Villarreal, "Mexican-American Vaqueros," p.11.

18. Sister Margaret Rose Warburton, "A History of the Thomas O'Connor Ranch, 1834-1939" (M.A. thesis), pp. 25, 34, 95, 111-116.

19. Lea, *King Ranch*, 2:483

20. J. Frank Dobie, "Ranch Mexicans," *Survey*, May 1, 1931, p. 170, and "The Mexican Vaquero of the Texas Border," *Political and Social Science Quarterly* 3, no. I (June 1927): 23.

21. William Hale, *Twenty-Four Years a Cowboy and Ranchman in Southern Texas and Old Mexico*, p. 137; John H. Culley, *Cattle, Horses, and Men*, p. 103; Dobie, *Vaquero of The Brush County*, pp. 54- 56; González, "Social Life," p. 11; Hunter, *Trail Drivers,* 2:938-939.

22. Mary J. Jaques, *Texan Ranch Life*, pp. 361-362.

23. Ibid., p. 61.

24. Hunter, *Trail Drivers*, I:187.

25. Lea, *King Ranch*, 2:497, 638-639; also *100 Years*.

26. Dobie, "Ranch Mexicans," p. 168; see also John Hendrix, *If I Can Do It Horseback*, p. 32.

27. Dobie, *Vaquero of the Brush Country*, p. 69; Graf, "Economic History," p. 625.

28. Miller, Sixty Years, pp. 15, 175.

29. Daniell, *Types of Successful Men*, p. 340.

30. Zamora O'Shea, *El Mesquite*, p. 59.

31. F. J. Turner, *The Frontier in American History*; Webb, *Great Plains,* pp. 206-207.

32. See Haley, *Charles Goodnight*, p. 16, for critiques, see George Rogers Taylor, ed., *The Turner Thesis*, esp. the contribution by Stanley Elkins and Eric McKitrick, for a Brazilian critique of the theme of "*La democracia Gucacha*," see Fernando Henrique Cardoso, *Capitalismo e escravidáo no Brasil merdional*, pp. 119-132.

33. See Jordan, *Trails to Texas*, pp. 145-146; Webb, *Great Plains,* p. 230; Joe B. Frantz

and Julian Ernest Choate, Jr., The American Cowboy, pp. 10, 105-106.

34. Biggers, *From Cattle Ranch*, esp. pp. 94-101; also Kerr, *Scottish Capital'* P- 189.

35. Gressley, *Bankers and Cattlemen*, p. 77; C. L. Douglas, *Cattle Kings,* pp. 52, 132-141, 218-225, 243, 252-253; Haley, *Charles Goodnight*, pp. 344-350.

36. Hunter, *Trail Drivers*, I:439; Frantz and Choate, *American Cowboy*, pp. 105-106.

37. John Upton Terrell, *Land Grab*, pp. 225-226; Ruth Allen, *Chapters in the History of Organized Labor in Texas*, pp. 35-38; William Bennett Bizzell, *Rural Texas*, pp. 126-127, 132-133; for incidents, see Dobie, *Longhorns*, pp. 51-60, or *Vaquero of the Brush Country*, pp. 9-10.

38. See Webb, *Texas Rangers*, pp. 429-437; Fenley, *Oldtimers*, p. 246; Chester Allwyn Barr, "Texas Politics, 1876-1906" (Ph.D. diss.), pp. 92-94, 130-131.

39. Cited by Allen, *History of Organized Labor*, p. 37.

40. Ibid., pp. 35-39; also Haley, *Charles Goodnight*, pp. 363-380; Gressley, *Bankers and Cattlemen*, pp. 123-125; William Curry Holden, *The Spur Ranch*, p. 102; Arthur Stinchecombe, "Agricultural Enterprise and Rural Class Relations," *American Journal of Sociology* 67 (September 1961): 174-175.

41. For a sociological discussion, see H. Hoetink, *Slavery and Race Relations in the Americas*, pp. 76-83.

42. Jonathan Speed, "The Hunt for Garza," *Harper's Weekly*, January 30, 1892, p. 103; Davis, *West from a Car-Window*, pp. 41-45.

43. Jaques, *Texan Ranch Life*, p. 38; Seymour V. Connor, *Texas: A History*, p. 269; Don M. Coerver and Linda B. Hall, *Texas and the Mexican Revolution*, p. 14; García, *Desert Immigrants*, pp. 14-17; Jordan, "1887 Census," pp. 271-278; Riegel, *Story of the Western Railroads*, pp. 1-16.

44. Holden, *Spur Ranch*, p. 90; Webb, *Great Plains*, p. 240; in U.S. Congress, House, *Range and Ranch Cattle Traffic*, p. 101.

45. B. Youngblood and A.B. Cox, *An Economic Study of a Typical Ranch Area on the Edwards Plateu of Texas*, pp. 308-312; A. Ray Stephens, *The Taft Ranch*, p. 130; Hunter, *Trail Drivers*, 2:853-854; Dobie, "Mexican Vaquero," p. 20.

46. Andrew García, *Tough Trip through Paradise*, 1878-1879, p. 6; J. Thompson, "A 19th Century History," p. 112; Dobie, "Mexican Vaquero," p. 23.

47. Allhands, *Gringo Builders*, p. 257; also Zamora O'Shea, *El Mesquite*, p. 65.

48. E. Johnson, *Commercial and Industrial Development.* p. 131.

49. Taylor Collection, no. 137-726.

50. Quoted in Corpus Christi, p. 153.

51. Davis, *West from a Car-Window*, p. 27.

52. Knox, *Economic Status*, p. 4; Johnny M. McCain, "Mexican Labor in San Antonio, Texas, 1900-1940" (typescript), p. 7; Jaques, *Texan Ranch Life*, p. 38.

53. Knox, *Economic Status*, p. 7.

54. Hunter, *Trail Drivers*, I: 461.

55. Chester Allwyn Barr, "Occupational and Geographic Mobility in San Antonio, 1870-1900, *"Social Science Quarterly* 51, no. 2 (September 1970): 401.

56. Holden, *Alkali Trails*, p. 64; M.T. García, *Desert Immigrants*, pp. 16, 156-157; Connor, *Texas*, p. 269; Coerver and Hall, *Texas and the Mexican Revolution*, p. 14.

57. E.R. Tarver, *Laredo*.

58. Hinajosa, *Borderlands Town*, pp. 118-119.

59. Walter B. Stevens, *Through Texas*, p. 72, R.O. García, *Dolores*, pp. 36-39; Hinajosa, *Borderlands Town*, pp. 68-71; also Wilkinson, *Laredo*: Da Camara, *Laredo*.

60. Gressley, *Bankers and Cattleman*, pp. 30-35; J. Thompson, "A 19th Century History," p. 79.

61. Graf, "Economic History," pp. 407-408; also see J. Thompson, "A 19th Century History," pp. 37, 60-61; Lea, *King Ranch*, I:54, 248-252.

62. J. Thompson, "A 19th Century History," pp. 106-110; Graf, "Economic History," p. 7; Edwin J. Foscue, "Agricultural History of the Lower Rio Grande Valley Region," *Agricultural History* 8, no. 3 (July 1934): 135; Lea, *King Ranch*, I:252.

63. Chatfield, *Twin Cities*, p. 3.

64. González, "Social Life," p. 82; J. Thompson, "A 19th Century History," p. 70.

Thomas E. Sheridan traces the history of Chicanos in southern Arizona and reveals the process of subordination since the late 19th century. Although his study is confined to southern Arizona similar trends leading to subordination were underway in other regions of the Southwest. He elaborates upon patterns of racial and economic subordination, dual processes insitutionalized by the middle 20th century. Sheridan also explores Mexican and Chicano resistance "in a variety of ways ranging from political organization to cultural preservation."

Race and Class in a Southwestern City: The Mexican Community of Tucson, 1854-1941
Thomas E. Sheridan

In July, 1892, a prominent Mexican rancher named Ramón Soto wrote a series of influential articles in *El Fronterizo,* Tucson's leading Spanish-language newspaper. In these articles, Soto passionately urged Mexicans in Tucson to set aside their differences and unite into one single politically powerful community. Soto called his vision of Mexican solidarity *la Colonia Hispano-Americana.* He wrote:

> All of us in general believe that this country is the exclusive property of the Americans, any one of whom arriving from New York, San Francisco, or Chicago has the right to be sheriff, judge, councilman, legislator, constable or whatever he wants. Such an American can be Swiss, Irish, German, Italian, Portuguese, or whatever. Always, in the final analysis, he is an American. And ourselves? Are we not Americans by adoption or birth? Of course we are. And as sons of this country, being born here, do we not have an equal or a greater right to formulate and maintain the laws of this land that witnessed our birth than naturalized citizens of European origin? Yes. Nevertheless, the contrary occurs.[1]

In one sense, Ramón Soto's plea for unity was answered less than two years later, when Mexican businessmen, intellectuals, and politicians met to form the *Alianza Hispano-Americana.* One of the primary purposes of the *Alianza* was to protect Mexicans against the rising tide of racism in the United States; at its height, in the 1930s, it was the largest Hispanic mutual-aid society in the nation. On a more fundamental level, however, Soto's dream never really came true. Mexicans in Tucson may have remained a majority of the city's population until the early 1900s, but they never exercised political or economic power in proportion to their actual numbers. *Tucsonenses* found themselves caught up in an increasingly hierarchical society, one that discriminated against them on the basis of class as well as race. Soto blamed Mexican powerlessness on political apathy, but the reality of Mexican subordination in southern Arizona was much more complex. In the following presentation, I want to explore some of the underlying factors-- demographic, economic, educational, and political--responsible for that subordination. I also want to suggest a few of the reasons why Soto's vision of a united *Colonia Hispano-Americana* remained just that--a vision and little more. In the process, however, I need to discuss the very nature of southern Arizona society in general, for only then can the particular history of Mexicans in Tucson be understood.

From Sonoran to Territorial Tucson

Tucson was founded in 1775, and for the first eight decades of its existence, it remained the northernmost outpost of Spanish, and later, Mexican Sonora. Its first non-Indian settlers were presidial soldiers and their families. They were tough, resourceful men and women who knew exactly what life was going to be like in the Tucson Basin when they moved up the Santa Cruz River from their former garrison at Tubac. Most of these individuals had grown up in the Sonoran Desert fighting Apaches, forming alliances with neighboring Pimas and Papagos, planting their crops of wheat, corn, beans, and squash along the floodplain of the Santa Cruz itself. In some cases, these families were descendants of pioneers who had first moved into southern Arizona in the early 18th century. Unlike the Anglos who followed them, Tucson's Hispanic pioneers settled the area as seasoned desert dwellers rather than immigrants from a foreign land.

At times, their experience and their endurance were the only qualities that enabled them to survive on the Apache frontier. For most of its history, Sonoran Tucson was a tiny finger of Hispanic society jutting north into harsh and hostile territory. With the exception of Tubac forty miles to the south, the only other Hispanic settlements in southern Arizona were scattered ranches and mines that contracted or disappeared whenever Apache raiding intensified. Contact with the rest of Sonora was sporadic, contact with the Hispanic communities of California and New Mexico almost nonexistent. As a result, Sonoran Tucson never developed into an urban center like Magdalena, Arispe, Hermosillo, or other Sonoran communities to the south. Instead, it remained an isolated frontier garrison of soldiers and the farmers who supported them.

Such isolation came to an end in 1854. Not satisfied with the territory it had won by force during the War with Mexico, the United States dispatched railroad speculator James Gadsden to Mexico City in 1853 to negotiate a further cession of Mexican land. Bankrupt and desperate, Mexican president Santa Anna accepted the offer that transferred the least amount of Mexican soil to the United States--30,000 square miles encompassing southern Arizona and the Mesilla Valley of New Mexico. Sonoran Tucson had survived Apache attacks, Mexican Independence and war with the United States. Suddenly, however, a mere stroke of a pen transformed Tucsonenses from citizens of Sonora into residents of the United States.

Luckily for the Tucsonenses, that transformation was not as traumatic as it was for Mexicans in other areas of the Southwest. In California, for example, Mexicans were overwhelmed by hordes of forty-niners, losing both land and power to the Anglo newcomers as they became a small minority in their native land almost overnight (Pitt 1966; Camarillo 1979; Griswold del Castillo 1979). The situation of Mexicans in Texas was even more desperate, as they were a "race of mongrels" to the victors of the Texas Revolt (Acuña 1981; De León 1982). Tucson, in contrast, did not attract many Anglo immigrants at first. There were no gold fields, no vast tracts of fertile land, no easy access to national and international markets. More to the point, the hostility of the Western and Chiricahua Apaches made life on the Arizona frontier a precarious proposition at best. As a result, Mexicans in Tucson often seemed to assimilate Anglos rather than vice versa in the wake of the Gadsden Purchase.

Nonetheless, the pattern of Anglo dominance and Mexican subordination began to emerge as early as 1860. That year, according to federal census manuscripts, Anglos constituted less than 20 percent of Tucson's total population of 925. However, they possessed 87 percent of the real and personal property in town. Within six years of the Gadsden Purchase, Anglo capital dominated Tucson's economy. Once in control, it never let go.

Part of the reason for this dominance was demographic. Of the 168 Anglos in Tucson in 1860, 159 were adult males, most of whom were in the prime of their lives. Tucson's Mexican population, on the other hand, was much less skewed; its male/female ratio was roughly equal while 37 percent were children fourteen years or younger. In a sense, early territorial Tucson was a dual, almost schizophrenic settlement: a Mexican community organized into families contrasting sharply with a typically frontier population of young aggressive Anglo males. Anglos consequently made up a disproportionate share of Tucson's work force--36 percent. More to the point, they were able to devote their energy and their capital to business enterprises without worrying about the constraints of family life.

But demography alone does not explain Anglo economic ascendancy. One of the most enduring myths about Arizona history is the myth of the rugged individual--the two-fisted, gun-totin' pioneer who wins fame and fortune on the Arizona frontier. Detailed historical research, on the other hand, paints a much different picture. Most of the capital that developed Arizona originated somewhere else. Anglo merchants settling in Tucson often had ties to larger business firms outside of the Arizona territory. Native Tucsonenses, in contrast, had nothing but their Apache-thinned herds of livestock and their small floodplain fields. As a result, most native-born Mexicans did not have the financial resources to successfully compete with the Anglo newcomers.

71

Most of the prosperous Mexicans in territorial Tucson were in fact immigrants themselves. Estevan Ochoa, partner in one of the biggest freighting companies in the territory, came from Chihuahua. The four Aguirre brothers, who established some of the largest ranches in southern Arizona, were also Chihuahua-born and bred. Leopoldo Carrillo, Tucson's premier urban entrepreneur, and Mariano Samaniego, the town's most successful Mexican politician, migrated from Sonora. Like their Anglo counterparts, these successful Mexican immigrants brought their own capital with them. Most native Tucsonenses, on the other hand, remained tied to a subsistence agrarian economy that was just about dead by the end of the century.

The Southern Pacific Railroad

During the 1860s and 1870s, a number of Mexicans, including Ochoa, Carrillo and Samaniego, were able to compete on a relatively equal footing with the Anglo merchants and freighters in southern Arizona. According to the 1870 federal census, Carrillo was the wealthiest individual, Mexican or Anglo, in Tucson. Five years later, Ochoa became the only Mexican elected mayor of the town following the Gadsden Purchase. Those two decades witnessed the creation of a uniquely bicultural society as Anglos and Mexicans formed partnerships with one another, married into each other's families and, perhaps most importantly, fought the Apaches together. Mexicans continued to be a majority of Tucson's inhabitants, and Spanish served as the *lingua franca* of the southern Arizona frontier. Because of the strength of Mexican society in Tucson, Anglo ascendancy was not as rapid or as brutal as it was in other areas of the Southwest.

But that was before the arrival of the Southern Pacific Railroad. On March 20, 1880, the leading citizens of Tucson turned out to welcome the railroad into town. Charles Crocker, vice-president of the Southern Pacific, proclaimed that Tucson's frontier days were finally over. "From California we will bring you her cereals," he stated, "and from the eastern terminus emigrants to people your valleys and explore your mountains, and to carry both ways your mineral wealth." Crocker was right. The railroad destroyed Tucson's isolation, linking the little community to national and international markets. For the first time in Tucson's history, goods could be shipped in and out cheaply by rail, rather than hauled by pack train or freight wagon. The result was a regional boom in southern Arizona's two major industries, mining and ranching, and an explosion in the economy of scale. Native Tucsonenses had been unable to compete with the immigrant merchants who rode into the area after the Gadsden Purchase. After the arrival of the railroad, no Mexican, immigrant or otherwise, could challenge the great copper or land-and-cattle companies that soon made Arizona a colony of East and West Coast business interests.

One of the most important consequences of this economic revolution was a voracious demand for cheap labor. The railroads needed workers to lay and maintain track. The mining companies needed laborers to dig gold, silver, and especially copper ore. At first, the empire-builders imported Chinese immigrants to perform these jobs. But Anglo and Mexican workers quickly reacted to this threat to their livelihoods by attacking the Chinese and destroying the camps they lived in. Anglo and Mexican newspaper editors soon joined the anti-Oriental crusade, deriding the Chinese as "*chinacates*" or "sons of the Celestial Empire" who stole jobs, spread strange Asiatic diseases, and sent all their money across the sea. In the words of Tucson newspaper *El Fronterizo*, "The Chinaman is a fungus that lives in isolation, sucking the sap of the other plants."[2]

What was happening in Arizona, of course, was the brutal but effective creation of an economic pecking order organized largely along ethnic lines. At the top were the owners and operators of the railroads, the mining corporations, and the land-and-cattle companies. All of these individuals, without exception, were Anglo. In the middle were the small businessmen, ranchers and farmers, most of whom were Anglo, but with a few Mexicans as well. And then, at the bottom, were the men and women who owned no land or businesses but possessed only their own labor to sell.

But even among the working class there were divisions, with Anglos pitted against Mexicans, Mexicans against Native Americans, and everyone against the Chinese. By the end of the 19th century, the ethnic configurations of this pecking order were clear. Anglo workers dominated the relatively good-paying jobs such as railroad engineer or underground miner. Mexicans maintained the tracks, picked the crops, and ran herd on the cattle. The Chinese, on the other hand, had been driven off the railroads and out of the mines. From then on, Mexicans, not Orientals, performed most of the lowpaying jobs in southern Arizona.

The Subordination of the Mexican Working Class

In Tucson, the establishment of this economic hierarchy was modified in part by the nature of the town's economy, which was commercial rather than extractive. Tucson never became a one-industry town like the mining communities springing up across Arizona, nor did it develop into an agricultural center like Yuma or the Salt River Valley. Consequently, the exploitation of Mexican labor was not quite as stark as it was in other areas. Nonetheless, Tucson's economy still depended upon cheap labor and an abundant labor supply.

No other measure reflects the subordination of the Mexican working class better than the occupational structure of Tucson. By analyzing federal census manuscripts and Tucson city directories, my colleagues and I on the Mexican Heritage Project were able to determine where Mexicans fitted into Tucson's economic hierarchy through time. The results of that analysis reveal that despite major changes in Tucson's economic structure between 1860 and 1940, most Mexicans remained trapped in low-paying, blue-collar jobs. Such occupational stasis contrasts sharply with the significant upward mobility experienced by Anglos during this 80-year period.

Tucson's economy in 1860 was relatively undeveloped, with most members of the work force (77 percent) employed in what today would be called blue-collar occupations. Only seven percent, on the other had, were merchants, traders, or shopkeepers, while a mere five percent were professionals or clerks. In short, most individuals in early territorial Tucson, Anglo or Mexican, worked with their hands.

But even in 1860 there were pronounced differences in the Anglo and Mexican occupational structures. For example, the proportion of Anglo white-collar workers (32 percent) was nearly double that of the Mexicans. Furthermore, 47 percent of the Mexican work force toiled at what could be classified as unskilled jobs, compared to only 27 percent of the Anglos. The disparity between the Mexican and Anglo work forces therefore began soon after Tucson became a part of the United States.

Twenty years later, the year the railroad arrived, the gap between Anglo and Mexican workers had widened. In 1880, the percentage of Anglo white-collar workers increased slightly from 32 to 36 percent. During the same period, the proportion of Anglo unskilled laborers dropped significantly from 27 to 19 percent. Mexicans, on the other hand, registered only a slight gain in the general white-collar category--from 17 to 21 percent--while experiencing a major increase in the proportion of unskilled labor--from 47 to nearly 60 percent. Even before the railroad transformed Tucson's economy, the subordination of the Mexican work force was well under way.

The structural changes triggered by the Southern Pacific increased the economic mobility of both Anglo and Mexican workers during the next two decades. The proportion of Mexican unskilled laborers declined from 60 to 40 percent between 1880 and 1900, while the percentage of skilled workers doubled from nine to 18 percent. Despite these genuine gains, however, it is clear that Mexican upward mobility lagged far behind that of the Anglos in Tucson. At the turn of the century, nearly half of all Anglo members of the work force occupied white-collar positions. Only about one in five Mexicans, by contrast, held such jobs.

The evolution of Tucson's economic structure continued during the first two decades of the 20th century. By 1920, 62 percent of all Anglo workers fell within white-collar categories, compared to 28 percent of all Mexican workers. Meanwhile, the percentage of Anglo unskilled laborers continued to decline--from 12 percent in 1900 to seven percent in 1920. The Mexican unskilled labor sector, on the other hand, remained about the same. Moreover, much of the apparent upward mobility from the blue to the white-collar categories occurred at the lowest levels of the white-collar world, the stratum labelled as "sales/clerical." In 1900, only three perent of the Mexican and seven percent of the Anglo work forces worked as clerks or salesmen. Twenty years later, those figures had jumped to 14 percent among Mexicans and 22 percent among Anglos. As Tucson developed into a commercial center of the Southwest, the city's economy demanded clerks, secretaries and salesmen rather than factory workers or farm laborers.

Meanwhile, Anglos continued to dominate the highest positions in Tucson's economy, occupying 95 percent of the prestigious white-collar jobs such as doctor, lawyer, engineer and government official. Mexican entry into the sales/clerical world did not serve as a stepping stone to the upper echelons of Tucson's economic or political hierarchy.

And even the limited upward mobility of the early 20th century stalled during *la Crisis*--the Great Depression of the 1930s. Between 1920 and 1940, the percentage of Mexican white-collar workers declined slightly from 28 to 27 percent, while the proportion of unskilled Mexican laborers rose from 38 to 41 percent. During that same period, the number of Mexican-owned businesses declined by 18 percent even though the Mexican population jumped from 7,500 to 11,000. Thus, on the eve of World War II, the Mexican community of Tucson was not substantially better off than it had been 80 years earlier. The proportion of Mexican blue-collar workers in 1940 remained essentially the same as it had been in 1860. More to the point, four out of every ten Mexicans continued to labor at low-paying, often temporary, unskilled jobs. Tucson was growing but most of the fruits of that growth were falling into Anglo hands.

The Institutionalized Subordination of Mexicans in Tucson

Part of the disparity between the Mexican and Anglo work forces may have been due to Mexican immigration. It is possible that Mexican residents in Tucson may have enjoyed significant upward mobility from one generation to the next but that the steady flow of Mexicans from south of the border continually replenished the unskilled labor pool. In order to test that hypothesis, researchers would have to chart the occupational movement of particular Mexican families. If sons did tend to secure better jobs than their fathers, then the immigration hypothesis would be vindicated.

In my opinion, however, Mexican immigration alone cannot explain the stubborn persistence of Mexican economic subordination. Between the Gadsden Purchase and World War II, far more Anglos than Mexicans poured into town. Many of those Anglo newcomers may have been better educated than the Mexican immigrants, but they also encountered far fewer impediments--linguistic, economic or political--to their occupational advancement. The major conclusions of my research, in fact, suggest that Tucsonenses, like Mexicans across the Southwest, found themselves in a society that institutionalized their subordination in countless subtle and not-so-subtle ways.

By "institutionalized subordination" I mean subordination woven into the everyday fabric of society. Such subordination is "institutional" in the sense that it is entrenched within and perpetrated by formal organizations such as school systems, political parties, labor unions, businesses, and city, state and national governments. But it also operates on other levels as well, encoded in racial and ethnic stereotypes, reflected by the mass media, latent or overt in most personal transactions between members of the dominant and subordinate groups.

I have carefully chosen the term "institutionalized subordination" rather than "institutionalized discrimination" in order to distinguish between the apartheid-like subjugation of Blacks and Native Americans, which was often legally mandated, and the less overt political and economic subordination of working-class Mexicans. Mexicans were not prohibited from eating in certain restaurants or sitting where they liked in certain theaters in town. Moreover, researchers have yet to uncover any residential covenants that expressly excluded Mexicans from living in certain neighborhoods in Tucson, even though many such covenants banned Orientals, Native Americans, and Blacks. And even though the Operating Brotherhoods of the Southern Pacific did refuse to admit Mexican members, thereby preventing them from holding such jobs as railroad engineer, it is not yet clear whether other businesses overtly barred Mexicans from certain occupations. In Tucson, then, a Mexican Jim Crow system did not exist, at least not on the books.

Ethnic Enclavement

Nevertheless, equality de jure did not ensure equality de facto. Quite the contrary. Nearly every social index available reveals that strong and enduring mechanisms were at work to keep Mexicans in Tucson, especially working-class Mexicans, politically and economically subordinate.

The most visible manifestations of that subordination were the residence patterns of the Mexicans themselves. When Tucson became a part of the United States in 1854, most Tucsonenses lived within the adobe walls of the old presidio in order to protect themselves against Apache raids. Almost immediately, however, a complex process of displacement began as Anglo merchants and artisans settled in and around the presidio while Mexican families moved south. That process accelerated during the next two decades. By 1881, a year after the railroad arrived, most Mexicans in Tucson lived in a roughly rectangular area that began several blocks south of the old presidio and extended as far as 18th Street. The western boundary of this Mexican neighborhood was Main Avenue, the eastern boundary, Stone Avenue.

Meanwhile, the rest of the town was developing according to patterns that still prevail today. The presidial district became the nucleus of Tucson's commercial center, the area where most of the town's major businesses were located. And of those 139 enterprises, Anglos owned 112, or nearly 81 percent. Anglos also occupied most of the downtown residences. At the same time, Anglo households were expanding eastward, drawn by the inexorable pull of the Southern Pacific railroad tracks. According to Tucson historian Don Bufkin, the Southern Pacific "acted like a magnet after 1880, drawing new development east and northeast from the old presidial center."[3]

The geographic dualization of Tucson grew even more pronounced by the turn of the century. Anglos remained in control of the central business district, owning from 70-100 percent of the businesses and residences there. However, by 1900 a second major Anglo neighborhood had developed in the vicinity of the old Military Plaza, where nearly 89 percent of all households were Anglo. Populated in part by employees of the Southern Pacific, this neighborhood soon attracted several of the city's most modern recreational facilities and commercial establishments including the Santa Rita Hotel, the Carnegie Library, and Armory Park.

No other urban development so accurately reflected the priorities of Tucson's city fathers. During the 1880s and 1890s, the most elegant urban oasis in Tucson was Carrillo's Gardens, which was located southwest of the commercial district. As Tucson became more and more of an Anglo town, however, the Gardens withered while eastern neighborhoods bloomed. Geographic distance therefore aggravated the social and economic distances already separating the two major ethnic groups in town.

By 1920, Tucson was essentially cleft in half by ethnic neighborhoods. Anglos continued to dominate the downtown commercial district, but they were also expanding north and east from their base in Armory Park. Health seekers, railroad employees, land speculators, and businessmen mostly turned their backs on the barrios and moved into new neighborhoods on the other side of the Southern Pacific tracks. The march to the Rincons and the Catalinas had begun.

Mexicans, in contrast, kept on moving southward. South Meyer Street--*la calle Meyer*--remained the commercial axis around which the southern barrios turned. But Mexicans were also beginning to settle along the Santa Cruz floodplain, creating semi-rural enclaves on both sides of the ravaged river channel. Furthermore, a major Mexican neighborhood was evolving north of the old presidial district where the Southern Pacific tracks swung north toward Phoenix. This neighborhood--Barrio Anita--soon became a solid working-class district just west of Davis Elementary School and Holy Family Church.

Twenty years later, on the eve of World War II, most of Tucson's modern Mexican barrios had been established. The neighborhoods south of the downtown area persisted as largely Mexican enclaves, even though Blacks and Native Americans were settling in some of the poorer sections. At the same time, Mexican households dominated Tucson's west side, occupying most of the residences in Menlo Park, Kroeger Lane, Barrio Sin Nombre, and the El Río district. Anglos, in contrast, continued to expand north and east.

The reasons for this geographic dualization were complex, involving cultural as well as economic factors. Contrary to stereotype, most Mexican barrios were not slums. Pockets of desperate poverty existed, especially in neighborhoods south of the commercial district such as El Convento, La Meyer, and Barrio Libre. Neighborhoods like Barrio Anita, Millville, El Río, and Menlo Park, on the other hand, were relatively prosperous working-class and middle-class districts. Even the poorer barrios contained large networks of relatives, *compadres*, neighbors, and friends who helped each other weather individual and collective hard times. In most cases barrio life was a positive response to discrimination and subordination. Within them, Mexican society flourished, and many elements of Mexican culture were preserved.

For all their vitality, however, the barrios still symbolized the ethnic enclavement of Mexicans within a larger society dominated by Anglo politicians and Anglo businessmen. Even though many Mexican families would not have left the barrios even if they could have, they were not free to live anywhere in town. First of all, most could not afford to purchase homes in the most exclusive Anglo neighborhoods; the economic subordination of Mexicans therefore restricted their residential options. Secondly, the real estate industry itself may have had a tacit understanding not to sell Mexican families homes in certain areas. Whatever the situation, boundaries of both race and class reinforced each other to concentrate Mexicans on the southern and western sides of town.

Educational Subordination

One of the results of ethnic enclavement was the high concentration of Mexican children in barrio schools. Again, such concentration was not mandated by law as it was in the case of Blacks. And years later, in the 1970s, when Mexican plaintiffs in a lengthy school desegregation case accused Tucson School District One of a wide range of discriminatory practices, the evidence they presented was inconclusive. Tucson Unified School District, on the other hand, commissioned a series of detailed quantitative studies demonstrating considerable levels of integration in supposedly segregated schools. Until more sophisticated studies of the Tucson public school system are undertaken, the available evidence suggests that the high percentage of Mexicans in certain schools was the result of residence patterns rather than school district policies.[4]

But even if the public schools did not intentionally segregate Mexican students, those institutions still were not able to provide Mexican children with equal educational opportunities. As a result, many Mexican pupils fell far below their proper grade levels and eventually dropped out of school. To its credit, the public school system developed a number of programs to rectify the situation, but those programs were not sustained and were not comprehensive enough to surmount the enormous problems they confronted.

One of the problems was economic. As Superintendent C.E. Rose pointed out in the 1920s:

Several hundred of the Mexican and Indian children each year are taken from school by their parents in order to help with work in the cotton fields. These children are out of school and beyond the jurisdiction of our attendance officers for periods varying from one to three or four months.[5]

When these children returned to Tucson they lagged far behind other students. In such fashion, the children of migrant laborers remained trapped in the same world as their parents, unable to get the education they needed to escape the cotton fields.

The second major problem was linguistic. Again, according to Superintendent Rose:

The school situation in Tucson is an unusual one in the fact that over 50 percent of the school children as a whole are Spanish-speaking. The 24th St. School (Ochoa) just established this year, is entirely made up of children of foreign blood, Mexican and Indian, who could not speak nor understand a word of English at the opening of the school year. The Drachman school is 99 percent foreign, the Davis school about 85 percent, the Mansfield about 60 percent, and the Holladay about 30 percent. Beginning English classes have been established in all these schools, and thirteen teachers were employed to do the work of these classes alone.[6]

Those beginning English classes were the notorious 1C courses that gave so many Mexican children their first taste of public education in Tucson. Introduced in 1919, the 1C program became the foundation of the school system's attempt to incorporate Mexican students into the English-speaking world. Not until 1965, in fact, were the 1C classes replaced by more sophisticated programs of bilingual education.

Perhaps the greatest problem of all was the attitudes of the teachers and administrators themselves. To begin with, it is illuminating to note that Superintendent Rose referred to his Mexican and Indian pupils as "foreign," even though many of the Mexican children and nearly all of the Papago ones came from family lines that had resided in Arizona long before the Gadsden Purchase was signed. No other phrasing better captures the cultural arrogance of educators like Rose and his colleagues. During the early 20th century, one of the primary goals of the public school system was the "Americanization" of immigrants to the United States. As Rose himself stated:

The supervisor and teachers of these children have been persistent in their efforts to get English into the homes and to awaken in the parents an interest to learn English and to learn and to assimilate the high ideals and customs of this country.[7]

Implicit in such a statement is the assumption that "American" ideals and customs are superior to Mexican ones. Prior to World War II, nearly all teachers and administrators in the Tucson public schools were Anglos. And most of these Anglos, no matter how well-intentioned they might have been, carried their derogatory stereotypes of Mexican culture and Mexican children into the classrooms with them.

Nowhere are those stereotypes clearer or more blatant than in a series of master's theses prepared for the University of Arizona's College of Education. At least four such theses written between 1929 and 1946 directly concerned Mexican children in Tucson public schools. Because those theses were approved by the College of Education, they must have reflected widespread attitudes in Arizona educational circles. As such, they constitute a rather damning indictment of Anglo school personnel.

For the purposes of this presentation, I will briefly discuss only two of the theses: Erik Allstrom's "A Program of Social Education for a Mexican Community in the United States," written in 1929, and Rachel Riggins' "Factors in Social Background which Influence the Mexican Child in School," written in 1946. Together they demonstrate the range of attitudes toward Mexican children among Anglo educators--attitudes ranging from outright racism to sympathetic paternalism. What they lack, however, is any awareness that their own attitudes may have contributed to the problems they sought to address.

Allstrom's thesis begins with the chilling sentence, "There is a Mexican problem in the United States." He then goes on to say, "The people of the United States represent the democratic development of seven hundred years since the Magna Carta. The Mexican is the product of the autocratic individualism of the Latins, plus the pride and exclusiveness of the American Indian" (Allstrom 1929:1-2). What follows is a breathtakingly simplistic analysis of Mexican history and culture, leading Allstrom (1929:4) to conclude that Mexican children are "exceedingly individualistic," lacking in "formal play," preoccupied with "sex thoughts," and "ignorant of the most fundamental social concepts."

Allstrom's solution to the problem was to "socialize" Mexicans in the United States by giving them "an opportunity to understand" the "democratic ideals and practices" of their adopted country. In his own inimitable words:

> This socialization, in my opinion, will best begin with socialized play and supervised reading in the formative years of childhood and adolescence. Play among the Mexicans in the normal Mexican atmosphere is chiefly gambling with cards and dice and on the holidays and Sundays cock fighting and bull fighting at which gambling is a major element. Play as it is known among Anglo-Saxon people is virtually unknown among the Latins. Small children are given over to the care and supervision of servants, who come from the lowest classes both socially and economically, and who are utterly unfit because of lack of knowledge to have the care of any children. These servants fill the minds of the children with filthy stories and with warped ideas of sex, and when the children arrive at the free-play age of Anglo-Saxon childhood they loaf about with nothing to do but discuss sex (Allstrom 1929:17).

It is not hard to imagine what kind of a teacher Allstrom or others like him must have been: racists with little or no understanding of their Mexican pupils. The destructive effect of such attitudes in the classroom must have been immense. Rachel Riggins, on the other hand, was a much more sympathetic observer of Mexican society and culture. A social worker in Tucson during the Depression, Riggins was familiar with the desperate poverty of many Mexican working-class families. She therefore recognized the obstacles many Mexican children faced in their pursuit of an education: poor nutrition, inadequate medical care, cramped and dilapidated housing and the necessity of older children having to quit school in order to work and support their families. As such, her analysis served as a welcome balance to the pseudoscientific nonsense of a man like Allstrom.

Unfortunately, however, Riggins fell into the same trap that has ensnared other, more sophisticated researchers. Foreshadowing the "culture of poverty" school of thought associated with such scholars as Oscar Lewis and Daniel Moynihan, Riggins believed that the economic conditions of the barrios created a cultural milieu that prevented many Mexican children from progressing in school. In her opinion, Mexican students were hampered by a

> mental attitude or mind set which develops rather naturally in such limited homes, retaining the flavor and customs of a culture based on folklore and superstition rather than on scientific knowledge and which tends, therefore, toward vague, mysterious generalization and unquestioning acceptance of ideas rather than careful examination of facts or a desire to prove or disprove them (Riggins 1946:38-39).

The danger in such a viewpoint is that it makes attitudes rather than external conditions the locus of social change. If Mexicans--or, by extension, any other minority in the United States--could just alter the way they thought, or their child-rearing practices, or their patterns of family life--then the rewards of the American Dream would soon be theirs. Such an outlook gives primacy to the consequences of poverty and discrimination rather than to their causes. Moreover, it tends to "blame the victim" for his or her own subordination. What Riggins and others failed to understand was that attitudes change in response to changing social and economic conditions, not vice versa.

No matter how good-hearted an educator like Riggins was, she and people like her undoubtedly conveyed the message that Mexican culture was somehow inferior to "American" culture. Such a message, whether it was blatantly communicated by washing children's mouths out with soap for speaking Spanish in the classroom, or more subtly transmitted through the glorification of "Anglo-Saxon" civilization, must have convinced many Mexican students that they were personally inferior as well. Those feelings of inferiority, combined with very real economic and linguistic disadvantages, deprived many Mexican children of the education they deserved. As one prominent Tucsonense later said, "It was a terrible waste of brainpower."[8]

Mexican Resistance in Tucson

So far, I have talked primarily about what happened to Mexicans in Tucson between the Gadsden Purchase and World War II. It is important to realize, however, that Tucsonenses never passively accepted the processes of subordination discussed above. On the contrary, Mexicans actively resisted those processes in a variety of ways ranging from political organization to cultural preservation. Their resistance, in fact, undoubtedly prevented the entrenchment of more overt forms of discrimination afflicting other Mexican populations throughout the Southwest.

One of the primary forms of Mexican resistance was vigorous participation in city and county politics. Contrary to stereotype, Mexicans were not politically apathetic. Instead, they joined both the Democratic and Republican parties in large numbers, supporting Mexican candidates and organizing Mexican political clubs. As a result, Mexican politicians won election to many important offices during the late 19th and early 20th centuries. Mariano Samaniego, for example, served as territorial legislator, county assessor, city councilman, and chairman of the county board of supervisors. He was also chosen as a member of the University of Arizona's first board of regents, a position he was particularly well-qualified for because he was one of the few inhabitants of frontier Tucson, Mexican or Anglo, with a college education. Other successful Mexican politicians included Estevan Ochoa, Joaquín Legarra, Perfecto Elías, and Nabor Pacheco, who served as Pima County Sheriff and Tucson Chief of Police.

But despite those successes, Mexican candidates were frustrated more often than they were rewarded. The number of Mexican elected officials peaked around the turn of the century; in the decades that followed successful candidacies were rare. Between 1904 and 1927, for instance, no Mexican was elected to the Tucson City Council. Tucsonenses like Bernabé Brichta continued to run for office, but they increasingly found that the avenues to political power were closed to all but a handful of the Mexican elite.

One response to the thwarting of Mexican ambitions through conventional political channels was the creation of Mexican organizations, especially the mutual-aid societies, or *mutualistas*. Those mutualistas were part of worldwide phenomenon involving industrialization and the widespread migration of people from the countryside to the cities. As immigrants left traditional networks of support such as extended families or peasant corporate communities, they created new institutions to provide themselves with the security they needed in strange and often hostile environments. Mexican mutual-aid societies sponsored social events, and offered low-cost life and burial insurance to their members. More importantly, they furnished an organizational structure that enabled their members to protest many of the manifestations of discrimination and subordination sweeping across the Southwest.

The largest of these mutualistas in Tucson--indeed, throughout the entire United States and northern Mexico--was the Alianza Hispano-Americana. But the Alianza was joined by other important organizations as well, including the *Sociedad Mutualista Porfirio Díaz*, the *Sociedad Amigos Unidos*, and the most politically active of them all, the *Liga Protectora Latina*, which was founded in Phoenix in 1914. Together, these mutualistas became the most important political instruments of Arizona's Mexican middle-class.

During its heyday, the mutualista movement engaged in a number of important crusades: protecting Mexican nationals from the military draft, protesting derogatory stereotypes of Mexicans in Hollywood movies, campaigning against discriminatory hiring practices in Arizona mines, struggling to win pardons for Mexican prisoners condemned to death in Arizona jails. Organizations like the *Liga* served as forerunners of more activist Mexican organizations such as the League of United Latin American Citizens (LULAC) or the GI Forum, which developed after World War II. Above all, they gave Mexicans an organized voice in Arizona politics at a time when the political climate in Arizona was growing increasingly racist and conservative.

The Politics of Race and Class in Tucson

It is important to note that most mutualistas in Tucson served middle-class rather than working-class interests. At times those interests intersected; the Liga, for example, strongly opposed a series of attempts to exclude Mexicans from running machinery or working underground in the mines. On the other hand, the mutual-aid societies did not appear to take an active role in the organized labor movement, at least not in Tucson. Protesting discriminatory hiring practices or the execution of Mexican convicts was one thing those manifestations of racism affected the status of all Mexicans regardless of class. But the organs of Mexican middle-class opinion were much more ambivalent about basic economic issues such as labor unions and the right to strike.

As early as 1878, for example, the editors of *Las Dos Repúblicas*, Tucson's first Spanish-language newspaper, condemned "workers' societies," contending that they consisted of "idle and depraved people" who wanted "a repetition of the 1792 Revolution in France."[9] Carlos Velasco, founding father of the Alianza Hispano-Americana, echoed those sentiments in a speech given on the Alianza's first anniversary. According to Velasco, one of the organization's major goals was to imbue the Mexican working class with a "hatred of vagrancy" and a "love of work."[10] Such observations stood in stark contrast to the revolutionary rhetoric of the Flores-Magón brothers and other radicals organizing Mexican workers on both sides of the international border.

And Mexican workers did organize, even when they were ignored by Anglo labor unions and opposed by Mexican middle-class intellectuals and businessmen. People familiar with the history of the Mexican Revolution remember the bloody strike in the Cananea copper mines in 1906. Many historians, in fact, consider the Cananea strike to be a precursor of the Revolution itself. But Mexican miners also carried out the first major strike in Arizona--the Clifton strike of 1903. They did so despite the fact that unions like the Western Federation of Miners had largely written Clifton-Morenci off as a "Mexican town."

Even in Tucson, where the economy was commercial rather than industrial, Mexican workers banded together to protest wage cuts and layoffs. Their biggest target, not surprisingly, was the Southern Pacific, the largest employer of Mexican labor in town. In 1920, for example, 27 percent of all Mexican workers worked for the railroad, usually in the shops or section gangs. The following year, when the Southern Pacific threatened to cut their wages by as much as thirty cents an hour, they decided to walk out on strike. *El Tucsonense*, the most important Spanish-language newspaper in Tucson, urged them not to do so, arguing that reduced wages were better than none at all. Eighteen hundred workers disagreed, and in July, 1922, the strike began.[11] The controversy between Mexican railroad workers and a middle-class Mexican newspaper reveals how differences of class often weakened bonds of ethnic identity among Mexicans in Tucson. The Southern Pacific workers, like workers throughout the world, believed that strikes were often necessary to achieve their goals. Mexican businessmen, on the other hand, viewed strikes and organized labor with alarm. First of all, Mexican merchants did not want the wage structure of southern Arizona to rise too sharply; otherwise, their own labor costs would have risen as well. Secondly, they saw strikes as threats to their own economic well-being, even when the strikes were not directed against them. Striking workers, after all, received no paychecks, and no paychecks meant no business in barrio stores. Larger firms could weather widespread strikes or layoffs. Many small, struggling barrio businesses, however, could not. In the final analysis, then, Ramón Soto's vision of a united *Colonia Hispano-Americana* was undercut by the conflicting interests of Mexican workers and Mexican businessmen, making it more of a chimera than a reality.

But even if all Mexicans in Tucson had come together to protest their subordination, the political and economic deck was stacked against them. Prior to World War II, Arizona's economy was dominated by three major extractive industries: mining, ranching, and agriculture. All three of these enterprises--the producers of Arizona's famous "Three C's": copper, cattle, and cotton--converted Arizona's natural resources into raw material to be shipped and processed somewhere else. And like most extractive industries, they depended upon cheap, abundant, often seasonal labor. An attempt to import Chinese workers failed in the late 1800s. Thereafter, Mexicans on both sides of the international border served as the reserve labor supply upon which Arizona's industries drew.

And since the Arizona economy relied upon cheap labor, the major source of that labor had to be subordinated in order to keep labor costs down. The results were differential wage scales for Mexican and Anglo workers, the manipulation of immigration policies to control the flow of Mexicans across the border, and most importantly, the pitting of Mexican and Anglo workers against each other in order to weaken the organized labor movement in general. Ethnic conflict and proximity to Mexico therefore served as two of the most important tools whereby Arizona industries and industries across the southwestern United States, kept workers tractable and wages low.

Moreover, there was no compelling reason to provide those workers with much more than an elementary education. Consequently, little pressure was put upon the public schools to improve their programs and prevent so many Mexican students from dropping out. On the contrary, too much education might have opened other avenues for many workers, thereby threatening the labor supply. In such fashion, derogatory stereotypes about Mexican children were fueled by the need for cheap labor, and even the most gifted of Mexican pupils often found themselves channeled into vocational courses rather than prepared for college and the white-collar world.

It is important to note that the subordination of the Mexican working class in southern Arizona was not the result of any conspiracy masterminded by Phelps-Dodge or the Southern Pacific. On the contrary, it was a much more complex phenomenon, one that developed because of many factors--cultural, political, demographic, and above all, economic--intersecting in the region. Many well-meaning people, even today, do not understand how subtle and pervasive racism really is. They believe that once discriminatory laws are struck down, racism ceases to exist. But what racism really is is a system of attitudes, symbols, and beliefs designed to justify the subordination of one group of people by another. Once rooted in a society, the system becomes extremely difficult to eradicate because it penetrates nearly all aspects of life and thought. Moreover, it operates on unconscious as well as conscious levels, affecting individuals and institutions in ways they often cannot comprehend. Tucson public schools, for example, may not have deliberately segregated Mexican children or intended to offer them inferior educations. Nonetheless, the destructive effects of the attitudes of teachers and administrators themselves must have been incalculable. In a sense, the institutional manifestations of racism are the least insidious because they can be identified and eliminated. It is far more arduous to change the basic assumptions people make about others, especially since many of those assumptions are unconscious and unquestioned.

Above all, racism must be viewed as a cultural construct, not a biological given. And like all such constructs, it is a form of adaptation to changing political and economic realities, the ideological manifestation of a set of historically determined power relationships that change through time. In the Southwest, an aggressive expanding nation dominated by Anglos encountered the sparsely populated frontier of another nation that had not yet recovered from a destructive war for independence. The economic and demographic strength of the one nation collided with the economic and demographic weakness of the other, resulting, not surprisingly, in conquest and colonization. As in all such situations through history and across the world, the conquerors were not honest enough to justify their actions on the grounds that might makes right. They therefore had to develop elaborate rationalizations for the subordination of the people they came to control. It is beyond the scope of this presentation to examine the range of those rationalizations. What I have tried to do here is merely present some of the consequences of race and class in Tucson, consequences that still influence the social, political, and economic life of the community today.

Notes

1. *El Fronterizo*, July 9, 1892. Soto's other two articles appeared in *El Fronterizo* on July 16 and July 23 of the same year.
2. *El Fronterizo*, August 4, 1894.
3. Don Bufkin, "From Mud Village to Modern Metropolis: The Urbanization of Tucson", *Journal of Arizona History* 22:72 (1981).
4. The plaintiffs' case, as well as the studies commissioned by the Tucson Unified School District in defense, is located in the archives of TUSD. The desegregation case is summarized at greater length in Sheridan, 1986.
5. Report of the Superintendent, 1923-24, p. 18. These reports are located in the Special Collections of the University of Arizona's Main Library.
6. Report of the Superintendent, 1920-21, p. 43.
7. Ibid., p. 46.
8. Fred Acosta, quoted in the *Arizona Daily Star*, July 16, 1978.
9. *Las Dos Repúblicas*, August 24, 1878.
10. *El Fronterizo,* January 19, 1895.
11. *El Tucsonense*, October 20, 1921. *El Mosquito*, July 1, 1922.

Bibliography

Acuña, Rodolfo
    1981, *Occupied America: A History of Chicanos.* New York: Harper & Row.
Allstrom, Erik
    1929, A Program of Social Education for a Mexican Community in the United States. Master's thesis, College of Education, University of Arizona.
De León, Arnoldo
    1982, *The Tejano Community, 1836-1900.* Albuquerque: University of New Mexico Press.
Griswold del Castillo, Richard
    1979, *The Los Angeles Barrio, 1850-1900.* Berkeley: University of California Press.
Pitt, Leonard
    1966, *The Decline of the Californios: A Social History of the Spanish-Speaking Californians, 1846-1890.* Berkeley: University of California Press.
Riggins, Rachel
    1946, Factors in Social Background Which Influence the Mexican Child in School. Master's thesis, Department of Education, University of Arizona.
Sheridan, Thomas
    1986, *Los Tucsonenses: The Mexican Community in Tucson, 1854-1941.* The University of Arizona Press.

Nuevomexicano apprehension in the 1890s over a future dominated by "los extranjeros" crystallized discontent into the formation of the first Chicano political party, El Partido del Pueblo Unido. In this article Robert Rosenbaum reveals how El Partido coalesced discontent over land encroachments, political bossism and erosion of their traditional way of life and sought to stem the tide through electoral politics. El Partido produced striking political victories in northern New Mexico but ultimately splintered and collapsed as factions and individuals joined the dominant political parties.

El Partido del Pueblo Unido
Robert J. Rosenbaum

The thirty-four names affixed to the call for delegates to the county convention of El Partido del Pueblo Unido signaled a realignment in the San Miguel political arena and a transition from terroristic to electoral politics.

The White Cap raids halted Anglo American "progress" in east-central New Mexico; the authorities could not combat the phantom movement, and public opinion supported the White Caps against land thieves. Investors and settlers paused en route to San Miguel County, waiting to see which tack *mexicano* resistance would take.

Conceivably, Las Gorras Blancas could have continued their violent attacks. During the summer, cut fences and burned barns were reported with increasing frequency, and Governor Prince received warnings of unrest spreading to neighboring counties. Fearful *americanos* predicted a war for independence: ". . . quite a large number of them are dreaming . . . that New Mexico can achieve her independence of the United States by driving out the Americans . . . They say,' . . . this county . . . is ours, and we don't propose to have any Americans interfering with our rights.' Ever since the annexation . . . a few hotheaded ignorant Mexicans have talked like the above, but since the labor organizations have come into existence . . . these extreme men have become more numerous and bolder in their declarations." [1]

There is no evidence that the idea of secession, however appealing, was seriously entertained. Las Gorras Blancas held sway only in San Miguel County. Bands appeared in adjacent regions, *los hombres pobres* shared common resentments and grievances, and in the summer of 1890, White Caps enjoyed marginal dominance in a disrupted county. But White Cap supremacy was more apparent than real. It rested on the uneven cornerstones of intimidation and popular sympathy. The first was concrete, but touched only a small segment of the county's population; the second was widespread but intangible and could disappear quickly.

The bitter, angry residents of the countryside saw their way of life being destroyed by incomprehensible methods that violated standards of order and morality. One purpose overrode all others in drawing the bands of horsemen together: restoration of the traditional use of the common land. Their success threatened to dissolve their organization held together by immediate problems and bounded by local landmarks: with the fences down, the problem no longer existed, and their unity weakened.

Juan José Herrera coordinated common complaints, methods, and leadership into a body capable of obstructing change and expressing discontent, not one that could sustain creative action. By the end of August others recognized that Las Gorras Blancas could go no further. The night riders had exposed serious problems to the full light of the New Mexican sun, and they had created a power vacuum. But Las Gorras Blancas could not fill the void, and El Partido del Pueblo Unido stepped forward to take advantage of White Cap successes. It assumed the mantle of Las Gorras Blancas' moral position by embracing, in form at least, two issues emphasized in the platform of the preceding March: the land question and political bossism. To this nucleus the party added the national anger against monopolies and corporations soon to solidify around the Populists and presented itself as a reform party committed to the welfare of all the people.

Membership

A mixed bag of Las Vegas *politicos* signed the call for the convention. White Caps Herrera and his brother Nicanor joined young, ambitious native Democrats Felíx Martínez and Nestor Montoya. Anglo Knights of Labor and Anglo lawyers and businessmen of the Democratic Party mingled with renegade Republicans unhappy with county leadership. *Jefes* like Lorenzo López saw a chance to increase their power.[2] Idealism, dissatisfaction, patronage, and power spurred the alliance of old antagonists. Opposition to the Republican Party as run by Eugenio Romero in San Miguel and Thomas Catron in Santa Fe was the only point of agreement among the leaders of the party that capitalized on the White Cap outbreaks.

Juan José Herrera. Felíx Martínez. and Lorenzo López represent three distinct types within El Partido del Pueblo's upper councils. Herrera, an active man of middle age. was willing to substitute votes and elected officials for raids and posted warnings if doing so would protect and enhance the interests of *los pobres*, but he was wary of Anglo practices. The traditional rights must be maintained; Herrera would support no change in established patterns until it was clearly demonstrated that the people, his people, would benefit.[3]

Felíx Martínez had a different vision of the coming order. Born in Taos and educated at a "commercial school" in Trinidad, Colorado, Martínez had come to Las Vegas in 1880 at the age of twenty-two and quickly made a mark as an entrepreneur and active Democrat. By 1890, he had served one term in the New Mexico House, another as county assessor, and was on the Democratic Territorial Central Committee. Martínez used his position in the county to plead for the masses in general and *mexicanos* in particular. But where Herrera viewed all aspects of Anglo America with suspicion, Martínez welcomed Anglo political institutions, commercial and technological innovations, and social services like public education. Martínez was not opposed to progress; he only wanted his people to control it in New Mexico.[4]

Lorenzo López was neither a leader of the people nor a proponent of integrating *mexicanos* into the American Dream. Born in 1837 to a wealthy local grazier, López combined the advantages of birth with a strong interest in politics and a judicious marriage into the powerful Romero family. By 1890, he was one of the top two Republican *jejes* in the county, controlling, in Catron's estimation, four hundred votes directly[5] able to command a large following among the lesser *jefes* and *patrones,* and alternating with his in-laws in the most lucrative and influential county offices. Friction with the Romeros prompted his move to the new party. At "daggers-points" with his wife's family since 1888, Lorenzo López saw in the new party a chance to control San Miguel County without having to share with Eugenio Romero.[6]

El Partido del Pueblo formed out of coalition of middle-class Hispanos, Anglo laborers and lawyers, and some old style *jefes políticos*, founded upon an angry and rebellious mass of *los hombres pobres*. The *Optic* called it the "mongrel" party and characterized the campaign as one of equal parts "free whiskey, free sheep and intimidation.[7] The newspaper branded El Partido del Pueblo Unido as the party of the White Caps: "'Down with the fence cutters, the despoilers of our citizens,' says Nestor Montoya. All right Don Nestor. That is certainly sage counsel; but then, the people would have more confidence in the sincerity of your purpose, if you would first remove the said persons from your county ticket."[8]

The Election of 1890

A good partisan newspaper, the *Optic* each day predicted crushing defeat for the upstarts. Even after preliminary returns promised a sweeping victory for the new party, the *Optic* remained optimistic. Eugenio Romero was not worried, the paper assured its readers, for the returns from the outlying precincts were sure to bring victory to the Republicans.[9]

Romero was wrong. Running on an anticapitalist, antimonopolist platform, which in New Mexico meant anti-land-grabber, anti-railroad and anti-Santa Fe Ring, the United People's Party captured every office by an average of 60 percent of the vote. The party supported Democratic incumbent Antonio Joseph for delegate-in-Congress, and this tie with Democrats was maintained through cooperation in the territorial legislature and continued participation in the Central Committee.

The precinct returns underscore the importance of the land issue; *mexicano* communities on threatened grants provided the largest margins for El Partido del Pueblo.

The returns also point to an independence on the part of the *nativo* voters: almost every precinct made distinctions between candidates, with Anglos generally faring worst.[10]

Despite the decisive victory and glowing predictions of future success, El Partido del Pueblo did little to change county administration. The legislative delegation gained some victories, particularly Nestor Montoya's fence law which made it a crime either to destroy a fence on land of good title or to erect one on property not owned in fee simple, but they were defeated by Catron over the abolition of the three-hundred-dollar exemption for heads of households-a severe setback to people who did not own three hundred dollars' worth of property-and the concomitant jury law which forbade anyone who had not paid taxes to sit on a jury.[11]

If county administration did not change appreciably and the legislative impact was less than earthshaking, El Partido del Pueblo did remain embroiled in the land question.

The Land Issue

For several years, territorial officials and businessmen had petitioned Congress for a special court to settle the confused property situation in New Mexico. The People's Party supported the creation of a U.S. Court of Private Land Claims, in hopes that it would untangle land titles and end large-scale speculation. Created in 1891, the court did not meet in New Mexico until 1892. Charged with ascertaining the validity and extent of Spanish and Mexican land grants in New Mexico, Colorado, and Arizona, the court sat until 1904 and heard cases involving a total of 235,491,020 acres. Unfortunately for *mexicanos*, it viewed most claims with suspicion; at the end of its term, only 2,051,526 acres remained as grant land, with the balance classified as public domain.[12']

As the court was just beginning in 1891, and as it had no jurisdiction over grants that had been patented by Congress-the Las Vegas Grant was one-New Mexicans involved in land controversies sought other avenues.

The territorial legislature offered a possible solution in an act of February 26, 1891. This act provided for the incorporation of a grant upon petition by inhabitants, and empowered a board of trustees, elected from the precincts within the grant, to determine legitimate owners and the extent of their private holdings, and to administer the common lands and other corporate matters.[13] El Partido del Pueblo used its strength to control the membership and policies of various committees formed to investigate this possibility.

The rights of *los hombres pobres* gained support from a decision rendered by Judge O'Brien in the case of *Millhiser et al. v. José Albino Baca et al.* The Millhiser group had not quit after the 1889 decision, but continued to bring suit against grant residents in, as the *Optic* put it, an apparent attempt to bankrupt every grant inhabitant. O'Brien ruled that the law of ten years' limitation, that is, ten years of unchallenged occupancy, gave all known native New Mexican residents on the Las Vegas Grant clear title to their holdings, even in the absence of documentary proof.[14]

The decision prompted the formation of a committee which began to identify all legitimate occupants of the grant under the law of ten years' limitation. A convention in July, 1891, resolved to petition for incorporation under territorial law and drafted the machinery for choosing the board of trustees. It also passed five resolutions proposed by Félix Martínez. These reduced the minimum tenure for legitimacy to five years and provided that those who could not meet this standard would be allowed to remain until they had established title; it made the maximum amount allowed any one individual 160 acres and stipulated that the proper tribunal would determine each claimant's holdings up to this amount. The fifth resolution stated that anyone settling after the date of the meeting would be an intruder, and that no uncultivated land could be allocated without the approval of proper authority.[15]

El Partido del Pueblo controlled the convention, and its proposals reflected the impact of Las Gorras Blancas: they stressed the rights of *los hombres pobres*, including the uncultivated or common land, and devised machinery that would in theory allow grant residents self-determination. Yet the resolutions really reflected an anti-corporate thrust rather than pure White Cappism. Four of the five emphasized size of the holdings and length of residence; the size was small, a victory for *los pobres*, but residence was short, thereby potentially including some Anglos. The last provision, although alluding to common land, provided for future settlement-something that Las Gorras Blancas had not fought for.

Political Jousting

Organized violence died down. Sporadic attacks on fences or crops occurred, fights and killings with political overtones continued as part of the scheme of things, but the coordinated bands that had roamed the countryside during the previous two years were no more. Some Anglos thought that *mexicanos* had refined techniques of harassment. One complained to Governor Prince that it cost him a yearly tribute of sixty-five dollars to keep his fence upright.[17] But in general the victory of El Partido del Pueblo brought quiet to San Miguel County.

The opposition countered by equating the party and Los Caballeros de Labor with all lawlessness throughout the territory; by building an organization, the Sociedad de los Caballeros de Ley y Orden y Protección Mutua,[18] which competed for members in the same communities that supported the White Caps; and by putting forth *El Sol de Mayo* to rival *La Voz* for the Spanish reading public.

By the winter of 1891, Republicans blamed the White Caps for every violent incident in the territory, from the mysterious burning of the new territorial capitol building and the shooting of Territorial Senator J. A. Ancheta to collusion between administrations and bandit gangs in several counties.[19] *La Voz* denied that the White Caps existed. "*Pobres Gorras Blancas*!" exclaimed one editorial and went on to say that the name came from an isolated raid on the San Miguel courthouse some years before and had become a catchall to include all the "thieves, assassins, and usurpers" in New Mexico.[20] Yet in its continual denials of any connection between the Knights and violence, *La Voz* never failed to stress that the real villains in New Mexico were not the "vandals or masked highwaymen" but the "despotic oppressors . . . hidden technically by the law . . . "[21]

Much of San Miguel's political activity for the next three years revolved around rhetorical duels between *La Voz* and *El Sol* and recruitment competition between the Knights of Labor and the Society of Law and Order. As the clear-cut issue of fences on the common land melted into a slough of litigation, meetings, and proposals, reintroduced factions and attendant bickering punctuated with frequent switches in allegiance and individual skirmishes characterized the conflict. Both newspapers featured confessions from people who had joined the wrong organization and now saw the error of their ways; El Partido del Pueblo scored the biggest coup with the defection of Enrique Armijo, the first editor of *El Sol*.[22]

Both groups expanded their operations. Herrera bought *El Defensor del Pueblo* in June, 1891 , and began to publish it in Albuquerque as the official organ of the Knights of Labor. Law and Order chapters appeared in Mora, Bernalillo, and Santa Fe counties, countered by assemblies of the Knights of Labor and local People's Party organizations. The latter, which by mid-1892 ranged from the Spanish strongholds in the north to Las Cruces on the southern Rio Grande, mirrored the San Miguel experience both in terms of their mixed support and emphasis on local considerations, and in their recognition of the themes of native control of New Mexico, hostility to Anglo economic competition, and ethnic pride.[23]

The paradox of rising group consciousness elsewhere in the territory and the reappearance of internecine feuds in San Miguel did not escape *La Voz*. "*Es necessario que obremos . . . todos como hermanos*," pleaded the paper, in order to better our condition and keep "*los extranjeros*" from dominating.[24] *Los neo-mexicanos* must stop personal and family wars, must ignore politics except during elections, and must work industriously. *Nativos* must learn English, not to replace Spanish, but to allow them to compete in the new order; New Mexicans must supplement farming and grazing with a knowledge of Anglo crafts and trades. For *La Voz,* progress was good, and technological skills, joined with political control through unity, were the ways to reach peaceful prosperity.

The national People's Party, founded on agrarian discontent and champion of the people against capitalists, inspired El Partido del Pueblo in much the same way that the national Knights of Labor encouraged Las Gorras Blancas. Beginning in the summer of 1891, peaking during the election of 1892, and continuing until 1894, El Partido del Pueblo made common rhetorical cause with the Populists on the issues of wealth, racial harmony, land, silver, and the worker. Cultural differences, racial antagonisms, and realities of power prevented a union between the two "people's" parties, however; they fought on the same side, but always as distinct armies.[25]

Land remained a continual issue, dying down and then flaring up as factions jousted for control of the grants. The Las Vegas Grant remained unsettled despite the meeting in 1891, and it would remain so until 1903. Debate centered around the definition of "community grant." Many Las Vegas businessmen, regardless of any party affiliation, argued that "community" meant the town of Las Vegas, because they wanted a settlement that would give the town control of and profit from the grant. Félix Martínez was willing to go along with this interpretation if "anglo-americans . . . would not in any way alienate the rights of hispano-americans."[26] Herrera rejected this proposal, asserting that "community" meant all of the residents of the grant, as defined in the grant document and buttressed by the laws of the Indies, and that Las Vegas had no more land rights beyond its corporate boundaries than did the City of Denver.[27]

Concerted action had dissipated, but the wellspring of resentment remained. Thomas Catron served as its most effective focus. During the fall term of the district court, Catron employed the jury law that he had sponsored in the preceding legislature to dismiss the jurors in a case in which he was involved. Using the imperative "Sal" ("Get out"), the form used for dogs, Catron ordered the jurors from the courtroom *con la arrogancia de un rey.*"[28] Two public meetings denounced both Catron and the jury law; an incident the following spring further enflamed most of San Miguel's *nativos* against the man.

On the night of May 29, 1892, Francisco Chaves, sheriff of Santa Fe County and grand master workman of the Knights Labor for the territory, was killed from ambush. A rising Democratic politician who had built a strong opposition organization to the Santa Fe Ring, he had been killed by the Borrego brothers, known associates of Catron. *La Voz* lost no time in charging Catron with the murder and connecting the Law and Order Society to the assassins. Since Catron was the Republican candidate for delegate-in-Congress in the fall, the county girded for a bitter campaign.[29]

The Election of 1892

Local personalities and the land grants had dominated the 1890 election. In 1892, Catron's shadow covered everything else. Pilloried for his enormous wealth based on land stolen from *los pobres*, his intimidation of *mexicano* jurors, and his use of harassment and assassination, Catron symbolized in San Miguel County the worst evils of Anglo encroachment; he lost by the widest margin of any candidate.[30]

El Partido del Pueblo again swept the election but, except for the delegate race, did not enjoy the superiority of 1890. Republican inroads in the 1890 areas of strength hinted that county politics were beginning to return to their old patterns.[31]

Still, El Partido del Pueblo faced the next two years with confidence. With a Democratic administration in Washington, the party leaders judged the time right for statehood-which would mean home rule for *mexicanos*. They added free silver and a wool tariff to their past programs, reflecting their adjudged self-interest among the trends affecting the nation.

Local confusion, however, contributed to the fragmentation that had begun in 1891, and national factors exacerbated it. The long depression and low purchasing power of agricultural and laboring sectors of the country's economy combined with foreign demands on U.S. gold reserves and a decline in railroad investment to produce one of the worst depressions in the nation's history. In New Mexico, the Panic of 1893 was compounded by the Wilson-Gorman tariff which placed wool, the territory's most important product, on the free list. Las Vegas businessmen refused to extend credit to *los pobres*; the Knights of Labor charged the merchants with inhumanity and an evil use of human suffering to break the back of the union.[32]

For the eighteen months after the 1892 election, factional bickering and personal animosities chipped away at *La Voz's* dream of a united *mexicano* people, *todos como hermanos*. E. H. Salazar, son-in-law of Lorenzo López, left *La Voz* and began another paper, *El Independiente,* for no apparent reason other than personal dislike of Martínez; Carlos Rudulph, clerk of the probate court, feuded with E. C. de Baca and earned sharp public censure from Los Caballeros de Labor.[32] Recognizing that their only hope lay in unity, Martínez supported an ethnically homogeneous mixture of Republicans and El Partido del Pueblo *políticos* for the school board in April 1894.[34] The following July brought an incident that almost united the whole *mexicano* population of the county.

The Billy Green Disturbance

"*Encuentro Fatal*" screamed the headline of *La Voz* on Saturday, July 28; "*Tragedia Sangrienta*" echoed *El Independiente*.[35] Both stories described a series of events that had taken place the preceeding Wednesday and Thursday. Billy Green, a notorious Anglo ruffian, had shot Nestor Gallegos, one of two brothers suspected of belonging to the Vicente Silva gang and charged with the murder of Patricio Maes.[36] Green and his brother Eli had been active in attempting to earn the $300 territorial reward for the arrest of anyone suspected of belonging to the Silva gang, or Gavilla Silva. Gallegos did not die until the following day, and in the interim he swore before Justice of the Peace Pablo Ulibarrí that Green had shot him without cause. Constable José Martínez and two deputies went after Green, backed by a warrant.[37]

The killer, his brother, and a Chihuahuan named Jesús Villezea, were eating in a restaurant in West Las Vegas when the officers approached. Green promptly shot one of the deputies and barricaded himself in the kitchen. East Las Vegas Marshal T. F. Clay hurried across the Gallinas River to bring the three into the more congenial custody of the Anglo "new town"; Sheriff Lorenzo López, his deputies, and a large number of townspeople went to the aid of the constable. While the two contingents struggled for the right to make the arrests, District Attorney L. C. Fort appealed to the regular army, stationed in Las Vegas to protect the railroad. The army tipped the balance in favor of the new town, and Clay returned across the river with the Greens, leaving Villezea as a sop for the wounded pride of county authority.[38]

The incident was important because of the racial hostilities it unleashed. Both *El Independiente* and *La Voz* branded it as a conflict *"entre el americano y el mexicano"*; racial epithets denigrating the *"pueblo mexicano"* filled the air, accompanied by rocks, scuffles, and bayonet stabs.[39] The *Optic* called it an unauthorized use of the military; *mexicanos* called it race war.[40]

A mass meeting the following Monday united all *mexicano* factions behind two resolutions; Juan José Herrera's signature appeared alongside Eugenio Romero's. The first proposal was for unity. Attributing the gradual impoverishment of the people to political divisions among them, it resolved that all factions would unite in one party. The second resolution focused specifically on the Billy Green incident and condemned "those persons who . . . delivered speeches as a pack of seditious agitators; their insults were directed candidly against the Mexican people, and their attempts to incite the race question places them on the same level as the Greens."[41]

Tension remained high on both sides of the river for the next month. The Greens' supporters clamored for their appointments as deputy U.S. marshals, a fitting reward, remarked *El Independiente* sarcastically, for "killing two Mexicans in the same day." Both papers stressed the end of past political wars, motivated by greed and jealousy, that had allowed *"el extranjero"* to take advantage of the people. "There will be no further mention of the factions of Don Eugenio or Don Lorenzo," promised *El Independiente*."[42]

News of the union in San Miguel spread throughout the territory: Guadalupe County *mexicanos* wrote that they were following their neighbors' example; from Rio Arriba County came news first of a strike against "capitalists," then of support of the united movement.[43]

Unity did not last into the month of September. Disagreements about the party platform and fights for leadership fragmented San Miguel *políticos* more sharply than ever before.[44] Eugenio Romero and Félix Martínez lined up under the banner of El Partido de Union, while Lorenzo López, E. H. Salazar, and others bolted to form El Partido Independiente. Calling each other the "partido bastardo," both presented strange alliances to the San Miguel electorate. The Unionistas gathered Eugenio Romero, Félix Martínez, and Juan José Herrera on one ticket; the Independientes countered with an equally con-fusing alignment of Lorenzo López, Miguel Salazar (prosecutor of the White Caps in 1890), and Knights of Labor officer Aniceto Abeytia. To further compound the issue, all candidates retained their original affiliations for territorial offices--Romero supported Catron for delegate, while Martínez continued to stand with Joseph.[45]

It was an alignment that benefited only Catron, who won. In San Miguel, the Unionistas prevailed in a hotly contested race, losing only one place, but the county never recovered from the confusion produced by the attempted union.[46] Politics returned to the factionalism of old that allowed the gradual impoverishment of *el pueblo*. Martínez soon repaired to El Paso to seek his fortune and illness drove Juan José Herrera to Kansas City.[47] Herrera's brother Pablo had been killed by the ubiquitous Bill Green, and Nicanor retired to his ranch near Ojitos Frios.[48]

Strengths and Weaknesses

The election of 1894 signaled the end of planned and coordinated resistance to Anglo American encroachment in San Miguel County. The movement failed for two reasons: the struggle over land, the fundamental issue that welded *los hombres pobres* into effective units, changed from direct physical confrontation to drawn-out, complex litigation; and class animosities and aspirations divided *los pobres* and *políticos* too sharply for any but the most serious and direct of threats to overcome.

For the people who rode with or supported Las Gorras Blancas, land was the issue. The raids of 1889 and 1890 brought speculation to a standstill; the territorial laws providing for incorporation of grants and the creation of the U.S. Court of Private Land Claims helped to defuse the hostility produced by the arbitrary fencing of the 1880s. Abrupt, crude changes ceased, and inconsistent court decisions or subtle conspiracies shrouded the fate of the grants. On the San Miguel del Bado Grant, for example, two years of power struggles resulted in a suit before the Court of Private Land Claims. The court ruled in 1894 that the San Miguel was a community grant. Victory for the people, exclaimed *La Voz*. Final settlement, however, did not come until 1904, when, after an appeal by the federal government, the U.S. Supreme Court ruled that only 5,024 acres--the land under ditch--would be allowed. Interpreting the grant as applying only to "house lots and garden plots" ignored the concept of common pasturage and destroyed the economic utility of the land for its residents.[49]

The Las Vegas Grant remained in similar limbo. Interior Secretary John W. Noble disallowed the attempt at incorporation and ruled that Congress had patented the grant "so that the proper parties in interest could perfect their title to their lands"; Noble ordered the remainder resurveyed and opened to settlement "under the general land laws."[50] Lack of funds kept the surveyor general of New Mexico from acting, and the Las Vegas was never declared "free land." Finally, in 1903, the San Miguel delegation to the territorial legislature got a bill passed that gave the district court of San Miguel County the power to appoint and supervise a board of trustees to manage the grant. The board could issue deeds and had the power to "lease, sell or mortgage any part of said tract" at its discretion. The land not actually occupied was sold, and *los pobres* on the Las Vegas, like their neighbors on the San Miguel, retained only house lots and garden plots.[51]

Políticos and *los pobres* did not embrace each other wholeheartedly. Men like Felíx Martínez, Nestor Montoya, and E. H. Salazar had some education and shared a vision of the future made up of equal parts liberal-democratic ideology and pure laissez-faire economics founded on a unified Hispanic population. Theirs was a movement toward "progress" with themselves in the vanguard, and with a sense of class and appropriate leadership graphically illustrated in the 1894 election: *La Voz* apologized for having Gregorio Flores, *un pobre agricultor*, on the ticket, but he was so scrupulously honest that "the people have honored him with this high distinction."[52]

If the Martínezes saw themselves as a kind of intelligentsia for the general *mexicano* population, *los pobres* saw them as *políticos*, an epithet with the same negative connotations that "politician" carries in many quarters today. With the fences down, the movement became political, and the *políticos* took over the movement. *Los hombres pobres* retreated to their homes and watched with a cynicism that proved well-founded. The sense of ethnic cohesiveness and shared outrage was there, strong enough to support the White Caps for more than a year and to inflame the county for a month after the Billy Green fiasco. But it never permanently transcended class divisions, factional alignments, or personal animosities in one volatile county.

Born in violence, the movement envisioning a united *mexicano* front against the *americano* advance ended in violence. To be sure, violence did not disappear completely. Land was still wrenched from its traditional use, and *los hombres pobres* were still hungry. In 1903, three hundred masked horsemen rode through Antonchicho before going up on a mesa northeast of the village and leveling the fence of an Anglo cattle company.[53] Singly or in groups, *los hombres pobres persisted*, at least until 1926, in cutting fences put up where none had stood before.[54] But never again did *mexicano* outrage achieve the coordinated success of the heady summer of 1890.

Notes

1. O. D. Barrett to General Benjamin Butler, July 21, 1890, *Terr. of N.M.*, Reel 8.

2. See Appendix G.

3. Herrera could have been no younger than his teens in 1866, when he was accused of adultery, making forty his minimum age in 1890. Miguel A. Otero, Jr., said that he was too old to lead the White Caps in 1895. See Miguel A. Otero, Jr., *My Life on the Frontier*, Vol. 2, p. 267.

4. From a campaign biography in *La Voz del Pueblo* (Las Vegas), October 24, 1892. See also Appendix G.

5. Thomas B. Catron to Stephen B. Elkins, August 15, 1892, Catron Papers.

6. *La Voz*, October 24, 1892; Otero, *My Life*, Vol. 2, p. 224.

7. *Optic*, October 22, 1890.

8. Ibid.

9. Ibid., November 5, 1890.

10. See election returns in Appendix F, Tables F-1--F-4. See also Robert J. Rosenbaum, "*Mexicano versus Americano*: A Study of Hispanic-American Resistance to

Anglo-American Control in New Mexico Territory, 1870-1900" (Ph.D. diss., University of Texas at Austin, 1972), pp. 229-248, for a discussion of the 1890 returns.

11. *La Voz*, March 7 and 14 and July 4, 1891.

12. "Report of the U.S. Attorney General," *House Executive Documents*, 8th Congress, 3rd Session, Document 9, Vol. 32, pp. 95-109. See also Bradfute, *Court of Private Land Claims*.

13. *La Voz*, July 4, 1891.

14. Ibid., April 25, 1891.

15. Ibid., July 11, 1891.

16. S. A. Clark to Governor Prince, May 30, 1892, Prince Papers. Clark wrote: "One of my neighbors is obliged to pay $65 per year to the man that cut his fence down last year, with the understanding that he is not to cut it up again."

17. Ibid. According to Clark: "The Mexicans boast of cutting fences and burning houses and if we say anything of taking it to court they tell us that the Jury (sic) do not take Americans' testimony and the Mexicans do not tesfy against each other."

18. The Society of Gentlemen of Law and Order and Mutual Protection.

19. For an example of the confusion in the minds of Anglos, see a telegram and supporting letter from Governor W. T. Thornton to Secretary of the Interior Hoke Smith (September 29 and October 1, 1894) requesting U.S. troops to remain at Fort Marcy in Santa Fe to aid local authorities. Thornton implied that the burning of the capitol building, the murder of Santa Fe County Sheriff Francisco Chaves, the attempted assassination of territorial Senator Ancheta, the Vicente Silva gang, and every other example of the era of "unprecedented crime" that had occurred under his predecessor's administration were the products of a secret organization of *mexicanos*. *Terr. of N.M.*, Reel 8.

20. *La Voz*, March 28, 1891.

21. Ibid.

22. Ibid,, October 3, 1891. Armijo wrote: "I say frankly that the perfidy and ill-breeding with which one of those members [of the Law and Order Society] has treated me, had led me to believe that there is no equality or good intentions in the organization," and he concluded that the People's Party "is the party that brings well-being and happiness to the people."

23. The newspaper *Estandarte* of Springer (Colfax County) reported that Eugenio Romero, *jefe* of "*las gorras negras*," was in the county trying to organize a chapter of the Law and Order Society. Reprinted in *La Voz*, April 2, 1892. See also *La Voz*, September 19, 1891, and August 13, 1892 Herrera owned *El Defensor* for about a year (June, 1891, to May, 1892), and he often wrote for the paper, although Pedro G. de Lama was the editor. Herrera maintained his residence in San Miguel County, however.

24. The full sentence, translated, reads: "It is necessary that we are all united, all as brothers, all as members of the same family." *La Voz*, May 16, 1891.

25. Robert W. Larson, *New Mexico Populism: A Study of Radical Protest in a Western*

Territory, pp. 34-47, dates the formation of the party from 1888, when it served as a front for the Republican Party (p. 43). As the turmoil of 1890 created realignments, and as it switched its territorial support to the Democrats, it ought more properly be dated from 1890. Larson calls it "the first genuine People's Party in the territory" (p. 47). That may be true, but that does not mean it was part of the National People's Party. The San Miguel party, like the Knights of Labor, became increasingly an ethnically oriented, native New Mexican organization. *La Voz* might print Populist boilerplate, but Anglo Populists were increasingly excluded from the party, particularly because they wanted community grant land declared public domain and opened for settlement.

26. *La Voz.* November 25, 1893.

27. Ibid., December 16, 1893.

28. "With the arrogance of a king." See *La Voz*, November 21 and 28 and December 5, 1891.

29. Ibid., June 4 and 11, 1892. The Borregos led an organization known as the Button Gang. The assassination of Chaves was mentioned repeatedly during the campaign of 1892. The trial of the Borregos lasted until 1897, with Catron fighting very hard for acquittal, Catron's enthusiasm led him to excesses-even by his standards-and disbarment proceedings were brought against him that very nearly succeeded.

30. *La Voz*, October 1, 8, 15, 22 and 29 and November 5, 1892.

31. See Appendix F, Tables F-5 and F-6; and Rosenbaum, "*Mexicano versus Americano*," pp. 282-293.

32. *La Voz,* September 16 and 30, 1893.

33. Ibid., October 14, 1893.

34. Ibid., June 2 and 9, 1894.

35. "Fatal Encounter"; "Bloody Tragedy."

36. Patricio Maes had been hanged from the bridge over the Gallinas River by his fellow gang members, as they suspected him of being on the verge of turning informer. His murder inaugurated the gradual unveiling of Silva's operations. See de Baca, *Vicente Silva,* pp. 16-18. See also *La Voz,* October 29, 1892.

37. *La Voz* and *El Independiente,* July 28, 1894.

38. The Pullman Strike had occurred shortly before, and railroad workers in New Mexico, especially at Raton, had launched violent attacks against the Santa Fe Railroad. Troops had been dispatched from Fort Marcy to quell the disturbances. See "Report of the U.S. Attorney General" (1896) *House Executive Documents,* Document 9, pp. 154-166; U.S. Adjutant-General's Office, *Returns from U.S. Military Posts, 1800-1916* (N.A. Microfilm Publication, Microcopy No. 617), Reel 747, Returns from Fort Marcy; *La Voz* and *El Independiente,* July 28, 1892.

39. "Between the american and mexican." *La Voz* and *El Independiente,* July 28 and August 4, 1894.

40. Ibid.; *Optic,* July 27, 1894.

41. *La Voz* and *El Independiente*, August 4, 1894.

42. *El Independiente*, August 11, 1894.

43. Ibid., August 11, 18, and 25, 1894.

44. Ibid., and *La Voz*, September 8 and 15, 1894.

45. Ibid.

46. See Rosenbaum, "*Mexicano versus Americano*," pp. 310-318.

47. *La Voz*, April 13, 1895.

48. *El Independiente*, December 29, 1894; *La Voz*, September 7, 1895.

49. *La Voz*, April 28, 1894; "Report of the U.S. Attorney General" (1905), p. 95-109; Leonard, *Role of the Land Grant*, pp. 104-106.

50. Secretary of the Interior Noble to Commissioner of the General Land Office, December 5, 1891, BLM, Reel 15.

51. "An Act to Provide for the Management of the Las Vegas Grant, and for Other Purposes." C. B. No. 101, approved March 12, 1903, *Acts of the Legislative Assembly of New Mexico: Thirty-Fifth Session*, Chapter 47, pp. 72-74. In an interview, Donaldo Martínez, then district attorney of San Miguel County, said that the board of trustees consisted of three Anglos and two Hispanos. The Hispanos were Eugenio Romero and Lorenzo Delgado, whom Martínez called "bandidos." Martínez also used the phrase "house lots and garden plots." Interview, February 11, 1972.

52. *La Voz*, October 27, 1894.

53. Interviews with Don and Doña Antonio Ruiz, Don Eduardo Montaño, Antonchico, February 15, 1972; Don Pedro Gallegos, Delia, February 18, 1972; Doña Pedro Lucero and Don George Jarramillo, Antonchico, February 18, 1972; Don H. H, Mondragón, La Loma, February 18, 1972.

54. Interviews with Don Manuel Lucero, Tecolotito, February 15, 1972; Don H. H. Mondragón, La Loma, February 18, 1972.

II

Since 1900

Historians Richard Griswold del Castillo, Alberto Camarillo and David Montejano, among others, have uncovered patterns of downward mobility and stagnation for Chicanos during the 19th century. In this study, Douglas Monroy reveals strikingly similar patterns for Mexican immigrants and Chicanos in the early 20th century. He also uncovers patterns of occupational stratification and employment vulnerability inherent in low-wage, labor-intensive industries in southern California during the first decades of the 20th century. In these settings the traditional Mexican family met with new challenges which undermined parental authority and caused generational conflicts.

An Essay on Understanding the Work Experience of Mexicans in Southern California, 1900-1939
Douglas Monroy

Recently Chicano historians have statistically validated what many Mexican workers in Southern California, indeed in all the barrios and colonias of the United States, knew all along: Mexican workers suffered entrapment in dead-end, low paying jobs, under harsh working conditions. The concept of a segmented, stratified, or dual labor market system has helped to illuminate and understand how and why the Mexican work experience became structured in this fashion. A labor force which is segmented into a primary high wage sector and a secondary low wage sector provides the employer class with very real benefits. Certainly, lower wages mean higher profits. The competitive and service sectors of the economy, where profits are much lower than in the industrial, usually monopolized sector, desire low wage employees. Furthermore, by maintaining a divided workforce, employers gain a measure of assurance that workers as a group will not unite against them and threaten their profits or even their class privilege and position. Generally, employers have developed and exacerbated already existing racial and sexual divisions to maintain this profitable labor market. Notable exceptions were the Industrial Workers of the World (IWW) and the Congress of Industrial Organizations (CIO) which successfully united ethnically and racially diverse workers. The use of racially identifiable strike breakers and the encouragement of racist ideologies have typically produced for employers a divided and thereby tractable workforce.[1] Increasingly we are seeing how this situation prevailed among Mexican and Anglo workers in Southern California. We must now proceed to understand the meaning of this work situation for the lives of Mexicans in the United States.

The Mexican's Position on the Social Ladder

Between the Anglo conquest of California and 1900, Mexicans in Los Angeles enjoyed little social mobility. Richard Griswold del Castillo has effectively demonstrated how Mexican employment in this period in Los Angeles changed for the better for some, for the worse for others. Some were able to enter into skilled occupations as the local economy expanded and diversified. Others, particularly ranchers, farmers, shopkeepers, and merchants suffered decline which "probably cancelled out these gains for La Raza as a whole." Griswold del Castillo concludes that "During the American era, the Mexican American occupational structure was stagnant, with little opportunity for significant upward mobility."[2]

Albert Camarillo has arrived at similar conclusions in his study of Mexicans in Santa Barbara. For the early 1900s, Castillo shows how "Chicanos remained immobilized within the lowest occupational categories . . ." illustrating "the continuity that existed from the time Chicanos were first incorporated into the labor market during the late nineteenth century." Camarillo finds 64.2 percent of Mexicans working in "low blue collar" jobs in 1910, 68.6 percent in 1920, and 68.3 percent in 1930. In addition, Camarillo cites the California labor commissioner who found working "conditions even worse than reported," and how "so many children (were) in the orchards that the schools were all but depopulated."[3] The exigencies of the labor market also circumscribed education, the heralded vehicle for intergenerational mobility in America.

My investigation of the occupational structure of Mexicans in Los Angeles for the 1930s reflects the same striking trend. Based on marriage records of 1936, we find that 77.5 percent of those younger but probably more settled men worked as unskilled or semi-skilled laborers. Skilled occupations accounted for 9.5 percent of those in this sample and 13.7 percent worked in white collar jobs or had small businesses. The women who worked outside the home in the sample did even worse. A mere 1 percent worked in a skilled trade and 85.4 percent worked in unskilled jobs. In comparison, about 38 percent of Anglo men worked in unskilled and semi-skilled occupations at this time in Los Angeles.

These quantitative studies confirmed that Mexican workers toiled in the lowest paying and harshest jobs. Moreover, the American dream proved futile for them; Mexicans generally did not move up the social ladder nor did their children in the pre-World War II era.[4]

Hierarchy Within the Strata

Clearly, for Mexicans, job prospects were not good in the periods cited above. "Good," of course, is a relative term. Might certain jobs and employment patterns within the lowest strata have appeared significantly better than others to Mexican workers?

Steadiness and regularity of work appear to be the most important considerations differentiating employment for lower strata Mexican workers. Even within the secondary labor market, Mexican occupations differed significantly with respect to steadiness of work.

Agricultural work was most unstable. In the late 1930s, the Los Angeles County agricultural labor market required a maximum of 7,175 workers in June and a minimum of 2,300 workers in December. In fact, unemployed Mexican agricultural workers from all over the state made Los Angeles their winter home. The depression of 1907-08 first draw attention to this phenomena of winter unemployment of Mexicans who made Los Angeles their off-season headquarters from which they migrated in the spring. Paul Taylor even claimed that "In February, probably 80 percent or more of the Mexican population of the state is found there." This pattern repeated itself throughout the country.[5]

Fruit and vegetable canning, an urban agriculture-related occupation, further demonstrates this situation. In 1928, Mexicans comprised 23.5 percent of those employed in Los Angeles canneries. One cannot imagine a more seasonal industry. Using an index of 100 as the average for the whole year, the monthly average for the three middle years of the 1930s showed a range of from 16.2 and 17.9 workers employed in a December and a January week respectively, to 354.1 workers to one August week for California canneries as a whole. (This compares to rubber workers who deviated only 1.5 above or below the index of 100.) Statewide, 60,000 to 70,000 found late summer jobs in California canneries while only 10,000 to 13,000 did so in winter. Average time of employment amounted to a mere ten to eleven weeks per year.[6]

Cannery workers still managed to live on their meager earnings. With wages averaging $26.64 per week for men and $16.55 per week for women, 75 percent of the women and 50 percent of the men earned less than $300 per year. Cannery workers were not transients; they numbered few out-of-state workers, and average residence in California was a full fifteen years.[7]

One would think that many of these workers found winter work in other industries. They did not. The California Unemployment Reserves Commission of 1937 found that only 1 percent of male cannery workers surveyed found employment outside the canneries and only 10 percent worked the entire year in the canneries. It remains to be determined if Mexicans comprised much of this 10 percent. Fully 70.1 percent of the male cannery workers found only casual or no employment at all; 18.9 percent attended school. For women, cannery work may have been only a supplement to the family income as 61 percent did not work outside the canneries or the home and claimed no desire to do so, although 31.6 percent of those who did desire employment could not find any."[8]

We can see from these statewide figures how a seasonal industry such as canning left many Mexican workers underemployed or unemployed during the winter. Perhaps the Mexicans who comprised 23.5 percent of the cannery workers in Los Angeles did not suffer as grievously as those in the rest of the state because Los Angeles, as a hub for other Southern California agricultural counties, could count on a wider range of products to be canned, thereby tempering the effect of seasonal employment.

Aside from canning, other urban occupations in which Mexicans figured prominently also felt the effects of seasonal employment. Textiles, in which Mexican women comprised three-fourths of the women's clothing workers, was one of the more stable in total employment, though it was a volatile, competitive industry prone to a great deal of turnover. For California as a whole, the industry deviated from the average total employment by only 3.5 percent while the average for seasonal deviation for all of California employment was 2.7 percent. Furniture and cabinet work and woodworking had a seasonal pattern of about 10.5 percent deviation from the norm, but all had considerable unemployment. In the building and construction gangs Mexicans suffered a 12.7 percent deviation from the norm.[9] Importantly, all these figures are for each industry as a whole, and since Mexicans occupied the bottom rung of the employment ladder, we can expect them to have been pushed off the ladder first, pushing these figures upward for the seasonal unemployment rate of Mexican workers.

A trend is obvious for all these seasonal occupations employing large numbers of Mexicans: all the off-seasons occurred in the winter months. A cannery worker could not find winter employment on a construction gang or in a dress shop to carry him or her over for the winter months because it was the off-season there too. When added to the many agricultural workers who wintered in Los Angeles with friends or relatives, this substantial number of unemployed urban laborers in seasonal industry must have produced a substantial amount of surplus laborers in addition to those chronically underemployed or unemployed owing to the Depression.

Some Mexican workers did find steady employment in Los Angeles. For example, 10 percent of Teamster's Local No. 1 were Mexicans who had figured significantly in this important local since the early 1930s. Many Los Angeles cement workers were Mexicans who had been in the union local since it originated. Even in the Hollywood Ornamental Plasterers Local organized in 1928, Mexicans comprised 10 percent of the membership even though they worked at the lowliest jobs. In local packinghouses, many Mexican workers held grimy, but steady and skilled jobs and had the reputation of being "local residents of long standing in the industry." Likewise the business agent of the Lumber and Sawmill Workers Local in 1951 recalled that the Mexican workers were "an old local population which has been in the workforce since the thirties."[10] Clearly unionization did much to insure stability. However, other more informal factors, such as family contacts and informal relationships with employers and foremen, also produced stable employment for some Mexican workers in Los Angeles. Urban and industrial work, while often suffering seasonal variation, was certainly far more steady than agricultural work. Undoubtedly the length of time north of the border contributed to the accumulation of those various factors producing stable work. Camarillo suggests that U.S.-born Mexicans fared better on Santa Barbara's street paving crews than Mexican-born, though by no means as well as Anglo workers.[11] These workers had various skill levels, but they all appear to have achieved a significant measure of stability in their work. This achievement, perhaps a form of social mobility, set some Mexican workers off from the rest, at least as much, I would suggest, as skill levels. The skill categorization gives us a picture of an integral and crucial aspect of the structure of the Mexicano workforce. But this view of the variation in the stability of work gives us an impression of a factor as crucial to the Mexican work experience as labor market segmentation.

This factor of work stability probably figured importantly in status and material differences among Mexican workers in Los Angeles. For example, in El Monte most Mexican workers lived in the deplorable Hick's Camp, but some lived "in comfortable homes . . . where the houses and yards are well kept." These homes were "humble dwellings of four and five rooms, but so infinitely better than the rest." Mexican home ownership was not unusual in Los Angeles in the 1930s. According to a special census of 1933, 18.6 percent of Mexican families in Los Angeles lived in homes they owned as opposed to only 4.8 percent and 8.6 percent for Japanese and Chinese families respectively.[12] Also, a 1933 study of ninety-nine Mexican families found a fairly wide divergence in annual income. Of these families, twenty-one had incomes between $500 and $900, thirty-five between $900 and $1,200, twenty-four between $1,200 and $1,500, and seven over $1,800. For those between $500 and $1,500, the average number of gainful workers per family did not vary significantly--1.43 to 1.34 to 1.58. Those families with incomes over $1,800 had an average of 3.28 gainful workers in the family. The average family net income amounted to $1,204 per year.[13] This wide variation in mean income and home ownership cannot be accounted for by the skill differences of the chief earners alone. The fact that some Mexican workers found steady work explains this wide divergence in annual earnings which in turn brought different families different levels of consumption, home ownership, and physical and psychological security.

Moving Up from Agricultural to Industrial Labor

Given the greater stability and higher wages, urban industrial work constituted a step up the social ladder for the Mexican worker within the secondary sector of the labor market. Many urban workers began as agricultural workers in Los Angeles proper or in outlying areas such as Palmdale or San Fernando. Usually recent immigrants went first to the fields and then to better and steadier urban jobs. For example, Manuel Hernández came from Mexico in 1926 to the fields around Los Angeles. Then, in 1934, he and his family moved to a small steel mill community in the city and became an industrial laborer. Similarly, Camarillo finds that recent migrants dominated agricultural work in Santa Barbara. However, even by 1950 the break from agricultural labor was not complete. Women and especially older children from the community in which Manuel Hernández lived would often "go to the fruit" to earn extra money as would whole families in times of strikes at the steel mill. "The walnut season" recalled one Mexican from Santa Barbara who migrated from the city to the field for thirty to forty days, "was the only time of the year us poor people could get a little ahead." [14] Moreover, one finds this pattern repeated in other industrial centers. In the Chicago-Gary region of the Midwest, the same advantages of industrial work drew Mexican workers from the sugar beet fields to the city. In Detroit, the higher wages of the factory attracted Mexicans from agricultural as well as from railroad track labor.[15]

Indeed, the evident desire of Mexican workers for industrial work over agricultural, and the fact that length of residence north of the border related to the achievement of urban work, show that Mexican workers perceived an important and clear-cut difference between different jobs within the secondary labor market. While little social mobility up and out of the low-wage sector occurred until unionization and World War II, Mexican workers' wages, comfort, and status improved relatively and diversified as some found steadier, usually urban jobs. Such mobility, of course, was hardly the end-all. Work continued to be alienating, typically much more so than what Anglo workers experienced.

Understanding the meaning of the structure of work certainly does not complete our task here. People exist in society in relation not only to their factory, but in relation to their families, their neighbors, their enemies, and their gods. These things exist in people's private realms, an area largely closed to historians generally concerned with external circumstances. Yet, to fully understand the meaning of the Mexican work experience, we must see how work affected this private realm.

Discussion of the transition from agricultural to urban industrial labor bares most clearly the connection between the family and work. Though many Mexican workers before World War II had mostly known industrial labor, many had worked in agriculture before they came to the city. The transition affected more than merely their work lives. Agricultural and industrial work patterns have different affects on family structure and patterns of familial interaction. In nonindustrial situations, the family, not the individual family members, is the productive unit. The family produces most of what it consumes. In industrial labor or even in capitalist farming, where private property and the introduction of wage labor replaces more communal forms such as these of Mexico and New Mexico, individuals leave the family in order to earn an industrial wage. Now the family depends on the market for its consumption needs. The transition from the family economy to an individualist economy becomes a mechanism for the breaking down of the organizational strength of the family. The individual, not the family, is the productive unit in industrial labor.

In the transition phase between the family and wage economies, family members commonly pool their individual wages. This practice persisted among Mexican families in the 1930s and after. Previous students of the effect of urbanization on Mexican families have noted the likelihood of a small, steady contribution, such as ten dollars, from older children, sometimes with the understanding that it was for room and board.[16] Industrial work patterns initiated this alteration of the traditional family economy and accelerated its more thorough dissolution after World War II.

Significantly, however, the journey north of the border did not automatically mean individualized labor for Mexicans. In a few areas beginning in the early 1920s, employers realized the greater efficiency they could derive from their employees by engaging whole families. Particularly in the Colorado sugar beet fields, employers hired large families at $23 to $25 per acre to work their allotted fields. In an attempt to discourage the use of labor contractors and gang labor, agricultural employers sought to make each family its own contractor and deal directly with them. Employers also found family labor more stable than solo labor and used family labor in the fields of the Arkansas and South Platte Valleys, Colorado, Wyoming, Idaho, Montana, Nebraska, the Dakotas, Iowa, Minnesota, and Michigan.[17] One does not find evidence of this practice of employing whole families rather than individuals in California. Yet, we still see the continuation, if not actual reinforcement, of the family economy among many agricultural laborers in the United States.

Certainly the fact that Mexican families moved together "following the fruit," reinforced a sense of the family as the economic unit even though they were employed as individuals. The well-known practice of families journeying in their old cars, from crop to crop, up and down the state of California, further demonstrates the structural reinforcement for the family that employment patterns gave to Mexican agricultural wage laborers in California and the rest of the Southwest. These aspects of agricultural, field factory labor maintained or even strengthened a sense of the family as the productive unit. Many Mexicans would bring this experience with them to urban employments.

This transition to industrial labor may even have produced a restrengthening of the family as a form of resistance to the imposition of the new labor system. Oscar Lewis noted an actual increase in family cohesiveness among some rural immigrants in Ciudad México. In general, however, the transition from the family economy weakens the family unit. Rudolfo Anaya in his novels, *Bless Me, Última* and *Heart of Aztlán*, portrays both the weakening of the family and efforts to reaffirm it in the face of individual wage labor. In *Bless Me, Última*, the father leaves the family and their New Mexican land each day to work on highway construction, and three of the sons go into the army. The family, rooted in the land, no longer is the productive unit, and this organizational weakening of the family, to the particular dismay of the mother, ultimately partly dissolves the historical

Mexican family. At the same time, the mother struggles to maintain their family, and her efforts save the Luna family from total destruction.[18]

Heart of Aztlán, set in Albuquerque in the 1950s, also portrays the influence that the pressures and expectations of city life and work have on the family. A daughter screams to her father: "It's about time I had something to say about the way things are run around here! I work too! I have my own money! So I will come and go as I want, and nobody will rule me!"[19] The family no longer produced as a unit; now it did not function as a unit.

Corridos also demonstrate both the weakening of old family patterns by urban, industrial labor and the consciousness and understanding of the process:

> Van las muchachas casi encueradas
> y a la tienda llaman estor
> llevan las piernas rete chorreadas
> pero con medias de esas chifón.
> Hasta mi vieja me la han cambiado
> vista de seda rete rabón
> anda pintada como piñata
> y va en las noches al dancin jol.[20]

So lamented a father about the changes in his family.

The pattern of work itself probably affected the patterns of familial interaction and bonding. Secondary market workers often do not have steady shifts at their workplace. Those at the bottom of the labor market structure are most often stuck with swing and graveyard shifts. In interviews conducted in 1949, Los Angeles Mexican housewives expressed the difficulty the odd shifts caused in their households. The pot never seemed to be off the stove and it seemed rare that the whole family sat down together for meals.[21] Now, in industrial labor, families not only did not produce as a unit, but they no longer took their physical sustenance together. In this manner an important agent of familial bonding became lost to recent Mexican immigrants.

The most apparent manifestation of this process of familial dissolution in urbanization is generational conflict. The second generation, influenced by the new, urban, individualist culture, find themselves estranged and isolated from their more traditionalist parents but unable to gain access to the larger society. They must then develop their own social units, a spirit of brotherhood of the peer group, to replace that of the family. This carnalismo often takes the destructive form of gangs. We see, therefore, the importance of the imposition of different work patterns on what are usually deemed "community" problems.

These new patterns also meant a first step towards the freeing of women and children from the patriarchy of the traditional family. However, nothing came along to replace the lost cohesion of the family resulting in gangs and familial conflicts. When women went to work outside the home in "la costura," the canneries, or other similar, unskilled occupations, their economic role changed. Now they had a direct, clear indication of how much they contributed to the family financially. This facilitated greater freedom of activity and more assertiveness in the family for Mexicanas. Such a step was at once positive and disorienting.

Certainly the move, geographically and metaphysically, to the city and urban labor wreaked havoc with the traditional Mexican family. Yet, the tradition was not totally destroyed. Families continued to care for and support its aged members, and family members did not view this endeavor in money equivalents. The "conservative norm" of child care and responsibility of older siblings for the younger, remained strong.[22] Changes in these norms do not appear to have occurred as quickly as economic ones. The family still remains the most important aspect of Mexican life. Because the family offers refuge for its individual members as they venture into a hostile outside world, it will probably remain so. Moreover, the greater power achieved by women through the partial weakening of patriarchy also strengthens them individually and will undoubtedly produce long-term positive results in Mexican communities. Mexicana feminism has its own dynamic and historical roots. Nevertheless, the family's corrosion by urbanization and industrial work patterns cannot be denied.

Conclusion

We see how complex a person's work life is, especially one as onerous and burdensome as that experienced by Mexican workers relegated to the bottom strata of the class. To be sure, the structure must be understood. More importantly, if we are to know the meaning of the Mexican experience in the United States, we must understand the perceptions of that structure and its meaning in the inner realm. From the description of the work lives of Mexicans, one imagines that such experiences must have been morally debilitating. Life and labor confused some into passivity and self-blame. Clemente, the father in *Heart of Aztlán,* cursed the city and blamed himself for ever having come to it.[23]

Just as surely this new life and labor angered others into active resistance; witness the tenacity and solidarity with which Mexicans participated in and led union struggles. Many, if not most, were probably motivated by both sentiments of assertiveness and passivity, supporting their more militant union leaders depending on the time and circumstances. Union organization changed people's private lives because it made possible higher wages, steady work, and for many, the opportunity to move into jobs previously reserved for Anglo workers. Such unionization was not achieved without a struggle. Through such activity many Mexican workers confronted and thereby transcended the structure of the labor market, restructuring their world with tangible gains, a new consciousness, and a new dignity.[24]

Notes

1. Mario Barrera, *Race And Class in the Southwest: A Theory of Racial Inequality* (Notre Dame, Indiana: University of Notre Dame Press, 1979), pp. 174-219, illucidates this and other theories of racial inequality.

2. Richard Griswold del Castillo, *The Los Angeles Barrio, 1850-1890: A Social History* (Berkeley and Los Angeles: The University of California Press, 1979), pp. 51-61.

3. Albert Camarillo, *Chicanos in a Changing Society: From Mexican Pueblos to American Barrios in Santa Barbara and Southern California, 1848-1930* (Cambridge, Massachusetts: Harvard University Press, 1979), pp. 166-74.

4. Douglas Monroy, "Mexican Labor in the Political Economic Development of Los Angeles," forthcoming; for the Anglo and Mexican populations see Faith N. Williams and Alice C. Hanson, *Money Disbursements of Wage Earners and Clerical. Workers in Five Cities in the Pacific Region, 1934-1936: Mexican Families in Los Angeles*, United States Bureau of Labor Statistics Bulletins, no. 639, part 2 (Washington, D.C., 1939), p. 88. This study also corroborates my statistics on the Mexican occupational structure. Mario T. García, "Racial Dualism in the El Paso Labor Market, 1880-1920," *Aztlán: International Journal of Chicano Studies Research* 6, no. 2 (Summer 1975): pp. 197-218, finds that the same patterns prevailed in El Paso. The 3.3 percent of the women who worked as "sales" or "saleslady" are included in the 13.7 percent who worked in the white collar category. Since sales was a fairly lowly occupation in status and wages, it would probably be better to include them in the unskilled category.

5. State of California, Department of Employment, *Agricultural Activities, Crops, and Labor*, compiled by Ellis S. Coman (Sacramento, 1939); Francis Cahn and Valeska Bary, *Welfare Activity of Federal, State, and Local Governments in California* (Berkeley, 1936), p. 203; Paul S. Taylor, "Mexicans North of the Rio Grande," *The Survey*, vol. 67, no. 3 (May 1, 1931), p. 140; and Norman D. Humphrey, "Employment Patterns of Mexicans in Detroit," *Monthly Labor Review*, vol. 61, no. 5 (November, 1945), p. 913.

6. State of California, Unemployment Reserves Commission, James L. Mathews, Chairman, *A Study of Seasonal Employments in California*, (Sacramento, 1939), pp. 46-51.

7. Ibid., pp. 51-53.

8. Ibid., p. 67.

9. Rose Pesotta, *Bread Upon the Waters* (New York: Dodd, Mead & Company, 1945), pp. 19-20; and State of California, Unemployment Reserves Commission, *A Study of Seasonal Unemployment*, pp. 37 and 86.

10. Scott Greer, "The Participation of Ethnic Minorities in the Labor Unions of Los Angeles County" (Ph.D. diss., University of California, Los Angeles, 1952), pp. 62-3, 69-70, 73, 89, 104.

11. Camarillo, *Chicanos in A Changing Society*, pp. 168-9.

12. Home Missions Council, *A Study of Social and Economic Factors Relating to the Spanish-Speaking People in the United States* (n.p., n.d., probably from the late 1920s), p. 23; and U.S. Bureau of the Census, *Fifteenth Census of the United States, 1930: Population, Special Report on Foreign Born White Families by Country of Birth of Head* (Washington, D.C., 1933), p. 212.

13. Williams and Hanson, *Money Disbursements*, p. 88.

14. Greer, "The Participation of Ethnic Minorities in the Labor Unions of Los Angeles County," pp. 77-78; Alice Bessie Cuep, "A Case Study of the Living Conditions of Thirty-Five Mexican Families of Los Angeles with Special Reference to Mexican Children" (M.A. thesis, University of Southern California, 1921), p. 45; Camarillo, *Chicanos in a Changing Society*, p. 166; and Richard G. Thurston, "Urbanization and Sociocultural Change in a Mexican-American Enclave" (Ph.D. diss., University of California, Los Angeles, 1957), pp. 33, 138.

15. Paul S. Taylor, *Mexican Labor in the United States: Chicago and the Calumet Region* (Berkeley: The University of California Press, 1932), p. 98; and Humphrey, "Employment Patterns of Mexicans in Detroit," p. 918.

16. Rena Blanche Peek, "The Religious and Social Attitudes of the Mexican Girls of the Constituency of the All Nations Foundation in Los Angeles" (Master of Theology thesis, University of Southern California, 1929), pp. 22, 31; and Thurston, "Urbanization and Sociocultural Change," p. 111.

17. Paul Taylor, *Mexican Labor in the United States: The South Platte Valley* (Berkeley, 1929), pp. 134-135, 154; Taylor, "Mexicans North of the Rio Grande," pp. 136-137; and Manuel Gamio, *The Life Story of the Mexican Immigrant* (Chicago: University of Chicago Press, 1931), pp. 145-146.

18. Oscar Lewis, "Urbanization Without Breakdown: A Case Study," *The Scientific Monthly*, vol. 75, no. 1 (July 1952), p. 36; and Rudolfo Anaya, *Bless Me, Última* (Berkeley: Tonatiuh, 1972).

19. Rudolfo Anaya, *Heart of Aztlán* (Berkeley: Editorial Justa, 1976), p. 38.

20. "Corrido Enganchado" in Paul Taylor, *Mexican Labor in the United States, Chicago and the Calumet Region,* pp. VI-VII. Translation: "The girls go about almost naked and call la tienda estor (store)/They go around with dirt streaked legs/But with those stockings of Chiffon,/Even my old woman has changed on me/She wears a bobtailed dress of silk/Goes about painted like a piñata/and goes at night to the dancing hall."

21. Thurston, "Urbanization and Sociocultural Change in a Mexican-American Enclave," p. 33.

22. Ibid., pp. 133-134.

23. Anaya, *Heart of Aztlán*, p. 43.

24. Douglas Monroy, "La Costura en Los Angeles, 1933-1939: The ILGWU and the Politics of Domination," in Magdalena Mora and Adelaida del Castillo, eds., *Mexican Women in the United States: Struggles Past and Present* (Los Angeles: Chicano Studies

Research Center, Occasional Paper Number 2, 1980), pp. 171-178; Douglas Monroy, "Anarquismo y Comunismo: Mexican Radicalism and the Communist Party in Los Angeles," forthcoming; and Luis Leobardo Arroyo, "Chicano Participation in Organized Labor: The CIO in Los Angeles, 1938-1950. An Extended Research Note, *Aztlán,* vol. 6, no. 2 (Summer 1975), pp. 277-303.

Exploring push and pull factors of the early 20th century, Ricardo Romo describes Mexican immigration patterns in the context of United States immigration generally. As a result of significant increases in Mexican immigration, particularly during the 1920s, labor-intensive industries of the Southwest continued the growth momentum spurred by World War I. Mexican immigration was not only key to agricultural and industrial growth throughout the Southwest but was preferred above other labor sources. Opposition to Mexican immigration, principally from Restrictionist Leagues and organized labor complicated the free flow of Mexicans to the United States.

Responses to Mexican Immigration, 1910-1930
Ricardo Romo

One of the most striking and persistent phenomena of the Southwest in the 20th century has been immigration from México. Although well under way at the turn of the century, this immigration had its first major impetus during the period 1910-1930. In 1900, perhaps 100,000 persons of Mexican descent or birth lived in the United States; by 1930 the figure had reached 1.5 million.[1] The 1910 Mexican Revolution sparked a large exodus of laborers to the Southwest but this "push" factor only coincided with "pull" forces in the United States. Economic development in the Southwest, principally in California, Arizona and Texas, was spurred by greater irrigation, extension of transportation systems and the demands of World War I. Unsettled by social and economic conditions in their homeland, Mexican laborers were attracted by better wages in the United States; unskilled occupations southwestern industries often paid common laborers five to ten times more than similar industries paid in México.

This influx of more than a million Mexican immigrants during 1910-1930 led to a confrontation between southwestern industries which needed casual labor and organized labor which opposed Mexican immigration for economic and racial reasons. During three different years, 1917, 1921 and 1924, Congress curtailed Oriental and European immigration. However, agriculture, transportation, and mining industries successfully lobbied to prevent restriction of Mexican immigration. Throughout this era, Mexican laborers alleviated labor shortages in unskilled and skilled occupations in the Southwest and also in some industries in the Midwest. Immigration from México and the response accorded to these newcomers has not been sufficiently examined. This essay is a small contribution to that task.

I

Historians generally recognize three major immigration movements to the United States. The first two immigration waves occurred between the years, 1815-1860 and 1860-1890, and were periods in which Germany, Ireland, and Great Britain contributed most heavily to the population growth of the country.[2] Mexican immigration was significant at the end of the third movement which occurred between 1890 and 1914. Heavy northward migration of Mexican laborers began with the construction of Mexican railroads connecting U.S. border towns with México City and greatly increased with the completion of México's National Railroad to the border in the 1880's. Although the United States Immigration Service kept only partial records of Mexican immigration in the last half of the nineteenth century, the national Census estimated that more than 50,000 Mexicans came to the United States between 1875 and 1900.[3]

Many of the Mexicanos recruited to work on the railroads during the 1880's settled in Los Angeles. Several California historians have estimated that the Mexican population in Los Angeles in 1887 numbered about 12,000, while another 15,000 were estimated to be residing in surrounding areas.[4] Chinese labor gangs built the extension of the Southern Pacific Railroad to Los Angeles, but when construction reached the San Fernando Valley, railroad supervisors recruited "Mexicans and Indians [to] join the work gangs."[5]

The completion of the Transcontinental railroad to Los Angeles gave birth to an economic boom. Between 1880 and 1890, the overall population of Los Angeles grew from 11,000 to more than 50,000 despite the exodus of thousands of residents after an economic recession in 1888. This population explosion created a dramatic change in the city's ethnic composition. According to one observer: "This boom made a permanent change in the city's character. The hybrid Mexican-American pueblo was no more."[6] For the first time, the Mexican population in Los Angeles became a numerical minority.

While Mexican immigration to the United States before 1900 was less than one percent of the total immigration, by 1900 the Mexican population in dozens of southwestern cities had doubled. The Mexican-born population of the United States in 1870, estimated at 42,435, increased to over 100,000 by 1900.[7] Ninety percent of the foreign-born Mexican population lived in three states: Texas, Arizona, and California. In 1900, Texas had the largest Mexican population, nearly 69.0 percent of the total, while 2.0 percent of the Mexican-born population lived in California.[8] The Mexican population of California grew rapidly over the next thirty years and by 1930 had increased fourfold, giving California 15.2 percent of the total Mexican population in the United States.[9]

After 1900, most Mexicans entered the United States through Texas. Many, after having temporarily resided along the border, then traveled on to Arizona and California. In 1903, a Texas railroad official stated that Mexican immigrants had been recruited in El Paso for several Years and railroad employers had substituted them for Italians and Blacks in the Southwest.[10] A few years later, a roadmaster working in Southern

California reported that Mexicans had been employed in his division "four or five years and were displacing other laborers." He observed that he preferred them to other available laborers especially the Japanese.[11]

At the turn of the nineteenth century, nativists in California had raised the issue of the "yellow peril," and thereby unwittingly aided the demand for Mexican laborers. The issue was later well summarized by Charles A. Thomson, a San Francisco minister who wrote in 1926 :

> The Mexican is the preferred of all the cheap labor available to the Southwest. On Oriental labor, Chinese and Japanese and Hindu, the verdict has already been cast. California has swung our national jury to an almost unanimous vote.[12]

Racially, Mexican laborers were more acceptable in California than Japanese or Chinese laborers.

During the period 1900-1910, nearly 50,000 immigrants from México officially crossed the international line. Mexican immigration represented 0.6 percent of the total immigration to the United States during this period.[13] However, as one observer noted, they constituted one sixth of the section hands and extra gangs on the railroads in the Western division. Railroad companies took Mexican laborers to work as far north as Illinois and Colorado. Given the seasonal nature of some track work, the companies often paid the expenses of any worker who wished to return to México.[14] Thousands of Mexican laborers during this period traveled back and forth across the border, but an increasing number began to settle during the off-season in cities such as Los Angeles.

During the decade of the Mexican Revolution, 1910-1920, twice as many Mexicans entered the United States than in the previous decade. An analysis made in 1912 by journalist Samuel Bryan emphasized that "immigration from México was due to the expansion of [the transportation] industry, both in México and the United States.[15] Moises González Navarro, a Mexican historian, wrote that the United States acted as a "safety valve" for México, for in times of political and social unrest thousands fled across the border into the United States.[16] Bryan explained Mexican migration in a similar manner, noting that Mexicans were pulled to the north by the expansion of industries, "drawing men from the farms and from the interior northward." This influx of immigrants, Bryan concluded, coincided with the economic expansion which took place in the southwestern United States.[17] The movement of immigrants to the border was facilitated by the use of the automobile and the railroad networks which connected the interior of México with the Southwest.

The railroad was the most common mode of transportation for the Mexican immigrant after 1910. Passage from central México to the U.S. border during the Revolution cost ten to fifteen dollars per person. In 1911 the average number of passenger miles traveled on Mexican railroads was 346, and by 1920 had increased to an average of 440 miles per passenger.[18] The increase in service and rail travel after the Revolution coincided with the general increase in Mexican immigration to the United States. Most of the immigrants going to California went by way of the Mexican border town of Juárez across from El Paso, Texas. Others also went by way of Nogales, Arizona and in the late 1920's through Calexico, California and Mexicali, Baja California.

Another popular means of transportation was the automobile. Many Mexican immigrants bought automobiles in border cities and then sold them or returned with them to the interior of México where United States automobiles were generally quite popular and always brought a good price. In one year alone, over five hundred Ford automobiles were taken back to México by returning Mexican laborers.[19] Automobile registration in México increased from over half a million in 1911 to over 8 million by 1920 and 17 1/2 million five years later, in 1925.[20] Frequently, immigrants bought automobiles in the United States in order to facilitate the migration of their members of their families, as did Ramón Lizárraga.

Lizárraga, a Mexican musician and an immigrant of the early twentieth century, utilized both the railroad and the automobile to emigrate to the United States. When Lizárraga first came to Los Angeles in 1903, he traveled by train. He returned to México in 1905 after having worked in Tucson and Los Angeles as a musician. In 1926, he again journeyed to Los Angeles by train, this time with enough money earned as a musician in México to enable him to purchase an automobile. He remained in the United States long enough to buy a "model T" Ford and returned shortly thereafter to México for his family. After selling his small farm in México, Mr. and Mrs. Lizárraga and their children loaded all their personal belongings into the old Ford and headed once again for Los Angeles.[21]

II

Unlike the Lizárraga family, the greatest number of Mexican immigrants streamed through the border station at El Paso, Texas. On occasion, as many as one thousand individuals per day went through the humiliating process of hot baths, medical examination, and literacy tests in El Paso. Vera L. Sturges commented:

> Everything possible seems to be done to keep them clean and sanitary; but when five or six hundred steaming people, men, women, and children, are crowded into the room at one time, sanitation becomes a farce.[22]

Seldom did the Mexican laborers emigrate with more than one or two family members due to the cost of $18 per person for visas and consular fees. In the 1920's, between sixty-five or seventy percent of the Mexican immigrants were males, the majority of them single.[23] Those with large families often brought them across the border surreptitiously. Some immigrants frequently left their families at the border on the Mexican side while the father found suitable and stable employment which would enable him to return for his family. Some immigrants, unable to pay or frustrated by long delays, crossed by night with the aid of a coyote.[24]

Once the immigrants crossed the border, labor agents or enganchadores competed vigorously to recruit them. These agents often made extravagant promises to induce immigrants to sign labor contracts with the companies they represented. One immigrant, now living in Los Angeles, recalled his crossing more than fifty years ago. He reminisced:

> They [the Texas Rangers] helped us cross [the Rio Grande] because they wanted workers from México. The companies perhaps gave them some money for allowing us to cross. The next day we found work [at the mines]. We were standing near the office when we were asked to go to work right away. But they did not pay very much--10 cents per hour, but not 10 cents in money, rather they gave us chits and you took them to the [company] store and bought your groceries.[25]

Enganchadores recruited workers according to instructions given to them by various employers. Helen W. Walker, a social worker in Los Angeles, observed that it was not uncommon for the enganchadores and employment bureaus to use "unscrupulous methods" to recruit Mexican laborers, since "their object [was] to get as many men as possible."[26] The recruiters, Mrs. Walker found, gave "no guarantee of the length of employment" and rapid turnovers were common.[27] Some farmers in Texas instructed their agents not to hire Mexicans who came without their families, while other farmers preferred immigrants coming across to the United States for the first time.

Workers often signed up with one firm in order to receive transportation to more favorable areas of employment. Ramón Terrazas, a resident of Los Angeles since the 1920's, left El Paso along with several hundred fellow Mexican laborers. Upon reaching the Imperial Valley in California, Terrazas jumped from the train as it stopped and proceeded to look for work on his own.[28] In earlier years, some workers transported to an area left their jobs before completing their contracts. One farmer complained that he "lost an entire gang after paying $12.50 fare a head, before they reached the job, to which they had been sent."[29]

III

In 1911 and 1912, nearly eighty percent of all emigrants who left México went to the United States.[30] In those two years Mexican immigration records show that some 135,125 Mexican immigrants, most of them single males, crossed into the United States, and interestingly, almost as many returned to México at the end of the year.[31] In contrast, the United States Census data reported only 40,785 Mexican immigrants during the same period.[32] The Mexican figures are perhaps more reliable because all persons entering México had to register at the border or face charges of illegal entry, a serious crime during the Revolution. Illegal entrants to the United States, on the other hand, were merely deported. It seems obvious that large numbers of Mexicans entering the United States crossed illegally. Jay S. Stowell, a close observer of border affairs, estimated that as many as 75 percent of the Mexican immigrants entered illegally.[33]

As military activities intensified after the assassination of President Francisco Madero, movement across the border took on new and expanded dimensions. High loss of men through battle casualties and desertion plagued Mexican armies. The U.S. Department of Labor reported in 1914 that "approximately 8,000 panic-stricken aliens, mainly of the Mexican race, entered the United States at Eagle Pass, Texas within a few hours" after fleeing from the Federal forces "who were reported about to attack the town of Piedras Negras."[34] Countless hardships were related by immigrants who sought safety on the U.S. side of the border. The Los Angeles *Times* reported one story which was not at all typical of the refugees' experiences:

> Scores of women camp followers [of the civilian refugees] had lost their children in the scramble and were crying piteously in the corral proved for them on the American side. They were without clothing sufficient to protect them from the cold and were drenched from wading through the river. The scene of disorder was almost as bad on the American side as on the Mexican.[35]

During the years that many Mexicans fled to the United States as war refugees, thousands of others left because of social and economic disruptions. Unlike the seasonal laborers recruited by industry and agriculture, these refugees came from the middle and upper classes of México and intended to remain in the United States for a longer period. J. B. Gwin, an officer for the Red Cross, stated:

> The Mexican refugees have surprised all beholders with their healthy conditions, their quiet polite manners and especially with their failure to appear as half-starved, poverty-stricken people from a desolate land . . . They probably represent the best element there is in México today, the farmers and small businessman who have taken no part in the wars.[36]

Most refugees generally preferred to work in communities with Mexican settlements. Many Mexican immigrants stayed in the Southwest to work, rather than travel on to the Midwest, in order to remain close to México where many of them had left relatives. In the Southwest, the immigrant also had the advantage of finding more places where his language was spoken and his culture persisted.

Many of the refugees who entered the United States--sometimes only slightly ahead of the advancing Mexican armies--found themselves confined for days and even weeks in United States Army processing camps. Few labor agents visited these camps to bid for laborers thus giving the refugee camp immigrants limited employment options. In 1914 the Los Angeles *Times* reported that "the Mexican Federal soldiers . . . in the custody of the United States border patrol forces at Presidio, Texas [would] be transferred to Ft. Bliss and [would be] interned there indefinitely."[37] In the article entitled "Making Friends of Invaders," J. B. Gwin wrote: "the camp is growing smaller rapidly. Over fifty have left with their families to go on the 'regancia' railroad work. Another forty have gone to the mines of New México.[38] Stories of the "invading hordes" constantly appeared in the Los Angeles *Times* during the years of the Mexican Revolution. Five thousand Mexican refugees crossed the "international Line," the *Times* reported one year, "enticed [by] Three Square Meals." The bill for feeding these refugees, the *Times* continued, would be sent to the Mexican government.[39]

IV

After the opening of the Panama Canal, boosters in California predicted "a large influx of South [sic] European immigrants by the way of the Panama Canal."[40] The boosters had hoped to replace Mexican laborers with Southern European immigrants. However, the outbreak of World War I crushed their hopes. Southwestern employers interested in inexpensive labor continued to send labor agents to México. "Each week five or six trains are run from Laredo," the Los Angeles *Times* stated in 1916, "carrying Mexicans who have been employed by labor agents, and similar shipments are being made from other border points." The demand for these laborers, concluded the *Times* "is so great that they are employed as fast as they cross the Rio Grande. Men, women and children are gathered up and placed upon the trains and shipped to the fields . . . "[41] The efforts of the labor agents in México proved to be very successful. In California, Mexican farm laborers had displaced other ethnic groups within a few years.

In 1917, the Immigration Restriction League pressured Congress to pass an immigration law over the objections of President Woodrow Wilson. The act doubled the head tax to $8.00 "and added chronic alcoholics, vagrants, and 'persons of constitutional psychopathic inferiority' to the list of excluded classes."[42] Most significantly, the act required immigrants to pass a literacy test which restrictionists knew would curtail non-English speaking groups. For mining, agriculture and railroad interests, the law did two things: first, it cut off the supply of cheap European labor; second, it all but spelled an end to the surplus supply from México which had been activated after the outbreak of the Mexican Revolution. Railroad and agricultural interests lobbied in Congress for the exemption of Mexican labor from the Immigration Act of 1917 in order to insure once again the availability of cheap labor from México. Their efforts did not go unrewarded.

Acting as special interest groups, railroad, agriculture and mining companies employed several strategies in order to insure the continued availability of Mexican laborers. One plan of action called for frightening the public about food shortages; proponents of this plan argued that the curtailment of Mexican farm laborers would bring about a serious decline in food production. The Los Angeles *Times*, whose owner employed hundreds of Mexicans, sided with those who acknowledged a need for cheap labor. In 1917, the *Times* carried an article which warned of serious consequences due to the "exodus" of Mexicans from Texas: "The exodus has reached a serious phase, particularly as it relates to the growing of crops and attending of live stock interest upon many millions of acres upon the Texas border."[43]

A member of the California Fruit Growers' Exchange claimed in May, 1917, that unless prompt action was taken to mobilize farm labor in California, a serious shortage of workers would hamper the harvest of bumper crops in Southern California."[44] During the same week, the Los Angeles Chamber of Commerce sent a telegram to immigration Commissioner A. Caminetti in Washington requesting that Mexican laborers be excluded from Section 3 of the 1917 Immigration Act which denied admission to aliens who could not read the English language. In the opinion of growers in Los Angeles, the law seriously restricted the necessary supply of agricultural workers from México.[45]

Within six months of the passage of the Immigration Act of 1917, Congress yielded to the pressure exerted by southwestern industries and gress yielded the decision to include Mexicans in the restrictive clauses. Congress allowed the United States Secretary of Labor to suspend the literacy test, the contract labor clause and head tax of the 1917 law. Interest groups that had argued for suspension actually wanted permission to tap the reserve labor pool available in México; they used as a pretext the existence of a labor shortage created by the outbreak of World War I.

Conditions in the United States during World War I made extensive immigration from México expedient. J. B. Gwin, an officer of the Red Cross, reported that after the Mexican Revolution of 1910, "the next impetus to immigration from México came as a result of the scarcity of laborers in the United States during the World War." Indeed almost twice as many Mexicans came during the period 1915-1919 than in 1911-1914.[46]

During the first World War Mexicans performed a valuable service to the United States and her allies. They manned railroads, helped construct new military bases and picked cotton used in gunpowder and clothing. Mexicans who worked in mines of the Southwest also helped to provide a steady flow of copper, lead, and other minerals needed in the war effort.

Thousands of Mexicans who entered the United States during the war years as temporary laborers remained after their six-month permission had expired. Of these remaining in California after the war, according to historian Robert G. Cleland, most of them settled in the Los Angeles metropolitan area, and by 1925 the former Spanish pueblo had become, next to México City itself, the largest Mexican community in the world.[47]

Those who used the war as a reason to hire Mexican laborers profited handsomely in return. Southwestern employers paid Mexican laborers low wages and provided them with poor housing. Vernon McCombs of the Home Council wrote in 1925:

> On the tuberculosis chart for the city [Los Angeles] there is a black cloud about the Plaza region. The causes are clear: low wages, seasonal employment, high rent, overcrowding, and inadequate nourishment. The average family has five members and the average house has two rooms, for which exorbitant rents are charged. In Los Angeles 28 percent of these Mexicans' homes have no running water 79 percent have no bathrooms, and 68 percent no inside toilets-many cases, six or eight families use a common toilet.[48]

Southwestern employers also violated the conditions of the immigration law under which Mexicans had been temporarily admitted. Mexican laborers were kept under employment longer than the government had sanctioned while the law clearly called for only temporary admission of Mexicans. The United States Secretary of Labor later extended the length of time allowed in the United States for Mexican workers involved in all forms of mining and all government construction work in the states within the southern department of the United States Army.[49] Abuses of these immigration restrictions frequently occurred, but violators generally escaped penalties.

However, the end of the war caused a surplus of Mexican workers in urban areas. Four million men at the rate of over 300,000 a month returned to civilian life after the signing of the Armistice on November 11, 1918.[50] The sudden return of so many men into civilian life put thousands of Mexican laborers out of work. Only in agriculture, transportation, and mining were Mexicans still in demand.

Moreover, successful pressure by interest groups in 1920 resulted in an extension of the "Exclusion Clause" of the 1917 Immigration Act, thus enabling a greater number of Mexican laborers to enter the United States. These workers, interest groups argued, were needed to keep pace with the increase in agricultural production. The cotton crop in California, for example, increased in value from $11,744 in 1909 to $9,237,182 ten years later. Arizona, whose irrigation works had been built by Mexican laborers, achieved even greater increases in cotton production, from an output valued at $730 in 1909 to $20,119,989 in 1919.[51]

Massive migration of southern Blacks to the North forced some southern and southwestern labor recruiters to go south of the border for workers. Midwestern states also began to rely more heavily on mexican labor and competed with southwestern states in recruiting Mexican workers. Aggressive recruitment of Mexicans to the sugar beet fields in Colorado exemplified this competition. In 1918, the United States Department of Labor cooperated with Colorado beet growers in developing a plan for securing Mexican laborers who were considered "admirably adapted to this work" according to a department spokesman.[52] In the fiscal year 1919, farmers recruited more than 10,000 of the 20,000 laborers admitted under the exclusion clause of the 1917 Immigration Act. Another 9,998 of these went to work on railroad maintenance.[53] According to United States officials, 50,852 Mexican immigrants entered this country between 1917-1920, and about half of them found employment with the railroads. While the law required these Mexicans to return to México within six months, nearly half of them remained, and in 1920, nearly 23,000 were still employed in the United States.[54]

V

After 1921, it became virtually impossible to hold back the influx of both legal and undocumented workers or "illegal aliens" from México. Gerald B. Breitigam, a journalist for The New York *Times*, reported in 1920, that since 1913 "more than five hundred thousand [had] entered the Southwest."[55] Another writer estimated that over a period of seven months in 1920, "more than one hundred thousand Mexicans . . . had crossed into the United States, relieving our farm labor shortage."[56]

Mexican immigrants came to the United States because they expected to find a more stable existence there and earn higher wages as well. The "higher wages have been effective stimulus," wrote sociology professor Emory Bogardus.[57] "Three dollars a day, for instance, in 1929, looked large to a Mexican accustomed to receiving the equivalent of fifty cents."[58] Economics professor Constantine Panunzio found that the average family income per year of one hundred non-migratory Mexican wage-earners' families was $1,337.35 for the year 1929-1930 in San Diego, California.[59] In the mid-twenties, Bogardus, found that although wages varied greatly according to occupation and "to the types of Mexicans employed," the median wage appeared to range between $2.75 and $3.25 a day.[60] Some industries such as railroad and agriculture had high labor turnovers, despite relatively high wages, and working conditions which were far from suitable. The following corrido or ballad sung during the 1920's illustrates the disappointment over working conditions experienced by numerous Mexican laborers in the United States:

The Immigrants
(Los Enganchadados -- ("The Hooked Ones"))

On the 28th day of February,
That important day
When we left El Paso,
They took us out as contract labor.

We arrived on the first day
And on the second began to work.
With out picks in our hands

We set out tramping.

Some unloaded rails
And others unloaded ties,
And others of my companions
threw out thousands of curses.

Those who knew the work
Went repairing the jack
With sledge hammers and shovels
Throwing earth up the track.

Said Jesús, "El Coyote,"
As if he wanted to weep
"It would be better to be in Juárez
Even if we were without work,"

These verses were composed
by a poor Mexican
To spread the word about
The American system.[61]

Nonetheless, Mexican laborers served as the principal work force in the industrialization and development of agri-business in the Southwest. Without Mexican labor, high profits and large-scale expansion in industries, transportation and agri-business would have been impossible. The Commissioner General of Immigration in the United States understood the role of the Mexican laborers, stating that while "Mexican immigration was not very extensive . . . it played an important part in the labor supply of the Southwest." In fact, the Commissioner added, "much of the movement is made up of those whose coming and going is regulated by the demand for labor in the border states."[62] As has been shown, economic interests were able to successfully modify Immigration Laws in order to meet the demands for a source of cheap labor. However, vociferous and sharp opposition to Mexican immigration developed within the United States and México.

VI

The continuous flow of emigrants across the border during the Mexican Revolution was not always viewed favorably by the Mexican government. The *Christian Science Monitor* reported in 1920, "the Mexican government threatens to prevent by military force the exodus of workmen to the United States and . . . nevertheless hundreds leave daily because of the unsettled conditions of the country."[63] The great loss of life during the Revolution, a drop in the birth rate, and a need for laborers to help rebuild the nation prompted México to restrict emigration. Toward the end of the Revolution, at a time when U.S. laws favored the immigration of Mexicans, President Carranza "notified the [state] governments of Northern México that they must prevent the increasing exodus of laborers to the United States."[64] President Carranza had every reason to be alarmed; one report stated that a recruiter for a sugar-beet company from California had raided Carranza's army and returned to the United States with 1,400 Mexican soldiers.[65]

The Mexican government failed to keep citizens from leaving their villages and farms in México because the government could not provide jobs or political stability; something Mexicans hoped they would find in the United States. Nevertheless, Mexican officials made various attempts to persuade Mexicans to stay home. Citizens were warned of the difficulties encountered in the United States by Mexicans. The Los Angeles *Times* commented in March of 1920 that the Mexican government had warned "the women not to leave México, stating that they would receive no protection from the American government, that justice would be denied them, and that they would become victims of mob violence if they went to the United States."[66] The *Times* stated that the exodus to the United States was causing alarm. Northern Mexican states sent news that there was "serious danger to numerous industries in Northern México through non-use and to large areas of farm land through lack of cultivation."[67] In March 1920, the Federal government instructed the governors of Northern México "to wage a publicity campaign to stop the emigration."[68] The campaign failed. Immigrants continued to cross into the United States, probably because conditions in México were still such that despite unfavorable publicity in the Mexican press, Mexicans preferred the risks of finding employment and housing in the United States to the hardships in México.

However, Mexicans did indeed encounter hardships in the United States: For example they, like most U.S. citizens, were adversely affected by the economic recession of 1921. But they survived and by the mid 1920's were working in midwestern cities that twenty years before had never seen a Mexican. Thousands of Mexican laborers had entered the industrial labor force in the Midwest by completely by-passing the border areas. Recruitment of Mexicans to the Midwest helped to draw them into urban areas of Illinois, Michigan, Kansas and Indiana. For example, by 1930, the Mexican population of Illinois numbered 28,906; Michigan listed 13,336, while Kansas had 19,150 and Indiana 9,642.[69] Important railroad connections from St. Louis and Kansas City to El Paso partially explained the movement of a large number of Mexicanos to those midwestern cities. In 1930, Kansas City, Missouri, and Kansas City, Kansas, both claimed Mexican communities of more than 5,000.[70] Edwin R. Brown, a Baptist minister from Los Angeles, California, commented on the movement of Mexicanos to the Midwest:

During the past fifteen years of revolution [in México], no less than "five million Mexicans have come into the United States, and of these, some two million have returned to México. Each year now, from fifty to ninety thousand come north across the border so that today there are over three million Mexicans in the United States, scattered from the border northeast to Chicago and beyond.[71]

As Mexican immigration grew, however, opposition from various elements of U. S. society intensified.

The strongest opposition to unrestricted Mexican immigration came from organized labor. During the years before World War I when Mexican immigration amounted to less than one percent of the total immigration to the United States, organized labor all but ignored the influx of Mexican immigrants. In 1913, for example, the American Federation of Labor's (AFL) annual convention entertained a resolution by a San Diego labor organizer to solicit the membership of Mexican laborers in the area. These workers, the representative said, "are forced to work for wages below standard, thereby lowering the wages for all labor. Labor [in southern California] is mostly performed by workers of Mexican nationality." He urged the International Unions to admit Mexicans into their locals. The delegate also expressed a need for a Spanish speaking organizer to assist him in working with Mexicanos.[72]

In 1917, the AFL adopted the request of several of its delegates, including a Mexicano, C. A. Vargas, to work toward the organization of Mexican miners in the Southwest. Mexican miners already were organized in the Clifton-Morenci-Metcalf area in Arizona, with locals, 80, 84, and 86, representing more than five thousand men. The delegates urged the AFL leadership "to do everything in their power to organize the entire fourteen thousand Mexican miners" in Arizona, and throughout the Southwest.[73] The outbreak of World War I dealt a blow to the efforts of the AFL members supporting the recruitment of Mexicans into their locals. As more Mexicans crossed the border, organized labor changed its position toward Mexican workers. The AFL came to view Mexican workers more as competitors for jobs held by native Anglos than as potential union members.

When World War I broke out, Samuel Gompers, head of the AFL, became concerned over the thousands of Mexican workers being admitted to the United States to replace those workers engaged in combat. Harry W. Fox, a labor delegate to the AFL Annual Convention in 1919, perhaps best expressed Gompers' fear of Mexican immigration. Fox reported to the AFL Executive body that Mexicans in the sugar-beet industry not only held down wages, but "accepted employment in different lines of efforts [non-agricultural], to the detriment of labor standards."[74] The lowering of wages and the displacement of native labor were probably the main objections of the AFL to the admission of Mexican labor during the war. Gompers feared that Mexicans would not be content to remain in farm labor, and would soon enter semiskilled and skilled trades. Fox believed the movement of Mexicans into other employment was "detrimental to the best interest of the country."[75] The AFL Executive body advised immigration officials to be careful to turn away those without proper permits. There was also a resolution introduced which criticized the use of Mexican laborers in construction crews at Fort Bliss, Texas. The delegate who brought up this resolution warned of the "necessity of employing red-blooded American citizens . . ," for he found the Mexicans "not only un-American in their ways, and non-union, but also aliens, owing their allegiance to another country."[76]

In addition to being seen as those who lower wages and displace native labor, Mexicans were also viewed as strike-breakers. For example, in the steel strike of 1919, steel companies in Chicago and Gary recruited labor from México. While it seems that some unwary Mexican workers became strike-breakers, they were but a small number and do not appear to have hindered union bargaining efforts. According to economist Paul S. Taylor, the number of Mexicans hired from 1916 to 1919 in the Chicago-Gary area was insignificant compared to the number of Southern Blacks.[77] In 1916, there were 18 Mexicans and 558 Blacks employed in the two major steel plants in the Chicago-Gary area. Three years later, during the nationwide steel strike, only 142 Mexicans and 2,699 Blacks worked in the two plants surveyed by Taylor in Gary, Indiana. By 1921, while organized labor pressed for the curtailment of European and Mexican immigrants, only 49 Mexicans and 1,375 Blacks labored in the previously mentioned steel mills.[78] Indeed Mexicans and Blacks suffered from the economic recession of that year, as well as from the successful campaign of organized labor to exclude them from industrial occupations.

Still, Mexican immigrants continued to arrive in large numbers. Their search for better work opportunities took them to states farther and farther away from the border. According to one observer, they were:

> probably recruited from the backway of the beet industry there are now about 8,000 Mexicans employed in various industries in Detroit. There are many in the automobile industry employed as unskilled laborers chiefly in the Ford Rough plant and the Briggs Mfg. Co. [sic] where parts are made for all cars.[79]

Organized labor was not the only sector of society to oppose large-scale Mexican immigration.

During the 1920's dozens of articles critical of the admission policies of the Immigration Service appeared in the United States. The concern voiced by those in opposition to Mexican immigration was typically expressed by *The Survey* of April 10, 1920:

> Amid wild gestures and mutual accusations between México City and Washington, Mexican laborers are leaving their own country for the United States in ever increasing numbers . . . They do not come singly but en masse, not from adjoining

districts but often long distances. Whole villages emigrate together.[80]

This increase in Mexican immigration led restrictionists to organize vicious campaigns to end the unrestricted flow of Mexicans to the United States.

In 1920, President Warren Harding signed into law the Johnson Act, the first immigration quota law in U.S. history. This law limited the number of entrants admitted annually to three percent of the number of foreign born of that nationality already in the United States, according to the census of 1910. Mexicans, as well as Canadians and other immigrants from the Western Hemisphere, were protected from the Johnson Act through the efforts of strong special interest groups in the Southwest.

Those individuals favoring open Mexican immigration to the United States argued that it was relatively small compared to that of European nations. Mexicans represented less than 4.0 percent of the total immigration to the United States between 1911 to 1921.[81] Those who favored the exemption of the Mexican from the quota laws contended that Mexicans returned to México much like "homing pigeons." Others argued that the Mexican was less visible in the United States because he was geographically isolated and therefore did not present a racial problem to society. More than 90 percent of the Mexicanos lived in the three states of Texas, Arizona, and California, while the core of the Restrictionist movement was on the East Coast and concerned itself with non-nordic European groups such as italians, Jews, Slavs, and Greeks.

After the passage of the 1924 European Immigration Law, the question of Mexican immigration became more complex. Opponents of Mexican immigration became adamantly concerned about the failure of Congress to include the Mexican on the quota list. As the Restrictionists gathered strength, representatives from agriculture and railroad companies took an active role in defending the free flow of Mexican laborers into this country. A popular argument used by defenders of immigration from México rested on the premise that "White" men would not perform menial work. "White men" refused this work because of the "character of the toil, rather than the scale of wages."[82] Another supporter of Mexican labor added a somewhat contradictory statement when he argued: "We can't get good white labor at our common labor rate, 35 cents an hour."[83] In 1920, the Department of Labor conducted a survey to determine whether or not Mexican labor was in fact displacing Anglo labor. The department hoped to settle the issue by submitting the following:

Our investigation proves beyond a reasonable doubt that White men are averse to accepting and refuse to accept (as they have the right to do), employment as unskilled or common laborers . . .[84]

Other strong opponents of Mexican immigration included those who considered Mexicans non-assimilable or undesirable as an ethnic group. A statement by

Congressman Albert Johnson in 1929 serves as a good example of this sentiment. Speaking before a group in New York, Congressman Johnson noted that "the time [had] come again when it [was] necessary for Congress to save California for Californians." To this statement, Roy Garis, writing in the *Saturday Evening Post*, added, "and the entire Southwest for Americans."[85] Remsen Crawford, expressed similar views when they said that "in various localities of the Southwest, there [was] almost perfect unanimity on the main point that these people can never be assimilated with white people.[86] A sociologist, W. Garnett argued against the introduction of Mexican laborers into Texas: "Negroes and Mexicans, of course, constitute our main non-assimilable population elements . . ." and would "bring racial complication to a section which heretofore [has] been blessed with freedom from this vexatious problem."[87] Other opponents of Mexican immigration warned the public of possible health problems, racial miscegenation, and displacement of Anglo workers.

Both organized labor and Restriction Leagues considered the exclusion of Mexicans from the quota laws a grave mistake. Kenneth L. Roberts, well known to *Saturday Evening Post* readers for his articles on European Immigration, voiced the concern of the Restriction Leagues. Roberts wrote that since the restriction of European immigrants, "the brown flood of Mexican peon immigration--the immigration of Mexican Indians and Mexican mestizos, or halfbreeds--has risen from year to year."[88] Aware of the congressional hearings regarding the admission of Mexicans into the United States, Roberts visited several cities to investigate the issue. In Los Angeles, Roberts reported, one can:

> see the endless streets crowded with the shacks of illiterate, disease, pauperized Mexicans, taking no interest whatever in the community, living constantly on the ragged edge of starvation, bringing countless numbers of American citizens into the world with the reckless prodigality of rabbits . . .[89]

By the early 1920's organized labor's opposition to Mexican immigration had become unequivocal. Failing in its bid to have México included in the quota acts of 1921 and 1924, the AFL pursued the matter from another angle. Samuel Gompers, a long time "friend" of México, called upon leaders of the Confederación Regional Obrera Mexicana (CROM), México's largest labor union, to attend a meeting in Washington.[90] Gompers hoped that he could convince México to restrict the emigration of her citizens in a manner similar to the Gentlemen's Agreement of 1905 with Japan. Little came of the negotiations with México, and Mexican labor leaders often used the sessions to express disapproval of the treatment of Mexicanos in the United States. CROM leaders argued that Mexican workers often worked for lower wages than native Anglos because the AFL would not allow Mexicanos into their unions. After the death of Gompers, and the assassination of President Obregón in México, the two groups discontinued efforts to come to an understanding.[91]

VII

Immigrants "have always played an important role in United States history, and Mexican immigrants have proven to be no exception. From the early 1880's, railroad companies employed Mexican laborers in construction and maintenance of railroad lines throughout the Southwest. At the turn of the century, the entrance of Mexicanos into the United States increased significantly, and so did the number of industries dependent upon their labor. Beginning in 1910, and continuing to 1930, social and economic dislocations in México drove thousands northward while even stronger economic factors associated with the expanding Southwest lured those emigrants into the United States. Immigration from south of the Rio Grande increased tremendously between 1900-1930 due to U.S. requirements for labor during the war years. This influx, however, did not come without some opposition. Organized labor accused Mexicanos of taking jobs from U.S. citizens. At the same time, other restrictionist organizations labeled Mexicans thriftless and prone to accept charity. Notwithstanding this opposition, Mexican laborers played an important role in the economic development of the Southwest. While debate in Washington D.C. over the restriction of immigration continued throughout the 1920's, perhaps a million Mexican immigrants entered the United States. Eventually not legislation but the economic depression after 1929 finally caused a marked decrease in Mexican immigration. By 1929 Mexicanos, moreover, had firmly established themselves in urban and rural communities throughout the Southwest and Midwest.

Notes

1. U.S. Bureau of the Census, *Fifteenth Census of the United States: 1930. Abstract of the Census* (Washington D.C.: U.S. Government Printing Office, 1932), pg. 130.

2. See for example, Maldwyn Allen Jones, *American Immigration* (Chicago: University of Chicago Press, 1960), Ch. 4 and 7; Robert A. Divine, *American Immigration Policy, 1924-1952* (New Haven: Yale University Press, 1967), Chapters 1-4.

3. U.S. Bureau of the Census, *Fifteenth Census*: 1930, pg. 130.

4. Carey McWilliams, *Southern California Country: An Island on the Land* (Santa Barbara: 1973), pg. 69, originally published in 1946; and Leonard Pitt, *The Decline of the Californios* (Berkeley: University of California Press, 1970) pg. 256.

5. Pitt, pg. 256.

6. WPA Writers Program, *Los Angeles: A Guide to the City and Its Environs* (New York: Hastings House Publishers, Inc., 1941) pg. 45

7. California Governor's Office, "Mexican Fact-Finding Committee," *Mexicans in California* (California State Printing Office, 1930), pg. 29.

8. Ibid., pg. 31.

9. Ibid.

10. Victor S. Clark, *Mexican Labor in the United States* (Washington, D.C.: U.S.Government Printing Office, 1908), pp. 477-478.

11. Ibid., pg. 478.

12. Charles A. Thomson, "The Man from Next Door," *Century Magazine*, Vol. 3 (January, 1926). pg. 279.

13. U.S. Bureau of the Census, *Fifteenth Census of the United States: 1930 Abstract of the Census, Population*, pg. 173.

14. Jeremiah W. Jenks, *The Immigration Problem* (New York: Funk, 1912), pg. 212.

15. Samuel Bryan, "Mexican Immigrants in the United States," *The Survey* (September, 1912), pg. 727.

16. Moises González Navarro, unpublished manuscript, 1973. (México D.F.:), pp. 735 and 738.

17. Samuel Bryan, "Mexican Immigrants," pg. 727.

18. México, Dirección General de Estadística, *Anuario Estadístico 1942* (México D.F., 1942), pp. 1054-1055; and Alfredo B. Cuéllar, *La situación financiera de los ferrocarriles nacionales de México con relación al trabajo* (México D.F.: 1935), pp. 42-45.

19. Manuel Gamio, *Mexican Immigration to the United States* (Chicago: University of Chicago Press, 1930), pg. 225.

20. México, *Anuario Estadistico 1942*, pp. 1081-1083.

21. Interview with Mr. Ramón Lizárraga, San Fernando, California, November, 1972.

22. Vera L. Sturges, "Mexican Immigrants," *The Survey* (July 2, 1921), pg. 470.

23. U.S. Bureau of the Census, *Fifteenth Census*: 1930, pg. 173.

24. Coyote: A person who engages in smuggling undocumented persons.

25. Interview with Mr. Valente S. Ramírez, December, 1972, in East Los Angeles, California.

26. Helen W. Walker, "Mexican Immigrants as Laborers," *Sociology and Social Research*, Vol. 13 (September, 1928), pg. 57.

27. Ibid.

28. Interview with Ramón Terrazas, August 1972.

29. Victor S. Clark, *Mexican Labor*, pg. 472.

30. México, *Censo general de la población*, resumen 1930 (México D.F., 1939), pp. 149-155.

31. Ibid., Table 44, "Entrada y salida, registradas en el país, durante el periodo 1908-1928," pg. 145.

32. U.S. Bureau of Immigration, *Annual Report of the Commissioner-General of Immigration to the Secretary of Labor, 1912-1913* (Washington D.C.: U.S. Government Printing Office, 1913), pp. 40, 54, and 92.

33. Jay S. Stowell, "The Danger of Unrestricted Mexican Immigration," *Current History*

(August, 1938), pg. 763.

34. U.S. Bureau of Immigration, *Annual Report of the Commissioner-General of Immigration to the Secretary of Labor, 1914*, pg. 458.

35. Los Angeles *Times*, January 2, 1914.

36. J. B. Gwin, "Making Friends of Invaders," *The Survey*, Vol. 37 (March 3, 1917), pg. 621.

37. Los Angeles *Times*, January 13, 1914.

38. J. B. Gwin, "Making Friends of Invaders," pg. 622.

39. Los Angeles *Times*, January 17, 1914.

40. Henry Alvin Millis, *The Japanese Problem in the United States* (New York: Macmillan Company, 1915), pg. 124.

41. Los Angeles *Times*, September 18, 1916.

42. Maldwyn A. Jones, *American Immigration*, pp. 269-270.

43. Los Angeles *Times*, June 10, 1917.

44. Los Angeles *Times*, May 19, 1917.

45. Los Angeles *Times*, May 30, 1917.

46. J. B. Gwin, "Social Problems of Our Mexican Population," *Proceedings of The National Conference of Social Work: 1926*. pg. 328.

47. Robert Glass Cleland, *California in Our Time* (New York: Alfred A. Knoph, 1947), pp. 251-252.

48. Vernon McCombs, *From Over the Border: A Study of the Mexican in the United States* (New York, 1925), pg. 35.

49. U.S. Bureau of Immigration, *Annual Report of the Commissioner-General of Immigration to the Secretary of Labor, 1918*, pp. 692-693.

50. George Soule, *Prosperity Decade, From War to Depression: 1917-1929* (New York: Holt, Rinehart, & Winston, Inc., 1968), first published in 1947. See Chapter IV, "The Postwar Boom."

51. U.S. Bureau of the Census, *Fifteenth Census of the United States: 1930 Agriculture. Volume II, Part 3* (Washington D.C.: U.S. Government Printing Office, 1932), pg. 516; and U.S. Bureau of the Census, *Fifteenth Census: 1930*, pp. 674-675.

52. U.S. Bureau of Immigration, *Annual Report, 1918*, pg. 692.

53. U.S. Bureau of Immigration, *Annual Report of the Commissioner-Gernal of Immigration, 1920*, pp. 7-8.

54. U.S. Congress, Hearings of the Senate Committee on Immigration, *Restriction of Western Hemisphere Immigration*, on S. 1296, S. 1437, S. 3019. 70th Congress, 1st Session, 1928, pp. 89-91 and 160; and U.S. Bureau of Immigration, *Annual Report*, 1920, pp. 7-8.

55. *The Literary Digest*, (July 17, 1920), pg. 53.

56. Ibid., pg. 39.

57. Emory Bogardus, *The Mexican in the United States* (Los Angeles: University of

Southern California Press, 1934), pg. 39.

58. Ibid.

59. Constantine Panunzio, *How Mexicans Earn and Live* (Berkeley: University of Clifornia Press, 1933), pp. 14-15.

60. Emory Borgardus, "The Mexican Immigrant," *Journal of Applied Sociology*, Volume 2 (1926-1927), pg. 473.

61. Manuel Gamio, *Mexican Immigration to the United States* (Chicago: University of Chicago Press, 1930), pg. 84.

62. U.S. Bureau of Immigrant, *Annual Report of the Commissioner-General of Immigration, 1918-1919*, pg. 61.

63. "Mexican Immigrant," *The Survey* (April 10, 1920), pg. 81.

64. G. Bromley Oxnam, *The Mexican in Los Angeles* (Los Angeles, 1920), pg. 21.

65. John R. Martínez, "Mexican Emigration to the United States, 1910-1930," (Ph.D. dissertation, University of California at Berkeley, 1957). See 1971 reprint, R and E Press (San Francisco, 1971) for quote, pg. 46.

66. Los Angeles *Times*, March 5, 1920.

67. Ibid.

68. John Martínez, pg. 48.

69. U.S. Bureau of the Census, *Fourteenth Census: 1920. Population, II* (Washington D.C.: U.S. Government Printing Office), pg. 731; and U.S. Bureau of the Census, *Fifteenth Census: 1930*, pp. 98-99.

70. U.S. Bureau of the Census, *Fifteenth Census: 1930*, pp. 98-99.

71. Edwin R. Brown, "The Challenge of Mexican Immigration," *The Missionary Review of the World*, Vol. 49, (March, 1926), pg. 192.

72. American Federation of Labor, *Proceedings of the 33rd Annual Convention*, 1913 (herein cited by date), pg. 164

73. AFL, Proceedings, 1917, pg. 264.

74. AFL, Proceedings, 1919, pg. 247

75. AFL, Proceedings, 1919, pg. 249.

76. AFL, Proceedings, 1919, pg. 242

77. Paul S. Taylor, "Some Aspects of Mexican Immigration," *Journal of Political Economy*, vol. 38 (October, 1930), pg. 614.

78. Ibid.

79. John McDowell, *A Study of Social and Economic Factors Relating to Spanish-Speaking People in the United States* (Home Missions Council, n.d.), pg. 15.

80. "Mexican Immigrants," pg. 81

81. Marion T. Bennett, *American Immigration Policies* (Washington: Public Affairs Press, 1963), pp. 61-62.

82. Gerge Marvin, "Monkey Wrenches in Mexican Machinery," *The Independent*, Vol. 120 (April 14, 1928), pg. 352.

83. Paul S. Taylor, *Mexican Labor in the United States*, Vol. VII, University of California Publications in Economics. (Berkeley: University of California Press, 1934), pg. 81; and Paul S. Taylor, "Monkey Wrenches in Mexican Machinery," pg. 352.

84. "Result of Admission of Mexican Laborers," *Monthly Labor Review* (November, 1920), pg. 1097.

85. Roy Garis, "The Mexicanization of American Business," *The Saturday Evening Post* (February 8, 1930), pg. 182.

86. Remsen Crawford, "The Menance of Mexican Immigration," *Current History* (February, 1930), pg. 904.

87. William Edward Garnett, "Immediate and Pressing Race Problems of Texas," *Proceedings of the Southwestern Political and Social Science Association* (Austin, 1925), pg. 35.

88. Kenneth L. Roberts, "Mexican or Ruin," *The Saturday Evening Post* (February 18, 1928), pg. 43.

89. Kenneth L. Roberts, "The Docile Mexican," *The Saturday Evening Post* (March 10, 1928), pg. 43.

90. Harvey A. Levenstein, *Labor Organizations in the United States and México* (Westport, Conn.: Greenwood Publishing Co., Inc., 1971), pg. 117.

91. Harvey A. Levenstein, "The AFL and Mexican Immigration in the 1920's: An Experiment in Labor Diplomacy," *Hispanic American Historical Review* (November, 1968), pg. 212.

El Primer Congreso Mexicanista, a political conference organized in southern Texas in 1911, is the focus of José E. Limón's study. In response to a climate of social oppression, Tejanos, under the leadership of Nicasio Idar, sought to convene influential Tejanos to confront a myriad of issues of the era. Interestingly, the issues and resolutions have a surprisingly contemporary ring, pre-dating Chicano movement issues and resolutions by some six decades.

El Primer Congreso Mexicanista de 1911: A Precursor to Contemporary Chicanismo
José E. Limón

In its struggle for social change on behalf of the Chicano community, the contemporary Chicano movement has developed a broad coherent ideology to guide and legitimize its activity in the areas of schooling, labor, and organized politics. At least five major themes form the ideology that distinguishes this movement, composed largely of student groups such as MECHA and MAYO. This ideology consists of: (1) a critical attack on the social subordination of Chicanos as a holistic phenomenon; (2) a personal, artistic, and institutional affirmation of the special variant of Mexican culture found in the U.S.; (3) the assertion of a feminist position within the larger movement; (4) the search for a unified political solution to Chicano problems including at least a partial acceptance of radical politics; and (5) the somewhat unclear projection of a quasi-separate nation state as the final goal for this movement.[1]

Finding no adequate historical precedents within the community, scholars attribute a seeming novelty to this ideology. One influential study labels the 1848-1921 period as "apolitical." According to Alfredo Cuéllar, this period of organizational and ideological inactivity is followed by a series of organizations such as the Order Sons of America (1921), LULAC (1929) and the American G.I. Forum (1948).

However, these groups follow an ideology of adaptation and accommodation to Anglo American society--a practice not substantially altered by later groups such as MAPA (1959) and PASSO (1960). As such the 1921-1960 groups stand in marked contrast to the contemporary Chicano movement of the mid sixties and its new ideology of Chicanismo.[2] Or, as Cuéllar put it in 1970:

Until recently no Mexican-American had tried to define the problems of the community in any terms except those of assimilation. It is precisely these ideas of assimilation and social "adjustment" that the Chicano militant reject. As a new alternative, Chicanismo represents a conception of an autonomous and self determining social life for Mexican Americans. It is interesting to note that it was not until the 1960's that the Chicano leaders emerged to question some of the oldest and most fundamental assumptions of Mexicans in American society.[3]

This history of ideologies needs to be revised on the basis of new evidence furnished by *EL Primer Congreso Mexicanista* de 1911. In the present study I will argue that this early congress and its social milieu anticipate many of the major themes that define the supposedly new ideology of Chicanismo.

Background of the Congreso

El Primer Congreso Mexicanista was a political conference held in Laredo, Texas, on September 14-22, 1911.[4] It was convened by Texas Mexicans to express and act upon a variety of social grievances which were the culmination of an encroaching Anglo-American domination of Texas-Mexicans during the latter half of the nineteenth century and into the early twentieth. This period was marked by the transfer of almost all Texas-Mexican land into Anglo-Texan hands through various legal and illegal means.[5] Coupled with an intensifying Mexican immigration, this loss of economic position started the conversion of the Texas-Mexican population into a cheap labor pool for the developing Anglo-Texan ranching and farming interests.[6] Protected by his nearly exclusive control of the political order and reinforced by his visible economic dominance, the Anglo-Texan, with his embedded sense of racial and cultural superiority, created a pattern of local, officially sanctioned segregation between the two peoples.[7] Finally, by suppressing acts of native resistance such as those of Juan Cortina and Catarino Garza and physically intimidating the Texas-Mexican population as a whole, law enforcement and military authorities reflected and supported the new socio-economic order.[8] In response to this developing climate of social oppression, Sr. Nicasio Idar and his family initiated a campaign of journalistic resistance that eventually led to El Primer Congreso Mexicanista.

The Idar Family and La Crónica

Born in Point Isabel, Texas, near Brownsville on December 1853, Nicasio Idar moved to Laredo, Texas, in 1880, after living in Corpus Christi and attending schools there. He was primarily a journalist and commercial printer, although he also served as an Assistant City Marshall and a Justice of the Peace in Laredo. As a journalist he published *La Revista*, a Masonic review, and *La Crónica*, a weekly independent newspaper dedicated "al beneficio de la raza méxico-texana." In addition to his affiliation with the Mexican Masonry, he also belonged to the Sociedad Mutualista Benito Juárez in Laredo and was a vice president of a Mexican and Texas-Mexican fraternal lodge system known as La Orden Caballeros de Honor. According to his obituary he had also been active in labor organizing "hasta lograr la fundación de la primera asociación de Ferrocarrileros Mexicanos." He died on April 7, 1914, leaving his widow Jovita and eight children, one of whom eulogized him as a man who left a legacy of ideas "sanas, nobles, benéficas, que forman un tesoro inacabable, pródigo siempre en beneficios y enseñanzas."[9] At least three children had shared, not only their father's ideas, but his enthusiasm and zeal in defending the rights of the Texas-Mexican community. Jovita (named after her mother), Clemente and Eduardo joined their father in his work as editor and publisher of *La Crónica*. This remarkable newspaper covered local and area news, Mexico, and world wide affairs, although it was centrally dedicated to "el progreso y desarrollo industrial, moral e intellectual de los habitantes mexicanos en Texas."[10] Eduardo covered Brownsville and the lower Rio Grande Valley as a traveling correspondent, while Jovita and Clemente served in a general capacity including considerable staff writing.[11] There were other writers for *La Crónica* including guest writers and the newspaper reprinted significant articles appearing elsewhere. lt began publication sometime in the 1890's with Nicasio Idar as editor, although it is likely that he did not become its owner and publisher until 1910.[12]

La Crónica and Social Oppression.

Throughout the period 1910-1911, *La Crónica* launched a series of attacks on particular manifestations of the social conditions oppressing Texas-Mexicans. Five issues drew the Idar's interest and formed the immediate social context of El Primer Congreso Mexicanista: (1) the deteriorating Texas-Mexican economic condition; (2) the already perceptible loss of Mexican culture and the Spanish language; (3) general social discrimination; (4) the particular problem of educational discrimination; and (5) the pattern of officially tolerated lynchings of Texas-Mexicans. The latter two drew their principal attention.

On November 2, 1910, Antonio Rodríguez, probably a Mexican national, was arrested by sheriff's deputies near Rocksprings, Texas, and accused of having murdered an Anglo-American woman on a ranch near town. His guilt or innocence will never be known, because within hours a mob took him from the Rocksprings jail, tied him to a tree and burned him to death. The local coroner returned a verdict of death "at the hands of persons unknown.[13] A later investigation by the Texas Rangers would show that "the recent burning of the Mexican there was done entirely by Americans, . . ."[14] This atrocity had an impact on U.S.-Mexican relations and on the Texas-Mexican community.[15] *La Crónica* bitterly attacked the burning as a barbaric act, and denounced the inaction of the local authorities.[16]

On June 19, 1911 Antonio Gómez, age 14, was asked to leave a place of business in Thorndale, Texas. He refused, a fight ensued and a Texas-German was left dead with a wound from Gómez's knife. Gómez was arrested, but was taken from the authorities by a group of men who beat him to death and dragged his body around town with a buggy. *La Crónica* commented on this particular lynching and on the general condition of injustice:

> Este hecho bárbaro fue communicado a todo el mundo civilizado causando la consternación consiguiente. Se espera saber que hará el Gobierno de Texas pero hay que suponer que se encausará a los lynchadores y se les dejará libres bajo fianza y despues de cansar la opinión pública con simulacros de juicios, se desechará completamente la causa; pues hasta ahora no recordamos de americano alguno que haya sido castigado por el lynchamiento de un mexicano, á pesar de que se han cometido algunas.

La Crónica saw this incident as a particular case of the general racial hatred and contempt felt by most Anglo-Texans toward Mexicans.[17] In a later article, *La Crónica* attacked the Mexican consuls for timidity in entering the case and, noting that Thorndale Mexicans were retaliating by boycotting Anglo merchants, concluded:

> . . . no queda a los mexicanos mas que un remedio; el que han adoptado los hombres de todas las razas para hacerse respetar: La asociación.[18]

Later that month *La Crónica* took note of an Orden Caballeros de Honor meeting held in Bay City on the Texas Gulf Coast to discuss the Thorndale matter and the need to unify Texas-Mexicans. In attendance were delegates from Matagorda, Rockeye, Wharton, and Runge.[19]

    La Crónica took interest in a third criminal case. León Cárdenas Martínez was arrested and tried for allegedly murdering two Anglo women near Reeves, Texas, in July, 1911. According to George Estes, his lawyer, a mob forced Martínez to confess at gunpoint. A single jury member who dissented on the "guilty" vote was threatened, and Martínez was finally sentenced to death. Under personal threats to his own life, Estes appealed the case and the death sentence was reduced to thirty years in the penitentiary.[20] Texas-Mexicans had sent several letters, including one from *La Crónica*, to Governor O. B. Colquitt asking for clemency for the 16 year old Martínez.[21] Governor Colquitt received pressure from the other side as well:

> . . . a petition said to bear the signature of nearly every Caucasian in Reeves County has been sent to Governor Colquitt asking him not to commute the Mexican's sentence.[22]

The Martínez case would receive attention at the Congreso.

    The judicial injustices committed against Mexicans were a logical result of the general climate of social discrimination. According to *La Crónica*, even the *Houston Post* noted the effect of the Alamo syndrome on juries trying Mexicans. The Post concluded that there was very little sympathy for the "greaser" in this country. J. J. Mercado, the translator of the Post article commented:

> Lo sabiamos ya nosotros antes de que el Post nos lo dijera y lo hemos sabido siempre, que millares de fallos judiciales en los tribunales de Texas en contra del Mexicano, han sido inspirados en la sangrienta venganza que entraña el grito "Remember de Alamo" y en el concepto de "greaser" que naciera de la eterna predisposición contra la raza mexicana.[23]

Earlier in the year *La Crónica* had noted the general climate of racial discrimination particularly in central Texas where signs such as "No lots sold to Mexicans" and "No Mexicans admitted" were prevalent, and where, in Austin, State Representative J, T. Canales was called "the greaser from Brownsville" during a session of the legislature.[24] The "greaser" concept particularly affected the educational process. Toward the end of 1910 and on through early 1911 Clemente Idar wrote a series of articles exposing glaring discrimination in Texas public schools, particularly in upper southern Texas. He argued that Texas-Mexicans paid school taxes, but were not permitted to participate in the educational system. The Mexican consul in Laredo was asked to investigate, but confined his investigation to the largely Mexican counties of Webb, Starr, and Zapata and concluded there was no discrimination in Texas. Idar urged him to visit the rest of southern and central Texas as he himself had done, but this was never done. Idar continued to attack specific counties: Val Verde, Hays, González, Atascosa, Medina, Frío, La Salle, Dimmit, McMullen, Uvalde, and Wilson, and also the towns of Pearsal, Devine, Kingsville, Asherton, Kyle and Del Rio. In one significant article he interpreted this pattern of discrimination as a violation of the Treaty of Guadalupe Hidalgo. As a result of this extensive series *La Crónica* began to receive letters from its readers all over Texas confirming the existence of segregation in their communities.[25] However, *La Crónica* also recognized that even in inferior and segregated schools, an ethnocentric educational process was starting to anglicize Texas-Mexican children. It expressed deep concern about the loss of the Spanish language and Mexican history and culture, and in a strikingly modern tone, argued for bi-lingual education:

> Con profunda pena hemos visto á maestros mexicanos enseñando inglés á niños de su raza, sin tomar para nada en cuenta el idioma materno que cada día se va olvidando "más y cada día van sufriendo adulteraciones y cambios que hieren materialmente al oido de cualquier mexicano por poco versado que esté en la idioma de Cervantes.[26]

English should also be learned, but Spanish was fundamental:

> . . . lo que quisimos significar simplemente es que no debe desatenderse el idioma nacional, porque es el sello característico de las razas y las castas se hunden cuando se olvida la lengua nacional . . . No decimos que no se enseñe el inglés a la niñez mexico-texana, sea en hora buena, decimos que no se olviden de enseñarles el castellano . . .[27]

A second consequence of such mis-education would be a progressive cultural apathy and indifference:

> . . . si en la escuela americana á que concurren nuestros niños se les enseña la Biografía de Washington y no la de Hidalgo y en vez de hechas gloriosas de Juárez se le refieren las hazañas de Lincoln, por mas que estas sean nobles y justas, no conocerá ese niño las glorias de su Patria, no la amará y hasta verá con indiferencia a los coterranos de sus padres.[28]

Late in 1910, *La Cronica* had proposed a dramatic solution for the cultural problem created by ethnocentric Anglo-U.S. schools: the creation of a separate school system staffed by imported Mexican teachers where the primary language of instruction would be Spanish. The expenses for such a school system were to be borne by the Texas-Mexican community.[29] Replying to a Texas-Mexican critic of this radical idea, *La Crónica* approvingly pointed to educational efforts of this kind already underway within the community:

> . . . en las cuales se propone la creación de escuelas donde se instruya á la juventud mexicana exclusivamente en la idioma de Cervantes, como una medida eficaz para que no pierda terreno y siga siendo todo el tiempo la hija de 'labradores pobres' y por tanto la bestia del trabajo, triste condición á la que se le quiere condenar. . .[30]

This was a strikingly modern linkage between the non-use of the child's native language and his progressive failure in the schools and in society. The notion of community created schools would appear again a month before the Congreso:

> La niñez mexicana en Texas necesita instruirse. Ni nuestro gobierno ni el de EEUU pueden hacer nada por ella, y no queda otro recurso que el de hacerlo por nuestro propio impulso a trueque de no seguir despreciados y vejados por los extranjeros que se rodean.[31]

Another area of concern for the Idars was the steadily deteriorating economic position of Texas-Mexicans. They urged the people not to sell their land to the growing wave of,

> . . . agentes y compradores de terrenos, que hacen sus mejores especulaciones comprando propiedades de mexicanos a precios ínfimos, para traspasarlas a manos de otros individuos que nada tienen en común con nosotros, y el resultado lógico de esa actividad, inevitablemente será que en muy pocos años el número de nuestros hombres acandalados de hoy se habrá reducido en grande proporciones, y entonces, sus descendientes y sus hermanos serán los que sufren las consequencias de su imprevisión.[32]

Idar felt now was the time to reverse the tide and hold on to the land. Only in this way could Texas-Mexicans reach "el no lejano y glorioso provenir que espera a nuestra raza heróica y viril."[33] As a result of this host of issues, the Idars begin making plans for El Primer Congreso Mexicanista.

El Primer Congreso Mexicanista--Organizational Techniques

The Idars were active members in the Orden Caballeros de Honor (OCH), a Texas-Mexican and Mexican fraternal lodge, and they utilized the Texas wide system of lodges as a primary organizational base. The largest groups were in Brownsville (200), Corpus Christi (80) and Laredo (90).[34] In January, 1911 through *La Crónica* the Idars began calling for a convention of the various lodges and special guests--"los mexicanos mas ilustrados en las letras, residentes en Texas, a todos los periodistas mexicanos de Texas, y a todos los cónsules Mexicanos." This convention to be held in Laredo, was to take up the questions of: (1) school discrimination; (2) the need for teaching Spanish in community controlled schools with Mexican teachers; (3) the Mexican consular system; (4) ways and means to protect Mexican lives and interests in Texas; (5) the role of the Orden; (6) formation of women's groups under the auspices of the Orden; (7) the need for Texas-Mexicans to acquire land and hold on to that which they had; and (8) organizing a future meeting to be known as El Primer Congreso Mexicanista.[35]

By February, 1911, the Idars changed their minds and asked each OCH lodge to send a special delegation to the OCH conventions. These special delegations would convene separately as El Primer Congreso Mexicanista so that immediate steps would be taken toward solving the Texas-Mexican problems. Arguing that Texas-Mexicans could not depend on change in the Anglo-Texan community or on external help from México, *La Crónica* urged organization, unification and education of the Mexican masses as the only solution to "los problemas que afectan las vidas y los intereses de nuestros hermanos." An open invitation was extended to all Texas-Mexican organizations "que en algo se preocupen por nuestro bienestar." A special invitation was extended to the Texas-Mexican Masonic Lodges. Indeed, *La Crónica* urged Texas-Mexicans to organize themselves locally for the purpose of sending a delegation to the meetings.[36]

In the March 16th issue of the newspaper, the Idars printed letters of support from prominent individuals in various groups. They also received the support of the very important *sociedades mutualistas*. These self help social groups existed extensively throughout Texas primarily to provide an insurance service, a place for socializing and an organizational base for the celebration of Mexican holidays in Texas. During this month the decision was also made to hold the dual convention during the week of September 14-22, 1911. The symbolic value of the date is, of course obvious, but *La Crónica* also took note of the tactical advantages--lower holiday train fare and the presence of large numbers of visitors in Laredo to celebrate *las fiestas patrias*.[37]

In July the proposed *Congreso* received the support of the Agrupación Protectora Mexicana of San Antonio, led by Doneciano Dávila and Emilio Flores and dedicated to the defense of Texas-Mexicans especially on the issue of lynchings. Dávila and Flores called for a nation-wide political unification of all Mexicans in the U.S. so that,

> . . . unidos todos bajo los vinculos más estrechos de compañerismo y confraternidad nos pongamos á cubierto de los limites de la ley, de todo genero de infamias á injustícias que con nosotros se pretenda cometer.

Nicasio Idar thanked them for their support noting their previous efforts on behalf of Texas-Mexicans, particularly "en el asunto de Cortez" an obvious reference to the legal defense of Gregorio Cortez.[38] In this same month the Idars published the first estimate of the expected attendance at the meetings. We are told that "la asistencia será de 300-400 personas."[39] In August we learn that a Mesa Directiva was to be elected by a majority of those present and that after the *Congreso*, chapters were to be established "en todos las poblaciones mexicanas" under the central Mesa Directiva that would function as "el centro de protección de todos los mexicanos de Texas, por medio de él se demandará justicia cuando sea necesario . . ."[40] In early September, *La Crónica* also took note of growing local support in the form of financial contributions.[41] And, on the morning of the *Congreso*, *La Crónica* announced the presence of additional delegations from the Agrupación Protectora Mexicana of Houston and a Masonic lodge in México City.[42] That same morning a terse announcement entitled "Otra Víctima del Odio Yankee" appeared in the paper:

> El lunes último fue muerto en Corpus Christi por un americano, el laborioso y digno mexicano José Olivares, hermano por parte materna del Sr. Nicasio Idar . . .[43]

No further explanation was given of this incident personally affecting the Idar family.

El Primer Congreso Mexicanista--The Meetings

On September 14, 1911 the delegates finally met on the second floor of a building in the town square known as Los Altos del Mercado. Roughly about this time the city of Laredo, located on the Rio Grande border approximately 200 miles from the Gulf port of Brownsville, was described in these terms:

> . . . a healthy and pleasant climate, an industrious and law abiding population, abundant and cheap labor, supplied with all the modern appliances for comfort, water works, electric lights, telephone exchange, costly public buildings, churches, schools, and private residences, smelters, and scapling works, ice factories, machine and car shops . . . a population of 15,000 souls and a taxable wealth of $3,000,000.[44]

More importantly a general review of Laredo newspapers from this time period tells us of a city whose political, educational, and cultural life were significantly influenced, if not dominated, by Texas-Mexicans--a situation which continues to the present.

As the Congreso met, a journalist covering the events would articulate the fundamental reason for the meetings:

> Estar en tierra extraña, vivir á merced de la majoria que son los habitantes de la tierra en que están y no unirse y defenderse mutuamente es estar a merced de ellos, es entregarse manistados al primer explotador de conciencia elástica, pero unirse entre sí, formar una sola liga defensiva ofensiva es ser invulnerables, es triunfar en el campo de la razón y de la justicia.[45]

We do not have an exact count of the persons in attendance, although we do know the Idars were successful in gathering two delegates from each OCH lodge in twenty-four Texas localities. We can add to this an unspecified number of representatives from Masonic lodges, sociedades mutualistas, agrupaciones protectoras, other types of social groups such as El Club Internacional of Laredo, special visitors such as the delegations from México, the press, and of course an unspecified number of ordinary visitors.[46] The secretary of the Congreso spoke of "una gran multitud" present at the sessions.[47] After a welcoming address by Nicasio Idar, the convention moved to elect a Mesa Directiva for the Congreso and to express its gratitude to Clemente Idar for his leadership role in organizing the Congreso. The Mesa was composed of: José P. Reyes, President (Brownsville), Nicasio Idar, Vice President (Laredo), Lisandro Peña, Secretary (Laredo), and as vocales J. A. Garza (unknown), Isidro G. Garza (Kingsville) and Timoteo F. Gloria (Rio Grande).[48]

Unfortunately we do not have a detailed day to day account of the Congreso proceedings. We do have a program of events, short general descriptions of the sessions, and most importantly, a collection of the major speeches (see footnote 47). The remainder of this study will be based on this data.

The Congreso was composed of formal discursos rendered in a high oratorical style together with discusiones and conferencias or what we might call workshops. Music was used extensively and the Congreso opened with a chorus of children singing patriotic songs and the recitation of a patriotic poem by a young boy. The poem, and all of the major speeches are replete with extensive allusions to México and Mexican history and culture. This pervasive nationalistic style is one of the major themes of the Congreso.[49]

Eight other ideas emerged in the speeches. The call for unity against the oppressor was repeated again and again. Lisandro Peña, for example, exhorted the people so oppressed in the past to unite and claim that which was theirs in the face of "malvados y tiranos."[50] J. M. Mora also called for Unity:

. . . cuando se hayan establecido relaciones de alianza y fraternidad en todas las sociedades mexicanas del Estado de Texas, será una liga tan fuerte y poderosa, revistiendo un carácter tan imponente ante el cual doblegarían la cerviz los politicos más astutos de la época, y sobre todo tendría gran representatción social tanto aquí como en México, que llamaría la atención del mundo.[51]

A third major idea is a radical working class ideology again expressed by Mora representing la Sociedad de Obreros Igualdad y Progreso:

En esta ciudad existió no hace mucho, una gran organización, y vimos como el capital persiguio a los obreros, hasta exterminarlos. El Capital como los políticos, ven un peligro amenazador para sus intereses cuando se trata, como en el asunto que nos ocupa, de unir el elemento obrero. Urge, pues, unir a la clase obrera y principalmente a los mexicanos que residimos en este país.[52]

A fourth idea was language and culture. S. G. Domínguez proposed the establishment of schools to teach both English and Spanish.[53] The Houston delegation sought discussion on the question of whether or not it makes more pedagogical sense to teach children in their native language first.[54] On the program we also find discursos and conferencias on topics such as "Mexicanismo" and "Orígen y Civilización Azteca."[55]

Several speakers addressed themselves to the question of criminal justice and bitterly denounced the lynchings.[56] They were, in fact, seen as one of the motivating reasons for the Congreso.[57] Hortencia Moncayo spoke explicitly on this issue and was congratulated by the Agrupación Proctectora of San Antonio who saw her and other active women as "las descendientes de Doña Josefa Ortiz de Domínguez, la Correjidora de Querétero y de Doña Leona Vicario.[58]

Texas-Mexican women and their particular social problems received the attention of the Congreso. A special invitation had been extended to women in the Laredo area.[59] The education of women was a topic on the program and Prof. S. G. Domínguez supported the idea:

> . . . lo absolutamente indispensable es educar a la mujer de nuestra raza para que amolde la tierna inteligencia de sus hijos . . .[60]

Soledad Flores de Peña pursued this idea in addressing the assembly:

> . . . es necesario comprender bien los dedeberes de cada uno y obrar según ellos; yo, como vosotros creo, que el mejor medio para conseguirlo es educar á la mujer, instruirla, darle ánimo a la vez que respetarla.

In return, she promised, women would be true to the tradition of Mexican heroines and develop strength, pride, and intelligence in their children.[61]

A seventh major theme was the social discrimination experienced by Texas-Mexicans. A letter read at the meetings expressed this view:

> Dia a dia se ve cruzar el Rio Bravo por grandes grupos de mexicanos que ansiosos de mejor salario para el sostenimiento de la familia van a Texas, y si bien es cierto que consiguen comer y vestir mejor . . . tambien es cierto que con frecuencia son tratados con un vergonzoso desprecio de parte de los americanos trantandolos como a raza degenerada o inculta . . .[62]

And, with regard to the particular case of school discrimination, the Houston delegation urged the Congreso to make a formal protest to the State Superintendent of Schools.[63]

Finally Telésforo Macías of Laredo urged Texas-Mexicans to practice sound economics so that the community would not find it necessary to go "de rodillas a poner en el mercado de los traficantes del trabajo ajeno, nuestro sudor, nuestro esfuerzo y nuestras energias en publica subasta."[64] Macias also eloquently summarized all of the Texas-Mexican concerns that prompted the Congreso including the lack of criminal justice, discrimination, labor exploitation, cultural retention, and the need for unity.[65]

On September 20, 1911, this first state wide gathering of Texas-Mexicans took a first small step in response to their social grievances. Appropriately enough, it donated $17.35 to the legal defense of León Cardenas Martínez.[66]

The Role of Laredo

The success of the Congreso required at least four elements: dedicated organizers, a medium of communication, money and a protected environment. The Idars and their newspaper provided the first two. The City of Laredo contributed the others. Financial contributions totaling $118.77 had been obtained from small Texas-Mexican merchants in the city and these funds were used to pay for chairs, hall rental, decorations, music and printed materials.[67] The availability of funds, however, only revealed a more fundamental characteristic of the city. The Texas-Mexican influence in its political, social and cultural life provided a supportive context that would have been extremely difficult to obtain elsewhere in 1911 with the possible exception of Brownsville. Laredo's distinctive characteristics had been noted in a March issue of *La Crónica*.[68]

Reception in the Press

This narrative would not be complete without a discussion of the available newspaper coverage given to the Congreso. According to *La Crónica*, Spanish language newspapers such as *El Demócrata Fronterizo* (Laredo), *El Imparcial* (San Antonio), *El Gallo* (Falfurrias), *El Hachero* (Eagle Pass) and *El Porvenir* (Brownsville) supported the Congreso and its aims.[69] The Anglo-American press reacted somewhat differently, if we can judge this reaction using two major newspapers from the area. The *San Antonio Express* and the *Laredo Weekly Times* reported the general factual details of the Congreso such as the time and place of the meetings and the names of the speakers, but deliberately or otherwise, they missed or misrepresented the tone and content of the meetings.[70]

Throughout both newspapers we find the redundant use of the term *interesting* describe the speeches. Almost nothing was said about their content and what was expressed does not correspond with the evidence presented in this study. According to the small notices buried in the back pages of both newspapers, the Congreso gathered to celebrate the "Mexican holidays" and to develop educational and citizenship programs designed to elevate the "Mexican race." According to the *Express*, José Reyes, the president of the Congreso,

> . . . made an interesting speech in which he said the objects of the Mexican congress were of an uplifting character and that its principal work will be the enlightment and elevation of the Mexican element in the State of Texas with a view of making them more desirable and better citizens and a credit to the Texas cities in which they make their homes. Several other addresses were made along similar lines and the Congreso seems determined in the work it has undertaken.[71]

The Laredo Weekly Times reported that J. M. Mora spoke on ways to relieve Mexican misery and,

> . . . maintained that the best way to bring about this condition was by the carrying out of moral and elevating ideas among the Mexican people, the bettering of their social positions by their own individual efforts to thereby obtain from them a position among the people with whom they make their homes.[72]

Unfortunately we do not have a text of José Reyes' speech, but it would seem improbable that a man expressing such views would have been elected to the presidency of a Congreso gathered to discuss lynchings, discrimination, the loss of land, labor exploitation and cultural nationalism. Mora, as I have shown, clearly spoke of the need for Mexican labor to unite itself over and against capital interests.

Post Congreso Developments

In an effort to provide a continuous long range solution to the multiplicity of Texas-Mexican problems, the Congreso decided to create an on-going state wide organization with local chapters. According to its constitution, La Gran Liga Mexicanista de Beneficencia y Protección would have these objectives: (1) carry out culture and moral instruction among its members; (2) protect its members when treated unjustly by the authorities; (3) protect them against unlawful acts by other persons; (4) create a fund for the organization; and (5) prevent the exclusion of Mexican children from Anglo American schools, and its motto would be "Por la Raza y Para la Raza."[73] Structurally, La Gran Liga would be composed of a central governing mesa directiva and local chapters each with their own mesa. The central and local mesa would have the same official structure: Director, Vice Director, Secretary, Treasurer, and a Master of Ceremonies. The central mesa was to be elected annually by delegates from the local ligas to the annual convention on September 16th. The central mesa had only the power to carry out those policies already written into the constitution or adopted at the conventions, including the power to hire agents to start local ligas in places of its own choosing, although each delegate was supposed to carry out the task in his local community.[74] The rest of the constitution spelled out the requirements for membership and the rights and obligations of the members. The organization was not limited to U.S. citizens or to males. The first Mesa Directiva of La Gran Liga Mexicanista was composed of: Nicasio Idar, Presidente (Laredo), Basilio Soto, Vice Presidente, (San Antonio), Gerónimo Jiménez, Tesorero (Laredo), Lisandro Peña, Secretario (Laredo). A Master of Ceremonies was not elected and all of the delegates were named as vocales.[76]

This was not the only organization produced by the Congreso. The women were to be heard from again. On October 15, 1911,

Un grupo de damas tan respetables como bellas se reunieron el domingo como a las diez de la mañana en el Salon de la Respetable Sociedad de Obreros "Igualdad y Progreso" y bajo los auspicios del Congreso Mexicanista organizaron la primera Liga Femenil Mexicanista con el ardiente anhelo de luchar ellas tambien POR LA RAZA Y PARA LA RAZA.[77]

A debate was held to select a more specific name for this women's group and the biographies of several Mexican heroines were read including those of Josefa Ortiz de Domínguez, Leona Vicario, and Doña Manuela Aguado de Abasolo. Apparently no name was chosen. The officers of the new organization were: Presidenta: Jovita Idar, Vice Presidenta: Profa. M. de J. de Teón, Secretaria: Profa. Soledad F. de Peña, Tesorera: Profa. María Rentería, Consejera General: Maria Villarreal, Vocales: Sritas. Profas. Luisa Cabrera, Rita Tarvin, Aurelia Peña y Sra. de Silva.[78] Since a number of these women were teachers, the organization immediately undertook a project to provide free instruction for poor Mexican children who could not afford to attend school.[79]

This is as much as we presently know about El Primer Congreso Mexicanista and its offspring organizations. They do not appear to have met again in 1912. The issues of *La Crónica* that I have been able to locate run through December, 1911 with a single issue from April, 1914. No mention is made of the Congreso in this latter issue, nor is it mentioned in other local available newspapers from 1912-1913. Although there were limited, scattered reports of efforts to organize ligas in a few communities, we must presume that La Gran Liga Mexicanista did not thrive.[80]

Analysis

The data presented permits us to argue that El Primer Congreso Mexicanista de 1911 represents an early organizational effort that anticipated many of the major themes of contemporary Chicanismo. Clearly we have the same pervasive concern for the socio-economic plight of Chicanos. To take three examples: (1) although far more subtle, the problem of social discrimination, particularly in the schools, continues to be a matter of intense interest to Chicanos; (2) the restoration of the land, particularly in Nuevo México, and the plight of Chicano labor, continue to attract contemporary attention; and (3) present day protest against police brutality in Chicano communities echoes the Congreso's denunciations of officially tolerated lynchings in 1910-1911. Yet taken by itself, the common concern with the subordinate socio-economic position of Chicanos would not alone argue for the Congreso as a precursor to the Chicano movement. In their own way the post 1921 accomodationist groups, Order Sons of America, the LULACS, and the American G.I. Forum, were also generally committed to this basic cause.

The particularly firm and unique ideological parallels between the Congreso and the contemporary period are to be found in their mutual interest in cultural retention and a rejection of assimilation, the rights of women and political unification. Like today's insistence on a personal and institutional commitment to bi-lingual and bi-cultural education, the Congreso was equally dedicated to the teaching of the Spanish language and of Mexican history and culture. Indeed we can even find in the Congreso milieu a tendency toward alternative school systems controlled by the community bringing to mind contemporary Chicano efforts in Colorado, the lower Rio Grande Valley and Crystal City, Texas. Similarly today's activist Chicanas can find strong historical precedent for their work in the activity of the Congreso women and La Liga Femenil Mexicanista. Finally the cry for political unity can still be heard. The apparent failure of La Gran Liga Mexicanista to achieve the latter in no way diminishes its importance as an effort that anticipated the current struggle of the Raza Unida Party to provide a single unified Chicano political vehicle for obtaining the same basic goals of the Congreso.[81] The opening remarks of this study referred to the contemporary vision of a quasi-separate nationstate for Chicanos.[82] The Congreso did not evoke a utopian ideal paralleling the contemporary notion of Aztlán. Yet, given their insistence on cultural nationalism and a pure ethnic organization together with the developing Texas-Mexican numerical majority in south Texas, it seems likely that their hypothetical success would have led to a political and cultural Texas-Mexican domination of the area. If not Aztlán, at least a reasonable portion of that vision.

These common interests, the socio-economic position of Chicanos, cultural retention, women's rights and the unity of the people, argue for the precursory character of El Primer Congreso Mexicanista de 1911. This relationship can perhaps be seen with greater clarity if approached with a conceptual framework.

Professor Ralph Guzmán has provided a simple and useful scheme for categorizing historical Chicano political organizations according to two variables-participation in the U.S. political system and intention to assimilate.[83] The data and analysis in the present study permit us to fill in some of the vacancies in his conceptual grid. All of the evidence gathered so far points to an extremely low almost non-existent assimilative intent in the Congreso and the ligas. The U.S. when mentioned was perceived as a problem, an obstacle, an enemy. Learning English, when it was mildly favored, if at all, was a purely utilitarian matter and seemed to have no intrinsic positive value as did the use of Spanish. Indeed we should note the exclusive use of Spanish in the Congreso and in *La Crónica*. Finally, we have a constant appeal to the Mexican cultural past.

The potential and the organizational structure for political participation were clearly present in the Congreso and the ligas. Yet apparently they did not have the opportunity to participate directly in U.S. electoral politics. For these reasons they are characterized as "medium" in terms of this variable. Using low assimilative intent and medium political participation, the Congreso has been located in the appropriate square in a revised version of Guzmán's scheme.

In both respects the Congreso and its milieu greatly resemble the 1967-70 Chicano movement ideologically, particularly in Texas. They were both phenomena marked by a strong sense of cultural nationalism, and, therefore, a low assimilative intent. Neither, however, actively and fully participated in the political process. On the same two criteria, the contemporary movement has been located in the same conceptual category with the Congreso.[84] Had La Gran Liga Mexicanista developed and participated in the U.S. political process the same ideological grounds as the Congreso, it probably would have resembled the contemporary Raza Unida Party in Texas which developed directly from the Chicano movement.[85] Like Raza Unida, La Gran Liga would have been the institutionalized agency resulting from a formative ideological, organizational phase. The actual Texas Raza Unida Party and a hypothetically successful Gran Liga Mexicanista are conjoined.

Conclusions

These findings permit us to fill in previously empty historical and conceptual slots thereby altering the political history of Chicanos in a significant manner. Whereas before it was probably correct to speak of a pre 1921 apolitical period and of a unique and novel post 1965 period, we now have to contend with an organized, militant, nationalist, pro-feminist social movement appearing in 1911.

The Congreso's scholarly importance is clear, but in arguing its precursory relationship to the contemporary scene, this study perhaps has accomplished more than a scholarly exercise. Professor Juan Gómez-Quiñones has called for a "union of history as discipline and history as action on behalf of a community in its struggle for survival.[86] If this new knowledge of historical ideological precedents lends moral and intellectual support to the contemporary struggle, this work has responded adequately to this call.

Notes

1. Alfredo Cuéllar, "Perspectives on Politics" in *Mexican-Americans*, Joan Moore, ed. (Englewood Cliffs, N.J: Prentice Hall, 1970), pp. 137-156. See also Rodolfo Acuña, *Occupied America: The Chicano's Struggle Toward Liberation* (San Francisco: Canfield Press, 1972) particularly chps. 9-10, and Armando Rendón, *Chicano Manifesto* (New York: Macmillan, 1971).

2. Cuéllar, pp. 137-156. For broader yet similar analyses, see Rodolfo Alvarez, "The Psycho-Historical and Socioeconomic Development of the Chicano Community in the United States," *Social Science Quarterly*, Vol. 53, No. 4 (March, 1973), pp. 920-942: Jesús Chavarría, "A Precise and Tentative Bibliography on Chicano History" *Aztlán*, Vol. 1, No. 1 (Spring, 1970), pp. 133-141; Juan Gómez-Q. "Toward a Perspective on Chicano History; *Aztlán*, Vol. II, No. 2 (Fall, 1971), pp. 1-49; Ralph Guzmán, "Politics and Policies of the Mexican-American Community," in California *Politics and Policies*,

Eugene P. Dvorin ed. (Palo Alto, Cal.: Addison-Wesley, 1966), pp. 350-385, and Miguel D. Tirado, "Mexican-American Community Political Organization, the Key to Chicano Political Power," *Aztlán,* Vol. 1, No. 1 (Spring, 1970), pp. 53-78. Carey McWilliams, useful but incomplete *North From Mexico* has been superceded by Rodolfo Acuña's *Occupied America: The Chicano's Struggle Toward Liberation* (San Francisco: Canfield Press, 1972) and Matt Meir and Feliciano Rivera, *The Chicanos: A History Of Mexican Americans* (New York: Hill and Wang, 1972). Neither of these general histories departs significantly from the analysis cited above. A study that sees cultural retention as a basic concern of the so-called assimilationist period is Charles Ray Chandler's, "The Mexican-American Protest Movement in Texas," Ph.D. dissertation, Department of Sociology, Tulane University, 1968. However, Chandler does not deal with the contemporary Chicano movement.

3. Cuéllar, pg. 155.

4. Prof. David J. Weber has published a speech from the Congreso and a brief commentary. See "Por La Raza y Para La Raza--Congreso Mexicanista, 1911," in *Foreigners in Their Native Land: Historical Roots Of The Mexican American* (Albuquerque: University of New Mexico Press, 1973), pp. 248-251. This publication appeared independently and somewhat after my research note, "El Primer Congreso Mexicanista de 1911: A Note on Research in Progress, *Aztlán*, Vol. III, No. I (Spring, 1972), pg. 171. Weber's commentary misses some important issues discussed at the Congreso and incorrectly identifies León Cárdenas Martínez as the victim of the Thorndale lynching. (See pp. 5-6 in the present study.) To my knowledge this is the only scholarly work on the Congreso.

5. D. W. Meinig, *Imperial Texas: An Interpretive Essay in Cultural Geography*, (Austin: University of Texas Press, 1969), pp. 54-56.

6. Victor Nelson-Cisneros, "La Clase Trabajadora en Texas, 1920-1940, "(Unpublished Ms., Center for Mexican-American Studies, University of Texas at Austin), pp. 3-4.

7. Meinig, pp. 98-101.

8. Américo Paredes *With his Pistol in his Hand* (Austin: University of Texas Press, 1971), pp. 31-32. See also Carey McWilliams, *North from Mexico* (New York: Greenwood, 1968), pp. 112-114.

9. *La Crónica*, April 18, 1914, pp. 1-2.

10. See any masthead of *La Crónica* (1910-1911) Texas Newspaper Collection, University of Texas at Austin.

11. "El Primer Año de Vida" *La Cronica* (Jan. 1, 1910), pg. 1. The author is currently at work on the preliminary research for a collective biography of this remarkable family whose members continue to be active participants in Chicano affairs today.

12. *The Chaparral*, (Feb. 18, 1899), pg. 3. "Mr. N. Idar, Assistant City Marshall and Editor of *La Crónica*, we regret to state has been quite sick the early part of this week." See "Progreso de *'La Crónica*,'" LC (Sept. 3, 1910), pg. 1.

"Con elementos propios principiamos la publicación de nuestro semanario *la Crónica* en Enero del año pasado, viniendo a ser la segunda Epoca de su existencia. Nunca creímos que llegaría en un año de vida a sentar la reputación y popularidad de que hoy goza tanto en la frontera Norte de México como en Texas, California, Arizona, y Nuevo México."

13. *San Antonio Light* and *Gazette* (Nov. 4, 1910), pg. 1.

14. "All Quiet in Edwards County--Lynching at Rock Springs Done By Americans, Says Ranger Captain." *San Antonio Daily Express* (Nov. 22, 1910), pg. 10.

15. Stanley R. Ross, *Francisco I. Madero: Apostle of Democracy* (New York: Columbia University Press, 1955), pg. 137.

16. "Barbarismos" *La Crónica* (Nov. 12, 1910), pg. 1.

17. "Cobarde Infame e Inhumano Lynchamiento de un Jovencito Mexicano en Thorndale, Milam Co. Texas, *La Crónica* (June 29, 1911), pg. 1. The accused were found not guilty. See "Lo Mismo de Siempre" *La Crónica* (Nov. 16, 1911), pg. 1.

18. "Valiente Cobardia de los Linchadores de Thorndale, Texas, Los Estados Unidos y México Nada Pueden Hacer Para El Castigo de los Criminales Represalias Unica Solución Posible," *La Crónica* (July 13, 1911), pg. 1.

19. "Junta de Indignación--El Infame hecho de Thorndale gita á los Mexicanos de Bay City" *La Crónica* (July 20, 1911), pg. 6.

20. "Traducción: Integra de la narración que hizo el Lic. George Estes á algunos periodicos como defensor del niño León Cárdenas Martínez, Jr., en el Proceso que se le enstruyo en Pecos, Texas el 29 de Julio de 1911. *La Crónica* (Oct. 26, 1911), pg. 2.

21. "Solicitud de Indulto," *La Crónica* (Aug. 24, 1911), pg. 1.

22. "Claim Mexican Hand is Not Murderer" *San Antonio Light* (Sept. 12, 1911), pg. 1.

23. J. J. Mercado, "Facultad de Perdonar--Traducción" *La Crónica* (Sept. 21. 1911), pg. 4.

24. "La Labor de la Crónica" (March 2, 1911), pg. 5.

25. "Los Niños Mexicanos en Texas" *La Crónica* (Nov. 26, 1910), pg. 3; "La Exclusion de los Niños Mexicanos en la Mayor Parte de las Escuelas Oficiales de Texas es Positiva." (Dec. 17, 1910), pg. 1; "Tanto los Niños Mexicanos como los Mexico-Americanos son excluidos de las Escuelas Oficiales--ya se Olividaron los Tratados de Guadalupe?" (Dec. 24, 1910), pg. 1; "La Exclusión en el Condado de Guadalupe", and "Los Mexicanos de San Angelo Demandan a Los Sindicos de las Escuelas Públicas" (Dec. 31, 1970), pg. 1; "La Exclusión de los Niños Mexicanos de la Escuelas Americanas En Algunas Partes de Texas" (Jan. 26, 1911), pg. 3; "La Exclusión en las Escuelas de los Condados de Frio, Bee, Hays, Bastrop, Comal, Caldwell, Blanco, etc. etc." (Feb. 9, 1911), pg. 1.

26. A. V. Negra, "Por La Raza--La Niñez Mexicana en Texas," *La Crónica* (Aug. 10,

1911), pg. 1. See also J. J. Mercado, "El Mexicano en Texas" *La Crónica* (Sept. 14, 1911), pg. 2 expressing concern for the linguistic deterioration already underway.

27. A. V. Negra, "La Conservación del Nacionalismo," *La Crónica* (Aug. 17, 1911), pg. 1.

28. Ibid.

29. "En Pro de la Raza Mexicana del Estado de Texas," *La Crónica* (Nov. 26, 1910), pg. 1.

30. "A 'El Imparcial de Texas'," *La Crónica* (Dec. 10, 1910), pg. 4.

31. A. V. Negra, "Por La Raza--La Niñez Mexicana en Texas," *La Crónica* (Aug. 10, 1911), pg. 1.

32. Clemente Idar, "Nuestro Deber en Este País: Solidaridad y Altruismo," *La Crónica* (Dec. 24, 1910), pg. 1.

33. Ibid.

34. "Excitativa del Gran Concilio de la Orden Caballeros de Honor a la raza Mexicana," *La Crónica* (Dec. 17, 1910) oja suelta inserted in newspaper.

35. "A la Orden Caballeros de Honor de Brownsville, Texas," *La Crónica* (Jan. 12, 1911), pg. 3.

36. "Un Gran Excitativo Al Gran Concilio de la Orden Caballeros de Honor." *La Crónica* (Feb. 2, 1911), pg. 1.

37. "Los Elementos Mas Conspicuous de Laredo Influyen Cerca del G. Concilio de a Orden Caballeros de Honor," *La Crónica* (March 16, 1911).

38. Nicasio Idar, "Argrupación Protectora Mexicana," *La Crónica* (July 13, 1911), pg. 2. See Américo Paredes, *With His Pistol in His Hand*, (Austin: University of Texas Press, 1958) for the full account of Gregorio Cortez.

39. "Una Gran Convención Se Reúne en Laredo," *La Crónica* (Jul. 27, 1911), pg. 4.

40. "El Congreso Mexicanista. ¿Qué Es y Qué se Propone?" *La Crónica* (Aug. 24, 1911), pg. 2.

41. "Para El Congreso Mexicanista" *La Crónica* (Sept. 7, 1911), pg. 4.

42. "Mas Delegados" *La Crónica* (Sept. 14, 1911), pg. 1.

43. "Otra Victima del Odio Yankee" *La Crónica* (Sept. 14, 1911), pg. 4.

44. E. R. Tarver, Laredo, *The Gateway Between the United States and Mexico*, Laredo Immigration Society (1889), pg. 1.

45. "El Congreso Mexicanista" *Fiat Lux* (Sept. 15, 1911), pg. 1.

46. That morning a general invitation to the public had appeared in *La Crónica*. "Invitacion" *La Crónica* (Sept. 14, 1911), pg. 1.

47. *Primer Congreso Mexicanista, Verificado en Laredo, Texas, EEUU de A. Los Dias 14 al 22 de Septiembre 1911. Discursos y Conferencias Por La Raza Y a Para la Raza.* Tipografia de N. Idar (1912), pg. 1.

48. Ibid., pg. 5. We have no evidence concerning voting procedures and privileges.

49. Ibid., pp. 3-5, 10-13. *The San Antonio Express* (Sept. 17, 1911), pg. 6 reports a

number of patriotic speeches, the display of Mexican flags and shouts of: "¡Viva México!" and "Viva Hidalgo!" during the meetings on the 16th.

50. Ibid., pg. 13.

51. Ibid., pg. 17.

52. Ibid., pg. 16.

53. Ibid., pg. 19.

54. Ibid., pg. 31.

55. Ibid., pg. 4.

56. Ibid., pg. 26.

57. Ibid., pg. 1.

58. Ibid., pp. 26-27.

59. "A La Mujer Mexicana de Ambos Laredos" *La Crónica* (Sept. 14, 1911), pg. 1.

60. Primer Congreso Mexicanista, pg. 20.

61. Ibid., pg. 24.

62. Ibid., pg. 14.

63. Ibid., pg. 31.

64. Ibid., pg. 34.

65. Ibid., pp. 28-30.

66. "Al Beneficio de León Cárdenas Martínez," *La Crónica* (Sep. 21, 1911), pg. 1 .

67. "Corte de Caja," *La Crónica* (Sept. 28, 1911), pg. 4.

68. "La Labor de la Crónica," *La Crónica* (March 2, 1911), pg. 5.

69. See "La Convención de los Caballeros de Honor y El Primer Congreso Mexicanista" *El Demócrata Fronterizo* (Sept. 23, 1911), pg. 4, "Congreso de Mexicanistas" *La Crónica* (April 20. 1911), pg. 4, and "Comentarios de la Prensa Sobre el Congreso Mexicanista," *La Crónica* (Sept. 28, 1911), pg. 3.

70. There was only one exception. "Mexicans May Protest Against Separate Schools, Matter is Placed Before Congreso Mexicanista in Session Now at Laredo" *San Antonio Express* (Sept. 17, 1911), pg, 16.

71. "Form New Organization, Congreso Mexicanista is Brought into Existence" *San Antonio Express* (Sept. 16, 1911), pg. 9. See also *The Express* for Sept. 15, 1911 (pg. 9), Sept. 18. 1911 (pg. 7), Sept. 19, 1911 (pg. 2), and Sept. 20, 1911 (pg. 7).

72. "The Mexican Congress--Interesting Subject Discussed" *Laredo Weekly Times* (Sept. 24, 1911), pg. 4. See also the Times for Sept. 17, 1911 (pg. 10) and Sept. 24, 1911 (pg. 6., 10).

73. "Constitución de la Gran Liga Mexicanista de Beneficiencia y Protección" in Primer Congreso Mexicanista, pg. 39.

74. "Constitución. . . ," pp. 39-42.

75. "Constitución. . . ," pp. 39-40, particularly Cap. II, Art. 3 on pg. 39.

76. "Para Constituyentes de la Comisión Consejera Del Congreso Mexicanista" *La Crónica* (Sept. 28, 1911) pg. 4.

77. "Liga Femenil Mexicanista" *La Crónica* (Oct. 19, 1911) pg. 1.

78. Ibid., pg. 1.

79. "La Liga Femenil Mexicanista" *La Crónica* (Dec. 7, 1911) pg. 1.

80. See "*La Crónica* publicará Semanariamente Los Progresos del Congreso Mexicanista" *La Crónica* (Sept. 28, 1911) pg. 4 and "Liga Mexicanista, No. 2," *La Crónica* (Oct. 12, 1911) pg. 1.

81. Rodolfo Acuña, *Occupied America: The Chicano's Struggle Toward Liberation* (San Francisco: Canfield Press, 1972), pp. 236-237.

82. Armando Rendón, *Chicano Manifesto* (New York: Macmillan, 1971), pg. 168.

83. Ralph Guzmán, "Politics and Policies of the Mexican American Community," in *California Politics and Voices*, Eugene P. Dvorin, ed., (Palo Alto, Cal. : Addison Wesley, 1966), pg. 374.

84. There are also strong similarities in the social-behavioral determinants of these phenomena as social movements. The author is currently at work on a study of these relationships.

85. Acuña, pp. 234-236.

86. Juan Gómez-Quiñones "Toward a Perspective on Chicano History" *Aztlán*, Vol. 2, No. 2 (Fall, 1971), pg. 39.

Christine Sierra traces the early Chicano political experience in the United States from the Mexican American War through the early 20th century. Sierra also places major emphasis on the conditions and forces which shaped the Mexican immigrant experience in Mexico and the United States. Mexican immigrants, she argues, are distinct from traditional American immigrants by virtue of the distinct nature of their arrival and their response to conditions in the United States. Her study reveals how these immigrants adopted an array of political strategies to cope with economic and political subordination.

Chicano Political Development: Historical Considerations
Christine M. Sierra

Analysis of a group's political development often involves an examination of the group's political behavior, as it chooses to organize in various ways, drawing from a myriad of approaches. Yet, the exercise of choice, of deciding between alternatives, takes place within a larger context. That context consists of the structured political relationships developed over time between the group and the political system.

This study of Chicano political development provides an overview of such structural considerations: those political arrangements and processes, drawn from early periods of Chicano history, that have set the basic parameters in which contemporary political endeavors evolve. Identified as key factors are the following: (1) the nature of Mexicans' entry into U.S. society, (2) the nature of Mexican immigration, (3) the nature of the Mexican work experience, and (4) Chicano experiences with ethnic organizational structures. Political ramifications flow from each of these factors, producing a political history that sets apart the Mexican experience from the experiences of other minority groups in the United States.

Historical Conditions For Chicano Political Development
"People of Conquest"

Contemporary political developments evolve from conditions of the past. Several factors can be identified as setting the broad parameters within which contemporary Chicano political development evolved. The first factor to note is that Mexicans in the United States constitute a "people of conquest." A defining characteristic that allows Robert Blauner to distinguish between immigrant minorities and "colonized" minorities is the

159

nature of the group's *original* entrance into society.[1] The fact that Mexicans (and their land) became a part of the United States by conquest distinguishes Mexican political history from that of other ethnic and racial groups with the exception of the American Indians. Mexicans' "special" relationship to the land of the Southwest prompted one social scientist to state that Mexicans resemble more the "typical minority in Europe than . . . the typical European minority in the United States.[2]

That part of Mexican territory originally known as the Spanish borderlands provided the arena in which the full force of Anglo-American expansionist ideology, the relentless search for natural resources, and the malignant growth of cultural animosities[3] finally collided and burst forth in a bloody war. The Mexican-American War of 1846 ended "officially" with the signing of a treaty on February 2, 1848. However, as Carey McWilliams observes, "it becomes quite apparent that the Mexican-American War was merely an incident in a conflict which arose some years before and survived long after the Treaty of Guadalupe Hidalgo."[4]

The terms of the Treaty of Guadalupe Hidalgo of 1848 made America's belief in "manifest destiny" that much more real and concrete. Mexico ceded to the United States a vast territory, which included the present-day states of California, Arizona, New Mexico, Utah, Nevada, and parts of Colorado. Mexico also accepted the Rio Grande as its border with Texas, which had become part of the United States through "annexation" in 1846.[5] Shortly thereafter, "by the use of high pressure methods already painfully familiar to the Mexicans," yet another "bite of Mexican territory" was secured for the United States.[6] The Gadsden Purchase added parts of New Mexico and southern Arizona to the newly "acquired" lands, whose mineral wealth in gold, silver, and copper had not yet been fully recognized by either the Americans or Mexicans.

The territorial conquest of "El Norte de México" laid the foundation for the future political development of Mexicans in the United States. One political scientist characterizes the conquest as pushing Mexicans in the United States "into a permanent posture of defense."[7] The political significance of the conquest crystallizes when one looks at three resultant processes: the usurpation of land rights, the supplanting of Mexican institutional structures and procedures with Anglo-American ones, and the suppression of cultural autonomy.

All citizens of Mexico who resided in the ceded territory were to become U.S. citizens if, within one year after ratification of the Treaty of Guadalupe Hidalgo, they had failed to leave the area. Carey McWilliams states that "only a few thousand Mexican nationals, perhaps not more than 1,500 or 2,000, took advantage of this provision; the rest became "citizens-by-default."[8] Citizenship "by default," however, provided few long-lasting guarantees of anything, especially of rights to the land. There were essentially three ways in which land was confiscated from Mexicanos in the Southwest. First, Mexican land grants were vaguely defined and could not be defended on ownership grounds under Anglo-American land laws. Second, through the imposition of high taxes and various swindling schemes, land passed from Mexican owners to Anglo hands. Third, squatters coming from the east began taking over the land--"and the better land at that!"[9] Arturo Madrid vividly brings to life these various processes by stating:

> From the Matamoros haciendas near the Gulf of Mexico to the Petaluma ranchos off San Francisco Bay the landholding ricos were forced off their holdings . . . Those who survived the armed violence fell victims to the Land Law of 1851, which permitted settlers to stake out claims on land which "to the best of one's knowledge" was unused. Those who resisted the squatters impoverished themselves in the courtrooms and backrooms of the new legal system, confused by judges and commissioners, outmaneuvered by plaintiffs, swindled by lawyers. Those who won the legal battles lost their lands to moneylending, tax manipulating entrepreneurs who flooded the West after the Civil War. The few survivors, extended token and symbolic political and social recognition, became the models for the "fantasy heritage" of Silver Dons, gay caballeros and Spanish conquistadores created at the turn of the century by publicists for the railroads and land companies and nurtured by . . . romanticizers of the Southwest.[10]

Whether their land was secured from them legally or illegally, Mexican settlers rich and poor alike, "doubted a government that would not protect their person" or safeguard their property.[11]

The territorial conquest also brought a change in the institutional structures and procedures of the Southwest. Mexican laws and governmental structures and procedures, no matter how feebly enforced or followed in the borderlands,[12] were the legitimate foundations upon which Southwest society rested. Moreover, as one historian points out, although sparsely populated, the urban centers of the Mexican Southwest had achieved self-sufficiency and "were regarded by the urbanites in Mexico City as outposts of civilization on the edge of the frontier."[13] That self-sufficiency was accomplished within a Mexican legal governmental framework. The supplanting of Mexican laws and governmental bodies by those from an Anglo-American tradition "drove home" the political significance of the conquest. No doubt the use of Anglo-American laws to appropriate Mexican land highlighted this transformation.

Annexation by conquest is not the only historical experience that Mexicans and American Indians share. Both minority groups had their rights specifically safeguarded by treaty provision. The Treaty of Guadalupe Hidalgo gave Mexicans the right to retain their language, religion, and culture. Both McWilliams and Acuña emphasize that the treaty contained explicit guarantees to insure Mexican cultural autonomy. However, in reality, "no provisions were made . . . for the (legal protection and) integration of the native peoples as a group, as a society."[14]

No treaty on earth, however, could have prevented those cultural and racial animosities, rawly exposed during the Mexican American War, from becoming institutionalized in the very fabric of Southwestern society. "Anti-Catholic, anti-mestizo (the racial mix of Spanish and Indian), and anti-Indian prejudices of Anglo Americans helped to channel Mexican political development even further into a permanent posture of defense."[15] The right of conquest gave way to the imposition of other "rights" of Anglo racial and cultural superiority--which were felt by the "native" Mexican population and became an integral part of the political experiences of Mexicans in the United States.

The Nature of Mexican Immigration

The "special" relationship that exists between the United States, Mexico, and the Southwest sets apart Mexican immigration from that of other ethnic groups. It is this factor as well which carries implications for Mexican political development in the United States. The simple fact of Mexico's proximity to the United States generates the theme of continuity that underlies the distinctive feature of Mexican immigration, particularly in the early twentieth century. In a historical and geographical sense, the theme of continuity develops from the fact that the southwestern part of the United States once belonged to Mexico. The fact that the American Southwest, at its "birth," contained a "native" population of Mexicans influenced the nature of initial population movements from Mexico to the U.S. side. Several scholars have noted this influence by characterizing Mexican "immigration" as truly a process of "migration" instead.

Sociologist Rodolfo Alvarez refers to those who composed the first massive population movements to the United States from Mexico (during the period of approximately 1900 to 1930) as the "Migrant Generation." He asserts that although these people were in a legal sense "immigrants," they were not in a sociological and cultural sense. As they left the political upheaval in Mexico in search of the economic rewards American capitalist agriculture promised them, they did not enter a "fresh social situation where they were meeting the host society for the first time," as an ethnic or racial group. Alvarez explains that their entrance into the United States was already "predefined by the well established social position of pre-1900 Mexican Americans as a conquered people (politically, socially, culturally, economically, and in every other respect)." This situation differed to some extent from the experiences of the first-generation immigrant arrivals from Europe to the eastern shores of the United States. In some ways, Alvarez maintains, European immigrants entered, as a group, a relatively less defined social situation, as opposed to Mexicans. "Their place in the social hierarchy was, in a sense, freshly negotiated according to what the group as a whole could do here."[16]

The social and cultural milieu of the Mexican communities in the Southwest provided newcomers from Mexico with a basis for familiarity and rapid adjustment into a new environment. At the same time this process was occurring, the dominant "host" society viewed the "migrant generation" basically in the same fashion it viewed the Mexican

Americans who had been living in the Southwest long before the 1900s. All were the "same"; all were Mexican.[17]

The political significance of these two simultaneous occurrences lies in the fact that the seeds of internal divisions among Mexicans, on nationality and citizenship grounds, were planted. Organizations emerged in Mexican communities that reacted to the anti-Mexican animosities embedded in the Southwest, so well reinforced by the national atmosphere of nativist sentiment permeating the 1920s. Nurtured by the class divisions already forming among Mexicans in the American Southwest, organizations emerged that stressed their American orientation over their Mexican roots.

The League of United Latin American Citizens (LULAC) evolved out of southcentral Texas in the late 1920s. Its middle-class members stressed their American citizenship and "American values" in ways that would indeed set them apart from the vast flow of Mexican migrants desperately in search of the "better life" in the land to the north.[18] Ironically, then, those forces that lent the American Southwest a historical continuity with Mexico eventually gave way to undercurrents of division and discontinuity, which began to take shape in the early 1900s.

As previously mentioned, the special nature of Mexican "immigration" brings to attention the theme of geographical continuity as well. Once a part of "El Norte de México," the Southwest, especially in the early twentieth century, physically resembled the northern portions of Mexico, for "wars do not alter the facts of geography."[19] To some extent, the resemblance still persists. As McWilliams observes, "one can travel from Chihuahua to Santa Fe with scarcely any feeling of abrupt change in the physical environment."[20]

Geographical continuity provided the Mexican migrant with a relocation experience very different from that of the European immigrant. Emigration from Europe involved traversing an enormous physical obstacle, the Atlantic Ocean, while attempting to survive the miseries time and space inflicted upon the passenger.[21] The crossing represented "a severance . . . an abrupt transition" of the utmost importance.[22] The land entered was different from the land left behind. It was "foreign" to the immigrant in countless ways.

Relocation for the Mexican migrant meant a gradual transition within the confines of a familiar environment. No less important or significant than the European experience, the relocation process for Mexicans, however, did not entail a severe severance from the land of origin. To be crossed was a border described by McWilliams as "one of the most unrealistic borders to be found in the Western Hemisphere."[23] Across much of the territory between the United States and Mexico, the border was no more than an imaginary line. In those areas where the Rio Grande separated the two nations, the river could be crossed fairly easily during most of the year--a reality that still exists. In addition, not until the 1930s was an official transaction required to enter the United States, a stark contrast to the European experience of Ellis Island.[24]

The notion of permanence highlights an additional distinction between Mexican migration and European immigration. As Dinnerstein and other historians point out, some first-generation European immigrants came to the United States with intentions of returning home once they had made some economic gains. Some, in fact, were able to do so. Yet for most, the force of circumstances rapidly made a return to the Old Country a virtual impossibility.[25] For Mexicans, however, the proximity of Mexico to the United States and the railroad system built between the two countries made a return to Mexico both feasible and real. Thus, Mexican migration has really entailed a back and forth movement of people. It encompasses permanent, temporary, and intermittent migrations, patterns that are still evident today.[26]

An examination of the special nature of Mexican immigration yields some additional political observations. Rising from the theme of historical continuity is the observation that, to a large extent, Mexican politics remained a frame of reference for Mexicans in the United States. Despite a once-common social science conclusion that Mexicans "show no political interest," interest in political events was indeed evident in Mexican communities of the Southwest. Interest, in many cases, however, focused on political occurrences in Mexico, especially during the period of the Mexican Revolution of 1910. Spanish-language newspapers followed the developments of the revolution closely,[27] and political clubs in the United States took sides over which faction to support.[28] Moreover, organizational ties developed between political groups in Mexico and groups in the United States. The party founded by the Mexican revolutionary Ricardo Flores Magón established its first headquarters in the United States in San Antonio, Texas. Known as *El Partido Liberal Mexicano* (PLM), it sought to organize Mexican laborers on both sides of the border.[29] Another organization that followed a similar strategy was *El Congreso Mexicanista* which emerged in Laredo, Texas in 1911.[30]

Present-day realities necessitate a continuation of interest in Mexican politics. Although different in content and expression, interest in economic and political developments in Mexico persists in Chicano communities. Mexican immigration, the policies of U.S. twin plants along the border, and issues such as the appointment of a U.S. ambassador to Mexico continue to serve as catalysts to Chicano political involvement.[31] The historical link of political interest between Mexicans on both sides of the border continues to exist.

The proximity of Mexico to the United States has historically allowed for constant migration between the two countries. It has also provided for the perception of the Mexican population by U.S. authorities as "movable." The implementation of deportation and repatriation measures are of fundamental importance in the political history of Mexicans in the United States. From 1926 to 1939, approximately one million people were repatriated to Mexico, voluntarily and involuntarily.[32] The United States government undertook these repatriation measures in an attempt to alleviate the social and economic woes of the country during the Depression. And, unlike other ethnic and racial groups, Mexicans were an "easy target" for such a program.

Perhaps of even greater significance is the role deportations have played in Chicano history. Beginning in 1929, the Department of Labor launched an all-out effort to apprehend and deport Mexican laborers (without papers) who were "taking jobs away" from U.S. citizens. Los Angeles county was the focus of what amounted to a purge. All Mexicans in the area, U.S. citizens and noncitizens alike, were subject to federal harassment. In many cases, Mexican Americans who did not have proof of citizenship in their possession, and who could not speak English, were deported as well.[33]

Whereas the need to control the flow of labor provided the justification for the deportations, a political purpose was evident as well. Local and federal authorities used both the threat of deportation and its actual enforcement to undermine organizational activity among Mexicans. For example, during the mid-thirties, Mexican labor unions were most effective at laying the groundwork for organizing in the fields. Yet, "with scarcely an exception, every strike in which Mexicans participated in the [Southwest] . . . was broken by the use of violence and was followed by deportations.[34]

Approximately two decades later, with the wartime labor shortage having passed, deportations struck the Mexican areas of the country once again. Organizational efforts suffered immeasurable losses as their leaders were deported, this time with the fervor of "anticommunism" so prevalent in the 1950s. One such leader, Luisa Moreno, had been involved in labor union activity and in attempts to maintain a regional organization called El Congreso de Pueblos que Hablan Español (Congress of Spanish-Speaking People).[35] In total, deportations of Mexicans numbered around two and a half million for the years 1950-53. The sheer magnitude of the deportations in this "Red Scare" period no doubt led some organizations. like the Community Service Organization (CSO) in Los Angeles, to temper their activities, lest they be judged "unAmerican."[36]

The Nature of Mexican Work Experience

The nature of Mexican work experience is the third major factor that has set the basic parameters within which Chicano political development evolves. Both the nature of Mexican immigration and the nature of Mexican labor have been intimately intertwined throughout history. With this in mind, the focus now turns to the major occupations Mexicans have historically filled and those employment patterns and policies that have generated problems for organization.

As indicated previously, Chicanos overall do not figure very high in the present-day occupational structure of the country. Not surprisingly, this situation evolves from a history of restriction to a subordinated labor status in the economic order of the United States. It is this aspect of Chicano history that most clearly draws distinctions between white immigrant groups, on the one hand, and Mexicans on the other.

The restrictive uses of Mexican labor emerged early in the formation of the new class structure in the Southwest, shortly after the conquest of Mexican land. In his study of the development of capitalist agriculture in California in the latter part of the nineteenth century, Tomás Almaguer discusses the role racial minorities played in that economic order. During the period from 1870 to 1900, racial minorities primarily constituted contract labor. On the other hand, white immigrants during this period found employment in a variety of skilled and semiskilled occupations. In addition, it was largely this group who benefited from the sale of rancho lands, which created their small farms. As Almaguer notes, largely due to the economic alternatives accorded Anglo Americans, they were able to "avoid the type of labor status that befell racial minorities in California." As he explains, "with white labor largely unavailable, it was first the Chinese, then later the Japanese and Mexican who were relied upon to meet the seasonal labor needs of capitalist agriculture."[37]

The basic nineteenth-century employment practice of contracted Mexican labor continued into the twentieth century as well. The restrictive nature of contract labor becomes apparent when one notes that Mexican labor was sought "by particular employers, for employment in particular industries at particular tasks." From approximately 1900-1940, Mexican labor was confined primarily to three major sectors: agriculture, mining, and the railroad industry. A further observation emphasizes that "with few exceptions, only a *particular class* of employers has employed Mexican labor in the Southwest," that class represented by large-scale enterprises.[38] One scholar offers the following literary summary of Mexican occupational history from the late nineteenth to the mid-twentieth century:

> Rounded up in small villages on both sides of the border and herded to ever larger railway center, Mexicans were then bunched into boxcars and dispatched to man the section crews and extra gangs of the Southern Pacific and Santa Fe, formerly the job of the despised Chinese, to pick the cattle-displacing cotton of middle and west Texas, a task abandoned by northward-moving Blacks; to do the risky, dirty-digging in the Gila Hills of southern Arizona, a job disdained by Anglo miners; to harvest crops of the Great Western Sugar Beet Co. (and from there) to develop the empires of California's agri-businessmen ultimately to replace the Filipinos, who had before replaced the Japanese, who previously had replaced the Chinese, all of whom had become less manageable and therefore less desirable.[39]

In whichever major sector Mexicans held jobs (from the late 1800s to approximately 1940), three aspects of their labor bore implications for organization. These aspects are (1) the predominant characteristics of their work; (2) their employment as a group; and (3) their use as a "reserve army of labor." The basic characteristics their jobs shared were the migratory and transient nature of the work, extremely limited opportunities for advancement, and conditions of social isolation.

Mexican labor was migratory and transient in several respects. For example, work in the field and on the railroads entailed travel over vast distances as crops were picked and tracks were laid. Employment for most was either seasonal or casual. In addition, the migratory nature of the work encompassed the flow of the labor force itself. In response to the heavy recruitment efforts conducted on both sides of the border, Mexicans provided a constant flow of labor to various industrial sectors. What resulted was an occupational history riddled with instability and inconsistency-inherent obstacles to organization.

Few opportunities for advancement existed in those economic sectors that employed Mexicans. Mexican labor was largely unskilled, to begin with, and Mexicans worked in industries that were highly organized by big business interests and dominated by big capitalist investments.[40] Few opportunities for advancement lay ahead for field and packing-house employees in the farming industry or for those working in crews in the nation's smelters and refineries.

Employment as section-hands on the rail lines or as diggers in the mines often meant living and working in the physically remote desert areas of the Southwest. Social isolation also meant limited interaction with others outside of the work environment. The situation for many involved "traveling over a wide territory, usually in the company of other Spanish-speaking workers, bossed by a Mexican foreman, [and] living in a Mexican labor camp or shacktown."[41] Both the limited opportunity for advancement and the condition of social isolation imposed upon Mexican workers a certain degree of confinement. Combined with the migratory and transient aspects of the work, these characteristics promoted a general condition of "permanent" instability and inconsistency for Mexican workers. Thus, formidable obstacles were indeed laid for the development of political organization in Mexican areas of the United States.

Identified as a second major aspect of the nature of Mexican labor is the pattern of group employment imposed upon it. Industries employed Mexicans en masse, as a group and not on an individual basis. Families, including men, women, and children, worked the "factories in the fields." Mexicans worked in the mines, smelters, and railroads in gangs and crews. Occupational segregation was evident across industries as well as within certain enterprises. In California in 1930 within certain plants, Mexicans were used "exclusively in specific types of employment rather than being scattered through the plant."[42]

The resultant consequence for organization is that divisions among workers developed along racial lines. "Skilled labor groups regarded Mexicans as *group* competitors rather than as individual employees." Trade unions shunned the incorporation of Mexican workers. When Mexicans did manage to organize themselves and go out on strike, organized labor in many cases did not support them. Their organizations, for the most part, were not affiliated with either the CIO or the AFL.[43]

The third major aspect of the nature of Mexican labor is its use as an integral part of the nation's "reserve army of labor." In periods of intense labor needs, Mexicans were actively recruited into the industries of the Southwest.[44] A major portion of this Mexican work force came from Mexico as "imported" or migrant labor. Because of its mobility and availability, Mexican labor provided U.S. business and corporate interest with a manipulatable pool of reserve labor. As such, Mexican labor served political purposes as well.

The importation of Mexican labor often served two strategically important functions: to depress wages and to break strikes. With cheap labor readily and seemingly inexhaustibly available, large corporate interests were able to drive small farmers and tenants (predominantly Anglo) from agricultural land in west Texas. Divisions along racial lines "naturally" increased in what essentially was a clash of economic interests.[45] Labor conflict in the fields is replete with examples of the use of imported Mexican labor to break strikes. In more recent history, the development of the Bracero Program in 1942 added the full backing of the U.S. government to the economic game of supplying large amounts of labor at depressed wages (and miserable working conditions).[46] The use of Mexican immigrant labor in such exploitative situations has resulted in the creation of deep divisions among workers and internal splits within the Mexican community in the United States. The bottom line is that the focus of "blame" for these exploitative conditions has been directed toward the Mexican laborer and not on those economic interests and processes from which these conditions emerge. The nature of Mexican labor thus provides insight into how certain patterns and practices, structured over time, act as constraints on Mexican political development.

Organizational Experience in the "Immigrant Tradition"--Similarities and Differences

A fourth factor that has influenced the overall political development of Mexicans in the United States is the overall organizational experience acquired as an ethnic group in this country. The two organizational structures that scholars define as significant in the social and political history of ethnic or immigrant groups are the mutual aid society and the political machine. The way in which these organizations have penetrated Mexican communities in the United States thus becomes an important subject for analysis.

The significance of the mutual aid society was that it represented one of the first organizational efforts launched by newly arrived immigrants to help themselves as a group. By pooling meager resources together, mutual aid was offered in the provision of low cost funeral and insurance benefits, low interest loans, and other economic benefits. Although historians are apt to emphasize the social cohesion and organization that mutual aid societies lent to immigrant life, their contribution is political as well. Mutual aid societies provided a basis for the later development of trade unions and associations among the immigrant groups. And, of course, as immigrants maintained their societies, they picked up organizing skills along the way. As Oscar Handlin notes,

The first encounter with the practice of governing came in their local associational activities. In time each society acquired a constitution and by-laws, no doubt printed from stock forms . . . and no doubt frequently honored in the breach. Still, here they elected officers, and conducted debates, and made rules. If these affairs had little effect upon the world outside, they nevertheless gave the members a taste of what politics involved.[47]

Evidence shows that the mutual aid organization was also part of the Mexican experience as well. In Mexican communities, as early as the 1890s, *mutualistas* emerged to perform functions similar to their earlier counterparts on the east coast. *Mutualistas* in their initial stage of development in the Southwest directed their efforts toward the Mexican working class and, in some cases, proved to be very nationalistic. One historian notes that some *mutualistas* excluded non-Mexican nationals from their organizations.[48] The total extent to which *mutualistas* developed in Mexican communities is not known; however, it does appear that there were many indeed. In the 1920s one study on Mexican immigrants uncovered the existence of many Mexican mutual aid societies in various parts of the country. In Los Angeles alone there were forty-four in the late 1920s. Others appeared in areas such as Albuquerque, San Antonio, Chicago, Kansas City, and Michigan.[49]

Some societies did develop into explicitly political organizations. The anthropologist Manuel Gamio notes that a *mutualista* founded in Tucson in 1894 took on a political purpose. *La Alianza Hispano Americana* launched a campaign to replace those in power in Tucson politics with native Tucson residents of Mexican descent.[50] Shortly after World War I, in Los Angeles, members of the Lázaro Cárdenas Society held meetings to discuss community grievances. In Kansas City, La Liga Protectora Mexicana organized in a defensive posture to protect the rights of legal immigrants in the area.[51]

The development and evolutionary paths of *mutualistas* replicate in many those of the white immigrant societies on the east coast. The Mexican experience with the political machine, however, does not appear to follow as closely.

The vast amount of scholarly research on the political machine attests to the impact the machine had on the political development of white ethnic groups on the east coast and to a lesser extent on blacks in the north. In stark contrast, very little is known about the mere *existence* of political machines (much less about their overall impact and significance) in Mexican areas of the country. I will generate a tentative argument of how machine politics has figured in the political development of Mexicans in the United States.

In its most basic form, a political machine is a hierarchical party organization that distributes patronage and other inducements to win votes and thereby to control elections and government. It functions in a situation where mass suffrage exists. In its perhaps "classic" form, it existed in large urban areas (such as New York and Chicago) and drew its massive support from the immigrant voters. Its game was politics, its inducements were for the most part specific and tangible, and its overall effects were varied and multiple. A relationship of exchange existed between the political machine and its immigrant supporters. It was an exchange with economic, social, and political features.

The machine offered the immigrant voter certain economic benefits in exchange for a vote. Tangible benefits provided were jobs in the public and sometimes in the private sector, emergency aid, occasional monetary gifts, and the like. Political favors came in the form of personal help in dealing with the public bureaucracies, the police, and other representatives of officialdom. Social rewards came from having someone to turn to in time of need, for the precinct captain was on familiar terms with the voters in the local ward.[52]

In their critique of the political machine, Norman and Susan Fainstein note that while the machine "undoubtedly provided services to many proletarians," it did so by reaching out to them as individuals and not as a collectivity. For example, unlike trade unions, the machine "had no direct interest in increasing wages, or in opposing employers."[53] Several scholars also argue that because of the individualized and particularized nature of the reward extended them (plus other factors), immigrants were conservatively socialized in ways that prevented them from perceiving themselves as a class with common interests.

In spite of the individualized rewards, however, it seems apparent that the immigrants reaped some benefits as a group as a result of machine politics. Perhaps like no other mechanism, the machine furthered a process of *integration* into the political and social fabric of U.S. society for immigrant groups. Incorporation into the party organization provided some groups with an avenue for social mobility. The Irish, of course, are a case in point. "Many municipalities in the generation after the Civil War knew only Irish names among politicians." Irish domination in large cities extended to fire and police departments.[54] The fact that representatives of ethnic groups were brought into the party organization in itself meant that general recognition was given them as a group.[55]

In addition to those who moved up the ranks of the party organization, the general immigrant population enjoyed the benefits of political incorporation that the machine had to offer. In fulfilling its part of the bargain in the exchange for voters, the political machine set in motion the process of political acculturation for the ethnic minorities. As Cornwell indicates:

> The mere seeking out of the immigrants in quest of their support, the assistance rendered in getting them naturalized (when it was necessary to observe these legal niceties), and so forth were of considerable importance in laying the foundation for their more meaningful political participation later.[56]

In inducing electoral participation and turning immigrants into citizens, the machine furthered the political education of the ethnic minorities. Michael Parenti notes that campaigns, voting, and contacts with the local political clubs "gave the ethnic some small

170

sense of participation and practice as an American, some tenuous feeling that his voice counted with the powers that be, and some claim to legitimacy and equal status." In the end, the political system became "an arena for the maximization of ethnic interests."[57] Thus, machine politics facilitated the incorporation and integration of ethnic immigrant groups into city government and the political system.

Political machines also made their appearance in such predominantly Mexican areas as Laredo, El Paso, and the rural counties of south Texas in the late 1800s. Historian Mario García documents the emergence of machine politics in El Paso, Texas, as early as 1860. It was not until the 1880s, however, that one particular party organization, known as "the Ring," assumed control and remained in power until around 1915.[58] In south Texas, one man, Jim Wells, bossed the border counties from 1880 until his death in 1920. Another by the name of Manuel Guerra bossed Starr County in Texas until 1915.[59] The evidence points to the existence of political machines in some areas with large Mexican populations.

Questions remain, however, regarding the similarities between the "classic" form of machine politics and that occurring in the Southwest. In its "classic" form, the machine provided jobs, most of which were "unskilled governmental or private-sector which the machine did not create, but only distributed." Outside of creating jobs within its own structure, the machine primarily allocated jobs within the working class. Business interests reaped these benefits and more, as they were awarded government contracts and the like.[60] Thus, there was a symbiotic relationship between political and economic interests. There was a good deal but not total overlap between the two spheres.

In the case of south Texas, for a time the overlap was complete. Politics revolved around a ranching economy. The political boss was also the economic king of the area. In the case of the cattle barons such as Jim Wells, they voted *their* tenants and their laborers on election day.[61] The *patrón-peón* relationship carried the bosses' role to the extreme.

Machine politics in El Paso approximated the "classic" form more closely. Machine politicians, representing El Paso's business and professional class, provided supporters with public jobs in return for their support. However, a significant difference of degree emerged. García explains that patronage was awarded to certain Mexican-American políticos "in return for their ability to organize and deliver Mexican voters."[62] The patronage extended to Mexicans in El Paso was to a select few and apparently did not approximate the degree to which jobs were distributed among the white ethnic populations. This is important to note since "the most significant, tangible return which the *largest* number of [white] immigrants received from the machine was a job."[63]

A further observation is that those patronage jobs awarded Mexican-American políticos brought them only into certain county positions and did not incorporate them into city government. The Ring supported Mexican-American candidates and offered patronage jobs in the sanitation and police departments. The majority of Mexican-American officeholders, however, served in "minor county positions." They represented the county commissioners, justices of the peace, local precinct chairmen, and officials from the outlying rural areas of El Paso. García comments on this pattern in the following manner:

> While the Ring did not hesitate to endorse Mexican Americans for certain county offices where the selection of a Mexican would be practical and beneficial, it apparently refused to nominate them for city positions for fear of offending American voters.[64]

While the political integration of Mexican-American *políticos* seemed somewhat limited and controlled, it appeared totally absent for the larger Mexican population. Some sort of exchange relationship existed between the machine and white ethnic groups. In the solicitation or "buying" of their votes, the machine provided certain services and benefits to the immigrant voters. In El Paso machine politics, an "exchange relationship" is difficult to find. The "buying" of votes did not translate figuratively but literally. And the "payment" in exchange hardly constituted a "service." García provided the following account:

> Both Democrats and Republicans in the 1889 city election openly purchased Mexican votes not only in El Paso, but in Ciudad Juárez Mexico as well. Besides money, the politicians offered free beer and entertainment. According to one account, the festivities began on the day before the election and continued all night. On election morning, the Mexicans discovered to their surprise that the doors of the dance hall had been locked and that they could not leave until the polls opened and their votes registered. At seven in the morning, therefore, the politicians assembled the Mexicans and under guard conducted them to the voting precincts where they were handed a prepared ballot and paid three dollars.[65]

The large property owners of south Texas followed similar practices. In addition to "voting their Mexicans," they imported "droves of Mexicans across the border [and] held them under guard in corrals and stockades" until election day.[66]

The corrupt practices of these machines did not stop with their buying votes, registering Mexican nationals, and "imprisoning" the voters. In El Paso, the Ring fraudulently purchased poll taxes (required as of 1902) for their Mexican supporters. Later an investigation showed that "in many cases Mexicans acquired these illegal receipts with the understanding they could also be used to secure employment with the city or county governments."[67]

While the type of individual rewards granted to white ethnics in the form of personal favors and the like may have been extended to Mexicans by the machine bosses, it appears that the economic inducements were limited. The group benefits provided to the white immigrants, such as social mobility and integration into city government and the political system, do not apply to the Mexican case in Texas. Mexican immigrants gained little or nothing as a result of machine politics. They were not incorporated into the political arena; rather they were herded like cattle from one polling place to another and "rewarded" in liquor and small change. The political education they received most likely "proved" to them the sham of American government in action. As García concludes, "it was not the Mexican immigrants who experienced acculturation into American life out of their political ties with the machines, but rather the Mexican Americans."[68] It was from their ranks that a select few found social mobility and were reinforced in their belief in the efficacy of American politics.

The information presented here comes from two case studies on political machines in Texas. There is good reason to suspect, however, that these cases might be representative of how the machine functioned at its height in Mexican immigrant communities.[69] For one thing, Texas was the major funnel for early Mexican immigration to the United States. Texas cities, especially El Paso and Laredo, were the chief points of entry for Mexican immigrants in the early 1900s. In addition, this period, from 1910 to 1930, represented the first massive waves of immigration from Mexico.

When one compares the overall time frame for the massive immigrations from Europe and Mexico, the argument (drawn from the Texas case) that the machine did not offer to Mexicans what it did for European immigrants is strengthened. European immigration occurred much earlier than Mexican immigration. As many scholars agree, the massive waves of European immigration from the mid-nineteenth century to the early 1900s contributed greatly to the machine's emergence and longevity. Mexican immigration did not follow this time line. Its first peak years were from 1900-1930. This difference is significant when one notes that machine politics was on the *decline* in the 1920s. The urban reforms of the Progressives, the nationalization and bureaucratization of welfare services, and the virtual stop of European immigration in the 1920s robbed the machine of much of its power.[70]

The ascendancy of machine politics began as early as the mid-1800s, while such powerful machines as Tammany Hall in New York City reigned in the 1890s.[71] An urban, highly industrialized, densely populated region of the county set the basis for machine politics in the nineteenth century. In the Southwest, allowing for some regional variations, economic growth and transformation of the area "took off from 1910 to 1929. The urbanization process for Chicanos in the Southwest unfolded relatively recently, from 1900 to 1930. With the exception of Los Angeles and San Francisco, the Southwest in 1920 had no cities with a population of over 100,000. As machines "peaked" in their power in the last decade of the nineteenth century, "urban growth in the Southwestern states had reached only 50 percent of the level found in the eastern and midwestern regions of the country."[72]

In general, the timing of Mexican immigration and the particular development of the

Southwest created conditions for machine politics that differed significantly from those of the east coast. Political machines in the Southwest had less to offer, less resources at their disposal with which to "buy off" the Mexican population. Patronage jobs were few, and reform governments were taking over the cities. The first era of Mexican immigration coincided with the decline of the political machine. Mexican immigrants were not extended the benefits other ethnic groups gained from machine politics. As such, the organizational experience accorded white ethnic groups as a result of machine politics did not carry over to the same extent in the Mexican experience.

SUMMARY

Several historical factors, identified here, created the antecedent conditions to Chicano organizational development. The original "entrance" of Mexicans in the United States, the nature of Mexican immigration and labor history, plus their organizational experience as an "immigrant" group have set the parameters for Chicano political development. This listing, however, is by no means exhaustive; other factors, such as the role of the Catholic and Protestant churches, perhaps carry equal weight.[73] The contribution this study seeks to make is to provide a preliminary analysis of the structural preconditions to Chicano organizational development. As more research is undertaken, of course, the picture will become more complete.

Notes

1. Robert Blauner, *Racial Oppression in America* (New York: Harper and Row, 1972), ch. 2, pp. 51-81. Other defining characteristics include the nature of a group's labor history and its geographical location.

2. Carey McWilliams, *North from Mexico* (New York: Greenwood Press, 1968), p. 207. He attributes this observation to Dr. Carolyn Zeleny.

3. Ibid., p. 98. McWilliams refers to the "malignant conflict of cultures."

4. Ibid.

5. Rodolfo Acuña, *Occupied America: The Chicano's Struggle Toward Liberation* (San Francisco: Canfield Press, 1972), p. 28.

6. McWilliams, *North From Mexico*, p. 59.

7. Armando Navarro, "The Evolution of Chicano Politics," *Aztlán* vol. 5, nos. 1 and 2 (Spring and Fall 1974), pp. 57-84.

8. McWilliams, *North From Mexico*, p. 51.

9. Alberto Camarillo, lecture at Stanford University, January 13, 1976.

10. Arturo Madrid-Barela, "Towards an Understanding of the Chicano Experience," *Aztlán* vol. 4, no. 1 (Spring 1973), pp. 189-90.

11. McWilliams, *North From Mexico*, p. 110.

12. See Ibid., pp. 99-100. He argues that there was no tradition of self-government in the borderlands. He cites Texas, far removed from its capital of Mexico City, as a case in point.

13. Ricardo Romo, "The Urbanization of Southwestern Chicanos in the Early Twentieth Century," *New Scholar,* vol. 6 (1977), p. 183.

14. McWilliams, *North From Mexico*, pp. 51, 102. See also Acuña, *Occupied America* pp. 29-30, for further elaboration of explicit provisions in the Treaty of Guadalupe Hidalgo.

15. Madrid-Barela, "Towards an Understanding," McWilliams, *North From Mexico,* and Navarro, "The Evolution of Chicano Politics," all address the issue of racial conflict between Anglos and Mexicans in the Southwest.

16. Rodolfo Alvarez, "The Psycho-Historical and Socioeconomic Development of the Chicano Community in the United States," *Social Science Quarterly*, vol. 53, no. 4 (March 1973), pp. 927-28.

17. Ibid., p. 928.

18. LULAC restricted its membership to American citizens. English was used exclusively at meetings. Its motto was, "All for one and one for all."

19. McWilliams, *North From Mexico*, p. 208.

20. Ibid., p. 58.

21. See Oscar Handlin, *The Uprooted* (Boston: Little, Brown, 1973) for a vivid account of the difficulties and conditions of crossing the Atlantic.

22. McWilliams, *North From Mexico*, p. 58.

23. Ibid., p.59.

24. Alvarez, "The Psycho-Historical," p. 930.

25. Leonard Dinnerstein et al., *Natives and Strangers: Ethnic Groups and the Building of America* (New York: Oxford University Press, 1979). pp. 134-35 and following.

26. Alberto Camarillo, lecture at Stanford University, January 13, 1976.

27. Félix Gutiérrez and Ramón Chacón, papers presented at the Annual Conference of the National Association for Chicano Studies, The Claremont Colleges, Claremont, California, March 1978.

28. For example, Mexican social clubs in the United States engaged in political debates, dividing into factions supporting either Porfirio Díaz or Francisco I. Madero.

29. Juan Gómez-Quiñones, *Sembradores: Ricardo Flores Magón y El Partido Liberal Mexicano: A Eulogy and Critique* (Los Angeles: Aztlán Publications, University of California, Los Angeles, 1973).

30. See José Limón, "El Primer Congreso Mexicanista de 1911: A Precursor to Contemporary Chicanismo," *Aztlán* vol. 5, nos. 1 and 2 (Spring and Fall 1974), pp. 85-117.

31. The Carter Administration in January 1980 announced the appointment of Mexican-American educator Julian Nava to the post of ambassador to Mexico.

32. See Abraham Hoffman, *Unwanted Mexican Americans in the Great Depression Repatriation Pressures, 1929-1939* (Tucson: University of Arizona Press, 1974).

33. Hoffman, *Unwanted Mexican Americans*, and Alberto Camarillo, lecture at Stanford University, February 10. 1976.

34. McWilliams, *North From Mexico*, p. 194.

35. Two historians at Stanford University, Alberto Camarillo and Vicki Ruiz, are compiling oral interviews with Luisa Moreno, who still lives outside the United States under another name.

36. Alberto Camarillo, lecture at Stanford University, February 12, 1976. He stated that because of the "Red Scare" during the years 1950-1953, the CSO had to lessen its intensive activity in obtaining rulings against abuses committed by law enforcement officers in Los Angeles.

37. Tomás Almaguer, "Class, Race, and Capitalist Development: The Social Transformation of a Southern California County, 1848-1903," Ph.D. dissertation, Department of Sociology, University of California at Berkeley, 1979.

38. McWilliams, *North From Mexico*, p. 215.

39. Madrid-Barela, "Towards an Understanding," pp. 191-92.

40. See McWilliams, *North From Mexico*, p. 215.

41. Ibid., p. 213.

42. Ibid., p. 215.

43. Ibid., pp. 194, 216. Mexican workers did receive considerable support from the IWW, for example, in their organization in the California fields in the 1930s. However, both the AFL and the CIO were slow to respond to the needs of Mexican workers. For further insights into the history of Mexican workers and organized labor see Devra Ann Weber, *The Organization Of Mexicano Agricutural Workers: Imperial Valley and Los Angeles, 1928-34, An Oral History Approach*, reprint from *Aztlán*, vol. 3, no. 2 (Fall 1972), pp. 307-50; Luis Arroyo, "The CIO and the Mexican Worker," Ph.D. dissertation, Department of History, University of California, Los Angeles, 1979; and Emilio Zamora, "The American Federation of Labor and the Mexican Worker in Texas During the Early 1900s," chapter of Ph.D. dissertation, The University of Texas at Austin, 1979.

44. Almaguer, "Class, Race, and Capitalist Development," p. 86.

45. McWilliams, *North From Mexico*, p. 216.

46. See the work of Ernesto Galarza for a lucid explication of the Bracero Program: *Merchants of Labor: The Mexican Bracero Story* (Santa Barbara: McNally & Loftin, 1964).

47. Oscar Handlin, *The Uprooted* (Boston: Little, Brown, 1973), p. 185.

48. Alberto Camarillo, lecture at Stanford University, January 13, 1976.

49. Manuel Gamio, *Mexican Immigration to the United States* (New York: Arno Press and *The New York Times*, 1969), appendix VIII, pp. 242-45.

50. Ibid., p. 133.

51. See Miguel Tirado, "Mexican American Community Political Organization," *Aztlán* vol. no. 1 (Spring 1970), p. 55.

52. Elmer E. Cornwell, Jr., "Bosses, Machines, and Ethnic Groups," *The Annals of the American Academy of Political and Social Science,* vol. 353 (May 1964), p. 31.

53. Norman Fainstein and Susan Fainstein, *Urban Political Movements* (Englewood Cliffs, N.J.: Prentice-Hall, 1974), p. 18.

54. Michael Kraus, *Immigration and the American Mosaic* (Princeton, N.J.: D. Van Nostrand Company, 1966), p. 61.

55. Cornwell, "Bosses, Machines, and the Ethnic Groups," p. 27.

56. Ibid., p. 31.

57. Michael Parenti, "Immigration and Political Life," in Frederic Cople Jaher, ed., *The Age of Industrialism in America* (New York: Free Press, 1968), pp. 90-91, 95.

58. See Mario García, *Desert Immigrants: Mexicans of El Paso, 1880-1920* (New Haven: Yale University Press, 1980), ch. 7.

59. McWilliams, *North From Mexico*, p. 86. He refers to Manuel Guerra as Manuel Gerra.

60. Fainstein and Fainstein, *Urban Political Movements,* p. 17-18.

61. O. Douglas Weeks, "The Texas-Mexican and the Politics of South Texas," *American Political Science Review,* vol. 24, no. 3 (August 1930), pp. 610-11.

62. García, *Desert Immigrants*, ch. 7, p. 155.

63. Fainstein and Fainstein, *Urban Political Movements,* p. 18, footnote 52, my emphasis.

64. García, *Desert Immigrants,* ch. 7, p. 160.

65. Ibid., p. 4.

66. McWilliams, *North From Mexico*, p. 86.

67. García, *Desert Immigrants*, ch. 7, p. 164.

68. Ibid., p. 21.

69. The case of New Mexico would probably be a major exception. Due to the large "native" Mexican population at the time of the conquest, plus other factors, Mexicans have continued to remain a large and visible part of New Mexican politics.

70. See Cornwell, Jr., "Bosses, Machines, and the Ethnic Groups," pp. 27-39; J. David Greenstone and Paul E. Peterson, "Machines, Reformers and the War on Poverty," in James Q. Wilson, ed., *City Politics and Public Policy* (New York: Wiley, 1968), pp. 267-92.

71. Martin Shefter, "The Emergence of the Political Machines," in Willis Hawley and Michael Lipsky, eds., *Theoretical Perspectives on Urban Politics* (Englewood Cliffs, N.J.: Prentice-Hall, 1976), pp. 14-44.

72. Romo, "The Urbanization of Southwestern Chicanos," pp. 184-87.

73. There is a paucity of systematic research on this question. Generalization is virtually impossible concerning this important point.

Ricardo Romo traces the historic pattern of Mexican migration into the region to the north of Mexico since the early 17th century. He strongly asserts that the Chicano urban experience pre-dated American acquisition of the southwestern region by some two centuries. Romo also reveals fascinating information about the formation of urban barrio communities, occupational structures and the effects of the urbanization process on Chicano/Mexicano behavior.

The Urbanization of Southwestern Chicanos in the Early Twentieth Century
Ricardo Romo

Chicanos have not always lived in urban areas, but since 1609, at least, when their Spanish-Mexican ancestors founded the pueblo of Santa Fe, they have contributed to and have been a part of the urbanization process in the Southwest. One hundred years after the settlement of Santa Fe, Mexicanos participated in the establishment of two more important cities--El Paso and San Antonio. Within a few decades, Spain commissioned Mexican *pobladores* (settlers) to build a chain of *pueblos* along the California coastline. Although sparsely populated, these towns achieved self-sufficiency and were regarded by the urbanites in Mexico City as outposts of civilization on the edge of the frontier. When American forces marched into the Southwest following the outbreak of war with Mexico in 1846, the importance of the urban centers became evident as the Mexican defense of the province all but collapsed with the capture of the region's principal cities.

After this territory became a part of the United States, Mexicans immigrated in very small numbers and it was not until 1910 that the Chicano population increased significantly and began concentrating in urban areas. Although the rate of urbanization from 1900 to the present varied from state to state, by 1970 some 85% of the Chicanos in the Southwest lived in cities and suburbs.[1]

Today Chicanos are the fastest growing population group in the nation, and already in the Southwest they constitute the largest ethnic minority. In California, for instance, the Mexican population has grown by more than a million in the last seven years, to a total of 4.2 million.[2] As an ethnic group, Chicanos are distinct in that 90% of their nearly 10 million members live in the Southwest.[3] Moreover, as an urban group, Chicanos, like Blacks, generally live in segregated neighborhoods at a time when other ethnic enclaves have all but disappeared in this region.

Urbanization is a highly complex phenomenon which affects every sphere of personal and collective life, having demographic, economic, and sociocultural aspects. What follows is a discussion of the urbanization process of Chicanos in the Southwest during the period of greatest urbanization in the area, 1900-1930. For the purpose of this essay, three major components of urbanization--structural, demographic, and behavioral--will be considered.[4] Among the questions underlying this discussion are: Is the widely expressed belief correct that Mexican population in this country is composed of "late arrivals?"[5] Is the current popular image of the Chicano population as largely rural accurate? What factors accounted for the differential in urbanization between areas such as Los Angeles and El Paso? What were some of the cultural consequences of 20th century urbanization?

Structural Urbanization

Structural urbanization concerns the organization of communities and society. In the American West, the extensive employment of modern technology, expanding capital investment, and the creation of a labor surplus, together with the improvement in communication and transportation, contributed to the emergence of urban-industrial communities. Of course, within the states of Texas, New Mexico, Arizona and California which make up the Southwest, there existed regional variations in economic development and consequently, growth differentials among the principal cities.[6] Three variables that will be discussed under the concept of structural urbanization are: economic development, specialization of labor or division of labor, and the internal spatial structure of cities (functional specialization of people and places).

Economic Development

Economic activity in the Southwest by non-indigenous groups predates the founding of Plymouth Colony, although the urbanization of Southwestern Chicanos in large numbers did not begin until the early 20th century industrial period. Economically and politically isolated from the Mexican heartland in the early 19th century, the Southwest became a part of the United States in 1848. Nearly fifty years later, the region still had not experienced substantial economic transformation. The principal cause of this considerable delay in urban-industrial growth in the Southwest can be attributed to the absence of high population concentrations and a scarcity of markets for manufactured goods.

The population of the Southwest grew slowly during the late 19th and early 20th century as it attracted only a small number of European immigrants and other migrants. With the exception of Los Angeles and San Francisco, this region in 1900 had no cities with a population of over 100,000.[7] The population of the entire Southwest area at this time composed less than 10% of the national total. Overall urban growth in the southwestern states had reached only 50% of the level found in eastern and midwestern regions.[8] The larger cities of this region--Los Angeles, San Antonio, San Francisco, El Paso, and San Diego--did not experience rapid urbanization until after 1900. Furthermore, it was in the 1900-1930 era that these cities attracted Chicanos in record numbers.

Urbanization of Southwestern Chicanos

The urban areas that attracted the greatest number of Chicanos in this period were those which generally shared these common characteristics: diverse economic structure, proximity to the Mexican border, and labor distribution capabilities (favorable transportation and communication facilities). As Table 1 shows, of the fifteen largest centers of Mexican people in the United States, only Chicago and Detroit did not meet all three requirements. There were also differences in regional levels of urbanization due to the impact of economic factors, which contributed greatly to the attraction of potential urban dwellers. For example, although San Diego was closer to the Mexican border, Los Angeles had the clear economic advantage between the years 1900-1930, especially in terms of capital and a diversified economy. Los Angeles also had railroad connections superior to those in San Diego, a factor which facilitated industrialization and contributed to its importance as an interstate distribution center for Mexican laborers.

The explosive population growth of Los Angeles and simultaneous industrial expansion in the years between World War I and the Depression have been often described as nothing less than "miraculous." From 1900 to 1930 the population grew by ten times and the city added some 4,000 new factories.[9] The construction of a major port in San Pedro, the completion of a 230 mile-long aqueduct that brought badly needed fresh water to the city, and the discovery of major oil deposits in the county assured the city's prosperity and growth potential. With the arrival of the first ships through the newly completed Panama Canal at the onset of the World War I, the city became a world trade center. Excellent inter-urban and inter-regional rail networks also gave Los Angeles a command of regional trade distribution thus enhancing its advantages over its old rivals, San Diego and Santa Barbara, in the crucial manufacturing sector.

Like Los Angeles, two of Texas' largest cities, San Antonio and El Paso, also gained substantially in population during the period under consideration. Both cities had excellent rail connections, cheap fuel for industrialization, and ready access to a plentiful supply of Mexican labor. The regional markets in West Texas and South Texas showed less promise than those of southern California, but El Paso and San Antonio commanded a great share of the commerce and shipping of raw resources in their respective regions. Mario Garcia, in a study of the Mexican population of El Paso in the early 20th century, credits the arrival of the railroad and the discovery of copper and other metals, not only in Arizona and New Mexico, but also in the Mexican states of Sonora and Chihuahua, with greatly increasing the city's position as a dominant commercial center.[10]

Once the railroad came to El Paso, the city became the hub of an inland empire composed of north and west Texas, southern New Mexico, and eastern Arizona. With capital accumulated through refining, storing and transportation of raw resources such as metal ores and farm products, El Paso improved its inter-regional transportation network, and financed the type of expansion that attracted additional industries. Compared to other

----

TABLE 1 *Distribution of Chicanos in Urban Areas for 1920 and 1930*

	City	1920	1930
1.	Los Angeles	29,757	97,116
2.	San Antonio	41,469	82,373
3.	El Paso	39,571	58,291
4.	Laredo	N.A.*	23,482
5.	Belvedere	N.A.	20,125
6.	Chicago	1,265	19,362
7.	Houston	5,002	14,149
8.	Corpus Christi	N.A.	11,377
9.	San Diego	4,007	9,266
10.	San Francisco	3,908	7,922
11.	San Bernardino	N.A.	6,839
12.	Denver	1,722	6,837
13.	Detroit	683	6,515
14.	Dallas	2,838	5,901
15.	East Chicago	N.A.	5,343
16.	Austin	N.A.	5,014
17.	Ft. Worth	4,426	3,955
18.	Riverside	N.A.	3,942
19.	Santa Ana	N.A.	3,633
20.	Gary	169	3,486

*Data not available.
Source: U.S. Bureau of the Census, *Fifteenth Census of the United States: 1930. Population Volume I* (Washington, D.C., 1932), Table 23.

Texas cities, the economy of El Paso was quite diversified, with refineries, construction, and commerce employing the greatest portion of the workforce.

San Antonio, the axis of a major agricultural and cattle raising region in south and central Texas, ranked as the largest city in the state with a population of 53,321. From 1890 to 1920, San Antonio also had the largest concentration of Chicanos in the United States.[11] In the 20s Max Handman commented on the importance of San Antonio as a distribution center for Mexican workers: "Texas is the corridor and clearing house for most of the Mexican casuals that are distributed over the country. The government labor agent, who, however, keeps no records of his clientele, estimates that his agency had shipped out of San Antonio in one year over 200,000 Mexicans."[12]

In a study dealing with urbanization and regional economic development, David Ward suggested that after 1910, "the increased use of petroleum and natural gas energy, advances in the petrochemical and communications industries, and the development of long distance road and air transportation strongly influenced selective metropolitan growth and differences in rates of economic development."[13] In the case of San Antonio, these factors certainly applied, although the rapid urbanization of San Antonio in the post 1910 era was also related to a decision of the federal government to build several military bases on the peripheries of the city. Efficient and rapid movement of military personnel and supplies required excellent road and eventually air transportation facilities. Indeed, the federal government built one of the first air bases in San Antonio.[14] The city's ready access to oil and gas and the availability of cheap unskilled laborers from neighboring Mexico assisted in the construction and maintenance of military facilities during World War I, a time when much of the United States male work force had been sent overseas. After the war San Antonio continued to benefit from the large federal payroll. Moreover, the city profited from the improvement of transportation facilities during the war which further solidified its position as a major commercial center in south Texas.

In 1929, southwesterners could look back with pride at twenty years of extraordinary growth and development. With the admission of New Mexico and Arizona to statehood in 1912 and the completion of deep water port facilities in Los Angeles and Houston, the rest of the nation no longer thought of the Southwest as an underdeveloped frontier region. Improved transoceanic trade after World War I spurred economic activity in southern California, while the increase in automobile travel contributed to regional and national integration. Not surprisingly, Southwest cities attracted thousands of newcomers as the economy of the urban communities experienced unprecedented expansion. Chicanos participated in the economic transformation of the region; in substantially large numbers they manned machines, constructed new railroad lines, and extracted mineral wealth from the earth.

Specialization of Labor

A consequence of urbanization in this country has been the growing specialization of the work force. In the Southwest, as in every region of the country, the introduction of new sources of energy and raw materials, new supplies of labor and industrial skills, new machines and techniques of production eroded the 19th century pre-industrial class and occupational structure. After 1890, new employment patterns, based on the requirements of capital accumulation in areas such as steel-making, automobile assembly, and textiles, began to play a larger role in the economy of the Southwest region. With the introduction of factory production came increased concentration of workers in urban areas.

For the Southwest, the transition from extractive industry and agriculture to capital intensive manufacturing and service activities came slowly. From 1890 through 1910, the Southwest (excluding California) had the lowest proportion of workers employed in manufacturing of any region in the United States.[15] For instance, 48.0% of the work force in the New England states was occupied in manufacturing in 1890, while only 9.1% of southwestern workers earned their living in a similar manner. By 1910, the proportion of individual workers employed in manufacturing in the Southwest had risen by only 3%.[16] Not surprisingly most Chicanos living in the Southwest in 1910 held jobs primarily in agriculture, ranching, mining, and transportation.[17]

The most dramatic changes in the post 1910 urbanization process in the Southwest occurred within the Chicano community. As has been noted, prior to 1910 the majority of Chicanos living in the Southwest labored outside the urban-industrial job market. Even when they lived in cities, steady factory employment was scarce, forcing thousands to rely on casual agricultural employment in surrounding rural communities. In Texas, for example, many Chicanos who lived in the cities of San Antonio, Austin, Houston and Dallas migrated to work the crops in southern Texas, and some often ventured as far north as Wisconsin and Minnesota. Paul S. Taylor reported that it was not unusual for south Texas farmers to recruit Mexican pickers from the lower Rio Grande Valley, Laredo, San Antonio, and the Winter Garden District, and sometimes from as far as Del Rio and Houston.[18] However, as economic opportunities improved in cities like San Antonio and Houston, the Chicano labor force migrated less frequently to distant agricultural areas. As Robert McLean wrote: "The secondary recruiters of Mexican labor are the factories and foundries, and construction projects in the great cities." In 1929, McLean found that the Mexicans migrated to the cities when agricultural jobs were at their lowest ebb: "He finds employment on a construction gang, and hesitates to leave when the crop which recruited him originally is again calling."[19]

Chicanos entered more specialized urban employment as cities became less dependent on trade and commerce with their hinterlands and more dedicated to manufacturing industries. The opening of several new military bases in San Antonio during World War I, which had spurred urbanization, also created a flood of new specialized jobs in construction, shipping and manufacturing. A study in which 1,282 Chicano workers were surveyed in San Antonio showed that in less than a decade the majority of the Chicano labor force had shifted to the industrial sector. Although the largest number of Chicanos surveyed in that study (47%) held jobs as laborers, a sizable number worked in semi-skilled and skilled positions such as carpentry, masonry, tailoring, and baking. Some earned their living as storekeepers and clerks, while more than one hundred worked for the City of San Antonio mostly in unskilled and semi-skilled work such as street construction, sanitation, and building maintenance.[20]

Variations in the rate of job specialization occurred within cities of the Southwest. As Alma M. Garcia demonstrated in a study of occupational structure of the Mexican population of El Paso, the types of jobs that Chicanos held in various cities between the years 1900 and 1920 were significantly different. In El Paso, the proportion of Chicano service workers more than doubled between 1900 and 1920, while there were few employment changes in the mechanical industries (craftsmen and operatives).[21] In contrast, Santa Barbara, which attracted fewer industries and fewer Mexican migrants than El Paso, witnessed little transition in the occupational structure of Chicanos during a similar period. Albert Camarillo found "that Chicanos remained as a poor, predominantly unskilled and semi-skilled working class in Santa Barbara throughout the first thirty years of the twentieth century."[22]

In Los Angeles, Chicanos probably had greater opportunities to engage in specialized types of work than other urbanized Chicanos in the West. Already by 1890, manufacturing and mechanical industries employed 25% of the city's labor force.[23] Although Los Angeles ranked behind San Francisco and Denver at the turn of the century in terms of the proportion of the labor force employed in industrial work, Los Angeles is important because by 1930 its Chicano population was ten times greater than either of the other two western cities.[24] A survey of the Mexican work force in Los Angeles during World War I indicates that while a disproportionately high number of this group worked in unskilled labor, the majority of them earned their living in such industries as building trades, steel and iron, meatpacking, inter-urban transportation maintenance, and street-paving.[25]

By 1930, industrial establishments in California with 100 or more workers on their payroll employed the majority of Chicano laborers in non-agricultural work.[26] That year the United States Census showed that 30% of the Chicano labor force in California worked in manufacturing-related jobs, the highest proportion for any state in the Southwest. Indeed, 5,500 Chicanos in California held jobs in iron, steel, and clay-glass industries. Another 5,000 Chicanos labored in service related jobs. By 1930 only 37% of the Chicanos in the state worked in agriculture, and the majority of those agricultural workers lived in urban areas, commuting to rural areas to work.[27]

The introduction of new mining technology after 1900 also contributed to the increased specialization of the Chicano labor force of the Southwest. In the mining communities of Arizona, New Mexico and Texas, new machines and excavation techniques made possible the extraction of very low grade ores.[28] The new and extensive open pit mines required more complex facilities and the training of men in new operations. Victor S. Clark indicates that large New Mexican mining centers such as Fierro, Silver City, and San Antonio, where coal and iron as well as other metals were mined, relied heavily on Mexican labor. Clark estimated, for example, that mining companies employed about 1,000 Mexicanos in the vicinity of Laredo, Texas in 1907.[29] New and larger smelters necessitated the employment of a larger labor force which, in turn, required a major expansion of towns to accommodate those workers.

Beyond 1848

Internal Spatial Structure

Cities have changed tremendously in size and complexity over the past hundred years, but many of the spatial patterns associated with urbanization and distribution of human activities during this initial period have persisted. David Ward, a geographer, approached one of the major questions of urban space with the premise that "while the volume and source of the cityward movement varied from region to region and from city to city, the sources of urban employment tended to occupy similar locations."[30] An analysis of the functional specialization of southwestern cities requires an examination of the origins of their internal spatial patterns.

First it should be noted that the Spanish and Mexicans proved extremely successful as town builders. They selected sites carefully, and the survival and growth of cities at those sites evidence their good judgment. Some of those early Spanish-Mexican settlements include San Francisco, San Jose, San Diego, and Los Angeles in California; Tucson and Phoenix in Arizona; Santa Fe and Albuquerque in New Mexico; and San Antonio, El Paso, Laredo, and Houston in Texas. These are among the largest cities in the United States, and Chicanos remain a sizable proportion of the population in each.

Early influences of Spanish and Mexican settlement are evident in spatial patterns found in many western cities today. The government of Spain took an active interest in the location and planning of cities in the colonies. An early Spanish law (1523) prescribed the conditions for laying out new cities--prerequisites which included that slaughterhouses, stockyards, fish markets, tanneries, and "other dirty and illsmelling businesses" be placed outside the town's main precincts, "preferably on the other side of a river or on the seashore."[31] In most of these early cities, government authorities distributed lots to residents, reserving the less desirable locations for common use and newcomers. An account by E. Gould Buffum, a visitor to Los Angeles in 1850, provided some insight into the city's early spatial structure. "The northern portion of the town," he wrote, "is laid out in streets, and appropriated as the residence of the trading citizens, while the southern part is made up of gardens, vineyards, and orchards."[32] To this day, the administrative offices, courthouses, and other public buildings of cities like Los Angeles, San Antonio, and Santa Fe, are located in the general area laid out by the Spanish-Mexican town builders of the 18th century.

In cities throughout the Southwest, residential patterns of Chicanos varied. During the early 20th century, some lived in segregated enclaves or barrios, while others lived in ethnically mixed neighborhoods. Matthew Edel attributes the general selection of housing units to four basic components: the housing unit itself, neighborhood, location and political jurisdiction. However, the decision of where individuals will eventually live is subject "to incentives induced by taxes, regulations and prejudices."[33] The selection of housing proved one of the most difficult ordeals faced by the Mexican migrant to an urban area. In many cases the search did not begin until family members had a firm commitment of employment. The housing unit itself was of primary importance, since many of the Mexicans had sizable families. For example in the large cities, Los Angeles, San Antonio, and San Francisco, Mexicans often found housing units that had been converted from single family dwellings to multiple family type apartments or boarding houses.[34] At the same time, the neighborhood had to be appraised. Basically, the main factor governing the selection of a neighborhood, other than a desire among most of the Chicanos to live in an area of similar social class and ethnic characteristics, was not its intrinsic value but its nearness to the economic activities of the user. While contemplating the unit and the neighborhood, Mexicans had to reflect on the location. Chicanos with limited finances found the central city the most desirable because such a location minimized transportation costs. Naturally, for those working in industrial areas distant from the city, any area close to the plant was desirable. For Chicanos, as for other minorities, the factors crucial to the question of political jurisdiction were associated more with the legal constraints, such as restrictive clauses against certain minority groups, imposed on the neighborhood. A secondary issue was the question of tax rates or public services available.

Mexicanos, like Blacks and Asians, were severely limited in their selection of housing units by widespread discriminatory practices.[35] A Chamber of Commerce brochure used to attract outside industries to southern California typified prevailing exclusionary policies of the period stating: "Lynwood, being restricted to the white race, can furnish ample labor of the better class."[36] Another example of discrimination was reflected in an advertisement that appeared in 1922 urging Mexicans to buy lots in a new development near Belvedere. "Mexicans," the text declared, "this is the last opportunity to live among your compatriots, for our communities are exclusively Mexican."[37] In other southwestern cities, Mexicans found that real estate brokers used restrictive covenants to channel their movement into certain sections of the city.

In all southwestern metropolitan communities, newly arrived and longtime residents competed with industry and commerce for space. In some cities, industrial and commercial establishments proved more effective, however, than residential users in acquiring control of accessible sites. Chicanos often found that they had no alternative but to move into more crowded quarters away from the central district. In Los Angeles, some 40% of the Mexican population maintained its residential location near the central area until the middle 1920s largely because the city had sufficient land available in the more industrially desirable harbor area.[38] Commercial development of central Los Angeles intensified as dozens of new banks and department stores located there. By the end of the decade, the majority of Mexican residents had moved eastward into a relatively inexpensive, but very poorly situated residential area near the Los Angeles River. Belvedere, the largest of the Chicano working class suburban communities in Los Angeles, had a Mexican population of almost 21,000.[39] The extension of Henry Huntington's "red cars" to Belvedere contributed to its rapid growth. A number of new industries, such as the B.F. Goodrich plant, located their new facilities near Belvedere during this period, as did other industries from the old central business district. South of Belvedere, meatpacking companies, iron and steel plants, cement and tile factories, the major employers of Mexican workers in the city, sprouted up along a path several miles long. More extensive use of the automobile and improvements in the city's inter-urban transit system made it possible for eastside residents to live in the Los Angeles periphery and continue to work in the central area.

In other large cities of the Southwest, Chicanos constituted the greater proportion of the population. In El Paso, Chicanos comprised 56.9% of the population in 1930, and Mexican residents in Laredo formed 72% of the population. (Other than Belvedere, 60.9% Mexican, no California city registered a Chicano population higher than 18%.)[40] In cities such as El Paso, with a very high Mexican concentration, segregation by socioeconomic factors was more prevalent than ethnic segregation. Thousands of Mexicans clustered around the smelters and railroad yards of El Paso's southside. Mario Garcia has noted that most of the Chicanos not employed by the smelters or railroad companies lived in El Paso's "Second Ward." There the "construction firms, downtown retail or wholesale stores, laundries, and other employers, as well as American housewives found needed workers."[41] Although, El Paso had its congested barrios where workers--both Mexican and Anglo--lived in dilapidated housing, the city also had a substantial upper class neighborhood where wealthy Mexicans owned fashionable homes.

In San Diego, California's principal border community, Mexicans lived adjacent to the canneries and warehouses associated with intercoastal shipping. The Mexican population of this port city was relatively small during the 1900-1930 era (see Table 1). While the city had a population of 147,997, it included only 9,266 Mexican residents, or 6.3% of the population. Here Chicanos lived in small segregated enclaves. Constantine Panunzio found that the Mexican residents of the city, although socially and politically segregated, lived under "favorable" conditions in 1930. Panunzio noted the presence of moderately good sanitation facilities, wide streets and no serious housing congestion in the Mexican *colonia*. The area had a number of Mexican stores, churches, and pool halls, without, according to Panunzio, the "slum tenements" often found in eastern and midwestern cities.[42]

In contrast to the more complex internal spatial patterns that developed in El Paso and San Diego during the early 20th century, Laredo, a small border community in Texas, had only minor socio-economic and ethnic variations in its residential districts. An early traveler to Laredo commented that the presence of so many Mexicans offered "one of the glaring contrasts so common in Texas," for Laredo had "all the characteristics of Old Spain." He asserted that nearly all of the town's buildings were made of adobe, with low walls, flat roofs, and grated windows. The Mexican town dweller, he lamented, seemed "decades away from entering the American mainstream," for in Laredo, all the public signs were in Spanish and most of the residents, Anglos included, spoke only that language. In that observer's opinion, "no one traversing the streets of Laredo would imagine himself in the United States."[43] Indeed, by 1930, Laredo had the highest proportion of Mexicans living in any city of the United States, nearly 75%.

Each of the large southwestern cities where Chicanos lived in sizable numbers had unique features and all grew at different rates. The factors that appear most crucial to understanding differential patterns of spatial structure are the rate of urbanization, the quality of inter-city transportation, and the degree of suburbanization during the period under consideration.[44] Naturally, the way cities grew affected Chicanos, since during this period they were undergoing urbanization at an unprecedented rate. In many cities Chicano newcomers solidified older Mexican resident bases, while in other cases, they established totally new neighborhoods, which still survive today and for the most part remain ethnically segregated communities.

Demographic Urbanization

Demographic urbanization is best defined as the redistribution of population or the process of population concentration. An analysis of this process requires an examination of growth in numbers and sizes of cities under investigation, levels of urbanization or proportion of the population urbanized, migration factors, rates of urbanization, and fluctuation in the rate of urban increase. Chicanos are of special interest since they have been characterized by Irene Taeuber as "the least metropolitan of the large nationality groups," while "the Irish the most metropolitan."[45]

Chicanos in the southwestern states lived in hundreds of towns, although roughly from 25% to 35% of the total Chicano population was concentrated in four or five large cities in each state during the period 1900-1930. Twenty-five percent of the Mexican population of Texas, for instance, lived principally in four cities: San Antonio, El Paso, Laredo, and Houston. In California, more than a third of the Mexican population lived in Los Angeles, San Diego and San Francisco. The percentage of Chicanos living in each of these cities also varied. In San Antonio, Chicanos constituted 35.6% of the total population in 1930, but in Houston and San Francisco, they represented less than five percent of the total population.[46]

In contrast with later developments, there was nothing spectacular about the urbanization of the Mexican population in the United States prior to 1900. Indeed, it had taken until 1920, 310 years after the first settlement by Mexicanos in the Southwest, for the Chicano population to reach 500,000. A decade later, more than 700,000 Chicanos in the United States lived in urbanized communities.[47] During the 1920s the Chicano population more than tripled, increasing by twice as much as it had grown in the previous 300 years. The urban trend during the turn of the century focused mainly on Texas and California, with Texas having a higher number of urban residents. El Paso, for example had a Mexican population of 39,571 by 1920, some 10,000 more than the officially recorded Mexican population of Los Angeles and only 2,000 less than San Antonio.

Most writers concerned with the Chicano population in this era disputed the official census count for Mexicans in the larger metropolitan areas. It is certainly true that poor people, non-English-speaking immigrants, migrant and casual workers were more apt to be missed by census takers than other members of our society. Writing in 1931, Max Handman noted that 56% of the children enrolled in San Antonio's primary school bore "Mexican names." According to Handman, this figure gave a far more accurate picture of the presence of a large number of Mexicans in that city. A few years later George I. Sanchez used a similar technique to estimate the Mexican population of New Mexico which he argued was undercounted by nearly half. Indeed, estimates of the Los Angeles Mexican population recorded at 29,000 in 1920, seem low for that period. *La Prensa de Los Angeles* estimated the Mexican population in 1921 at closer to 86,000 than 29,000.[48] Despite the problems with census accuracy, it is nevertheless certain that by 1920 urban areas were absorbing Mexicans in extraordinarily large numbers.

TABLE 2 *Distribution of Urban, Rural and Rural Non-farm Mexican Population in Four Southwestern States, 1930.*

State	Urban	%	Rural	%	Rural Non-farm	%
Arizona	41,194	36.0	15,836	13.9	57,243	50.1
California	244,199	66.3	38,920	10.6	84,894	23.1
New Mexico	11,038	18.6	16,800	28.3	31,502	53.1
Texas	318,647	46.6	238,042	37.3	126,992	18.6
TOTAL	614,978	50.2	309,598	25.3	300,631	24.5

Computed from the U.S. Bureau of the Census, *Fifteenth Census, of the United States: 1930. Population. Volume II* (Washington, D.C. 1932), p.65.

The Mexican immigration era of 1900-1930 qualifies as one of the most important population shifts in southwestern annals. Slightly more than 10% of Mexico's population-- approximately 1,500,000 people--emigrated to the United States during these years. The significance of this period is shown by the fact that 94% of the foreign born Mexican population in the United States in 1930 had arrived after 1900. Some 62% of them arrived after 1915.[49]

Prior to 1920, better rail connections from Mexico to Texas made it possible for a greater number of Mexicans to settle in Texas than in other states. Emigrants leaving Mexico before World War I had a choice of several Texas ports, including Matamoros, Laredo, Eagle Pass, and El Paso. New Mexico and California had no direct lines to

Mexico, while Arizona had only Nogales as an inland port city. Thus between the years 1900 and 1920, 70% of the Mexican migrants crossing the border departed for Texas, while only 6.5% initially migrated to California.[50]

By 1920, Mexicans made up the largest foreign-born population in all the large southwestern cities, with the exception of San Francisco where Asian Americans held that distinction. In Los Angeles, residents born in Mexico numbered 21,598. The next largest groups were Canadians, English, and Germans. By 1920, in cities such as San Diego, Tucson, El Paso, and San Antonio, Mexicans were overwhelmingly the largest foreign-born group. The Mexican population in California in the years between 1910 and 1920 increased by 163.5% compared to a 39.1% increase for Italians, even though the latter were the second fastest growing immigrant group in the state.[51] Mexicans, because of the proximity of their homeland to the Southwest and the improvement in railroad transportation from Mexico to the United States, no doubt had an advantage over the Italians and other immigrants from Europe and other Western Hemisphere countries.

No city in the United States urbanized as rapidly during the early 20th century as Los Angeles, where the population grew from 102,000 in 1900 to a little more than a million by 1930. In the first decade of the 20th century, Los Angeles population increased by an incredible 212%. By comparison, Chicago recorded a 29% increase for the same period. Again in the decade of the 20s, Los Angeles led the nation with a 115% increase, while New York, San Francisco and Chicago each grew by an average of 25%.[52] In addition, after 1920 more Mexicans settled in Los Angeles than in any other city in the United States and the city's Mexican population more than tripled. By comparison San Antonio's Chicano population doubled. By 1930, more Mexicans resided in Los Angeles than lived in either New Mexico or Arizona.

Chicanos living in the Midwest and East were even more urbanized than Chicanos in the Southwest. Of the Chicanos who migrated to Indiana, for instance, 91% settled in either East Chicago or Gary. Some 67% of the Chicanos in Illinois lived in Chicago; and 61.7% of the Chicanos settling in Wisconsin preferred the state's largest city, Milwaukee.[53] Thus in areas where there were few Chicanos, most tended to settle in large cities which offered greater economic opportunities.

During the early periods of heavy Mexican immigration, many of the immigrants came without their families, partly because so many of them were employed seasonally, and partly because of the high cost of bringing entire families across the border. A general pattern seems to have been that the greater the distance from the Mexican border, the lesser the presence of Chicano women, and consequently of Chicano families. At one extreme was the state of Oregon, which had few Mexican communities, and in 1930 recorded 1,247 Mexican males and 321 Mexican females living in the state, or a ratio of 388.5 males to 100 females. The most equitable ratio in the nation was found in Texas, where there were 105.6 Mexican males for every 100 Mexican females.

TABLE 3 Males Per 100 Females in Selected Cities of the United States for the Mexican Population 1930.

Los Angeles	103.5	San Antonio	94.0
Oakland	116.2	San Francisco	115.0
San Diego	109.6	Chicago	170.6
El Paso	86.7	Detroit	179.0
Houston	113.3	Flint	149.0

Source: U.S. Bureau of the Census. *Fifteenth Census of the United States: 1930. Population. Volume II* (Washington, D.C., 1932), pp. 116-131.

In El Paso and San Antonio, the opposite situation prevailed. In El Paso, the Mexican male to female ratio was 86/100 in 1930 while San Antonio had a ratio of 95/100. As has been noted, both of these cities served as depots or labor "clearing houses" for Mexican workers. From 1910 to 1920 the two cities functioned as the most important recruiting centers for midwestern and southern agricultural interests. Thousands of Mexican men who lived in El Paso and San Antonio traveled to distant cities and communities outside of the state for work periods of six months to several years, frequently leaving their wives and children behind. This fact may also explain the extremely high ratio of Mexican males to Mexican females in midwestern cities like Chicago (170/100) and Detroit (179/100).[54] In later decades, more Chicano families migrated to Chicago and today, Chicago's Chicano population ranks as one of the largest in the United States.

Behavioral Urbanization

Behavioral urbanization can be seen as the changes in life styles and individual behavior associated with structural and demographic urbanization. When large numbers of individuals are concentrated in cities of different size and density, daily routines and sequences of activities change radically through progressive differentiation. The effects of urbanization on human behavior are profound, for people change their ideas, behavior and social values. In *The Urban Process*, Leonard Reissman submits that "urbanization is social change on a vast scale." Moreover, "society gives way to urban institutions, urban values, and urban demands."[55] Thus, the group and individuals undergo some transformation in response to new roles, social situations, and spatial locations.

Here, the factors to be considered are limited to some aspects of traditional customs, formal organization, sex roles and marriage, role of women in the labor force, and attitudes toward urban life. The problem of defining behavioral changes in the Chicano community is complicated by the fact that while the majority of the Mexican immigrants in the 1900-1930 era came from a rural background, it is not known how many of them may have had previous urban experiences in Mexico or in the United States before eventually settling down in the metropolitan communities of the Southwest. Nonetheless, Ernesto Galarza concluded that living in urban areas presented the newcomer with many different problems. "Statistics on urban trends do not, of course," wrote Galarza, "probe the significance of what they suggest--that with such massive shifting and compaction there come correspondingly profound changes in the quality of life."[56] An example cited by Galarza concerned the credit system in the Mexican urban communities. In cities, he noted, the migrants could not rely on "the traditional system of borrowing money," a variant of the traditional money lending at usury of rural Mexico, and "borrowing--since the poor must borrow--has presented an entirely new set of subtleties which baffle[d] the Mexican-American."[57]

Galarza was one of the few Mexican immigrants to document his experiences in urban America. He came from a small rural community in Nayarit, Mexico and settled in the "lower part" of Sacramento in 1910. He described his newly adopted barrio as "a kaleidoscope of colors and languages and customs that surprised and absorbed [him] at every turn."[58] In Mexico he had lived in a *vecindad*, where neighbors knew one another and where he also had the benefit of an extended family to care for him. In Sacramento, however, he found that "even in the alleys, where people knew one another better, the houses were fenced apart, without central courts to wash clothes, talk and play with the other children."[59]

Had Ernesto Galarza lived in San Antonio, Los Angeles, or El Paso, he would have found that many of the Mexican families did indeed live in *vecindades*, but for some reason, perhaps because of the prevalence of ethnically heterogeneous neighborhoods, *vecindades* never developed in Sacramento. Also to Galarza's dismay, the community did not even have a plaza, "only parks which had no bandstands, no concerts every Thursday, no Judases exploding on Holy Weeks, and no promenades of boys going one way and the girls the other."[60] Galarza's observations tell us much about the adjustment of a young boy and his family to an urban environment. Unfortunately, there are but a few such studies or autobiographies from which to draw conclusions.

One of the traits that most clearly distinguished urbanized Chicanos from rural Chicanos and Mexicanos was the inclination to join and participate in voluntary associations. Manuel Gamio, a noted Mexican anthropologist writing in the 1920s, commented on the popularity of mutual benefit societies among the Mexicans in the United States.[61] The immigrants found that clubs and societies especially served members in areas where collective action was necessary, or where they as individuals could not be as effective. In the southwestern cities, Chicanos had a variety of clubs and societies from which to choose. It was not uncommon to find an individual who belonged to several organizations--including a trade union (Mexican and/or non-Mexican), a political party, and still another to accommodate leisure interests (athletic association, social club, etc.).

Exactly what percent or how many of the Mexicanos joined these organizations is unknown, since few of the organizational records survive. Evangeline Hymer conducted a sample survey of Mexicanos in one of the *colonias* of Los Angeles and found that 75% had a "preference for clubs," although what was meant by "preference" is not entirely clear.[62] While no information as to the level of participation of the individuals interviewed by Hymer is known, newspaper notices and interviews with members of the Mexican community of Los Angeles suggest that many mutual benefit societies were active and successful.

The most prosperous Chicano organizations originated in urban areas. Perhaps the best known of these mutual benefit groups was the *Alianza Hispano Americana* founded in Tucson, Arizona in the 1890s. By the 1920s, 275 lodges had been established in the Southwest. Another important organization, *Orden Hijos de América* originated in San Antonio during the recession of 1921. At a time when Mexicans faced threats of deportation in that city and in other parts of the country, the *Orden* restricted membership to Chicanos who held American citizenship.[63] In El Paso, Chicanos organized political clubs such as the *Club Ortiz Politico Social* "a group within the Democratic party," which "helped deliver the Mexican vote."[64] The success of these organizations varied from community to community, but from information that is available, Chicanos took a great interest in the clubs, and to some extent, these organizations did succeed in bringing many urban newcomers in contact with others of similar socio-economic backgrounds. This function, no doubt, proved of immense value to those migrants new to urban living.

The participation of Chicanos in voluntary organizations was just one way in which newcomers adjusted to new life styles. Adaptation to urban values and urban demands seemed especially evident in changes resulting from greater migration of males over females to urban areas. For instance, Paul S. Taylor noted that there was in many cases a reversal of the usual age differential between husbands and wives living in the midwestern United States compared to couples marrying in Mexico. He provided the example of a 21 year old man who married a 50 year old woman.[65] In other cities, especially in the Southwest where the sex ratio of males to females was not overly unbalanced, there were fewer cases of this reversal in age differential among married Mexican couples. In Los Angeles, for instance, only 28 of 209 Mexican males marrying in 1918 took older wives.[66]

Constantine Panunzio investigated the consequences of unbalanced sex ratios from another perspective. He suggested that sex distribution was a primary factor in producing or preventing intermarriage. Panunzio concluded that when an ethnic or racial group has an unbalanced sex ratio, members will tend to intermarry. Panunzio found that 83% of Mexican marriages in Los Angeles during the 1920s were intramarriages (between Mexican males and females). Although the intermarriage rate between Mexicans and non-Mexicans was low, it was not as low as that of the Japanese who seldom married out of their group. Indeed, 97.7% of marriages in the Japanese community were intermarriages.[67] Moreover, it was more likely that a Mexican woman would marry outside of her ethnic group than a Mexican male. In Los Angeles during 1918, the number of marriages of Mexican women out of their group totaled 51, while for Mexican men it amounted to only 32.[68]

Another consequence of urbanization for Mexican families in the United States was the large scale entrance of women into the industrial labor force, especially after World War I. Although many Mexican women could find employment only in domestic work, thousands of women in Los Angeles, El Paso, and San Antonio found jobs in manufacturing and service industries. Fully a third of the California Mexican female labor force was employed in manufacturing by 1930. Nearly 2,000 Mexican women held jobs in the garment industry, the vast majority in the Los Angeles area.[69] In states where manufacturing jobs were less numerous and agricultural labor dominated the economy, the greater proportion of employed Mexican women were found in non-industrial jobs. While only 14% of the Mexican women in California were in the labor market, in three midwestern states, Minnesota, North Dakota, and Montana, the percentage of Mexican women in the labor market was the highest in the nation, ranging from 20% in Montana to 51.3% in North Dakota.[67] Mexican women migrating that far north were generally migrant laborers. While few of these field-workers remained for more than two or three months, it was not uncommon for them to work as family units.

For both Mexican men and women urban employment often was made difficult due to the great separation in time and space from work place and residence. In farming communities, parents could take their children with them when they worked in the fields, while in the city, the type of work and the distance from home and work place made this almost impossible. Yet in the cities, many women employed in textile and cigar factories solved that problem by taking older children along to work with them rather than leaving them at home or enrolling them in school. Linna E. Bresette reported that in one cotton mill in a southwestern city, the entire force of 400 was made up of Mexican women and girls. A cigar factory in another southwestern city employed 600 Mexican women, many of whom Bresette thought appeared "under the age limit set by Child Labor Laws."[71] In Los Angeles and San Antonio, pecan-shelling companies and textile factories commissioned piece work, and employees were free to take their work home with them. At home, the families enlisted the assistance of the children and the work was organized along familial systems.

Some of the newcomers' reactions to urban life in this period were recorded in *corridos* (folk ballads). An immigrant in San Antonio, for example, expressed his disapproval of the modern customs and dress taken up by his compatriots when he wrote these lyrics:

On the Farm Where I was Born

I don't care to dance in the halls
That you have here;
What I want is an earth floor
Like on the farm where I was born

I don't care for your silk shirts
That you have here;
What I want is a suit of blue jumpers [overalls]
Like on the farm where I was born

I don't like your wide trousers
That you have here;
I like them close to the skin
Like on the farm where I was born.[72]

Another immigrant recorded his reactions to the dress of Chicano women, whom he not only condemned for wearing outlandish dresses, but also criticized for failing to maintain traditional customs such as cooking. He wrote these lyrics to a *corrido* entitled THE FLAPPERS

Red Bandannas
I detest,
And now the flappers
Use them for their dress.
The girls of San Antonio
Are lazy at the *metate* [grinding corn by hand]
They want to walk out bobbed-haired
With straw hats on.
The harvesting is finished,
So is the cotton;
The flappers stroll out now
For a good time.[73]

Just as our knowledge about urban theory is constantly changing, our perceptions about the dynamics of the urban process are under continuous reevaluation. Some scholars reject the concept of a dichotomous model--looking at the experiences and behavioral changes from a traditional versus modern approach. No doubt the behavioral patterns exhibited by many Mexican newcomers were neither modern or traditional. In forming their own voluntary associations and publishing their own newspapers, Mexicans displayed strong nationalistic sentiments. In their *corridos* they sang about better days in Mexico and the lyrics exhibited skepticism about American life. As sexual norms changed and fertility rates decreased, efforts among women intensified in their search to combine traditional and urbanized behavioral roles. Many immigrant newcomers to the city reconstructed their own world "by fusing old and new behavioral strategies to meet the continuing demands of survival."[74]

Conclusions

The data presented here contests the notion that Chicanos are recent immigrants to the United States. A continuity clearly exists between those Spanish-Mexican settlers who first occupied the Southwest in the 17th century and Chicanos who now live in the cities of the same region. While immigration from Mexico has been intense in the 20th century, especially in the years between World I and the Depression, almost every community in the Southwest had Mexican *colonias* dating back to the 19th century or earlier. The *colonias* survived the influx of Anglo settlers and served as a haven for later Mexican immigrants.

Mexicans immigrating to the Southwest in the early 20th century came during a period of intensive economic development. Yet, as the evidence presented in this essay demonstrates, there were differential growth patterns for various southwestern cities. Prior to 1920 when the majority of the new Mexican immigrants settled in Texas, two cities in that state, San Antonio and El Paso, ranked first and second as the largest Chicano communities in the nation. After 1920 more and more Chicanos, both rural migrants from the Southwest and recent immigrants from Mexico, began to relocate in California and Arizona. More rapidly industrializing cities, such as Los Angeles, attracted the majority of those moving to urban areas. The ten largest centers of Chicano population were also the fastest growing cities in the Southwest.

The belief that Chicanos have only migrated in large numbers to urban areas since World War II has little substance. The unremitting influx of Chicanos to cities during the period 1900-1930 undoubtedly makes it difficult to support the thesis expressed recently by one scholar that Chicanos "have been grossly unprepared by anything in their past experience" to meet the challenges of our "highly organized, predominantly urban and industrial" society.[75] While the rate of urbanization varied from city to city due to economic development and regional industrialization, by 1930 more than 50% of Chicanos, both regionally and nationally, lived in cities. Moreover, the urbanization process continues. When we consider that the United States Chicano urban population grew by 6% from 1960 to 1970, it is possible that by 1980 at least 90% of the Chicano population may be urban residents.

The urbanization of residents of Mexican ancestry in the United States undermines certain stereotypes. Much of the labor history by Chicano historians centers on rural farmworkers. Only recently have some historians begun to examine the role of Chicanos in urban industries. Urban Chicano labor leaders have been all but ignored, while labor scholars have taken a greater interest in the union activities of agricultural labor organizer Cesar Chavez and his predecessors. As has been suggested in this essay, economic development and urbanization prompted geographic mobility and occupational differentiation among Chicanos. Only when researchers examine the experiences of the Chicano urbanite can we expect to explain other larger historical issues such as the contradictions of assimilation and social mobility.

Appendix

El Rancho Donde Yo Naci

No me gusta bailar en salones
Como al estilo de por aquí
a mi me gusta piso de tierra
como en el rancho donde yo nací.

No me gusta camisa de seda
como al estilo de por aquí
a mi me gustan las "yompas" azules
como en el rancho donde yo nací.

No me gustan los calzones anchos
como al estilo de por aquí
a mi me gustan pegados al cuero
como en el rancho donde yo nací.

Las Pelonas

Los paños colorados
Los tengo aborrecidos
Ya hora las pelonas
Los usan de vestidos.
Las muchachas de S. Antonio
Son flojas pa'l metate
Quieren andar pelonas

Con sombreros de petate.
Se acabaron las pizcas,
Se acabó el algodón
Ya andan las pelonas
De puro vacilón.

Notes

1. U.S. Bureau of the Census, *Census of Population*: 1970. PC (2)-lD, Table 2, (Washington, D.C.: U.S. Government Printing Office, 1973), pp. 4-6.

2. "California Becoming 'Third World State,' Dymally Says," *Los Angeles Times*. June 20, 1977.

3. U.S. Bureau of the Census, *Census of Population*: 1970. PC (2)-1C, Table 1, (Washington, D.C.: U.S. Government Printing Office, 1973), pp. 1-6.

4. In selecting these three concepts of urbanization, I have been guided by the work of Eric E. Lampard, especially his essay "Urbanization and Social Change: On Broadening the Scope and Relevance of Urban History" in Oscar Handlin and John Burchard, eds. *The Historian and the City* (Cambridge: MIT-Harvard Press, 1963), pp. 225-247.

5. The "late arrival" thesis has been expressed by several scholars, including Arthur F. Corwin, "Mexican-American History: An Assessment," *Pacific Historical Review* 42 (August 1973): p. 3; and Marjorie Fallows, "The Mexican-American Laborers: A Different Drummer?" in Leonard Dinnerstein and Frederic C. Jaher, eds. *The Aliens:: A History of Ethnic Minorities in America* (New York: Meredith Corporation, 1970), p. 313. The success of labor organizer César Chávez as well as the publicity given to Reies López Tijerina of the New Mexico land grant movement has left the impression with many Americans that Chicanos are mainly a rural population.

6. Regional groupings by economists interested in regional growth make it difficult to accurately compare the Southwest--the states bordering Mexico--with other regions of the United States. For example, in Harvey S. Perloff et al., *Regions, Resources, and Economic Growth*, (Baltimore: The Johns Hopkins Press. 1960), California is included with Washington, Oregon, and Nevada in the Far West region, while Oklahoma is considered part of the Southwest region along with the states of Texas, Arizona, and New Mexico.

7. U.S. Bureau of the Census, *Fifteenth Census of the United States*: 1930. *Population. Volume I* (Washington, D.C.: Government Printing Office, 1931). pp. 18, 19, 131.

8. Perloff, *Regions*, p. 124.

9. See for example, Garet Garrett, "Los Angeles in Fact and Dream," *The Saturday Evening Post* (October, 1930), pp. 6-7, 134-144; and James H. Collins, "'Los Angeles Grows By a Formula," *Southern California Business* (September, 1933), pp. 18-19.

10. Mario Trinidad Garcia, "Obreros: The Mexican Workers of El Paso: 1880-1920," (Ph.D. dissertation, University of California, San Diego, 1975), pp. 10-17.

11. *Fifteenth Census of the United States: 1930. Population. Volume I.* Table 23, p. 67.

12. Max Sylvanus Handman, "The Mexican Immigrant in Texas," *Southwestern Political and Social Science Quarterly* (1926), p. 334.

13. David Ward, *Cities and Immigrants* (New York: Oxford University Press, 1971), p. 45.

14. For a more extended discussion of this city's development, see Federal Writers Project in Texas, *San Antonio: An Authoritative Guide to the City and Its Environs* (San Antonio: Clegg Company, 1938) and Charles Ramsdell, *San Antonio: A Historical and Pictorial Guide* (Austin: University of Texas Press, 1968).

15. Perloff, *Regions*, pp. 172-184. See also Harvey S. Perloff, *How a Region Grows: Area Development in the U.S. Economy* (New York: Committee for Economic Development, 1963), p. 48.

16. Perloff, *Regions*, p. 179.

17. Victor Clark, "Mexican Labor in The United States" U.S. Bureau of Labor Statistics, *Bulletin*, 78 (Sept., 1908), pp. 477-496, *passim.*

18. Paul S. Taylor, *An American-Mexican Frontier: Nueces County, Texas* (Chapel Hill: University of North Carolina Press, 1934), p. 100.

19. Robert N. McLean, "Mexican Workers in the United States," *Proceedings of the National Conference of Social Work* (1929), p. 534.

20. William John Knox, "The Economic Status of the Mexican Immigrant in San Antonio, Texas," (Master's thesis, University of Texas, Austin, 1927) pp. 29-30.

21. From Mario T. Garcia's "Obreros," p. 154.

22. Albert M. Camarillo, "The Making of A Chicano Community: A History of The Chicanos in Santa Barbara, California, 1810-1930," (Ph.D. dissertation, University of California, Los Angeles, 1975), p. 256.

23. Robert M. Fogelson, *The Fragmented Metropolis: Los Angeles 1850-1930*, (Cambridge: Harvard University Press, 1967), p. 122.

24. *Fifteenth Census of the United States: 1930. Population. Volume I*, Table 23.

25. Ricardo Romo, "Work and Restlessness: Occupational and Spatial Mobility among Mexicanos in Los Angeles, 1918-1928," *Pacific Historical Review* 46 (May 1977): 164-167.

26. California, *Mexicans in California: Report of C.C. Young's Mexican Fact-Finding Committee* (Sacramento: California State Printing Office, 1930), p. 82.

27. Computed from the U.S. Bureau of the Census, *Fifteenth Census of the United States: 1930. Population. Occupation* (Washington, D.C., 1932), pp. 86-90.

28. D.W. Meinig, *Southwest: Three Peoples in Geographical Change 1600-1970* (New York: Oxford University Press, 1971), p. 72.

29. Clark, "Mexican Labor," pp. 486 and 489.

30. Ward, *Cities*, p. 85.

31. William Lytle Schurz, *This New World* (New York: E.P. Dutton, 1964), p. 343.

32. John and LaRee Caughey, eds. *Los Angeles: Biography of A City* (Berkeley: University of California Press, 1976), p. 119.

33. Matthew Edel et al., "Urban Concentration and Deconcentration," in Amos H. Hawley and Vincent P. Rock, eds. *Metropolitan America* (New York: John Wiley, 1971), pp.130-132.

34. See for instance, John Emmanuel Kienle, "Housing Conditions Among The Mexican Population of Los Angeles," (Master's thesis, University of Southern California, 1912).

35. For evidence, see Bert Ira Van Gilder, "Sociological Aspects of Mexican Immigration to the United States," (Master's thesis, College of the Pacific, 1931), p. 62; Kiyoshi Uono, "The Factors Affecting the Geographical Aggregation and Dispersion of the Japanese Residences in the City of Los Angeles," (Master's thesis, University of Southern California, 1927), p. 140; and Mark Reisler, *By the Sweat of Their Brow: Mexican Immigrant Labor in the United States* (Westport, Conn: Greenwood Press, 1976), pp. 140-142.

36. Statement of H.G. Randall, secretary of Lynwood Chamber of Commerce, Los Angeles Chamber of Commerce Files, Box R330-979, ca. 1925, Los Angeles City Administration Library.

37. *El Heraldo De Mexico* (Los Angeles), July 1, 1922.

38. Ricardo Romo, "Mexican Workers in the City: Los Angeles, 1915-1930," (Ph.D. dissertation, University of California, Los Angeles, 1975), pp. 92.

39. *Fifteenth Census of the United States: 1930. Population. Volume I*, p. 108.

40. Elizabeth Broadbent, "The Distribution of Mexican Population in the United States," (Ph.D. dissertation, University of Chicago, 1941), Table 11, p. 72.

41. Garcia, "Obreros," p. 213.

42. Constantine Panunzio, *How Mexicans Earn and Live: A Study of The Income and Expenditures of One Hundred Mexican Families in San Diego, California* (Berkeley: University of California Publications in Economics, vol. 13, no. 1, 1933), p. 4.

43. Lee C. Harby, "Texas Types and Contrast," *Harper's Magazine*, July, 1890, p. 243.

44. For a good discussion of this general subject, see Larry S. Bourne, ed. *Internal Structure of the City* (New York: Oxford University Press, 1971).

45. U.S. Department of Commerce, Irene B. Taeuber and Conrad Taeuber, *People of The United States in the 20th Century: A 1960 Census Monograph* (Washington, D.C., Government Printing Office, 1971), p. 124.

46. Broadbent, "The Distribution of Mexican Population," Table 11.

47. *Fifteenth Census of the United States: 1930. Population. Volume II*, p. 65.

48. Max S. Handman, "San Antonio: The Old Capital City of Mexican Life and influence," *Survey*, May, 1931, p. 164; George I. Sanchez, *Forgotten People* (Albuquerque: University of New Mexico Press, 1940), p. 30; and *La Prensa De Los Angeles*, May 7, 1921.

49. *Fifteenth Census of the United States: 1930. Abstract of the Census*, Table 94, p. 179.

50. Leo Grebler, "Mexican Immigration to the United States: The Record and Its Implications." Advance Report 2, Mexican American Study Project (University of California, Los Angeles, 1966), Table 23, p. 104.

51. *Fifteenth Census of the United States: 1930. Population. Volume II*, pp. 225.

52. *Fifteenth Census of the United States: 1930. Population. Volume 1*, pp. 18-19.

53. Broadbent, "The Distribution of Mexican Population." Table 11.

54. *Fifteenth Census of the United States: 1930. Population. Volume II*, pp. 116-131.

55. Leonard Reissman, *The Urban Process: Cities in Industrial Society* (New York: The Free Press, 1970), p. 154.

56. Ernesto Galarza, Herman Gallegos, and Julian Samora, *Mexican-Americans in the Southwest* (Santa Barbara: McNally & Loftin Publishers, 1969), p. 22.

57. Galarza, et al., *Mexican-Americans*, p. 22.

58. Ernesto Galarza, *Barrio Boy: The Story of A Boy's Acculturation* (Notre Dame: University of Notre Dame Press, 1971), pp. 198-199.

59. Galarza, *Barrio Boy*, p. 204.

60. Ibid.

61. Manuel Gamio, *Mexican Immigration to the United States* (Chicago: University of Chicago Press, 1930), p. 132.

62. Evangeline Hymer, "Study of the Social Attitudes of Adult Mexican Immigrants in Los Angeles and Vicinity: 1923," (Master's thesis, University of Southern California, 1924), *Passim*, chapter ii.

63. Miguel David Tirado, "Mexican American Community Political Organization," *Aztlán* 1 (Spring 1970), pp. 55-56.

64. Garcia, "Obreros," p. 273.

65. Paul S. Taylor, *Mexican Labor in the United States: Chicago and the Calumet Region* (Berkeley: University of California Press, 1932), p. 193.

66. Data computed from 1918 marriage license applications of the City of Los Angeles. These records include the age, occupation, nativity, and religious affiliation of the groom and bride. Data is in the author's possession.

67. Constantine Panunzio, "Intermarriage in Los Angeles, 1924-33." *The American Journal of Sociology* 47 (March 1942), pp. 692-694.

68. Data computed from 1918 marriage license applications of the City Los Angeles. The data is taken from a sample of 406 marriage applications.

69. *Fifteenth Census of the United States: 1930. Population. Occupation.* pp. 86-90.

70. *Fifteenth Census of the United States: 1930. Population. Occupation*; Table 4 of "Color and Nativity of Gainful Workers" and Table 10 of "Occupations General Report."

71. Linna E. Bresette, *Mexicans in the United States: A Report of a Brief Survey to the National Catholic Welfare Conference* (Washington, D.C., 1929), p. 11.

72. Gamio, *Mexican Immigration*, p. 88.

73. Ibid., p. 89.

74. See, for example, John Bodnar, "Immigration and Modernization: The Case of Slavic Peasants in Industrial America," *Journal of Social History* 10 (Fall 1976). p. 60.

75. Fallows, "The Mexican-American Laborers," p. 313.

During the Great Depression, the United States government sponsored a forced repatriation campaign aimed at Mexicans. Using various rationale, including their alleged illegal status, growing unemployment rates in the United States and the general antipathy toward the Mexican immigrant, the Mexican became the object of a forced return to Mexico. Abraham Hoffman enhances our vision of this era by placing return movements within the context of repatriation generally and restrictionist campaigns directed toward Mexican immigrants.

Closing America's Back Door
Abraham Hoffman

Throughout American history there are many examples of people who moved or were moved from one place to another, either on a voluntary basis or under compulsion. In the eighteenth century the Acadians were forcibly removed from Port Royal by the British; after the American Revolution, Tory sympathizers lost possessions and property. As settlers moved across the North American continent, dozens of Indian tribes lost their lands and were placed on reservations often far removed from the land their ancestors had known. Negroes who experienced the beneficence of the American Colonization Society "returned" to Africa to found the nation of Liberia. Mormons who endured the hostility of their neighbors were finally compelled to seek refuge in a Zion to the West. As part of the post-Civil War movement which brought thousands of people across the continent, displaced veterans left bankrupt farms and plantations in their search for new opportunities.

Events in our recent past show that population movements, involuntary or voluntary in their causation, still occur. The most notorious involuntary movement in recent years was the relocation of the Japanese-American population of the United States during World War II. On the other hand, voluntary movements are much more subtle and less sensational than blatant violations of constitutional rights. An example of the voluntary type of movement is repatriation.

Repatriation means a return to one's homeland--more than a return--a sending back. Repatriations carried out at different times have had different meanings, tailored for the occasion. This is especially true when applied to immigrants from Mexico who returned to their homeland. Writers dealing with Mexican repatriation have sometimes found it necessary to precede the word with "voluntary" or "forced," with quotation marks to distinguish the catalyst.[1]

Mexicans were not the only immigrant ethnic group to undergo repatriation. Although little has been written on the subject, other immigrants volunteered to return to their countries of origin to a degree that can be surprising to anyone who assumes that immigration to the United States was the culmination of a one-way dream. As many as four million immigrants, chiefly Englishmen, Germans, Greeks, Italians, and Poles, indicated their intention of going back to their homelands in the first two decades of the twentieth century. Between 1908 and 1922, 3,416,735 people classified as "aliens whose permanent residence has been in the United States who intend to reside permanently abroad" left the country.[2]

Inducements to Repatriate

Many aspects of the movement of Mexicans southward matched the return of European immigrants in motivation and circumstance, though with additional factors that should be noted. The closeness of the Mexican border, the convenience of railroad connections, and the nomadic nature of employment offered to Mexicans, promoted a two-way traffic across the border, as did the Mexican government's periodic announcements of agrarian reform programs. The chance to return to Mexico with relative ease to demonstrate the skills acquired and the possessions obtained, or to spend or invest the wealth earned, all contributed to a significant flow of Mexicans back to Mexico in the years preceding the depression.

Prominent agriculturists publicized the return of Mexicans to Mexico as part of the "cycle of migration" that occurred in a time of prosperity. Organized labor and opponents of unrestricted immigration, who noted the growth of the immigrant Mexican population in the United States, contested this viewpoint. The challenge of restrictionists affected the cycle of migration for Mexicans entering as well as leaving the United States. The fact that emigration from Mexico was abruptly reduced *before* the failure of the stock market deserves notice. Before the advent of the depression in 1929, attempts had been made to limit the number of Mexicans, particularly those classified as laborers, who were entering the United States.

Restrictionist Debates

Several recent studies have placed the movement for immigration restriction into historical perspective. Although the issue of a quota for Mexican immigration has been studied, it has not been described in any great detail. John Higham's *Strangers in the Land*, a study of American nativism from 1860 to 1925, presented a highly discerning examination of immigration and its restriction, but his book was concerned chiefly with immigration from Europe. Other books that included sections on immigration restriction for Mexico concentrated for the most part on congressional debates.[3] Nevertheless, a rich literature exists beyond 1924 that carries the argument on restriction to new heights (or depths) of polemical conviction, directed towards Mexicans.

Restrictionists included small farmers, progressives, labor unions, eugenicists, and racists, while large-scale growers of sugar beets, cotton, and vegetables, allied with railroads, chambers of commerce, and business associations generally favored unrestricted immigration. Both factions were prolific in their writings and verbose in their speeches, and both factions had politicians in their camps.

Passage of the Quota Act of 1924 had sealed off immigration from sections of Europe and Asia, but immigration from countries in the Western Hemisphere was not included in the law. With Mexico as the primary target, the American Federation of Labor, local governments with aliens on their relief rolls, and small farmers who felt they could not compete with growers who hired cheap Mexican labor, clamored to plug the hole in the law. They found a spokesman for their viewpoint in the House of Representatives, where John C. Box, a Democrat from east Texas, introduced one bill after another in successive sessions seeking to amend the Quota Act, only to see them die repeatedly in committee.

Box's initial effort was aired before the House Committee on Immigration and Naturalization during January and February 1926, but his bill ran into heavy opposition. Typical of the lobbyists who opposed immigration restriction was Samuel Parker Frisselle, a farmer owning five thousand acres of land in California. Frisselle's credentials included membership in the Fresno Chamber of Commerce, the California Development Association, and the California Federated Farm Bureau, all opposed to restriction. Frisselle declared that if the Box bill became law it would mean the end of agricultural development in the West. Crops grown there required large numbers of laborers to harvest them; white men would not or could not do the work, and the only source of labor came from Mexico.

Frisselle denied the existence of any established Mexican population in the San Joaquin Valley, believed the schools sufficient for the Mexican children, and, to questions regarding figures or statistics about the numbers of Mexicans, pleaded ignorance except to repeat that the Mexicans were "a transient population." He insisted, "We must have labor; the Mexican seems to be the only available source of supply, and we appeal to you to help us in the matter, imposing upon California the least possible burden."[4]

Other men took the stand to plead for unrestricted immigrant labor: farmers from Minnesota, Arizona, Texas, and other states asserted the lack of desire by white men to do farm laborer work, and their dependence upon the Mexican. In addition, by drafting the bill to apply to all countries in the Western Hemisphere, the bill's authors invited even more arguments against its passage. Box's first attempt never got out of committee.

At his earliest opportunity Congressman Box reintroduced the bill, amid speculation on the chances of the bill's being passed, or even heard. The first hearing date was set for 1 February 1928, in the Senate committee, and the first House date was three weeks after that.

Long before this, however, lobbyists favoring unrestricted Mexican immigration laid plans to meet the challenge. On 5 October 1927, some three dozen men met in Los Angeles under the auspices of the Los Angeles Chamber of Commerce. Many members of southwestern business communities, representing agriculture, railroads, and industry, were present. So were Senator Samuel Shortridge and Congressman Joe Crail of California. Unanimous in their opposition to the latest Box bill, the group voted its sentiments into writing: "The agricultural interests through the border and mountain states are a unit opposing this bill, realizing that it will interrupt and embarrass agricultural production throughout these states." The men pledged that their "whole endeavor, therefore, should be to kill it if possible." A conference of businessmen at El Paso held in November strongly upheld this position.

Agitation on both sides developed as the hearing dates neared. George P. Clements, manager of the chamber's department of agriculture, busily drafted publicity, sending mimeographed copies of antirestriction propaganda to congressmen and senators. He stressed the point that since the Mexican was an alien he could be deported, whereas Negroes, Filipinos, and Puerto Ricans, if brought into the Southwest to do agricultural work, would be there to stay.

The proponents of restriction also made their preparations. The *Saturday Evening Post*, a strong partisan of restriction, timed a series of articles by novelist Kenneth L. Roberts to appear in January, February, and March of 1928, during the hearings in Washington. Roberts reviewed not only the recent history of immigration but also the rise of southwestern agriculture, and questioned whether "the economic value in the Southwest's proposal to provide hypothetical profits for some farmers and manufacturers in 1928" was worth "the expense of saddling all future Americans with a dismal and distressing race problem." *The Post* also strongly editorialized on 7 January 1928, that "Every consideration of prudence and sound policy indicates that Mexican immigration must be put under quota restrictions."

Meanwhile in Washington, the Senate opened its Hearings on Restriction of Western Hemisphere Immigration on 1 February 1928, with Congressman Box's counterpart, Senator William J. Harris of Georgia, introducing S. 1437, "A Bill to Subject Certain Immigrants, Born in Countries of the Western Hemisphere, to the Quota under the Immigration Laws," and several related bills.

Lobbyists representing agricultural interests in California, Arizona, Texas, New Mexico, Idaho, Wyoming, and Colorado, in addition to lobbyists from the railroad, cattle, and mining interests, were present. Only the Department of Labor favored the bill; the Departments of State, Agriculture, and Interior all presented spokesmen against it. Chester B. Moore of the Vegetable Growers of Imperial Valley and Ralph H. Taylor, executive secretary of the Agricultural Legislative Committee of California, representing, as Moore later put it, "practically every producing Cooperative Association in California and representing about 175,000 farmers, orchardists, grape growers, milk and poultry producers," led the campaign against restriction.

The opposition to the bills proved more than the restrictionist could handle. Although both Moore and Taylor were interrupted any number of times by House or Senate committee members, their testimony and the statements of the other lobbyists carried the day. In 1928 the bills again did not get out of committee. On 2 April 1928, lobbyist Moore wrote back to the Imperial Valley growers, expressing his jubilation at the victory:

We were informed on our arrival in Washington that our efforts to stop legislation at this session of Congress would prove useless, and we felt the Immigration Committees were going to vote the bills out. Due to the splendid cooperation of the various states and industries interested in opposition to such legislation, we were able to make considerable impression on the Committees.

The controversy continued as proponents and opponents of restricting Mexican immigration delivered speeches, wrote articles, and petitioned their representatives in state and federal government. Before such groups as the Pasadena Women's Civic League and later the Interdenominational Council in Spanish Speaking Work, meeting at Pomona College in November 1928, Clements warned of the dangers inherent in importing the "Porto Rican Negro" for field work, preferring the "man who had no idea of becoming a citizen or a menace," the Mexican. "Should the immigration quota be applied to Mexico?" he asked his audience, and followed it with his emphatic answer: "Most assuredly NOT!"

Each side filled magazines with articles that upheld its position while denouncing the other.[5] In the war of print the restrictionists predominated, as more articles favoring restriction appeared than did those which opposed it. The *Saturday Evening Post*, with its huge circulation totalling over 2.7 million, frequently editorialized against Mexican immigration. "Readers in the Southwest continue to bombard us with requests that we redouble our efforts to make Congress see the imperative necessity for putting Mexican immigration upon a quota basis, or for restricting it sharply by other means," went a typical example in the 22 June 1929 issue.

Some reasons for restrictions were ingenious. One professor at the University of California, S. J. Holmes, wrote in the May 1929 issue of *North American Review* that he believed the present *illegal* migration sufficient to meet American labor needs and reason enough why the legal entries should be restricted. Other writers continued to warn of the dangers of miscegenation, or of an inundation of people who could not be assimilated.[6] Still others repeated economic arguments and debated the relative need for and benefit from Mexican labor.[7] The American Federation of Labor, on the state and national level, annually passed resolutions calling for restriction of Mexican immigration, since Mexican workers so often proceeded from agricultural to nonagricultural occupations, and were sometimes employed as strikebreakers, as had happened during the 1919 steel strike.

The advent of the depression brought a new urgency to both factions. In May 1930, during the second session of the Seventy-first Congress, Box again entered his proposals, this time in two bills. And again, they failed to come to the House floor. A joint resolution issued in the third session proposed a total restriction on *all* immigrants for two years. This resolution passed the House but failed to clear the Senate.[8]

Renewed Enforcement

Further attempts at restriction through legislation were rendered superfluous by an important new development: Mexican laborers were no longer entering the United States. The victory that proponents of restriction finally achieved did not come to them by act of Congress. While restrictionist attempts to secure a quota for Mexico were defeated, a partial success was achieved when consular officers, on orders from the U.S. State Department, began enforcing provisions of the Immigration Act of 1917 which in effect denied entry to most Mexicans who applied for visas. At the same time, Congress passed a law making illegal entry a punishable crime.

President Hoover had endorsed these measures as a way of solving the problem without the passage of restriction legislation that might be insulting to the government of Mexico. These moves indicated that the years of lax enforcement of the immigration laws on the United States' southern border were coming to an end.

The 1917 Immigration Act had excluded illiterates and had required payment of an eight-dollar head tax. Companies and agriculturists had once evaded these requirements by securing exemptions, but by the late 1920s the reception for Mexican immigrants at the border stations had changed considerably. Lax enforcement had allowed thousands of Mexicans to enter illegally. Mexicans who had lacked the eight dollars--and after 1924, eighteen dollars, with the imposition of a ten dollar visa fee--or for one reason or another had entered without applying through standard procedures, constituted a sizable if unknown quantity of Mexicans in the United States. There were also Mexicans living north of the border whose residence dated back to a time that preceded any regulations on border crossing procedure. "It is difficult, in fact impossible," stated the commissioner general of immigration in 1923, "to measure the illegal influx of Mexicans over the border, but everyone agrees that it is quite large."[9]

Besides the illegal entry of Mexicans, the Bureau of Immigration had to contend with the smuggling of Chinese, Japanese, and European aliens over the Mexican border, and French Canadians over the northern border. At this time of heavy border traffic, "bootlegging" came to refer to the smuggling of aliens as well as liquor.

The Border Patrol

No force existed to combat the widespread illegal entry until 1925, when Congress appropriated a million dollars for the creation of the Border Patrol. Handicapped at first by lack of uniforms, inadequate and unqualified personnel, and a high turnover rate, the Border Patrol, nevertheless, soon developed high standards of efficiency and morale. At first the patrol lacked sufficient officers and equipment; areas which required attention twenty-four hours a day were covered for eight at the most, if at all.

In 1926, with 472 men in the Border Patrol, Commissioner General of Immigration Harry E. Hull requested a force of 660; in 1927, with the force grown to 632 employees, he asked for at least 1,000. By mid-1928 the Border Patrol numbered 781 employees, of whom 700 were patrol inspectors. The service attracted veterans and men with a sense of dedication. By 1930 the Border Patrol had achieved a reputation for integrity and efficiency, with both its personnel and its appropriation almost double their original size.[10]

The work was dangerous. In the seven years following its creation, the Border Patrol captured over one hundred thousand illegal aliens, and over twenty-six hundred smugglers who had attempted to bring the aliens over the border. Of fifteen men killed while serving the Border Patrol, twelve met their deaths along the Mexican Border.[11] Despite the impressive record that was created in so short a time, the Border Patrol probably deterred few aliens from crossing illegally during the period when it lacked funds and personnel. Yet the rapidly expanding operations of the patrol helped serve notice that the United States intended to maintain the integrity of its borders.

Visa Refusals

A second key factor in the administrative restriction of Mexican immigration lay in the instructions issued to United States consular officers. Unlike the lax enforcement of earlier years, consular officers beginning in August 1928 denied visas to most Mexicans desiring entry into the United States. Three basic reasons were used as standards for rejection. The first was illiteracy; the second, a rigid interpretation of the "LPC"--the liable to become a public charge provision of the 1917 Immigration Act. If the consul decided that a visa applicant might become indigent in the United States the visa was refused, even if the applicant possessed funds at the time of his interview with the consul. The third reason for refusal centered on the issue of contract labor and placed the applicant in a dilemma. If he indicated an advance commitment for employment in the United States, his visa could be denied on the grounds that the commitment violated the provision forbidding the entry of contract labor (though following American entry into World War I this rule had often been waived); if he kept such a commitment a secret, his application might be denied anyway, with the consul invoking the LPC provision.

The effect of this new policy on legal entries was striking, as shown by Vice Consul E. F. Drumwright's report submitted to the State Department on 4 September 1931. Between 1923 and 1929 an average of 62,000 Mexicans a year had legally entered the United States. In the year the new visa policy was put into effect, the figure dropped to 40,013; and for the fiscal year ending 30 June 1930, the number had been cut to 11,801.

Between 1 July 1930, and 30 June 1931, only 2,457 Mexican immigrants were granted visas, a reduction of 94 percent from the 1929 figure.

More significantly, after March 1930 no visas at all were issued to Mexicans who were common laborers, unless they had resided previously in the United States; and 40 Percent of the visas granted went to Mexicans who did not represent new immigration, but included people who were regularizing an illegal status or had lived in the United States previously as a legally entered alien.

Thus a border patrol increasing in size and efficiency, coupled with a strict policy on visa applications, provided a double deterrence to Mexicans who sought employment in the United States. Furthermore, according to the Act of 4 March 1929, aliens who entered the United States by illegal means subsequent to that date were guilty of a misdemeanor punishable by a year in prison or a fine up to one thousand dollars. Under the same act, the attempted return of a previously deported alien was a felony charge.[12]

As a result of these changes in policy, there was a brief period before the stock market crash during which Mexican labor was in short supply. Mexican migrant workers in California's Imperial Valley conducted a brief but unsuccessful strike for better working conditions and wages in May 1928. Texas, having served for years as a huge labor reservoir for other states to draw upon, in 1929 passed a law which placed a tax on companies which sought to recruit workers from within her boundaries.

The Great Depression

The public debate over a quota for Mexico reached its zenith at the end of the decade. As consular officers asserted that their scrutiny of visa applications had curtailed immigration, the Border Patrol continued to guard the boundaries with horses and automobiles. While Congressman Box and the restrictionist pursued their goal of a quota for Western Hemisphere countries, the stock market began its downward spiral in the autumn of 1929. The United States, accompanied by the rest of the world, entered the Great Depression.

Mexican workers in the United States were among the first to be dismissed from their jobs. During the first year of the depression, thousands of Mexicans were compelled to evaluate the position, achievements, and status they had attained by living and working in the United States. The limited employment opportunities, and the nature of the work offered to Mexicans, have already been noted. Working in the fields, Mexicans performed backbreaking tasks for their American employers. The seasonal nature of agricultural work made earning an adequate income an uncertain possibility. Growers expected Mexicans to answer their calls for labor and to put in a ten-hour day. Even in nonagricultural occupations, Mexicans earned low pay for long hours of work, in the face of the enmity of labor unions and small farmers.

Yet the differential in purchasing power made the sacrifices worthwhile. Tied to

Mexico with bonds of birth, blood, and loyalty, many Mexicans spent years in the United States, periodically sending money back to their families and relatives in Mexico. In 1920, almost $9 million in postal money orders were remitted to Mexico; even during the agricultural depression of 1921, $4.5 million were sent. In 1928, before the depression, over $14 million in money orders were mailed back to Mexico. Individual amounts varied; some Mexicans remitted the full amount allowed by the post office, a limit of 207.25 pesos. Others might send as little as half a peso; still others sent nothing. Although some restrictionists claimed these remittances constituted a net loss to the United States, it was also pointed out that American industry and agriculture had benefitted greatly from the labor which the Mexicans performed for their earnings.[13]

Even as the Mexican immigrant had made his way to work in sugar beet fields and steel mills, his presence had provoked argument and hostility. In an age when neither the United States nor Mexico provided any meaningful supervision for laborers recruited by large companies, the Mexican worker might find himself stranded in a town whose mines had closed, or laid off during a slack period in railroad maintenance or harvesting. When this occurred, Anglo Americans were quick to complain about the presence of Mexicans on local relief rolls.

Where the English-speaking community on occasion offered active assistance, a lack of mutual understanding could occur. For example, in the spring of 1921, a period of unemployment in Fort Worth, Texas, the local Red Cross chapter noticed a large number of Mexican men in the bread lines. Anxious to do the right thing, the Red Cross offered beans to the Mexicans; unfortunately, since the Mexicans were mostly young single men, they were unable and unwilling to cook the beans, which had been given to them raw. The "bean line" was discontinued.

Some injustices and unfair practices were too much for a "docile Mexican" to tolerate. Occasionally remedies were available. California's State Commission of Immigration and Housing heard complaints from Mexicans regarding violations of contracts, fraud, interpretation of immigration laws, and wage disputes. The commission's complaint department reported that Mexicans more than any other nationality used its services, possibly because its clients could not afford to hire an attorney.

Mexico Beckons

The thought of returning to the homeland was apparently never far from the minds of most first generation Mexican immigrants. A return home prior to the depression meant short-term residents leaving after a season or two, or Mexicans who had been in the United States for years returning with material possessions and savings.

While the Mexican government endorsed a policy of repatriation from the time of Alvaro Obregón through the 1930s, the problems of Mexican politics prevented any organized program of repatriation from becoming fully implemented. Progress was made, however, in creating irrigation projects and constructing reservoirs. Projects in the states of Coahuila, Aguascalientes, Durango, Hidalgo, Chihuahua, Sonora, and elsewhere promised a revitalization of Mexican agriculture in the late 1920s and early 1930s.

Mexicans living in the United States were frequently invited to take part in the development of farmland in these projects. Announcements of both private and government-owned lands in Mexico being opened for purposes of agricultural development were made known to Mexicans in the United States through their local consulates. Although mention was occasionally made of donating land to destitute Mexicans who returned from the United States, most land offers required capital either for purchase or rental. An investment in seed, tools, and other necessities for farming meant that only Mexicans who were financially prepared to do so could accept the Mexican land offers of the 1920s.

Too often, however, American welfare agencies accepted these offers of land and employment at more than their face value. The idea that Mexicans were leaving the United States to partake of Mexico's offers of land became a rationale in which the departure was a positive act rather than one of possible embarrassment for welfare officials.

The movement of Mexicans southward was greatly accelerated by the depression. The first repatriates to return to Mexico during the winter 1929-1930 were not generally destitute, as can be seen by the many reports of *repatriados* returning with material possessions such as automobiles and furniture. Word of possible location on an agricultural colony established for repatriates by the Mexican government, desire to see family and relatives, the prospect of purchasing land in the homeland with money earned in the United States, and the Mexican government's periodic offer to indigents of free railroad transportation from the border to the interior were all factors in a Mexican immigrant's decision to return to Mexico.

The increased traffic southward was duly noted by the American consuls in the months following the crash and ensuing depression. Consul General William Dawson reported to the State Department in February 1930 that "over five thousand Mexicans, most of them possessed of some means," were gathered around San Antonio, Texas, and "preparing to return." The consul at Ciudad Juárez, W. P. Blocker, learned in August 1930 that the Mexican Migration Service had announced that a special train would deliver two thousand people at a time from the border to the interior of Mexico. This was the second such train in ten months, and it relieved Ciudad Juárez of an excess of population.

A year after the beginning of the depression, the numbers passing through the border stations were still on the increase. Robert Frazer, Dawson's successor as consul general, estimated that almost twenty-seven hundred repatriates had crossed through Nuevo Laredo in the first fifteen days of December 1930. With the start of 1931, consular dispatches continued to describe a torrent of people passing through their border stations, an amalgam of *repatriado* and deportee, with a growing percentage of them penniless and hungry. Ciudad Juárez's municipal government was feeding two hundred people a day. On a single day, 9 January 1931, eight hundred repatriates were counted entering Mexico through the ports of Nogales and Nuevo Laredo, divided among some two hundred automobiles.[14] Mexican border stations were swamped, and where an occasional special train had been sent to Ciudad Juárez or Nogales, the Mexican government now found it necessary to provide transportation on at least a weekly basis.

The American consul at Nuevo Laredo, R. F. Boyce, made a detailed analysis of the repatriates passing through his station and submitted his report to the State Department on 8 January 1931. He found Mexicans returning from a wide area in the United States, with Mexicans from Texas predominating, as might be expected from his location. Few of the repatriates were recording their departure with the American authorities, leading the consul to believe that "at least half and perhaps more of these repatriates were illegally in the United States." It may also have been that the repatriates did not expect to return, but planned on remaining in Mexico longer than six months. The consul observed that many *repatriados* were leaving "after many years residence in the United States. Nothing but an acute unemployment crisis could have forced them out of the United States. Nearly all have been without employment for several months and have come to Mexico because they see no indication of better conditions in the near future."

In fact, conditions were about to worsen considerably for the many thousands of Mexican immigrants who had not yet considered the idea of repatriation. Viewing the large number of aliens in the United States in a time of depression, the United States government commenced an active drive on aliens living illegally in the United States. While the federal government aimed its campaign at aliens in general, Mexican aliens--those in the country legally as well as those who were deportable--were to find themselves prime targets for the Department of Labor's Bureau of Immigration.

Notes

Unless otherwise noted, material in this chapter is from General Records of the Department of State, Record Group 59, National Archives, Washington, D.C.; and the George P. Clements Papers, bundle 7, box 62, Department of Special Collections, University of California, Los Angeles, California.

1. Norman D. Humphrey, "Mexican Repatriation from Michigan," *Social Service Review* 15 (September 1941): 497; Samuel E. Wood, "California Migrants," *Sociology and Social Research* 24 (January-February 1940): 253; Donald Young, *Research Memorandum on Minority Peoples in the Depression,* pp. 42-43.

2. Saloutos, *They Remember America,* p. vii. U.S., Department of Labor, Bureau of Immigration, *Annual Report of the Commissioner General of Immigration,* 1923, p. 12. A fascinating study of the Back-to-Africa Movement between 1890 and 1910 has been

written by Edwin S. Redkey, *Black Exodus: Black Nationalist and Back-to-Africa Movements, 1890-1910* (New Haven, 1969).

3. Maldwyn Allen Jones, *American Immigration*, pp. 290-93; Robert A. Divine, *American Immigration Policy, 1924-1952*, pp. 52-68.

4. U.S., Congress, House, Committee Immigration and Naturalization, *Hearings on Seasonal Agricultural Laborers from Mexico*, 69th Cong., 1st sess., 1925-1926, pp. 4-27, *passim.*

5. The antirestrictionist article by George Marvin, "Monkey Wrenches In Mexican Machinery," *Independent*, 14 April 1928, pp. 350-52, was rebutted by Richard L. Strout, "A Fence for the Rio Grande," *Indepdt.*, 2 June 1928, pp. 518-20. The pro-restriction articles by Kenneth L. Roberts in *Saturday Evening Post* were disputed by Charles C. Teague, president of the California Fruit Grower's Exchange, in "A Statement on Mexican Immigration," *Sat. Eve. Post,* 10 March 1928, pp. 169-70. Carleton Beals, "Mexico and the Harris Bill," *Nation*, 9 July 1930, pp. 51-52, also opposed a quota for Mexico.

6. C. M. Goethe, "Other Aspects of the Problem," *Current History* 28 (August 1928): 766-68; idem, "Peons Need Not Apply," *World's Work* 59 (November 1930): 47-48; Remsen Crawford, "The Menace of Mexican Immigration," *Cur. Hist.* 31 (February 1930): 902-907; Chester Rowell, "Why Make Mexico an Exception?" *Survey*, 1 May 1931, p. 180.

7. Roy L. Garis, "The Mexicanization of American Business," *Saturday Evening Post*, 8 February 1930, p. 46; idem, "The Mexican Invasion," *ibid.*, 19 April 1930, pp. 43-44; Garet Garrett, "Government by Tumult," *ibid.*, 16 March 1930, pp. 43-44; Garet Garrett, "Government by Tumult," *ibid.*, 16 March 1929, pp. 14-15; Jay S. Stowell, "The Danger of Unrestricted Mexican Immigration," *Current History* 28 (August 1928): 763-66. Some more objectively written articles were McLean, "A Dyke Against Mexicans," *New Republic*, 14 August 1929, pp. 334-37; Gamio, "Migration and Planning," *Survey*, 1 May 1931, p.174; Bogardus, "The Mexican Immigrant and the Quota," *Sociology and Social Research* 12 (March-April 1928): 371-78; Thomson, "What of the Bracero?" *Survey*, 1 June 1925, pp. 290-91; Thomson, "Restriction of Mexican Immigration," *Journal of Applied Sociology* 11 (July-August 1927): 574-78; Glenn E. Hoover, "Our Mexican Immigrants," *Foreign Affairs* 8 (October 1929): 99-107; and Louis Bloch, "Facts about Mexican Immigration Before and Since the Quota Restriction Laws," *American Statistical Association Journal* 24 (March 1929): 50-60. See also the brief article by Galarza, "Without Benefit of Lobby," *Survey*, 1 May 1931, p. 181.

8. U.S., Congress, House, *Congressional Record*, 71st Cong., 3d sess., 1931, 74-74, pt. 7: 6744.

9. Bureau of Immigration, *Annual Report, 1923*, pp. 16-19.

10. *Ibid., 1925*, pp. 14-21; *1926*, pp. 16-18; *ibid., 1927*, pp. 16-19; *ibid., 1930*, pp. 34-44.

11. *Ibid., 1930*, p. 41; *ibid., 1931*, p. 60.

12. U.S., *Statutes at Large*, vol. 45, pt. I, chap 690, pp. 1551-52; editorial in *Nation*, 24

September 1930, pp. 309-10.

13. Gamio, *Quantitative Estimate, and Mexican Immigration to the U.S.*, pp. 30-31.

14. *La Opinión* (Los Angeles), 10 Jan 1931. See also issues of 11, 12, 13, 15, 19, 20, and 21 Jan. 1931.

Mario García's study of the Asociación Nacional México-Americana offers a view of the issues and concerns of the Mexican American generation. Operating at a time of severe political repression, ANMA nonetheless militantly advocated for political unity among Mexican Americans with a strong working-class and union base. In many ways ANMA advocated political positions which challenged more conservative elements in their own community and American society in general. García's study also reveals striking similarities with Chicano goals two decades later.

Mexican American Labor and the Left: The Asociación Nacional México-Americana, 1949-1954

Mario T. García

I

The early development of the study of Chicano history during the late 1960s and early 1970s was accompanied by a strong emphasis on a radical tradition. Militant Chicano historians, as well as those in other disciplines, looked to a radical past to legitimize the emergence of a contemporary Chicano protest movement. Juan Gómez-Quiñones and other writers in *Aztlán,* for example, stressed the involvement of Mexican workers in labor conflicts during the early 20th century. In a study by Camarillo and Castillo, so-called "Mexican bandits" in 19th century California and elsewhere became "social bandits," and Chicano cultural heroes, such as Gregorio Cortez, were rediscovered in the early work of Américo Paredes. Gómez-Quiñones integrated the anarcho-syndicalist movement of Ricardo Flores Magón, especially during the Magonista exile in southern California at the time of the Mexican Revolution, into the Chicano radical tradition. In Rodolfo Acuña's *Occupied America,* Chicanos exemplified a colonized people fighting to liberate themselves from a system of internal colonialism. Such studies and others created an inspirational, albeit questionable, interpretation that assumed a direct link between the radicals of the past and those of the present.[1]

This attraction to a radical tradition is understandable given the militant temper of the late 1960s and early 1970s. Furthermore, what these studies lacked in original research was offset by a positive new orientation stressing, as anthropologist Octavio Romano urged in his classic essays in *El Grito* in 1967 and 1968, that Chicanos not only had a history, but one steeped in action and protest. Rather than being passive and

219

accommodating, Chicanos struggled for freedom.[2]

Since the appearance of these early studies over 10 years ago, we have witnessed a more sophisticated Chicano historiography influenced by the radical tradition but also moderating it. Monographs such as those by Martínez, Camarillo, Griswold del Castillo, de León, Romo, and Balderrama, with their focus on Mexican communities in the United States involving generational, class, political, and cultural variables, suggest that these communities rather than being unidimensional, as proposed by the radical tradition, have instead been multidimensional. They have displayed various political tendencies and ideologies, including radicalism, liberalism, and conservatism. Such monographs further suggest the differences, as well as the similarities, from one historical period to another, something avoided by the radical tradition. It is the emergence of such diversity that has given recent Chicano historiography a distinct quality.[3]

Radicalism in the Chicano experience is one aspect of this diversity. That Chicanos have participated in radical and left movements in this country is indisputable. Besides the earlier works cited, other, more recent studies reveal this history. Emilio Zamora, for one, has noted the involvement of some Mexican Americans in Socialist Party activities in Texas. Victor Nelson-Cisneros and Vicki Ruiz have discovered that Mexican Americans, many of them women, had both rank-and-file and leadership roles in United Cannery, Packing, and Agricultural Workers of America (UCAPAWA). This leftist union, with a Communist Party orientation, successfully organized in the agricultural and canning industries of the Southwest during the 1930s and 1940s. Cletus Daniel, in the best study on agricultural radicalism in California, has similarly examined the relationship between the Communist party and Mexican farmworkers. Douglas Monroy and Luis Arroyo have shown Mexican American activity in Los Angeles industrial unions that were led or strongly influenced by the Communist Party. And Acuña in his revised version of *Occupied America* has also introduced new information concerning Mexican American radical groups.[4] Yet although such research underscores a radical tradition, it needs to be complemented by an understanding that radicalism represents only one stratum in the ideological and political spectrum within Mexican communities in the United States.

II

Although the involvement of Mexican Americans in leftist unions and political organizations such as the Communist Party is beginning to be documented, almost nothing is known about specific, left-oriented Mexican American associations. This study is an attempt to fill this gap and concerns the Asociación Nacional México-Americana (ANMA), which arose during the Cold War years of the 1940s and early 1950s, a period Acuña labels "the decade of defense" for Mexican Americans.[5]

ANMA was indirectly organized by the International Union of Mine, Mill, and Smelter Workers through its national headquarters in Denver, Colorado. This militant and progressive union traced its origins to the Western Federation of Miners and by the 1940s had organized many of the major mining and smelting regions of the West and Southwest. Some of its national officers suffered political persecution, especially during the 1950s, as alleged Communists. The CIO expelled the Union in 1950, along with several other progressive unions, on the charge of being Communist-dominated.[6] In New Mexico and Arizona, as well as in El Paso, the Mine, Mill, and Smelter union members consisted almost exclusively of Mexican Americans and Mexican nationals. The three El Paso locals, for example, by the early 1950s contained over 2,000 workers, almost all of Mexican descent, led by Mexican American officers. With such an ethnic composition, it appears that the International Union believed that ANMA could function as its political arm in the Mexican American communities of the Southwest.

Fifty delegates organized ANMA at a two-day meeting in Phoenix on February 12 and 13, 1949. They came, according to an ANMA history, from the sugar beet fields of Colorado, from the factories of Los Angeles, from the mines of New Mexico, and from the cotton fields of Arizona and Texas. They had assembled to establish an organization that would provide a "new voice" for Mexicans north of the border. ANMA was to represent "a national association for the protection of the civil, economic, and political rights of the Mexican people in the United States as well as for the expansion of their education, culture, and progress."[7] Any person or organization, regardless of citizenship, nationality, color, religion, or political affiliation, that was interested in the progress of "el pueblo mexicano," could join ANMA. These requirements contrasted with those of middle-class-oriented Mexican American organizations such as LULAC, which insisted on American citizenship for membership. ANMA was to be governed by its annual national convention and administered by an executive committee, a national committee, and a national office. The executive officer, a national president, would preside over the national convention and the meetings of both the executive and national committees.[8]

The objective conditions for the founding of ANMA are to be found in the particular plight of Mexican Americans and Mexican nationals during the postwar period. Despite certain economic improvements and gains in political and civil rights, Mexicans in the United States still represented, according to ANMA, second-class citizens. ANMA recognized that racial minorities such as Mexicans and Blacks received special treatment in the form of greater economic insecurities, lower wages, inferior education, and suffered more than whites from recent rollbacks of New Deal welfare services. "What is even worse," ANMA proclaimed in 1952, "the Mexican people are objects of an accelerated program of discrimination, deportations, physical assaults, police brutality, and, at times, murder." In addition, they continued to be exposed to cultural discrimination and stereotyping as lazy, passive, and inferior people.[9]

ANMA concluded that the ascendance of political right-wing reaction in the country, made it imperative to organize all Mexicans into a national association for ethnic self-defense. This was no time for distinctions among the four to five million people of

Mexican descent. ". . . (W)e are all united by the chord of language, culture, and lifestyle," ANMA stressed.[10] Believing that earlier attempts at organizing Mexicans had been characterized by false leaders and by betrayals, ANMA emphasized that Mexicans, despite standard stereotypes, could in fact be organized. "We should learn the lesson that labor unions learned when they started to organize," one ANMA leader noted, "that strength lies in unity."[11] ANMA hoped to be the vehicle for such unity especially among workers, intellectuals, youth, and professionals.[12]

In a period of three years, ANMA sponsored two national conventions: its founding convention in Los Angeles on October 14 and 15, 1950, and another in El Paso on July 12 and 13, 1952. Local chapters also sprang up in six regions: Arizona, northern California, southern California, Colorado, New Mexico, and Texas. These locals included Phoenix, Tucson, East Los Angeles, Denver, Albuquerque, El Paso, San Antonio, and Chicago. ANMA claimed further contacts in Utah, New York, San Diego. and Dallas. In 1950 it reported a membership of 4,000 in more than 30 locals.[13]

Ideologically, ANMA voiced radical views within the context of Mexican American politics. Its interpretation of Mexican American history, for example, had a different emphasis from that of LULAC. Whereas LULAC, through the influence of historians such as Carlos Castañeda, concentrated on the Hispanic roots in the Southwest as a way of convincing Anglos of the integral role Hispanics had played in American history and of their cultural contributions; ANMA focused on the conquest of northern Mexico by the United States in the mid-19th century. For ANMA, Mexican American history had begun in violence, conquest, and the subjugation of the resident Mexican population.

Although not propounding what years later would be referred to as "internal colonialism," ANMA did emphasize the role of conquest. Because Mexicans had been annexed through force rather than voluntarily joining the United States, the Southwest possessed a culture and tradition quite different from the rest of the country. These differences had been recognized by the Treaty of Guadalupe Hidalgo ending the Mexican War in 1848 and promising to protect Mexicans' distinct culture and heritage. These guarantees, however, had not been fulfilled; arriving Anglos abused the Mexicans' culture, language, political rights, and economic holdings. Consequently, since 1848 Mexican Americans had been treated as an underclass of American citizens.

Such a legacy, moreover, continued into the 20th century when Southwestern economic concerns imported and exploited thousands of Mexican immigrant workers. Important as cheap labor during boom times, Mexicans also served as surplus labor and during the depressed 1930s faced unemployment, deportations. and forced repatriations. This historical experience, according to ANMA, had created much adversity for Mexicans in the United States. "This state of conditions has served to intimidate and oppress the Mexican worker throughout the Southwest," it concluded, "to force the Mexican to accept a low standard of life due to such exploitation and to impose on all other workers, especially in agriculture, to accept low wages due to the competition of Mexican labor."[14]

In addition, unlike other Mexican American civil rights organizations that stressed unity through citizenship as well as ethnic ties, ANMA emphasized unity through the fundamental working class nature of the Mexican population in the United States. Ninety-five percent of Mexicans north of the border were workers and ANMA believed this condition to be not only objective grounds for organization, but proof of the inescapable bonds between Mexican Americans and the union movement. Alfredo C. Montoya, ANMA's first president and an officer of the Mine, Mill, and Smelter Workers, observed in 1950 that recent gains by Mexican workers had been made possible through the assistance of Southwestern industrial unions. "With the help of the unions *el pueblo Mexicano* has eliminated many of the pre-existing wage distinctions [between Mexican and Anglo workers]," Montoya announced. "In many of the basic industries we have won the right to better jobs based on one's work and ability and at least (although not completely eliminated) we have broken the medieval control enjoyed by agriculture and mining interests over generations of Mexicans."

Just as the unions recognized that unorganized Mexicans only weakened the labor movement, Mexican workers realized that if the unions were destroyed they would also suffer. Montoya cautioned that he did not mean to imply that Mexicans should allow other groups to fight their battles for them, only Mexican Americans could achieve first-class citizenship for themselves. However, in their struggle, their natural allies were the unions.[15] ANMA did not proclaim what could be considered a revolutionary class position by calling on Mexican workers to overthrow capitalism and erect a socialist society. One could be indicted and sent to prison for espousing such views during the McCarthy period. Yet, it brought attention to the working class condition of most Mexicans, their class interests with other workers, and the exploitative nature of the class system in the Southwest. An economic elite exploited Mexicans as cheap labor and in turn amassed great profits. "The insufficient wages of the sugarbeet workers creates the vast wealth for corporations such as the Great Western Sugar Company that dominates the economic and political life of this state," one ANMA official in Colorado asserted.[16] ANMA believed, unlike such groups such as LULAC, that rectification of disparities in wealth and power could only be arrived at through a working class movement.

If ANMA recognized class in the formulation of its ideology, it also paid attention to the realities of race and culture. Mexicans were exploited as cheap labor and were oppressed as a distinct ethnic/racial community. ANMA in its short existence did not produce a sophisticated theory on race and class, but it did make it clear that Mexicans as well as Blacks faced double oppression. In a 1952 editorial, *Progreso*, ANMA's newspaper, commented that the Mexicans' participation in the class struggle had to contend directly with ethnic/racial segregation and discrimination. Such conditions aided in reducing the Mexicans' standard of living and forced them to accept hard, dirty, and cheap jobs.[17] Besides employment, Mexicans also faced discrimination in housing, education, political representation, and public services. Racism, according to ANMA, had become so pervasive and destructive that some Mexican Americans believed themselves inferior to Anglos and attempted to pass as "Spanish Americans" or "Nice Mexicans," as ANMA referred to them. These types of Mexican Americans either blamed other Mexicans for the existence of discrimination or else pretended it did not exist. ANMA observed, however, that few Mexicans, regardless of skin color and class background, successfully escaped prejudice. It recalled that even Edward Roybal, Los Angeles' only Mexican American city councilman, had been refused the sale of a home because he was of Mexican descent. ANMA further noted how the postwar housing boom permitted poor whites to purchase homes, but not Mexicans: "Today it is discovered that to be poor is not a great obstacle to buy a modest and decent house. But to be a Mexican is something else!"[18] "Why do such things exist?" ANMA queried. "It is not the fault of our people. Fault lies in discrimination-the discrimination which allows rich employers to pay us low wages and to divide us from other workers."[19] An exploitative class structure fueled racial/ethnic prejudice and discrimination. ANMA saw racism directly linked to a white ruling class and did not associate all whites, especially workers, with the perpetuation of such a system. ANMA would struggle alongside Anglo workers who also desired to eliminate racism. All workers would benefit from the elimination of an underclass of cheap labor.[20] To ANMA, both class and race had to be considered in developing a strategy for the liberation of Mexicans in the United States.

ANMA complemented these views by its discussion of culture. Deprived of an autonomous cultural development. Mexicans in the Southwest still possessed a distinct culture needing protection encouragement, and this uniqueness could be an objective basis for political organization. Employing a popular approach to culture, no doubt to distinguish it from the middle-class-oriented Mexican American organizations, ANMA promoted a form of cultural nationalism. It acknowledged the Mexicans' cultural heritage and praised efforts at cultural resistance.[21] Yet Mexican culture had come under more aggressive attack in the early 1950s. The Cold War and McCarthyism, in addition to bringing about violations of civil liberties and constitutional protections, created an irrational apprehension over anything considered "un-American." Consequently, Mexican Americans and Mexican nationals faced heightened cultural prejudice. "At the same time," *Progreso* warned in 1952,

> There is a subtle campaign, at times impudent, with the motive of desecrating our historical heritage, our culture and our language. All forms of the news media is being utilized to slandor [sic] and ridicule our people and our cultural institutions. At the same time there is a continual effort to negate, twist, and generally misrepresent our contemporary contributions as well as our historic economic and cultural ones in this country.[22]

ANMA observed that other ethnic groups whose families had arrived from Italy,

Ireland, or Germany remained proud of their heritage. So too should Mexicans. One ANMA official declared,

> We should understand and be proud of the rich culture of our ancestors and of Mexico-a culture of hard work, beautiful music, a culture that has produced the three greatest artists of the Americas-Orozco, Rivera, and Siqueiros. We know that Mexicans such as these are neither "sucios" (dirty), "flojos" (lazy), nor "estupidos" (stupid)-the usual untruthful characteristics generally attributed to Mexicans. ANMA struggles to preserve our culture and to promote dignity and pride in our nationality.[23]

Although ANMA favored cultural nationalism, it did not advance a theory of "nationhood" for Mexican Americans similar to that developed by the Communist Party for Blacks in the deep South. Rather, ANMA interpreted Mexican Americans more as a national minority, and stressed the integration of Mexican Americans through the acquisition of civil rights and the acceptance of a state of cultural pluralism whereby Mexican culture would be given due recognition in the United States.

In fighting for the rights of Mexican Americans, ANMA also encouraged an international consciousness, particularly with respect to Mexico and the rest of Latin America. It noted, for example, that the treatment of Mexicans in the United States represented a mirror reflecting United States attitudes and policies toward Latin America. If the United States treated Mexican Americans as second-class citizens, so too did it deal with Latin America as an inferior entity. Discounting particular differences, ANMA proposed that the relationship between Mexican Americans and Latin Americans was crucial and that the struggle for Mexican American liberation was linked with that of Latin America. ". . . (A)s long as this country takes unjust advantage of those people south of the Rio Bravo (Grande)," Alfredo Montoya concluded, "we shall never achieve what we are struggling for-first class citizenship."[24] Calling on Mexican Americans to shun the idea of a frontier between themselves and Mexico, ANMA proclaimed its defense of the rights of Mexican nationals in the United States and promised to develop ties of solidarity with Mexicans south of the Rio Grande.[25]

Domestically, ANMA advocated a united front. It opposed sectarianism and called for alliances with other Mexican American organizations subscribing to similar general principles and goals. A divided people would never alter their conditions, but united Mexican Americans could. "The situation and the times does not allow us the luxury of jealous, distrusts, and suspicions amongst us," Montoya appealed. "Such characteristics are almost semi-feudal vestiges which in the past have fatally damaged our cause. For this reason, our organization is ready to cooperate with others whose aim is to improve the lot of the Mexican people, and who believe in cooperation based on mutual respect and benefit."[26] ANMA, unlike middle-class-oriented Mexican American groups, also aspired to a united front with other oppressed peoples within the country, in particular Blacks and

Jews. Mexican Americans represented only one of several minorities, who in some cases were worse off than Mexicans. The struggle and gains of one minority aided those of the rest.[27] "We should unite with Blacks who suffers similar conditions as our own, and in this way reinforce both groups," an ANMA official exhorted.[28] Such a coalition, including progressive labor unions, ANMA believed indispensable to the Mexican American cause.

In conformity with its ideology, ANMA developed a varied political program. First and foremost, due to the undeclared war in Korea, ANMA called on Mexican Americans to support the peace movement in the country. President Montoya, writing in 1952, observed that the Korean conflict represented a major setback for workers and minorities even though a majority of Mexican Americans and other Americans opposed the war. Not only was the war costing the lives of thousands of Mexican Americans out of all proportion to their numbers in the United States, but it also affected the well-being and rights of the Mexican American community. Montoya noted that attacks on Mexicans had increased since the beginning of the war in the form of police brutality, racial discrimination, the victimization of Mexicans through the use of the so called anti-subversive Smith and McCarran Acts, the loss of economic benefits through the application of the anti-labor Taft-Hartley Act, and the loss of social services for the poor, the aged, and the young. In addition, minority groups had to unjustly bear the costs of the war through excessive taxes, prices, and decreased wages.[29] Consequently, ANMA believed the war had to receive priority attention since it affected and magnified so many other problems. "The Mexican people not only deserve peace," *Progreso* stated, "but they need peace for their happiness and well-being." ANMA urged nations to resolve their problems through negotiations. "This is more sensible and civilized than killing millions of lives including those of our youth." As part of the struggle for basic rights, ANMA included the right to peace.[30]

With its emphasis on working-class solidarity, ANMA supported particular struggles of Mexican American workers in the Southwest. In 1952 it publicized the triumphs of Local 890 of the Mine, Mill, and Smelter Workers of Bayard, New Mexico, in its 15-month strike for improved wages and working conditions. The Bayard strike, of course, would be immortalized in the classic film *Salt of the Earth*. The ANMA local in Denver, which had provided money and donations of clothes to the strikers, especially lauded the courageous role of the Mexican women who had taken over the picket lines after the workers had been barred from them.[31]

ANMA also called attention to the plight of migrant workers in Southwestern fields and supported a $1 an hour minimum wage for agricultural workers as well as a guaranteed annual wage.[32] As part of its concern for migrant labor, ANMA protested the bracero program whereby Mexico supplied field hands to American agriculture. ANMA considered the program to be a boon to agribusiness at the expense of both braceros and domestic farm workers. Braceros worked as peons, while Mexican American workers were forced to leave their homes in search of employment because they could not compete with cheaper bracero labor. ANMA advocated a suspension of the program and the involvement of both Mexican and U.S. labor unions in drafting an alternative solution to the need for agricultural labor in the Southwest.[33]

Finally, as part of its labor program, ANMA through its association with progressive labor unions encouraged unionism among Mexican Americans. Besides the Mine, Mill, and Smelter Workers, ANMA received support from such unions as the United Electrical Radio and Machine Workers of America, the National Union of Marine Cooks and Stewards, the International Longshoreman's and Warehouseman's Union, the Furniture Workers, Upholsterers and Wood Workers Union, and the Amalgamated Clothing Workers of America.[34]

The passage of anti-alien, anti-subversive, and anti-immigration laws in particular alarmed ANMA. In 1950 it officially protested the McCarran Act passed by the U.S. Congress. According to ANMA, such legislation, under the guise of controlling subversives, in fact aimed at destroying legitimate organizations such as labor unions working for peoples' rights. Anyone who protested against discrimination, police brutality, or injustices on the part of any governmental agency could now be accused of being a Communist and prosecuted under the McCarran Act. Minority groups would be especially vulnerable to unjust persecution.[35] Consequently, ANMA declared the McCarran Act to be a direct violation of the Bill of Rights.[36] As part of its 1952 platform, ANMA aided a successful campaign supporting four Mexicans in Santa Ana, California (the Sereno Case) who had been prosecuted as undesirable under the McCarran Act. ANMA further helped organize mass meetings against the Act, such as one in Los Angeles on March 13, 1952, attended by over 200 persons protesting the application of the McCarran Act to unfairly deport Mexican workers.[37]

Besides working conditions, ANMA sought other improvements in the quality of life for Mexican Americans. At least one ANMA local, for example, took up rent control as an issue.[38] The Lincoln Heights local in East Los Angeles was organized out of a struggle for improved housing.[39] In Denver, ANMA confronted local authorities regarding limited and segregated public housing for Mexican Americans.[40] Reflecting the increased educational aspirations of Mexican Americans, ANMA in Colorado questioned why less than 100 Mexican Americans attended all colleges and universities in that state. ANMA further observed that during the 1947-48 academic year only 78 Mexican American high school seniors could be found in Colorado. These conditions resulted not from lack of support for education by Mexican American parents, but from economic exploitation and discrimination that forced young Mexican American children to leave school at an early age to supplement the family income.[41]

Economic and social rights also needed to be complemented by effective political representation. ANMA thought it ironic that Mexican Americans were being asked to fight for democracy in Korea while being denied it in their own communities. The time had come for Mexican Americans to elect representatives from their own group rather than relying as in the past on politicians who had little or no interest in the problems of Mexican Americans. "This will reflect not only the revival of a civic consciousness," ANMA declared, "but a recognition that our progress is impossible without a voice and a vote within governing circles."[42] Responsible political representation, however, could only be achieved if Mexican Americans registered to vote and if they allied themselves with the labor movement and other minorities.[43]

This appeared to be happening and an encouraged ANMA noted in mid-1952 that in recent elections throughout the Southwest, Mexican Americans had not only voted in large numbers, but more Mexican Americans had run for office than ever before. These candidates conducted valiant, although mostly unsuccessful races, despite the fact that their opponents were in many cases supported by local chambers of commerce and other monied interests. The elections had revealed the potential political strength of Mexican Americans. "When the political power of five million Americans is freed from its bondage," ANMA promised, "then its voice will be heard."[44] In El Paso, ANMA organized a Poll Tax Committee to encourage Mexican Americans to pay their poll taxes and to use their vote to elect honest and capable representatives who would help alleviate problems associated with work, housing, health, and education.[45]

Youth work formed still another aspect of ANMA's political program. This was an especially important issue in light of continued cases of police harassment and brutality against young Mexican Americans. The Estrada Courts local in East Los Angeles, for example, had been organized is a result of an incident of police brutality.[46] Besides protecting against such injustices, ANMA attempted to organize youth as a way of preventing delinquency and of politicizing young people. Through its national youth director, it established ANMA youth clubs in at least two states. ANMA observed that young veterans in particular welcomed the opportunity for political work, since after returning from the battlefields they discovered that American society had little to offer them.[47]

Culturally, ANMA pursued a two-fold strategy. On the one hand, it attacked prevalent stereotypes of Mexicans, especially in the mass media. In its 1952 platform, ANMA announced a national campaign against the perversions of Mexican culture portrayed in the press, literature, radio, and television. It called particular attention to the Judy Canova radio show, which depicted Mexicans, through the character of "Pancho," as lazy and stupid.[48] Mexican Americans possessed a sense of humor, it being one of the few things enjoyed by poor people, and appreciated humor done in good taste, one ANMA official stated. However, the "humor" in the Canova show Mexican Americans could easily do without. "Behind the image of a stupid, lazy, and ignorant clown that is [Pancho]," Alfonso Sena of Colorado charged,

> there is a century of persecution and deprivation of our people. According to this
> humor our people should perform the most servile labor and receive the lowest

wages. This humor sustains the poor health of many of our children, the terrible shacks where we are forced to live, the lack of educational opportunities, the brutality of the police toward our youth, the segregation and many other indignities that are forced upon us.[49]

It was not funny, Sena added, that more than 80 percent of the Mexicans in Denver labored in unskilled jobs and that the average family income of Mexican Americans in 1949 was only $1,840 compared to $1,930 for a Black family and $3,020 for an Anglo family. Nor was it funny that the average family income of a migrant family in Colorado only amounted to $1,424.[50]

To protest comedy at the expense of Mexicans, ANMA, along with certain allied labor unions, initiated a national economic boycott of the Colgate Palmolive Peet Company, Canova's sponsors. They asked the public to pressure radio stations airing the show and to boycott such products as Palmolive soap, Cashmere Bouquet soap, Colgate Shaving Cream, Super Suds, and Fab. "One of the principal objectives of ANMA is the defense of our people's dignity and the just representation of the real Mexican-'el verdadero Mexicano,'" the organization proclaimed, "and the true Mexican is the deprived and exploited worker who has maintained the railroads, labored in the fields, and built the cities. For the Mexican people, their low economic standing, the negation of their rights, and the ridicule which they are subject to are one and the same."[51] Two months later, *Progreso* reported that due to the boycott and protests, the Canova show had been canceled.[52] To prevent such stereotyping in the media, ANMA, at its second national convention in El Paso, adopted a resolution urging the employment of Mexican Americans in motion pictures, radio, and television. "We must fight for jobs for our people in all cultural and mass communications to which their talents entitle them," the resolution concluded.[53]

To present a more positive image of Mexicans and to promote ethnic pride, ANMA sponsored cultural programs. Through its national director of culture it encouraged locals to organize functions that would tap the talents of Mexican Americans. Cultural centers, it suggested, might be established by each local.[54] According to ANMA, music represented the art form that engaged most people and should therefore be concentrated on by the locals. "More than art, dance, and even literature," *Progreso* editorialized, "music occupies first place in our communities." Mexican music, of course, consisted of many types, including corridos, huapangos, and jarabes. Some Mexican music was really American music, having nothing to do with Mexican culture. Despite such variety, ANMA recommended that local directors of culture identify the most popular forms of music in their communities as well as those who performed them. Having done this, the locals could stage community concerts that would involve not only performances, but education through teaching the audiences the music and words of songs so they could directly participate. In addition to music, local cultural committees could arrange lectures on hygiene, art, the care of children, and on other ethnic cultures.[55]

As an example of what could be done in cultural work, ANMA's national culture committee organized a "Semana de Historia y Cultura Mexicana" in Los Angeles to coincide with the celebration of the 16th of September (Mexican Independence Day) in 1950. ANMA sponsored a number of musical variety shows at Croation Hall in Belvedere. These shows featured its own group of artists including singers, dancers, and musicians under the direction of Crescencio Ruiz, the national director of culture. Black and Jewish performers also participated. Evening shows highlighted a musical-slide presentation depicting the history of music and art in Mexico from pre-Columbian times to the present. Movies about Mexico were also part of the week-long festivities. Finally, the most important exhibition of Mexican American and Mexican art ever held in Los Angeles, according to *Progreso*, accompanied the ANMA program. Artists, including ANMA members, displayed nearly 150 pieces of art at Centro Soto-Michigan.[56]

The publication of *Progreso*, ANMA's national newspaper, also constituted part of ANMA's cultural agenda. Written primarily in Spanish in order to reach most Mexican nationals and Mexican Americans and to promote the Spanish language, ANMA did publish some articles in English. Indeed, ANMA acknowledged that a bilingual format was best because of the heterogeneity of the Mexican population in the United States and the cultural erosion and language discrimination faced by Mexican Americans. "Some say that Mexican Americans should know how to read Spanish," Dr. Edward Lamar, the national editor of *Progreso* wrote,

> We agree with that, unfortunately many do not. Many older people can read neither language because education was not available for them in their youth. They must depend upon their children to read the paper for them. Many of their sons and daughters speak both languages but have been taught to read only English and are often even penalized for speaking Spanish in school. ANMA must correct this condition; we must also recognize that it exists.[57]

Accepting English as a fact of life and not being dogmatic in its cultural nationalism, ANMA incorporated the values and benefits of bilingualism and biculturalism. "We all want to learn to use both languages well," Lamar insisted, "to appreciate the culture of others, to be in a position for better jobs in either the U.S. or Mexico, and to be ready to take our place in active leadership in our community."[58]

Although ANMA apparently did not have a specific program or commission on women, it appears that women played active and important roles in the organization. Isabel González, for example, was elected the first vice-president of ANMA in 1949. Other women in national offices included Florencia Lamar, who was national treasurer. In the locals, women held leadership positions, although none seem to have been elected presidents of their chapters.[59] Applauding the role of women in the "Salt of the Earth" strike, one male official impressed on ANMA members the need to recognize the potential leadership capacities of women. "We should accept them as leaders with all the respect they deserve," he stressed. "We should assist them to develop to their fullest potential as leaders of our organization, and we should recognize the marvelous contributions that Mexican women have made to ANMA."[60]

Desiring a united front, ANMA pursued contacts not only with labor unions. but with other community organizations. Alfredo Montoya, President of ANMA, and Mauricio Terrazas, southern California Regional Director, both participated in the short-lived American Council of Spanish-Speaking People headed by Dr. George I. Sánchez of the University of Texas.[61] No evidence exists, however, of any association with prominent but middle-class oriented Mexican American organizations such as LULAC and the American G.I. Forum. It is not unlikely that these staunchly anti-Communist groups shied away from the leftist ANMA. While ANMA's united front with prominent Mexican American civic organizations was limited and in some cases nonexistent, its contacts with left-oriented, non-Mexican American groups was not. Progressive collectives supporting ANMA included the Independent Progressive Party (which in 1948 ran former Vice-President Henry Wallace for President of the United States), the Los Angeles Committee for the Protection of the Foreign Born, the Civil Rights Congress, and the Jewish Peoples Fraternal Order of the International Workers Order.[62]

Because of its ideology and reform program, plus its affiliation with leftist organizations such as the Mine, Mill, and Smelter Workers, ANMA faced much harassment and political persecution as a so-called "red-front" group. At its 1952 national convention in El Paso, for example, one local newspaper announced the meetings with a headline reading: "Red Front Leaders Gather for Meeting." Interviewed by the *El Paso Herald-Post*, President Montoya denied that ANMA was allied with any Communist organization but was repeatedly questioned on whether ANMA supported the Korean War. In a biased statement intended to discredit ANMA, the *Herald-Post* wrote: "Montoya refused to give a 'yes' or 'no' answer as to whether or not he or his organization favors action against Red aggression in Korea." The newspaper also attempted to link ANMA with potential violence by reporting that the Chief of Police was "keeping his eye" on the convention. "We can't stop them from meeting," the Chief stated. "There is nothing we can do unless they start a disturbance. If there is any trouble we will put an end to it in a hurry."[63]

The *Herald-Post* further attacked ANMA for its criticism of Mexicans in the media, especially the comic strip characters "Little Pedro" and "Gordo." In an editorial entitled "Spreading Poison," the *Herald Post* dismissed ANMA's position as pure propaganda intended to breed hate and distrust in American institutions. "There's nothing harmful in roly-poly, good-natured Gordo, who brings admiring smiles to his readers. And Little Pedro is a smart chap who has a way of doing the unexpected." The newspaper concluded that ANMA's aim was simple: "Create class hatred, stir up trouble that can be used to enlist more fellow travelers-that's the object of such speeches."[64]

Two years later, the U.S. Attorney General listed ANMA as a subversive group as had been done with many other progressive organizations. Before the listing, ANMA had been accused without evidence of representing a front for the Communist Party during the El Paso trial of Mine, Mill, and Smelter organizer Clint Jencks. At the Jencks trial, Alfredo Montoya had also been charged with being a member of the Communist Party. Convicted of filing false non-Communist affidavits, Jencks was later acquitted partly on the grounds that witnesses who had testified against him had lied and were paid FBI informers.[65]

Faced with such charges and political pressures, ANMA defended itself by accusing its opponents of being antidemocratic and of wishing to destroy community organizations and labor unions that supported social improvements and constitutional protections for minorities and workers. ANMA recognized that in order to achieve these gains it had to also protect the right of protest and freedom of speech even though this might involve being a victim of red-baiting. ANMA also attacked efforts by local governments to pass anti-Communist ordinances requiring municipal and county employees as well as others to sign anti-Communist oaths or to register as Communist Party members. In Los Angeles it strongly applauded the courageous stand of Councilman Roybal who in 1950 voted along against such an ordinance passed by the city council. This ordinance was later declared to be unconstitutional.[66]

By the middle of the 1950s, ANMA appears to have ceased to function. Its demise is linked to the general persecution of the Left in the United States, commonly referred to as McCarthyism. Although pursuing a basic reform program and declaring its loyalty to the democratic principles of the U.S. Constitution, ANMA, along with many other similar progressive organizations, was perceived as a threat by a paranoid ruling circle and hence could not be allowed to function peacefully. ANMA's brief history, moreover, has to be seen in light of the political attacks on the Mine, Mill. and Smelter Workers, its chief patron. Although the Union survived, its own efforts to protect itself during the early 1950s must have detracted from the attention and support it could provide ANMA. Acuña also suggests that the demise of ANMA was linked to the shifting policies of the Communist Party during the 1950s.[67]

It is, of course, conceivable that ANMA's own internal program may have had something to do with its limited life. For example, it naively assumed that both Mexican Americans and Mexican nationals in the United States held to a common identity and common interests. Its open alliance with labor unions and political groups regarded as "radical" may have underestimated the conservative nature of many Mexicans in the United States. The discovery of additional internal documents will, of course, shed light on this question. From what we know now, however, it would seem that external rather than internal pressures caused ANMA's decline. "The Chicano movement in the 1950s," Acuña correctly notes, "was in fact driven underground or forced to use calmer methods in order to counteract the highly undemocratic and unconstitutional pressures that existed during that time."[68]

Although we do not know the full extent of its influence and despite its demise, ANMA still represents perhaps the most important Mexican American leftist organization during the first half of the 20th century. In addition to its political program concentrating on the problems of working class Mexican Americans, ANMA was the only group that articulated a particular Mexican American leftist or radical political ideology. Although its program as a whole was limited to democratic reforms, due no doubt to its effort to achieve mass support and to the political persecution of Marxists at the time, ANMA nevertheless correctly stressed the working class conditions of most Mexicans in the United States and the exploitative class character of the American system. ANMA's attempt, moreover, at linking class, race, and culture in interpreting the Mexican American experience constitutes one of the first efforts to explore these fundamental themes by Mexican Americans. Finally, the history of ANMA is a testimony to the courage and dedication of those Mexican Americans who, by standing up for their rights as U.S. citizens and by refusing to be intimidated by the reactionary temper of the period, dared to challenge the contradictions of American society.

III

Beyond the discovery of a Chicano left in history is the issue of the extent and nature of its influence. This involves, for example, whether the relationship between Mexican Americans and the Left led to an ideology similar to that debated by Black Marxists during the 1930s. If so, did this ideology clashed with other dominant intellectual-political tendencies in the Mexican American communities, most notably, the political and cultural nationalism articulated by Mexican exile leaders and, by the 1930s, the Americanist ideology championed by LULAC and other middle-class-oriented Mexican American groups.

In addition to what already has been done in the historiography of the Chicano left, I would suggest the following points of departure for future work. First, it seems to me that the most important period for the study of the Mexican American left, aside from the recent past, includes the 1930s, 1940s, and 1950s. The most concerted activity among Mexican American leftists occurs during this time. The Great Depression of the 1930s not only created objective conditions for protest due to the increased hardships suffered by Mexicans in the United States, but it gave rise to a militant Communist Party that successfully organized among the unemployed, agricultural laborers, and industrial workers. Yet if radicalism marked one perimeter of this period, antidemocratic reaction marked the other, in the form of the Cold War and McCarthyism. As a result, the later stages of this period drove the Communist Party underground and weakened the leftist union movement. The years between 1930 and 1960 are therefore critical ones for evaluating the full extent of Mexican American participation in leftist politics and the influence of this activity within Mexican American communities.

From what we already know, let me advance what we will probably continue to discover. Although increased numbers of Mexican Americans and Mexican nationals joined leftist unions as well as the Communist Party, they concentrated primarily on basic economic, political, and civil rights for Mexican Americans within the context of the capitalist system. In so doing they did not effectively articulate a revolutionary political position aimed at successfully challenging what I interpret to be the dominant reformist tendency in Mexican American political circles, voiced by groups such as LULAC. Mexican American leftist leaders, although perceived as undesirable competitors by their middle-class counterparts, supplemented rather than superseded the reform movements of the period. This is not to suggest, however, that even had a revolutionary ideology been advanced it would have found fertile ground. Here I differ with Douglas Monroy's undocumented contention to the contrary.

One can make a case that both objective and subjective conditions for mass revolutionary consciousness among Mexicans in this country simply did not exist at that time. In this sense, Mexican American leftists, such as those in ANMA, represented true radicals in that they astutely understood the limitations of the conditions under which they worked and yet made the most of them in addressing the immediate interests of Mexican American workers. In any event, Mexican American leftist leaders found themselves too engaged in daily labor problems and in defending themselves against political persecution to develop an interpretation of Marxism/Leninism that might have challenged the hegemony of the reform Americanism espoused and supported by many Mexican Americans, especially after World War II. The absence, moreover, of a leftist Mexican American intelligentsia--something that would not arise until the 1970s--hindered the birth of a specific leftist politics. By contrast, nonradical reformers had access to a small number of Mexican American intellectuals and writers such as Carlos Castañda, George I. Sánchez, Alonso Perales, and Ignacio López, who presented a middle-class Mexican American world view. Only ANMA drafted a radical political platform, but even this was couched in reform language and limited by ANMA's brief existence.

Finally, it can be concluded that a Mexican American left emerged out of the 1930s, but it was one which focused more on reform than revolution. As a reform movement, the Mexican American left rather than being out of step with its time was very much a part of it. For reform and the achievement of the mythical "American Dream," not revolution, characterized the most politically active sectors of Mexican American communities between the 1930s and the early 1960s.

Notes

1. Juan Gómez-Quiñones. "The First Steps: Chicano Labor Conflict and Organizing

1900-1920," *Aztlán*, 3, 13-50; Ronald W. Lopez. "The El Monte Berry Strike of 1933, *Aztlán*, 1 (Spring 1970), 101-114. See special issue of *Aztlán* on labor history. especially Emilio Zamora Jr.. "Chicano Socialist Labor Activity in Texas. 1900-1920," 221-238; and Victor B. Nelson-Cisneros, "La clase trabajadora en Tejas. 1920-1940," 239-266. Also. see Albert Camarillo and Pedro Castillo, eds., *Furia y Muerte: Los Bandidos Chicanos* (Los Angeles: Chicano Studies Center. UCLA, 1972); Américo Paredes. *With his Pistol in his Hand: A Border Ballad and its Hero* (Austin: University of Texas Press. 1958); Gómez-Quiñones. *Sembradores: Ricardo Flores Magón Y El Partido Liberal Mexicano* (Los Angeles: Aztlán Publications. 1973); Rodolfo Acuña, *Occupied America: The Chicano Struggle Toward Liberation* (San Francisco: Canfield Press, 1972); José E. Limón, "El Primer Congreso Mexicanista de 1911: A Precursor to Contemporary Chicanismo, *Aztlán*, 5 (spring and fall 1974), 85-106.

2. See, for example, Octavio I. Romano, "Minorities, History, and the Cultural Mystique," *El Grito*, 1 (fall 1967), 5-11, and "The Historical and Intellectual Presence of Mexican-Americans," *El Grito*, 2 (winter 1969), 32-46.

3. Oscar J. Martínez, *Border Boom Town: Ciudad Juárez Since 1848* (Austin: University of Texas Press, 1978). Albert Camarillo, *Chicanos in a Changing Society: From Mexican Pueblos to American Barrios in Santa Barbara and Southern California, 1848-1930* (Cambridge: Harvard University Press, 1979). Richard Griswold del Castillo, *The Los Angeles Barrio: A Social History, 1848-1890* (Berkeley: University of California Press, 1980). Mario T. García, *Desert Immigrants: The Mexicans of El Paso, 1880-1920* (New Haven: Yale University Press, 1981). Arnoldo de León, *The Tejano Community, 1836-1900* (Albuquerque: University of New Mexico Press, 1982). Ricardo Romo, *East Los Angeles: History of a Barrio* (Austin: University of Texas Press, 1983). Francisco E. Balderrama, *In Defense of La Raza: The Los Angeles Mexican Consulate and the Mexican Community, 1929 to 1936* (Tucson: University of Arizona Press, 1982).

4. See Zamora, "Chicano Socialist Labor Activity," 221-238; Nelson-Cisneros, "La clase trabajadora," 239-266; Vicki Ruiz, "UCAPAWA and Mexican Women Workers" (Stanford, 1982); Cletus Daniel, *Bitter Harvest: A History of California Farmworkers, 1870-1941* (Berkeley: Univ. of California Press, 1982); Douglas Monroy, "Mexicans in Los Angeles, 1930-1941: On Ethnic Group Relations to Class Forces" (UCLA, 1978); Luis Arroyo, "Industrial Unionism and the Los Angeles Furniture Industry, 1918-1954" (UCLA, 1979); Acuña. *Occupied America*, revised ed., 1981.

5. Acuña, *Occupied America*, 213

6. Vernon Jensen. *Nonferrous Metals Industry Unionism*, 1932-1954 (Ithaca, NY: Cornell University Press. 1954).

7. See "Segunda Convención Nacional de la Asociación Nacional México-Americana." This and the other documents cited in the notes are in the author's possession.

8. Constitución de la Asociación Nacional México-Americana.

9. *Progreso*, June 1952, 2.

10. See document "Asociación Nacional México-Americana."

11. See Alfonso Sena, "Discurso Principal Conferencia Estatal de Colorado."

12. *Progreso,* December 1950, 1.

13. Ibid.; *Progreso*, October 1950, April 1950; "Convención Nacional Fundadora de ANMA," 6.

14. "Breve Historia del Pueblo Mexicano en E.U.," in *Progreso*, June 1952, 5-6. This history was taken from Isabel González, "Step-Children of a Nation" (American Committee for Protection of Foreign Born, 1947).

15. *Progreso*, October 1950, 2, 6.

16. Sena, "Discuro Principal."

17. *Progreso*, April 1952, 7.

18. Ibid., October 1950, 5.

19. Sena, "Discurso Principal."

20. Ibid.

21. *Progreso*, June 5-6.

22. Ibid., 2.

23. Sena, "Discurso Principal."

24. *Progreso*, December 1950, 2.

25. Ibid., 5.

26. Ibid., 2.

27. *Progreso*, June 1950, 8.

28. Sena, "Discurso Principal."

29. *Progreso*, April 1952, 4.

30. Ibid., 6.

31. Ibid., 1, 3; June 1952, 4.

32. Sena "Discurso Principal."

33. See document "Atención!" and *Progresso*, December 1950, 4.

34. See "Convención Nacional Fundadora" and "Segunda Convención."

35. *Progreso*, October 1950, 2.

36. Ibid., December 1950, 5.

37. Ibid., April 1952, 4, 6. For deportations of Mexicans under the McCarran Act, see also Acuña. *Occupied America,* 215-216.

38. *Progreso*, October 1950, 2.

39. Ibid., 4.

40. Ibid., June 1952, 4.

41. Sena, "Discurso Principal."

42. *Progreso*, April 1952, 1, 3.

43. Ibid.

44. Ibid., June 1952, 8.

45. See "Atención!" and press release, ANMA. El Paso, January 22, 1952.

46. *Progreso*, October 1950, 4.

47. Ibid., December 1950, 2.

48. Ibid., April 1952, 6.

49. Sena, "Discurso Principal."

50. Ibid.

51. *Progreso*, April 1952, 4.

52. Ibid., June 1952, 4.

53. *El Paso Herald-Post*, July 14, 1952, 1.

54. *Progreso*, December 1950, 4: April 1952, 8.

55. Ibid., June 1952, 3, 7.

56. Ibid., October 1950, 1, 5.

57. Ibid., December 1950, 3.

58. Ibid.

59. "Segunda Convención"; *Progreso*, December 1950, 3; April 1952, 8; June 1952, 6.

60. Sena "Discurso Principal."

61. *Progreso*, April 1952, 3.

62. See "Convención Nacional Fundadora" and "Segunda Convención."

63. *El Paso-Herald Post*, July 11, 1952, 1.

64. Ibid., 12.

65. Ibid., February 5, 1954, 1.

66. Ibid., October 1950, 4.

67. Acuña. statement to author.

68. Acuña, *Occupied America*, 213.

69. Douglas Monroy, "Anarquismo y Comunismo: Mexican Radicalism and the Communist Party in Los Angeles During the 1930s." *Labor History*, 24 (winter 1983), 34-59.

Carlos Muñoz Jr.'s article provides an interesting contrast between the goals of the Mexican American generation and its leadership and the emerging militancy of the early and middle 1960s. The contrasts are most apparent not only in the style of protest but in the contrasting redefinition of history which guided the direction of the movement. Surprisingly the politically militant stance and advanced reform programs are similiar to those esposed by earlier organizations covered in this section.

The Militant Challenge:
The Chicano Generation
Carlos Muñoz, Jr.

By 1950 the Mexican and Mexican American population in the United States had increased significantly--doubling in California, for example. World War II had resulted in an influx of Mexican and Mexican American labor from rural areas to the urban centers of the South and Midwest. The economic prosperity generated by the war had made possible some upward social mobility for a small sector of the Mexican American working class. But most Mexican Americans remained rooted in the semi-skilled and unskilled proletariat. Although many of the wartime employment gains they had made in industry had been lost by the end of the 1940s, Mexican American workers continued to make some progress through their participation in trade union activity.

The urbanization of the majority of Mexican Americans during this period was a major contributor to their 'Americanization'. The children of the Mexican American working class in particular came into direct contact with mainstream American culture through the dominant political institutions in the cities. Urbanization resulted in the acceleration of the acculturation and assimilation process and consequently the legitimization of the liberal capitalist ideology that underpinned the politics of accommodation and integration pursued by middle-class Mexican American organizations such as the League of United Latin American Citizens. These organizations had won victories in the courts in the late 1940s over *de jure* school segregation, decisions that had been hailed by LULAC as major victories for 'Democratic assimilation'.[1] *De facto* segregated schooling nevertheless remained the reality for most Mexican American youth.[2]

The Mexican and Mexican American rural proletariat continued to be the most oppressed sector within the ranks of labor. Under the leadership of Ernesto Galarza it struggled against the far greater power of Southwestern agribusiness. Galarza, who as a student activist in 1929 had spoken out in defense of Mexican workers, had gone on to become the first Mexican American to earn a Ph.D. in history and political science at Columbia University.[3] However, during the postwar years he became a labor organizer instead of pursuing an academic career. Galarza organized African American and white workers in Louisiana through the Southern Tenant Farm Union founded by the militant socialist H. L. Mitchell and was later assigned by Mitchell to organize Mexican American farmworkers in California in 1949. Together with Mitchell, Galarza struggled within the labor movement to obtain support for organizing farmworkers. In 1950, the AFL-CIO endorsed their efforts and appointed Galarza the executive secretary of the newly created National Farm Labor Union.

The politics of class struggle in the fields and in the cities did not move students of Mexican descent to participate in those struggles or follow in Galarza's footsteps. The politics of the 1950s were not conducive to radicalism anywhere, especially to participation in social struggles that could be easily characterized as 'communist inspired'. Like other young people of their generation, Mexican American student activists--the few in existence--were influenced by the politics of super-patriotism generated by the war against Hitler and fascism and reinforced by the Cold War against new enemies, Stalin and communism. The decade witnessed the rise of rightwing ideologues like Senator Joseph McCarthy of Wisconsin, who spearheaded an anticommunist crusade across the nation, and the passage of right-wing federal legislation like the McCarran-Walter Act, which resulted in the deportation of Mexican labor activists considered subversive of US national interests.

The Mexican American student presence on college campuses increased during the decade as a direct result of the G.I. Bill. Among the thousands of returning Mexican American veterans who took advantage of this opportunity to pursue a higher education were Americo Paredes, Octavio Romano-V., and Ralph Guzman. They were destined to become, along with Galarza, significant contributors to Mexican American intellectual life.

Few returning veterans who went to college became involved in organizing Mexican American students on campus. Those who did become political activists limited their involvement to mostly local community struggles and joined middle-class and professional organizations. They did not choose to identify themselves as students but as veterans. The politics of the times notwithstanding, the antiMexican racism in the larger society, although not as ugly as it had been during the 1920s and 1930s, compelled a few of the more progressive of them to speak out in defense of their people in the context of the liberal reformist political tradition typified by the LULAC organization and further developed and refined by the new middle class and professional organizations of the post-World War II era. Veterans played central leadership roles in those organizations. Their political consciousness was shaped by patriotic Americanism and the anticommunism then permeating society. They did not reject their Mexican origins but, like the generation of the 1930s, emphasized the American part of their Mexican American identity. In their minds, political accommodation and assimilation were the only path toward equal status in a racist society. Integration in education and at all levels of society would result, they believed, in the acceptance of their people as first-class citizens.

They acknowledged that Mexican Americans were victims of racism, but they did not promote a nonwhite racial identity for their people. Instead, they promoted the image of Mexican Americans as a white ethnic group that had little in common with African Americans. Some ignored their nonwhite Native American racial background for fear of being put in the category of 'people of color' and thus suffering the same discrimination as African Americans. They believed that by minimizing the existence of racism toward their people, they could 'deflect' anti-Mexican sentiment in society. Others rejected their nonwhite origins altogether and promoted a 'Spanish' or 'Latin American' identity.[4] As products of a racist society, others simply held anti-Black attitudes. Mass protest, confrontation, radicalism, and coalition politics with other people of color were therefore rejected as alternatives in the pursuit of civil rights and equal opportunity in jobs and education.

They perceived US society as democratic: all Mexican Americans had to do was to vote and elect their own to political office. LULAC, MAPA, and CSO, for example, were indeed able to elect a few of their members to office, but on the whole, Mexican Americans remained underrepresented in the political process and largely powerless. This was especially true in California.

From the ranks of the more progressive members of the Mexican American Generation emerged intellectuals who had a more critical attitude toward US democracy. Ralph Guzman personified these intellectuals. Like many of them he was a World War II veteran who had attended college on the G.I. Bill and had participated in the development of new middle-class organizations. He was a prominent member of CSO and worked as a journalist for the *Eastside Sun* community newspaper, where he first spoke out against injustices suffered by Mexicans and Mexican Americans.[5] He also served as director of the civil rights department of the Alianza Hispano-Americana, and in that capacity he engaged in litigation against the segregation of Mexican American children in the schools. During the 1950s he was one of the few Mexican Americans who spoke out against McCarthyism. In recognition of his work for civil rights, he became the first Mexican American appointed to the Board of Directors of the American Civil Liberties Union (ACLU). Guzman received much support from another World War II veteran, Edward Roybal, the first Mexican American to be elected to the Los Angeles City Council. Roybal jeopardized his re-election by courageously defending the rights of free speech and association during the McCarthy era and publicly criticizing the use of 'Red Scare' tactics against those who defended Mexican Americans against racist attacks. One of the most progressive members of the Mexican-American Generation, Roybal was a cofounder of CSO and MAPA and later became the first Mexican American congressman from California.

When John F. Kennedy declared his candidacy for president in 1960, he called Guzman and other leaders of the Mexican American middle-class and professional organizations for help. The Kennedy campaign thus marked the entry of this leadership into national politics. They played an important role in the campaign through the Viva Kennedy Clubs they organized in the southwestern states. The Kennedy campaign also recruited Mexican American college student activists into the Viva Kennedy Clubs and they became visible as well in middle-class organizations. Most important, it marked the beginning of a new era of politics that was to eventually produce the Chicano Generation: Mexican American student activists who would embark upon a new quest for identity and power characterized by a militant and radical politics.

The politics of the early 1960s differed markedly from those of the 1950s. The Kennedy presidency followed by the Johnson administration marked the end of McCarthyism and the beginning of a liberal political era in national politics. Liberalism nurtured the aspirations for political change on the part of African Americans and created cracks in the system of racial oppression in the South. The dramatic emergence of the civil rights movement generated reform in education and politics. Although chiefly aimed at benefiting African Americans, the movement created a political atmosphere beneficial to Mexican American working-class youth, for it gave them more access to institutions of higher education. Their access to college was no longer limited to patronage by the YMCA and the Protestant and Catholic churches, as had been the case in the 1930s, nor was it limited to veterans with G.I. Bill benefits, as it had largely been in the 1940s. There were now hundreds of youth of Mexican descent attending college as a direct result of federal educational programs made possible by the civil rights movement and implemented especially during the Johnson administration.

The growing numbers of Mexican American students on college campuses did not come close to representing a significant proportion of the Mexican American population: Mexican American youth remained severely underrepresented. Neither did they produce a visible Mexican American student activism. But from those numbers came a few student activists who, between 1963 and 1967, participated in some activities and organizations of the civil rights movement. Some of them became active indirectly or directly as members of the Student Nonviolent Coordinating Committee. For example, Maria Varela became a key SNCC organizer in Alabama, where she established an adult literacy project.[6] She was from New Mexico and before joining SNCC had been a cofounder of Students for a Democratic Society at the University of Michigan. Elizabeth ('Betita') Sutherland Martinez, a civil rights activist of Mexican descent, became the director of the New York City SNCC office in 1964 and also worked in Mississippi.[7] Others participated in the 1963 March on Washington organized by Dr. Martin Luther King, Jr. and the Southern Christian Leadership Conference. At San Jose State College in Northern California, a few Mexican American students joined a campus protest when a Black student was denied admission.[8]

In the mid-1960s, some of those who had participated in SNCC and other organizations or who had been influenced by the civil rights movement came to the realization that Mexican Americans were not a concern of the Black civil rights leadership and its allies. The War on Poverty programs created by the Johnson administration did not initially address poverty in the *barrios* of the South and Midwest. The first organized student effort in the nation to bring specific attention to the needs of Mexican Americans and youth in particular took place on the San Jose State College campus in 1964 when Armando Valdez organized the Student Initiative (SI). Valdez was a member of Students for a Democratic Society and a supporter of SNCC.[9] He recruited some students from the handful of Mexican Americans on campus at that time and others from the ranks of white liberal student activists. The objectives of Student Initiative focused on pressuring the campus administration to create programs to recruit Mexican American students and tutorial programs to help them survive once they entered college.

Mexican American student activists were also exposed to a more radical politics during the early 1960s as left political organizations resurfaced from the underground where they had been driven during the McCarthy era. Communist and socialist youth groups became visible on college campuses as did nonsocialist New Left groups like SDS. Campus protest against the Vietnam War was also becoming visible, as manifested in the 'teach-ins' organized by white liberal and leftist faculty and students.

In 1964 Luis Valdez and Roberto Rubalcava, student activists at San Jose State, became associated with the Progressive Labor Party (PL); as an undergraduate student Valdez had been active in the Viva Kennedy Clubs and in MAPA Valdez and Rubalcava travelled to Cuba as part of a PL delegation,[10] and their first-hand observation of the Cuban revolution inspired them to produce the first radical manifesto written by Mexican American student activists. The manifesto read in part:

> The Mexican in the United States has been . . . no less a victim of American imperialism than his impoverished brothers in Latin America. In the words of the Second Declaration of Havana, tell him of 'misery, feudal exploitation, illiteracy, starvation wages,' and he will tell you that you speak of Texas; tell him of 'unemployment, the policy of repression against the workers, discrimination . . . oppression by the oligarchies', and he will tell you that you speak of California; tell him of US domination in Latin America, and he will tell you that he knows that Shark and what he devours, because he has lived in its very entrails. The history of the American Southwest provides a brutal panorama of nascent imperialism.[11]

The manifesto represented a radical departure from the political thought of the Mexican-American Generation and a harsh critique of its political leadership:

> Spanish-speaking leaders are not leaders at all; Americanized beyond recall, they neither understand or care about the basic Mexican-American population, which has an identity of its own. As sons of Mexican manual laborers in California, we have travelled to Revolutionary Cuba . . . to emphasize the historical and cultural unanimity

of all Latin American peoples, north and south of the border. Having no leaders of our own, we accept Fidel Castro.[12]

Valdez returned from Cuba and after graduating from college joined the radical San Francisco Mime Troupe, where he continued to refine his critique of the assimilationist and accommodationist perspective of the Mexican American Generation and worked to develop a new cultural identity and politics for Mexican Americans. Some of that thinking came to fruition when he joined the farmworkers' struggle in Delano, California in 1965 and founded the Teatro Campesino. Many of the ideas behind the conceptualization of the Chicano identity and the development of the Chicano Generation of the late 1960s emanated from the ideas of Luis Valdez and the cultural work of his Teatro Campesino. Key members of the Teatro were student activists he recruited from college campuses in Northern California.[13] One of the most prominent of them was Ysidro Ramon Macias, an undergraduate activist at the University of California, Berkeley. Macias became one of the Teatro's original playwrights; his influential play *The Ultimate Pendejada* dramatized the rejection of the assimilationism of Mexican-American identity and the emergence of Chicano identity.

However, Valdez and Rubalcava were unusual in the early 1960s. Most Mexican American student activists remained very much in the mold of the Mexican-American Generation's political thought and identity. Middle-class and professional organizations reached Mexican American youth by directly recruiting them into their organizations or indirectly influencing their ideological direction through participation in community youth programs. LULAC, for example, had a youth group called the Junior LULAC for youth between the ages of fourteen and eighteen. Its purpose was defined as carrying 'forth the work of the LULAC at the teen-age level and serving as a training ground for the future leadership of the organization via participation in its 'social, civic, sports, and parliamentary activities.'[14] The LULAC constitution made clear that its youth auxiliary could not act 'contrary to the direction of the LULAC Supreme Council or the better judgement of its adult leadership.'[15]

Members of AMAE and MAPA and other professional Mexican American political activists, mostly social workers and teachers, promoted participation in the Catholic Youth Organization (CYO), Protestant church programs, and city youth programs. As in the 1930s, Los Angeles again became the site of a conference of Mexican American youth to provide 'citizenship training'. This time around the conference was not sponsored by the YMCA but was organized by the Los Angeles County Human Relations Commission under the leadership of Mexican American World War II and Korean War veterans who had become social workers and teachers.[16] These conferences were held in the summer at Camp Hess Kramer and were patterned somewhat after the YMCA Mexican Youth Conferences of the 1930s. The first conference was held in 1963.[17] In addition to promoting good citizenship, the conferences were forums for discussion of problems in the schools and communities of the participants. Speakers came from the leadership of middle-class and professional organizations, and they exposed the student participants to the politics of the times. However, unlike the YMCA conferences of the 1930s, the Camp Kramer conferences did not result in a publication similar to *The Mexican Voice*.

Most of the participants were bright, 'clean-cut' high school students selected for their leadership skills. After entering college some of them became participants in the formation of Mexican American student organizations on campuses in the Los Angeles area. These new organizations promoted Mexican American identity and the theme of 'progress through education' defined by the 1930s student activists.

Before these student organizations emerged, however, several other events occurred which, in addition to the civil rights movement, also had great impact on Mexican American student activists in the early 1960s. These included the dramatic emergence of the farmworkers struggle in California led by César Chávez, the land grant struggle in New Mexico led by Reies López Tijerina, and increasing discontent on the part of the Mexican American middle class leadership with the Democratic Party and other dominant political institutions.

On 16 September 1965, the anniversary of Mexican independence from Spain in 1810, the National Farm Workers Association (NFWA) met at a local Catholic church hall in Delano, California and voted to join the striking Filipino grape pickers in the area. Four days later, members of the NFWA led by César Chávez joined their Filipino brothers and sisters on the picket lines with shouts of 'Viva La Causa!'[18] Luis Valdez quoted the 'Plan de Delano' which proclaimed 'the beginning of a social movement in fact and not pronouncements'.[19] The 'Plan de Delano' defined the farmworker struggle as a nonviolent revolution 'for social justice' led by the 'sons of the Mexican Revolution' and called for the unity of all poor farmworkers across the nation:

> The strength of the poor is also in union. We know that the poverty of the Mexican or Filipino worker in California is the same as that of all farm workers across the country, the Negroes and poor whites, the Puerto Ricans, Japanese, and Arabians; in short, all the races that comprise with all the working men in the nation . . . to those who oppose us be they ranchers, police, politicians, or speculators, we say that we are going to continue fighting until we die, or we win. WE SHALL OVERCOME.[20]

Student activists, especially those on some of the larger college and University campuses in California, were moved by the upwelling of the farmworkers' struggle to begin support activities on behalf of the farmworker movement.

The increasing discontent of the leadership of LULAC, MAPA, and other middle-class organizations also had a significant impact on student activists associated with those organizations. The nature of this discontent was not ideological but was initially related to the lack of upward mobility within the Democratic Party and other institutions, lack of

Democratic support for Mexican American candidates for elective office, and the party's habit of taking the Mexican American vote for granted. MAPA and PASSO were in fact created by the middle-class leadership as a direct result of those realities. MAPA in California was the direct result of the Democratic Party's refusal to support the candidacies of prominent political leaders Edward Roybal and Henry López for statewide office.

The Viva Kennedy campaign in 1960 had been a watershed in the development of middle-class political organizations, since it marked the entry of their leadership into the arena of national politics for the first time. With the exception of California, Viva Kennedy Clubs had successfully mobilized the Mexican American vote for Kennedy. After Kennedy's election to the presidency, these leaders expected that some of their own would receive high-level appointments in the Kennedy administration. These expectations were frustrated. The Mexican American organizations were ignored by Kennedy and Democratic Party leaders. The leadership of MAPA bitterly criticized the Kennedy administration at the organization's fourth annual convention in November 1963, just days before Kennedy's assassination in Dallas. Edward Roybal criticized Kennedy for not doing anything he had promised during the course of the 'Viva Kennedy' campaign of 1960: 'It has taken the Kennedy Administration three years to appoint a coordinator on Latin American affairs, and it has done nothing for Mexican Americans in the Southwest who helped the President get elected.'[21]

It was not until the Johnson administration that some Mexican Americans were appointed to a specially created presidential committee named the Inter-Agency of Mexican American Affairs, but this committee had no power nor was it an integral part of the administration. To add insult to injury, Johnson's War on Poverty did not have Mexican Americans on its list of priorities but instead had a limited focus on the African American poor.

In Crystal City, Texas in 1963 the leadership of PASSO united with the predominantly Mexican American Teamsters union in a local election campaign. The result was the defeat of all the white candidates and the victory of all the Mexican American candidates endorsed by the two organizations. The Crystal City election was of historic significance: for the first time Mexican Americans had taken complete control of a city government in the Southwest. Crystal City was thus widely viewed as a 'revolt' against white political domination. Although those who took power were far from being radicals, their election did have a profound impact on student activists in Texas.[22] The Mexican American takeover of Crystal City's City Council lasted only two years, but it was training ground for Jose Angel Gutiérrez, at the time a nineteen-year-old undergraduate, who was to cofound MAYO four years later at St. Mary's University in San Antonio. He later returned to Crystal City to help found La Raza Unida Party, the first Mexican American political party in US history, and to lead a second electoral revolt with more permanence than the first.[23]

By 1966 the Mexican American middle-class leadership was prepared to take more public measures to express their discontent with the Johnson administration. On 8 April, at a conference called by the federal Equal Employment Opportunity Commission in Albuquerque, New Mexico, the presidents of LULAC, PASSO, and other organizations attacked the commission for not having a Mexican American leader as a member and for having only one on its Washington, DC staff. They also expressed displeasure that the commission did not take any action against the eight hundred major corporations in the Southwest that did not employ any Mexican Americans. The leaders presented eight demands to the Johnson administration for affirmative action on behalf of Mexican Americans.[24] After an hour at the conference, all fifty Mexican American leaders, representing organizations in all the southwestern states, walked out in protest.

The walkout in Albuquerque marked the first time that the middle-class leadership had engaged in an act of collective protest against the government. This action, while mild in comparison to what happened later in the 1960s, nevertheless had some impact on those student activists who were products of the Mexican-American Generation. It revealed a more critical political consciousness that was emerging among those who had not previously protested the contradictions of US democracy and who in particular had never used a civil rights tactic of public protest on behalf of Mexican Americans. The walkout did not represent a change in ideology on the part of the middle-class leadership, but it did encourage a more critical posture toward dominant political institutions among the Mexican American youth associated with those organizations.

A few of the middle-class leaders did make a radical departure from the ideology of the Mexican-American Generation. The most important of them was Rodolfo 'Corky' Gonzáles of Denver, Colorado. After a successful prize-fighting career, he had become a successful small businessman as a bail bondsman and was a Democratic Party politician well on his way to elective office. He had served as a Democratic precinct captain and was appointed the Colorado Coordinator of the 'Viva Kennedy' campaign in 1960. He served as the director of the War on Poverty program in Denver during the Johnson administration. By 1965, however, he had grown increasingly disenchanted with the Democratic Party leadership and resigned his party membership and posts as well as his position in the War on Poverty program. He explained his decision in a letter to the county chairman of the Democratic Party:

> The individual who makes his way through the political muck of today's world, and more so the minority representatives, suffer from such immense loss of soul and dignity that the end results are as rewarding as a heart attack, castration, or cancer. . . . I can only visualize your goal as complete emasculation of manhood, sterilization of human dignity, and that you not only consciously but purposely are creating a world of lackeys, political boot-lickers and prostitutes.[25]

After his resignation from the Democratic Party he founded the Crusade for Justice in 1965, the first Mexican American civil rights organization in the nation. He and his organization were to become extremely significant in the emergence of the Chicano movement.

On 5 June 1967, another major event took place that had an important impact on Mexican American student activists. It occurred in Tierra Amarilla, New Mexico where Race López Tijerina had been leading a struggle to recapture lands that had been stolen from the Hispano people (Spanish-Americans who were direct descendants of the original Spanish colonizers of New Mexico).[26] Tijerina had founded the Alianza Federal de Mercedes as the organizational vehicle of that struggle. On 5 June, a group of armed men from the Alianza took over the county courthouse, taking twenty hostages who they held for about an hour and then released. A jailer and a state police officer were wounded. Later Tijerina's men fled into the mountains. The National Guard was mobilized, and it carried out a massive manhunt, complete with tanks. Forty innocent Hispanos were arrested. This was the first militant armed action taken by Mexican Americans anywhere in the Southwest for over a hundred years, and it became a source of inspiration for some student activists, especially in New Mexico.

With all these events taking place between 1964 and 1967, Mexican American student activism was becoming more visible on the campus as well as in the community. Federally funded War on Poverty programs in the community became training grounds for many students, and they became participants in local community politics. Some of them were influenced by the grass-roots community-organizing approach of Saul Alinsky.

By 1966, student activists, though still relatively few in number, were seriously discussing the formation of distinct Mexican American student organizations on their campuses throughout the Southwest. By the fall of 1967 organizations had emerged on several college campuses in Los Angeles and on two campuses in Texas. At St. Mary's College in San Antonio, Texas it was named the Mexican American Youth Organization (MAYO).[27] At the University of Texas at Austin it was called the Mexican American Student Organization (MASO), later changing its name to MAYO.[28] In the Los Angeles area, chapters of the United Mexican American Students (UMAS) were formed at UCLA; California State College, Los Angeles; Loyola University; University of Southern California; California State College, Long Beach; and San Fernando State College. At East Los Angeles Community College, another group organized as the Mexican American Student Association (MASA).[29]

At about the same time, the Student Initiative organization at San Jose State College in Northern California changed its name to the Mexican American Student Confederation (MASC).[30] Chapters followed at Fresno State, Hayward State, and Sacramento State colleges. The following year, 1968, students formed a chapter of UMAS at the University of Colorado at Boulder,[31] and a MASC chapter at the University of California, Berkeley. By 1969 UMAS chapters were emerging in other parts of the Southwest. The first UMAS chapter in the Midwest was organized at the University of Notre Dame by Gilbert Cárdenas, a first-year graduate student in sociology and former undergraduate member of UMAS in California.[32]

Ideologically, most of these new student organizations had objectives similar to those of the Mexican Youth Conferences of the 1930s and the Mexican American Movement of the 1940s. They emphasized the theme of 'progress through education', and concentrated on activities related to recruitment of Mexican American students and helping them stay in college. The new student organizations worked with Mexican American professionals to raise scholarship funds for needy students, and sought their advice on matters relating to the education of Mexican Americans. Some of the student activists themselves attended college with help from scholarships made available by middle-class organizations like LULAC. With few exceptions, the new student groups mirrored the political consciousness of the Mexican American Generation of the 1930s and were committed to the development of a new generation of professionals who could play a leading role in the betterment of the Mexican American community within the context of middle-class politics.

These student organizations did not yet represent a student movement in political terms. But as they came into direct contact with community politics and learned more about the Chávez and Tijerina movements they came to represent a student movement in the making. By the end of 1967, the antiwar and Black Power movements had become other sources of growing militancy among some of the student leaders. The politics of the times were now characterized by mass protest, and the fact that the main protagonists in the unfolding drama were white and Black radical youth did not go unnoticed by the leadership of the Mexican American student organizations. Some of them joined with SDS and the Black student unions in planning campus protests.

But for the most part, UMAS, MASC, and MAYO stuck to Mexican American issues. They began to sponsor campus programs and demonstrations to support Chávez and Tijerina. Student caravans were organized to take food to Delano, where the headquarters of the United Farm Workers Organizing Committee was located. Student organizations provided much of the manpower on the picket lines at the Safeway stores and other markets during the grape boycott, and they demanded that colleges and universities boycott grapes. They brought Chávez, Tijerina, and Corky Gonzáles to speak on campuses throughout the Southwest.

The initial student support for the Chávez and Tijerina movements, however, was largely related to pride in the fact that two Mexican American leaders struggling for social justice had achieved national recognition and extensive mass media coverage. In 1967 Chávez was the first Mexican American leader to appear on the cover of *Time* magazine. He was promoted by the mass media and his followers as the 'Mexican American Dr. Martin Luther King, Jr.' since he was also a disciple of the Ghandian philosophy of nonviolence. Luis Valdez, who had proclaimed Fidel Castro as his leader upon his return from Cuba in 1964, became the most ardent promoter of Chávez as 'our first real Mexican American leader . . . [the one] we had been waiting for'.[33]

Support for Chávez also stemmed from the reality that most Mexicans and Mexican Americans had been farmworkers at some time in their lives. But the stark reality had to be faced that the farmworker movement was far from being a broad civil rights effort; Chávez was a union organizer and lent his increasing prestige and astute leadership abilities only to farmworkers--or to efforts that he saw as in the immediate interests of farmworkers. He consistently shunned responsibility for leading a movement broader than a union for farm workers, and he told student leaders that the issue of educational change was not on his agenda.[34] Many of his followers, however, including Luis Valdez, continued to embrace Chávez as the leader of all Mexican Americans and eventually as one of the leaders of the Chicano Movement.

Despite the inspiration provided by César Chávez and the farmworkers movement, student activists found it difficult to organize students solely around the issues related to the struggle of the farmworkers. The attention given to the farmworker movement by liberal politicians like the Kennedys and by the mass media contributed greatly to the movement's rise and the making of Chávez into a respected national leader. But it also reinforced the existing stereotype of all Mexican Americans as farmworkers. Although strongly supportive of the Chávez and Tijerina movements, student leaders on urban campuses were well aware that the vast majority of their people lived in cities. They therefore felt the need to build an urban movement to address the issues faced by the majority of Mexican Americans. Neither César Chávez and the farmworkers nor Reies Tijerina and the farmers of northern New Mexico truly addressed the needs of urban youth.

Rodolfo 'Corky' Gonzáles did. Gonzáles, founder and head of the Crusade for Justice, a civil rights organization in Denver, Colorado was in his early forties but younger than Chávez and Tijerina; in addition he was a product of an urban barrio. He had parted company with the Mexican American middle-class organizations he had worked closely with in the past and now spoke directly, and forcefully, to the issues facing the youth. His charisma captured the imagination of young activists, students and nonstudents alike.

In 1967 he wrote an epic poem entitled *I Am Joaquín*, which was distributed to the UMAS, MASC and MAYO student leadership throughout the Southwest by La Causa Publications in Oakland, California. This poem was published in book form in 1972. *I Am Joaquín* did not offer its readers a well-defined radical ideology, but it did provide a critical framework for the developing student movement through its portrayal of the quest for identity and its critique of racism. More than a poem, it was an ambitious essay that attempted to dramatize key events and personalities from important moments of Mexican and Mexican American history, beginning with the indigenous ancestors prior to the Spanish conquest. It ended with the adamant assertion that people of Mexican descent and their culture would continue to endure.

I Am Joaquín filled a vacuum, for most student activists had never read a book about Mexican American history--especially one that linked that history with Mexican history. The few books available on some aspect of the Mexican American experience were not yet part of the curriculum in colleges, much less elementary and secondary schools. The only book that presented the history of Mexican Americans had gone out of print long before the 1960s. That book was *North From Mexico* by Carey McWilliams, a white liberal who had supported the Mexican American civil rights struggles in California before becoming the editor of the *Nation* magazine.

The most significant aspect of *I Am Joaquín* was that it captured both the agony and the jubilation permeating the identity crisis faced by Mexican American youth in the process of assimilation. As Gonzáles explains in his introduction, 'writing *I Am Joaquín* was a journey back through history, a painful self-evaluation, a wandering search for my peoples and, most of all, for my own identity.'[35]

This search for identity and the dilemmas that it posed are the key to understanding the Chicano student movement of the 1960s. To a large degree, the movement was a quest for identity, an effort to recapture what had been lost through the socialization process imposed by US schools, churches, and other institutions. In order to create a new identity, as an alternative to the one defined by the Mexican American Generation, the more militant student leadership sensed the need to take on that socialization process. The following portions of *I Am Joaquín* were especially meaningful to the militant student leaders of the 1960s:

> I am Joaquín,
> lost in a world of confusion,
> caught up in the whirl of a
> gringo society,
> confused by the rules,
> scorned by attitudes,
> suppressed by manipulation,
> and destroyed by modern society . . .
>
> I have come a long way to nowhere,
> unwillingly dragged by that
>   monstrous, technical,
>   industrial giant called
>   Progress
> and Anglo success . . .
> in a country that has wiped out
> all my history,
>   stifled all my pride,

in a country that has placed a
different weight of indignity upon
        my
        age-
        old
        burdened back.

        Inferiority
is the new load . . .
        I look at myself
        and see part of me
who rejects my father and my mother
and dissolves into the melting pot
        to disappear in shame.
        I sometimes
        sell my brother out
        and reclaim him
        for my own when society gives me
            token leadership
            in society's own name.[36]

Gonzáles did not advocate a specific identity for Mexican Americans in his poem: at the time he wrote *I Am Joaquin* he believed it possible to organize a movement regardless of the question of a specific identity:

La Raza!
    Mejicano!
        Espanol !
            Latino!
                Hispano!
                    Chicano!
or whatever I call myself,
    I look the same
    I feel the same
    I cry
        and
sing the same.[37]

It was Luis Valdez who first gave concrete direction to the development of a distinct Chicano identity and its emphasis on the nonwhite legacy of the Mexican American people. Valdez argued that there was only one identity appropriate to the oppressed Mexican American, and that identity was rooted in the nonwhite indigenous past and in the working-class history of the people. He wrote that the Spanish conquest of Mexico 'was no conquest at all', that although it did shatter 'our ancient Indian universe . . . more of it was left above ground than beans and tortillas'.[38] Valdez thus stressed the Native American roots of the Mexican American experience and rejected those of the Spanish, who were European and white:

> Most of us know we are not European simply by looking in a mirror . . . the shape of the eyes, the curve of the nose, the color of skin, the texture of hair; these things belong to another time, another people. Together with a million little stubborn mannerisms, beliefs, myths, superstitions, words, thoughts . . . they fill our Spanish life with Indian contradictions. It is not enough to say we suffer an identity crisis, because that crisis has been our way of life for the last five centuries.[39]

Valdez, like Gonzáles, acknowledged that La Raza included all Mexican Americans, but he emphasized the working-class realities of the majority. As he put it,

> Our campesinos, the farm-working *raza* find it difficult to participate in this alien North American country. The acculturated Mexican-Americans in the cities, ex-raza, find it easier. They have solved their Mexican contradictions with a pungent dose of Americanism, and are more concerned with status, money and bad breath than with their ultimate destiny . . . they will melt into the American pot and be no more. But the farmworking *raza* will not disappear so easily . . . We are repelled by the human disintegration of peoples and cultures as they fall apart in this Great Gringo Melting Pot.[40]

During the same year that Corky Gonzales's poem was first distributed, a handful of student activists in Northern California, under the guidance of Professor Octavio Romano-V., an anthropologist at the University of California, Berkeley, published the first issues of *El Grito: A Journal of Contemporary Mexican-American Thought,* the first Mexican American scholarly journal to appear in the United States. One of their purposes in launching *El Grito* was to challenge the racist stereotypes of Mexican Americans that had developed and persisted within the social science disciplines. The journal was to be a forum for 'Mexican American self definition', a direct effort to deal with the question of identity, although in less political and more academic terms than those normally used by activists.

Identity and the discovery of one's roots were thus becoming crucial issues for student organizations as they emerged on campus after campus. And as student activists confronted the issue of Mexican American identity, they increasingly exposed the historic role of the schools in the undermining of Mexican American culture.

The Rise of Student Militancy

On the morning of 3 March 1968, shouts of 'Blow Out!' rang through the halls of Abraham Lincoln High School, a predominantly Mexican American school in East Los Angeles. Over a thousand students walked out of their classes, teacher Sal Castro among them. Waiting for them outside the school grounds were members of UMAS and various community activists. They distributed picket signs listing some of the thirty-six demands that had been developed by a community and student strike committee. The signs protested racist school policies and teachers and called for freedom of speech, the hiring of Mexican American teachers and administrators, and classes on Mexican American history and culture. As might be expected, the signs that caught the attention of the mass media and the police were those reading 'Chicano Power!', 'Viva La Raza!', and 'Viva La Revolucion!'. By the afternoon of that day, several thousand more students had walked out of five other *barrio* high schools to join the strike. The strike brought the Los Angeles city school system, the largest in the nation, to a standstill and made news across the country; a *Los Angeles Times* reporter interpreted the strike as 'The Birth of Brown Power'.[41] Over ten thousand students had participated by the time the Los Angeles 'blow-outs' ended a week and a half later.

But the strike accomplished something much more important than shaking up school administrators or calling public attention to the educational problems of Mexican American youth. Although not one of its original objectives, the strike was the first major mass protest explicitly against racism undertaken by Mexican Americans in the history of the United States. As such, it had a profound impact on the Mexican American community in Los Angeles and in other parts of the country, and it generated an increased political awareness along with visible efforts to mobilize the community. This was manifested in the revitalization of existing community political organizations and the emergence of new ones, with youth playing significant leadership roles.

Overnight, student activism reached levels of intensity never before witnessed. A few Mexican American student activists had participated in civil rights marches, anti-Vietnam War protests, and had walked the picket lines for the farmworker movement. But the high school strike of 1968 was the first time students of Mexican descent had marched en masse in their own demonstration against racism and for educational change. It was also the first time that they had played direct leadership roles in organizing a mass protest. The slogans of 'Chicano Power!', 'Viva La Raza!', and Viva La Revolucion!' that rang throughout the strike reflected an increasing militancy and radicalism in the ranks of UMAS and other student organizations. The nature of these concerns and the momentum built up among Mexican American students-both in high school and on college campuses-

-broke the ideological bonds that characteristically keep student organizations, and students in general, from questioning authority and the status quo. Membership grew as those organizations and their leaders became protagonists in struggles for change in Mexican American communities. The strike moved student activism beyond the politics of accommodation and integration which had been shaped by the Mexican American Generation and the community's middle-class leadership.

However, it was not student activists who conceived of the strike; the idea originated with Sal Castro, the teacher at Lincoln High School who had walked out with his students. Like Corky Gonzáles, he had become disillusioned with the Democratic Party and with Mexican American middle-class leadership. Also like Gonzáles, he had played a prominent role in the 'Viva Kennedy' campaign in 1960, serving as the student coordinator of the Southern California campaign. He was a Korean War-era veteran attending college on the G.I. Bill at the time. Like other veterans, he played a role in MAPA and was a founder of the Association of Mexican American Educators. He had been a firm believer in the 'American Dream' and was on his way toward a successful political career. In addition to the Kennedy campaign, he had worked on other campaigns and had been elected to the Democratic Party Central Committee.[42]

But by 1964 Castro had come to the realization that the Democrats did not have the interests of Mexican Americans at heart and that corruption was inherent in the political system.[43] A product of the barrio schools in East Los Angeles, Castro returned to the neighborhood as a teacher only to find that racism toward Mexican American youth remained virulent. Through the AMAE organization he worked hard to make reforms within the school bureaucracy but was not able to accomplish much. Like other middle-class leaders, he saw that the civil rights movement ignored Mexican Americans and that they were low on the agenda of the War on Poverty and in education reform plans. But unlike most other middle-class leaders, Castro came to the conclusion that his people needed their own civil rights movement and that the only alternative in the face of a racist educational system was nonviolent protest against the schools. He therefore prepared to sacrifice his teaching career, if necessary, in the interest of educational change for Mexican American children.[44] The strike made Castro one of the movement's leaders.

The strike of 1968 went beyond the objectives of Castro and others concerned only with improving education. It was the first loud cry for Chicano Power and self-determination, serving as the catalyst for the formation of the Chicano student movement as well as the larger Chicano Power Movement of which it became the most important sector. In response to the strike, one of Mexico's foremost intellectuals, Carlos Fuentes, wrote that

Mexican Americans . . . are reminding us all of the very powerful roots of our personality, of the very wide extension of our cultural image and of the community action that is required if that identity is to become something more than a passing reference in celebrations.[45]

After the strike the UMAS leadership urged the members to assume a more political role in both the community and on campus and to think in terms of being part of a student movement. In the first Mexican American student organization newsletter to be published and distributed throughout the Southwest, the UMAS chapter at California State College, Los Angeles, described its role:

UMAS is cognizant of the social, economic, and political ills of our Mexican people. The desire of UMAS is to play a vital role in the liberation of the Mexican American people from second class citizenship. To do this we see our role to stand united in the effort to affect social change for the betterment of our people. We believe the ills that beset our people are not products of our culture, but that said ills have been inflicted by the institutions which today comprise the establishment in the American society.[46]

This first newsletter urged students to participate in the Poor People's March on Washington scheduled for later in the spring of 1968 and to join the Mexican American delegation to it being led by Reies López Tijerina. It also called on students to support Sal Castro, who had been suspended by the Los Angeles Board of Education for his role in the strike and for his continued support for change in the schools. Finally, UMAS advocated an 'internal and external' plan of action for the student movement:

[Recognizing] that the system cannot be changed overnight, we feel it is necessary that we work within the existing framework to the degree that it not impede our effectiveness. It is historically evident that working within the existing framework is not sufficient; therefore, our external approach will consist of exerting outside pressure on those institutions that directly affect the Mexican American community.[47]

The term *Chicano* appeared often--mostly interchangeably with *Mexican American*--but UMAS advanced no particular ideology for the student movement at this point. The newsletter made clear that UMAS was 'open to all students who want to contribute to the betterment of the Mexican American' and that it had 'no political labels'.[48] UMAS continued to stress educational issues, involvement in the community to assist high school students and defend them from harassment by racist teachers, the need to establish tutorial programs, and efforts to increase enrollments of Mexican American college students. These goals illustrate UMAS's emphasis on reaching out to and being part of the Mexican American community.

In the weeks following the strike, the leadership of each UMAS chapter in the Los Angeles area formed a coordinating body called UMAS Central. The first newsletter of this group called on Chicanos to take pride in their Mexican identity and on students to see themselves as a political vanguard.

> We have begun to recognize our role as an organizational agent through which Chicano students are able to recognize themselves as Mexicans and to take pride in it. We are the avant-garde of the young Mexican American liberation movement: We formulate a philosophy for our people and we provide the hope for the future of Mexicans of all generations. We recognize ourselves as a generation of doers as well as thinkers. . . We are resolved to perpetuate an atmosphere of respect and dignity for our people. . . We are the agents of progress and unity. We demand social justice for a people too long oppressed.[49]

Militancy in the ranks of the developing student movement accelerated as a consequence of the response to the strike on the part of the power structure of the city of Los Angeles and the implementation of directives from the Federal Bureau of Investigation. On 4 March 1968, FBI Director J. Edgar Hoover issued a memo to local law enforcement officials across the country urging them to place top priority on political intelligence work to prevent the development of nationalist movements in minority communities.[50] Hoover's chief goal was to undermine the Black Power Movement, but his directive was considered applicable to other similar movements by the Los Angeles District Attorney, Evelle Younger, a former high official in the FBI and a Republican Party candidate for state attorney general at the time of the strike. The political intelligence units of the Los Angeles City Police and the Los Angeles County Sheriffs office were ordered to investigate the 'Brown Power' strike.

On 2 June 1968, three months after the strike and two days before California's primary elections, thirteen young Mexican American political activists who had been identified as leaders of the emerging 'Brown Power' movement were indicted by the Los Angeles County Grand Jury on conspiracy charges for their roles in organizing the strike. The indictments charged that the thirteen activists had conspired to 'wilfully disturb the peace and quiet' of the city of Los Angeles and disrupt the educational process in its schools.[51] They were characterized as members of communist 'subversive organizations' or outside agitators intent on radicalizing Mexican American students. Each of the thirteen activists faced a total of sixty-six years in prison if found guilty.

None of the 'LA Thirteen' were in fact communists or members of 'subversive organizations'. They included Sal Castro; Eliezer Risco, editor of a new community newspaper named *La Raza*; and Patricio Sanchez, a member of MAPA. The remaining ten were all student activists and key leaders of their respective organizations. They were Moctezuma Esparza of UCLA UMAS and four members of the recently formed Brown Berets organization (David Sanchez, prime minister; Carlos Montes, minister of communications; Ralph Ramirez, minister of defense; and Fred Lopez). Others were activists working with community War on Poverty programs: Richard Vigil, Gilberto C. Olmeda, Joe Razo, and Henry Gómez. At that time president of UMAS at California State College, Los Angeles, I was also a member of the LA Thirteen. Instead of preventing the rise of another 'nationalist movement', the indictments of the LA Thirteen simply fueled the fire of an emerging radicalism among Mexican American students.

Several weeks later, Mexican American graduating seniors at San Jose State College and members of the audience walked out during commencement exercises. Approximately two hundred people were involved in the demonstration. They denounced the college for its lack of commitment to the surrounding Mexican American community, as shown by the low enrollment of Mexican American students on campus. The walkout was also a protest against the inadequate training of professionals such as teachers, social workers, and policemen, who, after graduating, would work in the Mexican American community with no understanding of the culture and needs of that community, or--most important--of how their own racism affected their dealings with Mexican Americans.

Prior to the commencement, the student leadership had demanded that all graduating seniors be required to participate in intensive two-week sensitivity workshops so that they could learn something about Mexican American culture. The proposed workshops were to be taught by students from San Jose's Mexican American community who knew the problems awaiting anyone performing a job that required working with Mexican Americans. The student leaders called their protest the 'commencement' of a militant student movement that would struggle to change institutions of higher education responsible for perpetuating racism against their people.

That walkout was the first protest activity undertaken by Mexican American students on a college campus. Five months later, in November 1968, Mexican American students became part of the strike at San Francisco State College, organized by the Third World Liberation Front (TWLF). It was marked by violent confrontations between students and the police, and many students were injured. The strike began over issues initially raised by Black students and lasted until March 1969. Although the students' demands mostly focused on the needs of Black students, one demand called for the creation of a Department of Raza Studies under the umbrella of a proposed School of Ethnic Studies. The TWLF also demanded open admission for all third world students. The San Francisco State strike was significant because it marked the first time that Mexican American and other third world student activists united to create a politically explosive 'rainbow coalition.'

In October 1968, the Mexican American Student Confederation took over the office of Charles Hitch, president of the University of California system, to protest his refusal to discontinue the purchase of grapes while Chávez's farmworkers were on strike--part of a national campaign to boycott grapes in support of the UFW. The takeover of Hitch's office resulted in the arrest of eleven MASC members for trespassing and unlawful assembly. This was the first in a series of third world student confrontations with university authorities on the Berkeley campus, which eventually culminated in the formation of another Third World Liberation Front and student strike.

Patterning itself after the Third World Liberation Front at San Francisco State across the Bay, the TWLF at Berkeley organized its own student strike, which lasted from January through April 1969. It was the first major third world student confrontation within the University of California system, and one of the most violent to occur at any of the university's campuses: many students were arrested or became victims of police violence.

In contrast to the strike at San Francisco State, Mexican American students played a leading role in the organization of the Third World Liberation Front and the strike on the UC Berkeley campus. The strike was aimed at exposing the university's lack of commitment to meeting the educational needs of third world people. Although there were many differences within the TWLF, the strike demands incorporated previous issues raised by both African American and Mexican American student activists. The TWLF demanded the creation of a Third World College with departments of Mexican American, Black and Asian-American studies. It also demanded sufficient resources for the proposed college to involve itself in minority communities and contribute effectively to their development. TWLF demanded that the new college be under the full control of its students, faculty, and representatives of the community; 'self-determination' was to be its principle of governance. Other demands called for open admission for all third world people and poor working-class whites and the recruitment of third world faculty and staff.

There were other high school student strikes throughout the Southwest during 1969, patterned after the 1968 strike in Los Angeles. In Denver, Colorado and Crystal City, Texas, high school strikes also resulted in significant political developments beyond the immediate issues of educational change. In Denver, the strike contributed to the further development of the Crusade for Justice and made Corky Gonzáles a national leader of the emerging Chicano movement. In contrast to the relatively violence-free student strike in Los Angeles, the Denver demonstrations resulted in violent confrontations between police, students, and members of the Crusade for Justice, and Corky Gonzáles was himself arrested. After his release he praised the striking students for risking 'revolutionary' actions" to make history: 'You kids don't realize you have made history. We just talk about revolution. But you act it by facing the shotguns, billies, gas, and mace. You are the real revolutionaries.'[52]

In Crystal City, a high school strike contributed directly to the founding of La Raza Unida Party, a second electoral revolt in that city that resulted in the party's takeover of city government and the school system, and the making of José Angel Gutiérrez into another national leader of the Chicano Movement.

The movement was given further impetus by other events that took place in 1968, the year that was the turning point of the decade. The antiwar movement became a potent political force in national politics as mass protest against the war in Vietnam dramatically increased. Simultaneously, on the battlefields of Vietnam, US troops were being overrun in the Tet offensive, the largest Vietnamese attack of the war. As a result the Johnson administration was forced to agree to peace talks held in Paris later that year. It was also the year that Dr. Martin Luther King, Jr., led the Poor People's March on Washington, which included a contingent of Mexican Americans. Later in the year Dr. King and Senator Robert F. Kennedy were assassinated.

Even more important, 1968 was also the year of international student uprisings from Paris and Berlin to Tokyo to Mexico City. In Mexico City, the site of the Olympics that year, over four hundred students were massacred by the Mexican army. In Paris, students battled police and brought the entire city to a standstill, touching off a month-long nationwide general strike of ten million workers. Between 1968 and 1969, Mexican American student militancy intensified as more and more of them became convinced that they were part of an international revolution in the making.

From the ranks of these militant students came artists, poets and actors who collectively generated a cultural renaissance and whose work played a key role in creating the ideology of the Chicano movement.[53] In Oakland, California the first group of radical artists organized themselves as the Mexican American Liberation Art Front (MALAF). Elsewhere in the Bay Area, Jose and Malaquias Montoya, Esteban Villa, René Yañez, Ralph Maradiaga and Rupert García produced posters whose striking art reflected the movement's quest for identity and power. Other artists emerged in other parts of the nation, and by 1970 a distinct Chicano art movement was in full bloom, which, in addition to radical poster art included a Chicano mural art in the tradition of the Mexican revolutionary artists David Alfaro Sequieros, José Clemente Orozco, and Diego Rivera.[54]

Poets and writers produced campus and community underground newspapers, which replaced student organizational newsletters as the main form of movement communication. These newspapers led to the formation of an independent Chicano Press Association.[55] In addition to Berkeley's *El Grito*, radical poets and writers created other magazines such as *Con Safos* in Los Angeles and *El Pocho Che* in San Francisco.[56]

Student activists also created numerous campus and community based 'guerilla' theater groups patterned after the Teatro Campesino. By 1970 these groups had become part of a national Chicano theater movement called Teatros Nacionales de Aztlán."[57]

The student strikes in the community and on the college campus, in conjunction with the political upheavals of the late sixties, thus generated the framework for the eventual transformation of student activist organizations into a full-blown student movement with clear social and political goals and an ethnic nationalist ideology that came to be known as cultural nationalism.

Notes

1. Edward Garza, 'LULAC: League of United Latin American Citizens,' Master's thesis, Southwest Texas State Teachers College 1951, p.32.

2. Guadalupe San Miguel, Jr., *Let Them All Take Heed*, Austin 1987.

3. Muñoz, 'Galarza,' p. 15.

4. Mario García, 'Americans All: The Mexican-American Generation and the Politics of Wartime Los Angeles, 1941-45', in Rodolfo de La Garza et al., eds, *The Mexican American Experience: An Interdisciplinary Approach*, Austin 1985.

5. Rodolfo Acuña, *A Community Under Siege: A Chronicle of Chicanos East of the Los Angeles River*, 1945-1975, Los Angeles 1984, p. 121.

6. Clayborne Carson, *In Struggle: SNCC and the Black Awakening of the 1960s*, Cambridge, Mass. 1981, p. 119.

7. Betita Martinez, interview, January 1989.

8. Luis Valdez, interview, 11 August 1982.

9. Armando Valdez, interview, 6 January 1983.

10. Luis Valdez, interview.

11. Luis Valdez and Roberto Rubalcava, 'Veneceremos!: Mexican-American Statement on Travel to Cuba', in Luis Valdez and Stan Steiner, eds, *Aztlán: An Anthology of Mexican American Literature,* New York, 1972, pp. 215-16.

12. Ibid.

13. Luis Valdez, interview.

14. League of United Latin American Citizens, *Constitution, By-Laws, and Protocol*, n.p. 1977, p. 24.

15. Ibid., p. 26

16. Juan Gómez-Quiñones, *Mexican Students Por La Raza: The Chicano Student Movement in Southern California, 1966-67*, Santa Barbara 1978, pp. 16-17

17. Acuña, *Community Under Siege*, p. 119.

18. Ronald B. Taylor, *Chávez and the Farm Workers*, Boston 1975.

19. Valdez, 'Plan of Delano', in Valdez and Steiner, eds, *Aztlán*, pp. 197-201.

2O. Ibid.

21. Kenneth C. Burt, 'The History of the Mexican-American Political Association and Chicano Politics in California', unpublished MS, p. 62.

22. John Staples Shockley, *Chicano Revolt in a Texas Town*, Notre Dame 1974.

23. Armando Navarro, 'El Partido de La Raza Unida in Crystal City: A Peaceful Revolution', Ph.D. diss., University of California Riverside 1974.

24. 'Walkout in Albuquerque', Carta Editorial, vol. 3, no. 12, 8 April 1966, in Valdez and Steiner, *Aztlán*, pp. 211-14.

25. Stan Steiner, *La Raza: The Mexican Americans*, New York 1973, pp. 383-84.

26. Peter Nabakov, *Tijerina and the Courthouse Raid*, Berkeley 1970.

27. Navarro, 'La Raza Unida in Crystal City'.

28. César Caballero, 'A Historical Review and Analysis of U.T. MAYO's Social Change Activities', unpublished paper, 1974.

29. Gómez-Quiñonez, *Mexican Students Por La Raza*, p. 19.

30. Armando Valdez, interview.

31. United Mexican American Students, 'La Historia de UMAS', Boulder, Colo. 1970.

32. Gilbert Cárdenas Papers, author's files.

33. Luis Valdez, 'The Tale of La Raza', *Bronze*, vol. 1, no. 1, 25 November 1968.

34. In 1968 Chávez conveyed this message to a delegation of UMAS members who had gone to Delano in support of the United Farm Workers. The meeting was reported to the author in his capacity as president of UMAS.

35. Rudolfo Gonzáles, *I Am Joaquín: An Epic Poem*, New York 1972, p. 1.

36. Ibid., pp. 6, 10, and 51-52.

37. Ibid., p. 98.

38. Valdez, 'The Tale of La Raza'.

39. Ibid.

40. Ibid.

41. Dial Torgerson,'"Brown Power" Unity Seen Behind School Disorders: Start of a Revolution?', *Los Angeles Times,* 17 March 1968.

42. Salvador Castro, interview, 17 March 1982.

43. Ibid.

44. Ibid.

45. Letter from Carlos Fuentes to Prof. Donald W. Bray in response to his invitation to speak at a UMAS event at California State College, Los Angeles, after the strike. Bray had written to Fuentes on my behalf when I was president of UMAS.

46. Carlos Muñoz, Jr., *UMAS Newsletter*, California State University, Los Angeles, 17 April 1968, p. 1.

47. Ibid., p. 2.

48. Ibid., p. 1.

49. *UMAS Central Newsletter*, no. 1, 5 May 1968.

50. Baxter Smith, 'FBI Member Reveals Repression Schemes', *The Black Scholar*, vol. 5, no. 7, April 1974, p. 44.

51. Two years later, in June 1970, a California state appelate court dropped the charges against the thirteen activists. See *Salvador B. Castro et al., Petitioners, v. The Superior Court of Los Angeles County, Respondent; The People, Real Party in Interest.* 9 C.A. 3d 675; 88 Cal. Rptr.500, 1970, pp. 675-720.

52. Steiner, *La Raza.*

53. Tomás Ybarra-Frausto,'The Chicano Movement and the Emergence of a Chicano Poetic Consciousness',in Ricardo Romo and Raymund Paredes, eds, *New Directions in Chicano Scholarship*, Santa Barbara 1977.

54. Rupert García, 'La Raza Murals of California, 1963 to 1970: A Period of Social Change and Protest', Master thesis, University of California 1981. See also Shifra M. Goldman and Tomás Ybarra-Frausto, *Arte Chicano: A Comprehensive Annotated Bibliography of Chicano Art, 1965-1981*, Berkeley 1985.

55. Francisco J. Lewis, *The Uses of the Media by the Chicano Movement: A Study in Minority Access*, New York 1974.
56. Bruce Novoa, *Chicano Poetry: A Responce to Chaos*, Austin 1982.
57. Jorge Huerta, *Chicano Theatre: Themes and Forms*, Ypsilanti, Mich. 1981.

Richard Griswold del Castillo provides a focus on contemporary conditions and issues affecting Latinos and Chicanos during the past decade. Included is a discussion of demographic trends, increasing socio-economic diversity among Latinos and the growing underclass. Griswold also includes a review of the growing political influence of Latinos and their impact on American popular culture. In addition, Griswold explores bilingual education issues, movements against undocumented immigrants and the growing visibility of Chicanos and Latinos in the arts.

Latinos and the "New Immigrants," Since 1975
Richard Griswold del Castillo

In the summer of 1983 the *Los Angeles Times* published a series of articles examining the Mexican American experience in that city. In one feature article, the reporters explored the problem of preferences for ethnic labels and found a lack of unanimity about what Chicanos/Latinos/Hispanics/Mexican Americans/Mexicanos wanted to call themselves. Generally, the native born preferred the label "Mexican-American," followed by "Latino." The term "Hispanic" was third in preference. Mexican immigrants favored the term "Mexicano," also followed by "Latino." While a plurality could agree on the term "Latino" only a small minority (four percent) agreed that the term "Chicano" fit them.[1]

In the 1980s, "Latino" replaced "Chicano" as a term that most people could agree upon. "Hispanic," enjoyed popularity among the middle class but provoked sharp criticism from others who were sensitive to the Indian and mestizo backgrounds of most Mexican Americans. The occasional confusion and debate over terminology led to the use of a more neutral term "Latino." The *L.A. Times* poll indicated something of the increasing complexity of the city's population. It demonstrated changes in self perception, away from a parochial ethnic identity ("Chicano") towards a more pan-Latin American identity ("Latino"). "Latino" referred to a national Spanish speaking community, with a majority of Mexican ancestry but including large populations of Central and South Americans. The Latino communities extended to the Cuban American enclaves in Florida and the Puerto Ricans in New York and Chicago. More and more Chicanos recognized the cultural and linguistic bonds they shared with the hundreds of thousands of Latin American immigrants who had been flooding the city and the nation. Thus the waves of immigration to the U.S. from Central America and Latin America was bringing about a shift in ethnic self identification.

In the 1980s, a dramatic demographic explosion in the Spanish speaking population, fueled by a new wave of immigration from Latin America and Mexico, underlay the increased visibility of Latino culture. This so-called, "New Immigration" produced ambivalent reactions from the Anglo American mainstream. Elements of Latino culture gained nation-wide popularity but Latino immigrants became the targets of discrimination and rejection. This chapter will examine how new waves of immigration from Latin America affected the cultural and economic context of Mexican American history through the 1990s.

Demographic and Economic Shifts

Between 1975 and 1989 more than eight million immigrants entered the United States legally. About a third of these, three million, were Latin Americans and Mexico's share was about one million. More Asian than Latin American legal immigrants entered the U.S. during this period. If we were to include the migration of Puerto Ricans to the mainland (not officially counted as immigration) and the entry of estimated millions of undocumented Mexican and Central American immigrants, the number of entrants from Latin America undoubtedly was the largest group.

Rubén Rumbault, in his 1991 study, noted that this "new immigration" from underdeveloped regions of the world (Asia and Latin America) was changing the culture of ethnic America. "The American ethnic mosaic is being fundamentally altered, and ethnicity itself being redefined and its new images redefined in the popular media and reflected in myriad and often surprising ways. Immigrants from a score of nationalities are told that they are all "Hispanic," while far more diverse groups, from India and Laos, China and the Philippines--are lumped together as 'Asians.'"[2]

Latin American immigration contributed to a dramatic increase in the Latino population of the United States. A very high Latino birth rate, the highest of any ethnic group in the United States, contributed to this demographic surge as well. Between 1980 and 1988 the Latino population grew from 14.6 millon to 19.4 million, an increase of thirty-four percent compared with only a seven percent increase in the general population. Latin American immigration counted for at least two million of the increase. Another two million could be accounted for by undocumented immigrants who were settlers rather than sojourners, leaving a million explained by the excess of births to deaths. Of almost twenty million Latinos in the United States in 1988, those of Mexican descent accounted for sixty-two percent of the total. Puerto Ricans were about thirteen percent of the mainland Latinos and Cuban Americans were five percent; twelve percent of the total came from Central and South America and the remaining eight percent were counted as "Other Hispanics."[3]

The 1990 Census showed that the proportion of Mexican immigrants within the larger Latino population declined during the 1980s. This could be explained by the relative large flow of immigrants from Central and South America. For example, California by 1990 had become the most populous state in the union with 29,760,000 people and about one fourth of these were Latino. About thirty-eight percent of the Los Angeles County's population and twenty percent of San Diego County's were Latino. Projecting a steady high rate of growth, demographers have estimated that the Latino population would reach thirty million by the year 2000. In some states, such as California and Texas, the projected increase would, by the year 2010, make the Latinos almost half their population. Projections were that, by the year 2060, Latinos would become the nation's largest ethnic or racial group.[4]

The use of the word "Latino" to describe immigrant and non-immigrant Spanish speaking populations, created a false notion of unity. Not all Latinos regarded the new immigrants as brothers to be welcomed into the community. The attitudes of Mexican Americans towards this new immigration varied according to socio-economic class, education, and generational status. A survey conducted by a research group at Pan American University in South Texas in 1984, disclosed that the more affluent and educated Mexican Americans believed that undocumented immigrants were taking unfair advantage of social services, particularly public education. They did not regard job competition as serious a problem as did the working class Mexican Americans. Overall Mexican Americans regardless of socioeconomic class did not think that this immigration from Latin America was having a negative impact on their lives. The more acculturated and educated Mexican Americans, however, supported stricter immigration controls.[5] Rudolfo de la Garza, a leading analyst of Chicano political opinion regarding Mexico and Mexican immigration, concluded that while Chicanos were "the principal group openly defending the Mexican position on the issue of undocumented workers," there was still "historical antipathy between Chicanos and Mexicans."[6] Another study by Christine Sierra pointed out the diversity of Mexican American responses to proposals for immigration restriction. Native born Latinos were much more likely to support employer sanctions and stricter enforcement measures than foreign born Latinos. When compared to other racial and ethnic groups, however, the native born Latinos tended to be less supportive of strict immigration controls.[7] Apart from these few studies researchers knew very little about the relationship between Mexican Americans and Mexican immigrants in the 1980s. Impressionistic evidence, gathered from school yards and the work place suggested an ambivalent relationship characterized by antagonism and competition along with a shared language and racial background. Certainly more acculturated Mexican Americans continued to be intermediaries between the *recien llegado* (recently arrived immigrant) and the larger society and economy. Bilingual and bicultural Mexican Americans worked as the bosses, supervisors and contractors managing (and exploiting) monolingual Spanish speaking Latino immigrants.

A Growing Underclass

The new flood of immigration from Latin America had long term consequences for the economy of the United States. Between 1980 and 1987 one fifth of the nation's employment growth was because of increased Latino employment, especially of Latino women. In the 1980s Latinos were the nation's fastest growing work force. The non-Latino work force grew by ten percent but the number of Latino workers increased by forty percent. The inflow of Mexican and Latin American immigrants who sought out jobs at the bottom of the American occupational ladder fueled most of this occupational increase. Latino women had a much higher rate of employment gain than men, almost a fifty percent growth rate in the period, two and a half times that of the growth rate for non-Latino women.

Despite the growing numbers of Latinos entering the work force, Latino unemployment caused by technological innovation, job competition by new immigrants, and business failures, remained about one and a half times above that of the general population but below that of African Americans. Unemployment varied according to national origin: Cuban Americans had the lowest rate of unemployment, about five percent, and Puerto Ricans and Mexicans had the highest, about ten percent. Meanwhile the unemployment rate for Anglo Americans ranged from six to nine percent. In terms of occupational mobility for all Latinos there was no significant change in their status during the 1980s. The vast majority remained in the lower paid skilled and unskilled blue collar jobs. Although Latino women entered the mid-level sales and technical occupations faster than did Latino men, more than half of all employed Latino men continued to work in blue collar jobs.[8]

Scholars noted that most of the new Latin American immigrants who entered the U.S. came from the employed and skilled working classes in their countries of origin. The middle class Cuban refugees who arrived after 1959 followed this pattern, with heavy representation in the professional middle classes. (The Cuban immigrants (*Marielitos*) who arrived in the late 1970s, however did not). Nevertheless, in comparison to the relatively affluent U.S. working class, the immigrants entered at the bottom of the American socio-economic pyramid. Native born Latinos who were U.S. citizens such as a majority of the Puerto Ricans in New York, Chicanos in the inner city barrios, Hispanos in New Mexico's small towns, and Tejanos in South Texas also endured high rates of poverty and educational underachievement.

While immigration continued at a high level, the federal government cut social services funding. Latino poverty, school drop outs, and unemployment rose. By 1990, Latinos were collectively even worse off than they had been in 1980. At the beginning of 1980, thirteen percent of Latino families lived below the poverty line. By the end of the decade, the number rose to more than sixteen percent. Meanwhile, the Latino median income adjusted for inflation declined from $23,088 to $21,759. Thus, the Latino experience became more polarized with some success stories but many more tales of human tragedy and defeat.

The Latino Middle Class

Not all Latinos were impoverished immigrants or blue collar workers. During the late 1970s and 1980s one of the fastest growing economic groups in the United States was the Latino middle and upper classes. Affluent Latinos, those having annual incomes of more than $50,000 a year, grew from 191,000 in 1972 to 638,000, an increase of 234 percent. Most of the expansion during the 1980s came from the growth of the Latino middle class (with incomes between $50,000 and $100,000). The proportion of Latino families living in affluence grew from seven percent of all households in 1972 to eleven percent in 1988, surpassing the proportion of middle class blacks (which was ten percent in 1988) but remaining below the proportion of Anglo Americans' twenty three percent). The low average income of all Latinos tended to mask the growth of this small but important group.

Like most well-off Americans, most Latino affluent families had two or more paychecks to support their life-styles. Unlike the Anglo American middle class the Latino families tended to be younger, have more children and have less education than their Anglo counter parts (only twenty nine percent of the Latino middle class had a college degree vs. fifty percent for Anglo Americans). More Latino affluent lived in metropolitan areas than was true for Anglos. Those cities having the largest Latino middle class segments in 1989 were Honolulu, Hawaii (twenty five percent), Washington D.C. (twenty four percent), Detroit (eighteen percent), San Francisco (fifteen percent), San Jose, California (fifteen percent), Orange County (fourteen percent)[9]. In the 1980s this group's growth provided an important resource for the mobilization of a new kind of politics. Culturally, this group would be supporters of a more mainstream approach to Latino music and art.

Advertising agencies and corporate managers discovered the "Hispanic Market" in the 1980s. They generated a good deal of survey research to plumb the buying habits of Latinos and how they could best exploit this fast growing group. The collective buying power of Latinos grew to over $171 billion in 1989, increasing at ten percent per year. Businesses began to expand their portion of products in the Spanish language, using Latino images. This created new opportunities for Latino marketing firms and models, especially in the major Southwestern metropolitan areas.[10] The expanded economic clout of Latinos provided Latino political groups with additional weight as they pushed for expanded hiring of Latinos within key companies. In 1985, for example, six national Latino groups led by the League of United Latin American Citizens (LULAC) and the American G.I. Forum signed an agreement with the Adolf Coors Corporation. After a ten year boycott of Coors by Chicano activists because of its anti-union, anti-Mexican policies, Coors agreed to a minimum hiring level of Latinos and committed its company to invest in the Latino community in proportion to its increase in sales.[11]

Some governmental officials and businessmen labeled the 1980s "The Decade of the Hispanic," sounding an optimistic note based on the growing economic and political power of Latinos. Despite the affluence of the Latino middle class, the final record of this decade proved to be mixed concerning the overall progress for all. Latino society perhaps became more differentiated with regards to education, socio-economic status, upward mobility and acculturation.

Latino Politics

Obviously there was an important political motive for the widespread adoption of the terms "Hispanic" and "Latino," particularly among the middle classes. These terms allowed Latino politicians and middle class organizations to claim that they represented a much larger national constituency than if they remained identified with ethnic nationalism. In the 1980s scores of Hispanic and Latino political caucuses, professional associations and business groups organized as political pressure groups. In the U.S. Congress and in the state governments of Florida, California, Arizona, New Mexico and Texas, Latino legislators formed lobbies and caucuses to push for agendas that would benefit their constituencies.

Two of the most active Latino organizations in this period were the Mexican American Legal Defense and Education Fund (MALDEF) and the Southwest Voter Registration Project (SWVRP). Together, they began many legal actions to attack impediments to Latino electoral victories. Their attack on the at-large district election system was a strategy that would have profound political consequences. The at-large election system was a structure that forced candidates in local district elections to win their election at-large or in city-wide contests. This political practice handicapped Latino candidates who had limited resources for city-wide campaigns and who lacked political appeal outside their ethnic districts. In the 1980s, both MALDEF and SWVRP won hundreds of court victories overturning the at-large electoral system. They won by proving in court that this system discriminated against Latinos who were protected under the Voting Rights Acts of 1965, 1975 and 1982.

Another front in the political battle for fair representation was the struggle over redistricting. For decades, Latinos had been victims of gerrymandered electoral districts. Historically, Anglo American incumbents of both parties had diluted the Latino voting block to create "safe" districts and insure their reelection. Redistricting occurred every ten years, after the federal census, to readjust election districts to reflect population shifts. In 1981, Latino organizations through out the Southwestern states, spearheaded by MALDEF and SWVRP, launched major efforts to challenge redistricting procedures and overcome Latino political fragmentation. Other Latino groups such as the Puerto Rican Legal

Defense and Education Fund (PRLDEF) in New York and the Hispanic Coalition on Reapportionment (HCR) in Michigan and Pennsylvania also lobbied the state reapportionment commissions and presented their own reapportionment plans. Richard Santillan in his analysis of the politics of the redistricting struggles in 1981, argued that hard won victories in creating Latino electoral districts led to significant Latino electoral gains during the rest of the decade.[12]   Benefiting from the civil rights struggles of the previous decades and the victories against gerrymandering and at-large elections reenergized political strategies. Latino political organizations had unparalleled success in the 1980s in electing officials. The SWVRP's work in registering new Latino voters was important in many of these electoral victories. The decade saw the election of Latino mayors in Denver (Federico Peña), San Antonio (Henry Cisneros) and Miami (Xavier Suárez) and Latino governors in New Mexico (Toney Anaya) and Florida (Bob Martínez). The voters elected hundreds of other Latinos to local and state offices, primarily in the Southwest. There were enough Latino elected officials to form a national organization, NALEO (National Association of Latino Elected and Appointed Officials), which issued annual status reports on the growing electoral strength of Latinos. In 1987, NALEO reported that there were 3,317 elected Latino officials in the United States, a number double the number in 1980.[13] The four southwestern border states, California, Arizona, New Mexico and Texas had the majority of elected Latinos but Florida, New York and the Mid-West also voted in substantial numbers.

The preponderance of Latinos won elections at the local level, serving on school boards, county offices and city councils. While Hispanic women were underrepresented in public offices, a higher proportion of Latinas were elected (eighteen percent) than was true for women in the general population (twelve percent). Most of the Latino officeholders in the 1980s had first entered electoral politics in that decade but they were not, as a group, particularly young, having an average age of about forty-four years. Most Latino elected officials in this decade were native born citizens (ninety percent). These new leaders represented ethnic constituencies, districts of more than fifty-five percent Latino in population, but the new office holders also appealed to a broader spectrum of non-ethnic voters by their articulation of issues.[14]

Representing this new Latino political leadership were people like Gloria Molina, Henry Cisneros, and Xavier Suárez. They were highly educated, committed, and articulate leaders who had a broad appeal while retaining the solid support of voters within their ethnic communities.

Gloria Molina was a crusading Chicana in East Los Angeles who won her first election in 1982 in an Assembly race against Richard Polanco, who was a well entrenched establishment politician. Daughter of a California farm worker, she lived in the East Los Angeles barrio and had gotten grass roots political experience during the Chicano movement in the 1960s. In the state Assembly Molina fought long and hard against the construction of a state prison in her district. She ultimately succeeded by organizing a myriad of local groups and embarrassing the Latino politicos who had supported the prison in hopes of political favors. She ran unsuccessfully against Richard Alatorre in a 1986 Los Angeles City Council race but the next year she won a stunning victory in being elected to a newly created Los Angeles councilmanic seat. In 1991 she ran against her arch enemy Richard Alatorre for the Los Angeles County Board of Supervisors. She won that election with majority support of both men and women, Anglos and Latinos. This was the first time in more than 100 years that the voters had elected a Latino to this powerful office. Most observers predicted that from here she was in an ideal position to enter national politics.

Gloria Molina rose to prominence because of her passionate advocacy of women's rights and issues of community development. As an outsider to both the Anglo dominated political establishment and the old boy network of Chicano officials, she represented a populist and feminist approach to Latino politics who appealed to a wide variety of middle class non-ethnic voters.[15]

Henry Cisneros, a young professor of Public Administration, came much more from a conservative political background. Born in San Antonio, Texas, Cisneros descended from an old-line elite family who had immigrated during the Mexican Revolution. Cisneros attended a Catholic high school and Texas A & M, later earning two master's degrees and a doctorate degree from Ivy League universities. When he returned to Texas he worked as a professor at the University of Texas in San Antonio until he won election to the City Council in 1975 as part of a multi-ethnic coalition. His youthful optimism and charismatic style along with his management training and fiscal conservatism made him a favorite of the San Antonio Anglo middle class. Also he appealed to the working class Chicanos of San Antonio who identified with his success. He won reelection as a mayor of the city in 1981 with support of Anglos and a huge majority (ninety-four percent) of the Chicano vote. His ability to move in elite circles and his adept manipulation of complex issues made him an unusually attractive figure to national politicians. In 1983 President Reagan appointed him to the National Bipartisan Commission on Central America. He ultimately endorsed a report that justified the administration's policy. His conservative economic philosophy did not antagonize his Chicano and Mexicano constituency since he also lobbied for more jobs and education. In 1989 Cisneros decided not to run again for mayor, citing personal economic hardships in continuing. In the 1990s he devoted himself to building a Latino controlled financial management corporation called The Cisneros Group.

Xavier Suárez was a Cuban born, naturalized citizen who, in 1985, was elected mayor of the largest Latino majority city in the United States, Miami, Florida. Suárez was the ninth of 14 children from a middle class Cuban family. His father had been an engineer and a college dean. After the Cuban Revolution his family fled to the U.S. and settled in Washington D.C. Reportedly, Suárez learned English in only two months. He went on to earn a degree in mechanical engineering, a master's degree in Public

Administration and a law degree from Harvard. Moving to Miami he joined a law firm and soon got involved in local politics. With the support of wealthy Cuban bankers, he ran several times unsuccessfully for a seat on the Miami City Commission. In 1983 he ran against Maurice Ferré, the Puerto Rican born incumbent mayor who had been in office for 12 years. Ferré was supported by a coalition of Anglo, Black and Cuban voters. Ferré won that election but in the process alienated key members of his coalition. In the next election, Suárez succeeded in knocking off Ferré. The tone of Miami politics changed from its traditional anti-communist Cuban orientation towards local issues like drugs and unemployment. Along with Florida governor Bob Martínez and a host of other Cuban Americans who rose to local political office in the 1980s, Suárez represents a new generation of Latino leadership outside the four Southwestern states.[16]

Despite these success stories and optimistic trends, Latinos remain underrepresented at all levels of government. In California, for example, where Latinos comprise more than twenty percent of the population, less than two percent of the federal, state and county officials were Latino. In Texas where more than twenty percent of the total population are Latino, in 1983 they were less than six percent of the local municipal elected officials. The same kind of inequity continues to exist in every other Southwestern state with the possible exception of New Mexico.

Education

The existing educational system was one of the most important ways that immigrant and native born Latinos could escape the cycle of poverty and marginalization. There continued to be a devastating school drop out rate in public schools and relatively low numbers of Latinos attended and graduated from college. In the 1980s, white Americans "discovered" the educational problem as nation-wide reading and math scores declined for all groups. Several best selling books criticized the secondary schools and colleges' failure to teach basic literacy and numeracy. A well publicized government study stated that the failures of the educational system was placing our nation at risk.[17]

Chicanos and Mexican immigrants had been "at risk" for many decades. The influx of hundreds of thousands of new immigrants made the educational system's failure more visible. Long charged with the task of mainstreaming or "Americanizing" immigrants, the public schools proved unequal to the task as larger and larger numbers of Latino children failed to keep up with their Anglo American peers.

An example was the Los Angeles City School System. Perhaps one of the most multi-racial, multi-ethnic school systems in the nation, about half of the students were foreign-born in 1980. The largest contingent of the foreign-born, about 80 percent, were Mexican immigrant children, followed by Central American and Asian born students. Between 1970 and 1980 the Latino school population in Los Angeles had doubled to 267,000 students while white enrollment fell to 120,729. By 1990 the school population exceeded 300,000 Latinos while black and Anglo school enrollment continued to decline. Concentrated in segregated regions of the city, the Latino students had a school drop out rate of forty-eight percent. This compared with a national drop out rate (in 1980) of forty-five percent for Mexican Americans, twenty-eight percent for blacks and seventeen percent for whites.[18]

The educational environment in other school districts having large numbers of Latinos was not much better. In Texas a long tradition of segregation that led to the inequitable funding of non-white schools aggravated the high drop out rate. In Texas the poorest school districts were invariably Latino or black. Yet they were the districts saddled with the highest property tax rates and the lowest allocation of state funding. In 1973, the Supreme Court had ruled in *San Antonio School District v. Rodríguez* that this inequity did not violate the constitution. The problem of unequal funding continued to plague Texas' Latino school districts and resulted in increasing educational neglect for Latinos.[19]

In addition, legal discrimination against Mexican children continued. In 1975, the Texas state legislature added a statute to the Education Code declaring that only children of U.S. citizens and legal aliens could receive free public education. Many school districts subsequently began charging up to $1000 a year tuition to children of undocumented workers. In 1977, the Mexican American Legal Defense and Education Fund (MALDEF) filed a law suit to challenge this policy. In *Doe v. Plyler* MALDEF argued that the state's policy was unconstitutional, violating the 14th Amendment that states that no state shall "deny to any person . . . the equal protection of the laws" of the United States. Further, they argued that the Federal government, not the state, was responsible for enforcing immigration laws. In 1980, MALDEF won their case on appeal thus setting a precedent for the educational rights of undocumented immigrants.[20]

Educational experts were much better at describing the dimensions of the problem than at constructing remedies. Educators knew that there were many reasons for the high drop out rate for Latinos. The most important were related to the income and educational backgrounds of the parents, the recency of immigration and exclusive use of Spanish at home, and the characteristics of the school itself--class size, school facilities, and teacher motivation and training. The actual reasons for Latinos quitting school before graduation varied tremendously ranging from pregnancy to boredom, but almost all drop outs were below their grade level in reading and writing skills. This educational lag most often appeared by the third grade indicating that the most important remedies for the problem (primarily intensive tutoring in reading and writing skills) were to be addressed at the grammar school level.

Since the 1960s Chicano educators had argued in favor of reform of the elementary school system, in particular, through the institutionalization of bilingual education. Bilingual advocates argued that it was most important to teach Spanish-speaking students how to read in their native language first, and then, once students had mastered reading skills, it would be easier to teach them how to read in English. By using Spanish as the language of instruction in the grammar schools to teach native Spanish-speakers, teachers would be able to reinforce the family cultural values of immigrant children and create a more positive learning environment for the teaching of English and other subjects. Almost all Latino immigrant families wanted their children to learn English since it was obvious to them that this skill was important in getting a job.[21]

The bilingual advocates had support from the Supreme Court when the *Lau v. Nichols* decision in 1972 directed the schools to address the needs of the non-English-Speaking students. The Lau decision allowed school districts to determine the methods to be used in fulfilling this mandate. For the next twenty years a wide variety of bilingual programs arose (not only Spanish-English but also dealing with Asian languages) funded by local, state and federal funds. The funds however were never sufficient to meet the demand. Moreover, President Ronald Reagan's administration cut federal funding for bilingual education by a third. Experts estimated that by the end of the 1980s less than three percent of the Latino school age population had bilingual education programs.

Yet there was evidence that bilingual programs were having success in easing the transition from Spanish to English and in preventing drop outs. A 1984 Department of Education study, for example, tracked 2,000 Spanish speaking grammar school children over four years and found that they achieved skills at the same level as their English speaking peers. The study confirmed that bilingual programs, if managed correctly, were one way of combating the school's failure to educate. Other studies concluded that bilingual programs improved the self concept and cognitive functioning of students. Truly bilingual students outperformed their Spanish speaking peers who had been left to "sink or swim."[22]

Despite these successes, the modest diffusion of programs with the avowed aim to mainstream immigrant children, bilingual education came under attack. Many whites feared the implications of the massive immigration flooding the U.S. from so-called Third World countries. Nativists worried about the decline of "all-American" values that they linked to the school's failure linguistically to assimilate foreigners. Bilingual education and its assumptions of multicultural equity bothered those who feared the "balkanization" of American culture. In 1975, the U.S. Congress amended the Voting Rights Act to require that electoral information and ballots be multilingual. This provoked criticism from conservatives who argued that American citizens should be able to understand English in order to vote.

In 1978 Emmy Shafer was unable to communicate with any of the Spanish speaking clerks in the Dade County (Florida) administrative offices. In protest, she organized a local initiative that succeeded in making it illegal to translate official signs into a language other than English. This was the beginning of the English-Only movement, a conservative backlash against bilingual education, and Spanish speaking Latinos.

In 1982 Senator S.I. Hayakawa (R., Calif.) proposed a constitutional amendment to make English the official language of the United States. When Congress defeated his proposal, Hayakawa formed a private organization called U.S. English to implement English-Only laws through initiative procedures and lobbying state legislatures. U.S. English claimed a membership of over 300,000 and engaged in fund rasing and mass mailings to promote their cause. Eventually, more than seventeen states voted referendums to make English the official language. The states with the largest Chicano and Mexican immigrant populations, California and Texas, both passed English-only laws. New Mexico, with its long tradition of Spanish language and culture, passed instead an "English Plus" law stating that "Proficiency on the part of our citizens in more than one language is to the economic and cultural benefit of our State and Nation."[23]

The English-Only movement attracted nativists and members of the radical right and generated a good deal of patriotic and linguistic xenophobia. One nativist, Richard Viguerie mailed a letter to more than 240,000 homes asking for the repeal of federal bilingual education legislation. Included with his letter was a Mexican peso with the message, "I know the peso is worthless in the U.S. but I enclosed it to make an important point about a billion-dollar U.S. government program that's worthless too. It's called the Bilingual Education Act."[23]

Immigration and Nativist Response

The growing tide of immigrant workers flowing into the U.S. during the 1970s and 1980s led to intense debates over cultural and economic consequences. A large portion of the immigrant influx came as undocumented workers. In 1983, for example, the INS apprehended more than a million illegal entrants from Mexico. This represented only a small fraction of those who actually crossed in that year and was equal to the total number of legal entrants from Mexico during the decade of the 1980s.[26] The daily apprehension of thousands of these "illegal aliens" raised the specter of a nation unable to control its borders. In 1977 President Jimmy Carter asked Congress to consider drafting a new immigration law that would impose sanctions on employers for knowingly hiring undocumented workers and bolster the police powers of the Border Patrol. Included in his message was the suggestion that the Congress also draft a program to grant amnesty to undocumented immigrants already residing in the U.S. These basic points, employer sanctions, expanded enforcement and amnesty became the substance of several immigration bills later introduced into Congress.

The most long-lived proposal was the Simpson-Mazzoli bill, introduced in 1982. The Simpson-Mazzoli bill proposed a fine of $10,000 for employers who hired "illegal aliens" and would have granted amnesty to long term residents. Additionally the bill proposed a bracero-like guest worker program (H-2 Program) to import seasonal workers from Mexico and the Caribbean in case of a labor shortages. Special interests emerged in the debates in Congress over this bill. S. I. Hayakawa (R., Calif.) sought to attach an "English as the official language" provision to the bill. Labor unions generally supported the sanctions' provisions but were wary of the H-2 Program. Latino human rights groups opposed the penalty provisions fearing that they would be used by employers to justify their discrimination against Latino citizen. Church groups and those against U.S. support for the escalating war in Central America opposed the bill fearing the massive deportation of the thousands of Central American refugees who had fled to the U.S. to escape political terrorism. Other Latino groups were divided. The American G.I. Forum supported the idea of immigration restriction and increased support for the border patrol and they were opposed by groups like the San Diego based Committee for Chicano Rights. MALDEF supported immigration reform but opposed many of the provisions of the Simpson-Mazzoli bill. The League of United Latin American Citizens (LULAC), a conservative middle class organization, voted to boycott the Democratic Party's convention in 1984 unless the delegates voted to oppose the Simpson-Mazzoli bill.[26] The "Latino Lobby," composed of the leaders of the National Council for La Raza, LULAC, MALDEF, and the United Farm Workers Union opposed different aspects of the immigration proposal. They worked in coalition with other immigrant rights groups to advance their interests.[27]

Eventually, legislators introduced alternative bills to meet the objections of the various lobbies. The result was the passage in 1986 of the Immigration Reform and Control Act (IRCA). This law provided for employer sanctions, a strengthened border patrol, a guest worker program and amnesty for undocumented workers who arrived before 1982. It also had provisions to review the implementation of the law to see the extent of violation of the rights of Latino citizens and Central American refugees.

A surge in nativist attitudes accompanied the long debate over various provision in the immigration bills. Community spokespersons portrayed Mexican and Central American immigrants as a threat to "the American way of life." They believed that the immigrants were responsible for rising crime rates, disease, unemployment, rising welfare costs, moral decay and decline in the quality of life. Despite a large body of social scientific studies that contradicted these assertions, a kind of paranoia regarding immigrants swept the country. The Democratic governor of Colorado, Richard Lamm, coauthored *The Immigration Time Bomb* and argued that the U.S. should curtail immigration from Latin America because it was undermining the nation's economy, corrupting American values and fragmenting the social fabric of the country.[28] In San Diego, California, Tom Metzger reorganized the Ku Klux Klan as the White Aryan Resistance. They distributed hate literature in high schools and public meetings warning Mexicans to go back or face violent consequences. Attacks against undocumented immigrants grew in number, not only by local racists, but by Border Patrol officers who had a war zone mentality. Sadly many of the attacks also came from Chicano and Mexican thieves (some of them Mexican officials) who preyed on the undocumented crossers. In the 1980s, the U.S. Mexican border region became the most dangerous terrain in America as every year hundreds of undocumented immigrants were robbed, beaten, raped and killed as they tried to cross.

Despite the anti-immigrant rhetoric, the U.S. increasingly needed immigrant labor in order to keep as economy prosperous. The *Wall Street Journal* in 1976 had said that ". . .illegals may well be providing the margin of survival for entire sectors of the economy." By 1985 the *New York Times* reported that respected economists believed that "illegal immigrants" had become the backbone of the economy.[29] Demographers, like Leo Estrada at UCLA, warned that the nation faced a severe labor shortage in the 1990s, particularly in the blue collar occupations, as the general population grew older and had less children. A work force augmented by immigration was the only way that the U.S. could continue to be competitive in a world economy. Undocumented and legal immigration from Mexico and Latin America provided the surplus labor that employers could use to lower their operating costs and expand production. The money spent and taxes paid by the "new immigrants" in turn created more jobs and helped fund social services. David Hayes-Bautista, for example, found that in California the population of working younger Latinos, including immigrants, was increasingly responsible for supporting social programs for the aged Anglos.[30] Other researchers found that those areas of the country that had the greatest economic growth and the least unemployment were the same areas that had substantial immigration. James Cockcroft's book *Outlaws in the Promised Land* (1986) reviewed the literature on the economic impact of Latin American immigration during the first half of the 1980s. He concluded, "In general, U.S. citizens benefit disproportionately from not just the migrants' labor and consumption but all the tax and benefit program checkoffs paid by immigrant workers."[31]

One of the effects of the debates over immigration restriction in the 1980s was to educate millions of U.S. Latinos about the importance of this "new immigration" to their political and cultural survival. Latinos joined Central American refugee support groups like CISPES (Committee In Support of the People of El Salvador) and included demands for amnesty for Central American refugees along with demands for police reform and Affirmative Action programs. MALDEF and The SWVRP targeted immigrant communities for future citizenship and voter registration drives. The generally anti-Mexican tenor of the debates in Congress mobilized many middle-class Latino organizations to take a stand in favor of immigrant rights.

Maturation of Latino Arts

The demographic, economic and political prominence of the Latino during the 1980s provided a context for a florescence and maturation in the performing and visual arts. Generally speaking, Latino artists joined the mainstream. Bolstered by the new creative energies coming from the Cuban, Puerto Rican and Latin American cultures, Mexican American creative artists enjoyed a new popularity. One important aspect in "the boom" in Latino visual and performing arts was the growth of a Latino market. For the first time it was possible for many Latino artists to earn a living from their work by selling their art to other Latinos. The main impetus in the change in Latino arts, however, came from the artists themselves who made a conscious choice to expand beyond the barrio and movement audiences to gain acceptance and recognition from the larger society.

Perhaps the most dramatic evidence of the emergence of Latino culture was in the film industry. After having Hollywood's exclusion of Latinos from producing and directing major productions for decades, the 1980s saw the exhibition of major motion pictures written, directed, or starring Latinos based on Latino themes. Perhaps the most artistically powerful statement tying the immigration to Latinos was the movie *El Norte* (1983), a moving saga about a Guatemalan brother and sister and their adventures in fleeing through Mexico to the U.S. Produced and directed by Gregory Nava, a Chicano, and staring a well-known Mexican actor, Pedro Arisméndez, the film made powerful statement about the tragedies experienced by Latino immigrants in the U.S. It also highlighted the competitive and exploitative relationship between the Chicano and the newly arrived immigrant. *El Norte* had limited distribution. The first in a series of box office hits was *La Bamba* (1987) written and directed by Luis Valdez about the life and tragic death of Ritchie Valens, a popular rock and roll star of the 1950s. Earning more than fifty five million dollars, the film showed Hollywood that Latino themes could sell. Next, Cheech Marin stared in the movie *Born in East L.A.* (1987) a comedy with serious undertones about Mexican immigrants and their relationship to Latinos. This also was a modest financial success. In 1988 Hollywood produced three major films starring Latinos and developing Mexican American cultural themes. Robert Redford with Moctezuma Esparza did *The Milagro Bean Field War* with a large Latino cast and starring Rubén Blades, a well-known Latino recording artist. Ramon Menendez directed *Stand and Deliver*, staring Edward James Olmos, based on the true story of a successful barrio high school math teacher and Raul Julia starred in the film *Romero*, a moving account of the life and assassination of Archbishop Romero in El Salvador. In 1989 other films emerged to capture a portion of the market. Raul Julia and Sonia Braga (Brazil) starred with Richard Dryfus in *Moon Over Parador*, a satire about a Latin American dictatorship and Jimmy Smits with Jane Fonda starred in Carlos Fuentes' *Old Gringo,* a story set during the Mexican Revolution.

A consequence of these and other films being produced in the 1980s was the promotion of new Latino film stars, many of who had been languishing in stereotypical minor roles. One of the most promising of these was Edward James Olmos, who had grown up in East Los Angeles of Mexican immigrant parents. After several number of small parts in television series, Olmos was "discovered" by Luis Valdez who cast him as the Pachuco in the 1978 play *Zoot Suit*. For his acting, Olmos won a Tony nomination and a Los Angeles Drama Critics Circle award and this led to his being cast in supporting roles in the films *Wolfen* (1981) and *Blade Runner* (1982). Olmos had a commitment to accept only roles that presented positive images of Latinos. His most important films in this regard were *The Ballad of Gregorio Cortez* (1982), a drama based on Américo Paredes' book, and *Stand and Deliver* (1988). He accepted of the role of Lieutenant Martin Castillo on the popular television series *Miami Vice* in 1984 only after promises that he would have creative control of the character. By the end of the decade, Olmos had established his own production company with the goal of making Latino movies that were artistically powerful and as well as socially responsible.

In the area of music, a growing Latino population meant more of a domestic market for Latino sounds, but the non-ethnic mainstream also picked up on the beat. Latino groups and artists sought to find a popular audience by mixing and crossing over. The Miami Sound Machine sold 1.25 million albums with their pop salsa rhythms. Los Lobos, an East L.A. Chicano group, provided the music for the hit movies *La Bamba* and *Salsa* and sold millions of albums of their unique blend of rock and roll, Tex-Mex, and Mexican corridos. Rubén Blades, the Panama-born recording artist, made his first album in English, *Nothing But the Truth*, keeping the rhythm and style but reaching the non-Latino audience. Linda Ronstadt, from the Tucson-Sonora Ronstadt family, had a big hit with her *Canciones de Mi Padre*, ballads sung in Spanish with the Mariachi Vargas de Tecalitán from Mexico.[32]

While retaining an ethnic tone and message Latino films and music appealed to large mixed audiences. The same tendencies were true for the performing arts. Perhaps the best example of this was the play *Zoot Suit* (1978), the first Chicano play to be performed on mainstream stages in Los Angeles and New York City. Written and directed by Luis Valdez, *Zoot Suit* was based on the Sleepy Lagoon incident in 1943. Incorporating music and dance of the 1940s, *Zoot Suit* had a social-political message but was entertaining as well. It was immensely popular in Los Angeles, running forty six weeks and having an audience of over 400,000. It was less so in New York, perhaps because of their lack of familiarity with Chicano culture. This play and subsequent ones by Valdez like, *I Don't Have to Show You No Stinking Badges*, and *Corridos* sought to entertain larger audiences while remaining faithful to Mexican and Chicano ideals.

Aside from Valdez, several Chicano playwrights contributed their talents to producing an authentic Chicano theater that could be appreciated by non-Latinos. Carlos Morton wrote a series of plays and won the Hispanic Playwrights Festival Award, New York Shakespeare Festival. Rubén Sierra wrote *La Raza Pura o Racial, Racial (The Pure Race or Racial, Racial)* and with Jorge Huerta, *I Am Celso*, Fausto Avedaño wrote *El Corrido de California* and Estela Portillo Trambely *Sor Juana* and *Blacklight*, the latter winning second place in the American Theatre Festival in New York.

Jorge Huerta established the nation's first Master's in Theater Arts specializing in Hispanic/Latino theater at the University of California in San Diego. Besides training a cadre of professional actors, directors and playwrights, he worked with the local Old Globe Theater and San Diego Repertory Theater to produce original Chicano productions and productions of noted Latin American playwrights.

Nicolás Kanellos, a literary critic and historian, aptly summarized the state of Chicano theater in the 1980s:

"[T]he days of teatro as an arm of revolutionary nationalism are over. The revolutionary aims of the movement have resulted in modest reforms and certain accommodations. Luis Valdez now sits on the California Arts Council. Many other teatro and former teatro people are members of local arts agencies and boards throughout the Southwest. Former teatristas are now professors of drama, authors, and editors of scholarly books and journals on Chicano literature and theater."

If Chicano literature did not produce a best seller or a poet laureate during this era it was not for lack of talent or productivity. The big publishing houses, located in New York, remained impervious to the literary merits of Latinos. The national appeal of Latino works had yet to be proven. A major breakthorugh, however, occurred in 1989 with the publication of the *The Mambo Kings Play Songs of Love* (1989) by Oscar Hijuelos, a Cuban American resident of New York City. Hijuelos' book won the Pulitzer Prize for literature and became a best seller for Harper Row Publishers. It was a lyrical and sorrowful story of a couple of Cuban musicians in New York during the 1940s and 1950s as they became part of the Latin music boom of that era. Hijuelos' passionate and rich style evoked a barrage of sensual images that captured people's imagination. Concurrent with the success of this book, Gabriel Garcia Marquez (Colombia) and Octavio Paz (Mexico) won Nobel Prizes for their literature and this sparked a surge in English language translations of their works.

Despite this modest Latino "boom" in literature, most Chicano writers did not have large commercial success. Many may have eschewed it. Most Chicano writers were university professors whose orientation tended to be away from the marketplace. Most of the well known Chicano fiction writers of the previous decade continued to publish short stories and novels but there emerged a new group of writers. Nash Candelaria wrote a triology based on New Mexico's history. *Memories of the Alhambra* (1977), *Not by the Sword* (1982) and *Inheritance of Strangers* (1985) tracing the history of José Rafa's family through 400 years. The main themes of the Rafa trilogy were conquest, conflict and identity while underscoring the Chicano's links to universal humanity. Arturo Islas created *The Rain God: A Desert Tale* in 1984 as a historical-autobiographical novel set in El Paso and Lionel García wrote *Leaving Home* in 1985 about a Latino baseball pitcher in the 1930s and 1940s and *A Shroud in the Family* in 1987 about a Tejano searching for his identity in family relations.

Latinas also made important contributions to the development of fiction. Gloria Anzaldua wrote *This Bridge Called My Back* and *Borderlands/Fronteras* (1987) exploring issues of sexual and cultural politics. Irene Beltrán produced *Across the Great River* (1987), dealing with the experiences of an undocumented immigrant family as seen through the eyes of a young girl. Denise Chávez, in *Face of an Angel* (1990), wrote about the survival strategies of a career waitress and Ana Castillo's *Sapagonia* (1990) reflected on the meaning of being a Mestizo in the Americas. There were many collections of short stories written by Latinas published by the two most prominent Latino editorial houses, Arte Publico Press and Bilingual Review Press.

Modern Chicano literature continued to be intensely personal. The most controversial, and so best selling, autobiography of the 1980s was *The Hunger of Memory* (1982) by Richard Rodríguez. This book, more than any other, perhaps, challenged the values of the Chicano movement. In the book Rodríguez described his alienation from the main Chicano activists and his willingness to abandon the Mexican culture and embrace Anglo American values. His book was about language and the importance of learning a public language (English) rather than preserving a private one (Spanish). He attacked bilingual education, Affirmative Action and ethnic politics. Praised by the Anglo American critics for his literary style and power, *The Hunger of Memory* came under attack by Chicano intellectuals because of its conservative message. Rodríguez wrote several essays that appeared in national magazines, and he narrated television documentaries on Mexican culture. Because of his literary skill he became, ironically, the most well-known Chicano writer in the U.S.

Writing for a smaller audience, Chicano poets turned away from didactic political messages and became more introspective. A major development in these years was the emergence of an energetic group of Chicana and Latina poets. Bernice Zamora published *Restless Serpents* (1976) that explored the contradictory and conflictive feelings about being a woman in a male dominated culture. Zamora linked Chicana poetry to American literary works, with frequent alusions to the mainstream tradition. Alma Villanueva wrote *Bloodroot* and *Poems* in 1977 and *Mother, May I?* in 1978, poetry that was intensely personal and confident, powerfully asserting female sexual superiority and creative power while emphasizing her identity as a woman rather than as a Latina. Another prominent Chicana poet of these years was Lorna Dee Cervantes who wrote *Emplumada* (1981), a complex array of feminist poems that developed themes springing from barrio life.[34]

The most prolific and widely-acclaimed poet in the 1980s, however, was Gary Soto. Born in the San Joaquin Valley, Soto's poems moved away from the overt political declamations of the Chicano movement years and explored personal themes using vivid and evocative language. Critics acclaimed his first collection *The Elements of San Joaquín* (1977) as a masterpiece that captured the essence of rural landscapes and people. *The Tale of Sunlight* (1978) was more psychological in character and *Father is a Pillow Tied to a Broom* (1980) evoked more somber and sorrowful tones. *Where Sparrows Work Hard* (1981) and *Black Hair* (1985) and *Who Will Know Us, New Poems* (1990) were all major advances in the use of language. Soto won national and international prizes for his work. His collection of short stories, *Living Up the Street* (1985), about his childhood in Fresno, California, won the National Book Award.

Latino visual artists had somewhat more success than fiction writers in gaining national recognition for their work. The diversity of artistic expression multiplied and mural art declined as the dominating form for Chicanos. In 1987, a national touring exhibition of Latino artists, "Hispanic Art in the United States: Thirty Contemporary Painters and Sculptors," showcased the rich imagery and vitality of modern Latino artists of diverse Latin American backgrounds. Another national touring exhibition, opening in 1990, "CARA: Chicano Art Resistance and Affirmation" interpreted the Chicano art movement (1965-1975) within a larger historical and cultural framework. Another historical retrospective organized by the Bronx Museum in 1990 was "The Latin American Spirit: Art and Artists in the United States, 1920-1970" that focused on the international influences of Latin American art and artists in the United States. These shows, and many other locally organized art exhibits, publicized the emergence of new talent and energies and challenged the conservative dominions of the American art academy. In 1991, the Mexican government organized a major historical and contemporary touring exhibit of visual art entitled "Mexico Splendors of Thirty Centuries." This exhibit made the public even more aware than ever of the traditions of Latino art.

The main aesthetic directions of Chicano art in the 1980s was towards the private and away from the public. Artists sought commercial success in creating canvas paintings not public murals. A host of new talent sold their work in galleries in Los Angeles, Austin, San Francisco and San Diego. As art collectors began to bid thousands for works by artists such as John Valadez, Luis Jimenez, Carmen Lomas Garza, and Carlos Almaraz, Chicano graduated from the streets to the salons.

Conclusions

Immigration from Latin America and a dramatic growth in the Latino population shaped the years following the decline of the heightened political sensibilities of the Chicano movement (1965-1975). The economic, linguistic and national diversity of the U.S. Spanish speaking population expanded. The new immigrants filled an important niche in American economy and, at the same time, the general Latino population became more economically polarized. The middle and upper class Latino classes grew. So too did the Latino underclass. The new wave of immigration led to new political activities. MALDEF and the SWVRP made an intense effort to enlarge Latino representation within the existing political system. Instead of demonstrations they used the courts and the ballot boxes. Latino immigration provoked a nativist backlash that resulted in a new immigration law in 1987 that promised to "cure" the problems attributed to the newcomers. The conservative political and social tone of the Reagan years had its reflection in Latino politics. Large national organizations made deals with multinational corporations to help fund their activities. With some notable exceptions, Latino politicans increasingly joined the mainstream and eschewed radical ethnic approaches. The Chicano renaissance of the

1960s and 1970s became a Latino "boom" in the 1980s.

Mainstream America became more aware of the rich cultural expressions of Latino artists in the movies and music. The mood of the 1980s was to commercialize ethnicity and seek ways of selling it. Meanwhile a fundamental contradiction remained between the underclass of working class Latino immigrants and native born and the growing Hispanic middle classes.

Notes

1. The series was reprinted as *Southern California's Latino Community* (Los Angeles: Times Mirror Co., 1983). See Frank Sotomayor's, "A Box Full of Ethnic Labels," p. 27-28.

2. Rubén Rumbaut, "Passages to America: Perspectives on the New Immigration," in *America at Century's End: American Society in Transition* by Alan Wolfe, ed. (Berkeley: University of California, 1991).

3. *La Red/The Net*, Vol. 2, no. 2 (1989), p. 20.

4. "U.S. Hispanic Population: The Year 2080," *Hispanic Business,* 9:3 (March 1987), 50.

5. Lawrence W. Miller, Jerry L. Polinard, and Robert D, Wrinkle, "Attitudes Toward Undocumented Workers: The Mexican American Perspective," *Social Science Quarterly*, 65, no. 2 (June 1984): 483-493.

6. Rudolfo O. de la Garza, "Chicanos and U.S. Foreign Policy: The Future of Chicano-Mexican Relations," *Mexican-U.S. Relations: Conflict and Convergence*, Carlos Vásquez and Manuel García y Griego, eds. (Los Angeles: UCLA Chicano Studies Reseach Center and UCLA Latin American Center Publications, 1983), pp. 401-403.

7. Christine Marie Sierra, "Latinos and the 'New Immigration': Responses from the Mexican American Community," *Renato Rosaldo Lecture Series 3: 1985-1986* ed. Ignacio García (Tucson: Mexican American Studies and Research Center, University of Arizona, 1987), pp. 42-55.

8. Peter Cattan, "The Growing Presence of Hispanics in the U.S. Work Force," *Monthly Labor Review* (August 1988), pp. 9-13.

9. William O'Hare, "The Rise of the Hispanic Affluence," *American Demographics*, Vol. 12 (August 1990) pp. 40-43.

10. George Swisshelm, "U.S. Hispanics Move to Rediscover their Ethnic Roots," *Television/Radio Age* Vol. 36 (July 1989): A1-A47.

11. Tom Díaz, "Coors Get on Board Hispanic Trend," *Nuestro* (January/February 1985), pp. 12-18.

12. Richard Santillan, "The Latino Community in State and Congressional Redistricting, 1961-1985," *Journal of Hispanic Policy*, Vol. 1, no. 1 (1985), pp. 52-65.

13. Harry P. Pachon, "Overview of Hispanic Elected Officials in 1987," *1987 National Roster of Hispanic Elected Officials* ed. by National Association of Latino Elected and

Appointed Officials (Washington D.C.: NALEO Education Fund, 1987).

14. Harry P. Pachon, "Overview of Hispanic Elected Officials in 1987," *1987 National Roster of Hispanic Elected Officials* ed. by National Association of Latino Elected and Appointed Officials (Washington D.C.: NALEO Education Fund, 1987), pp. xv-xxiv.

15. *Los Angeles Times*, February 20, 1991, A18.

16. *Nuestro*, Jan./Feb. 1986, pp. 15-17.

17. See National Commission on Excellence in Education, *A Nation at Risk: The Imperative for Educational Reform* (Washington D.C., April 1983); also Erick Hirsh, Cultural Literacy: *What Every American Needs to Know* (Boston: Houghton Mifflin, 1987); Charles Sykes, *Profscam: Professors and the Demise of Higher Education* (Washington D.C.: Regnery Coteway, 1988).

18. Thomas Muller and Thomas J. Sepenshade et. al., *The Fourth Wave: California's Newest Immigrants* (Washington D.C.: The Urban Institute, 1985), pp. 80, 82.

19. Rudolfo Acuña, *Occupied America: A History of Chicanos* (New York: Harper & Row Publishers, 1988), pp. 389-90.

20. *MALDEF Newsletter*, Vol. X, No. 4 (Fall 1980): 1:1.

21. For an excellent discussion of drop outs and educational statistics see selected essays in Pastora San Juan Cafferty and William C. McCready, *Hispanics in the United States: A New Social Agenda* (New Brunswick, New Jersey: Transaction Books, 1985).

22. Pastora San Juan Cafferty, "Language and Social Assimilation," in *Hispanics in the United States: A New Social Agenda*, pp. 102-4; describes the evaluation of bilingual programs. For a more recent study see "Bilingual Students Held to Do Well," *Los Angeles Times,* February 12, 1991: 1:2.

23. Mark R. Halton, "Legislating Assimilation: The English-Only Movement," *The Christian Century*, Vol. 106 (November 29, 1989), p. 1119.

24. Raul Yzaguirre, "The Perils of Pandora: An Examination of the English-Only Movement," *Journal of Hispanic Policy*, Vol. 2 (1986-1987), p. 5.

25. David Reimers, *Still the Golden Door: The Third World Comes to America* (New York: Columbia University Press, 1985), p. 203.

26. James D. Cockcroft, *Outlaws in the Promised Land: Mexican Immigrant Workers and America's Future* (New York: Grove Press, 1986), pp. 218-227.

27. Christine Marie Sierra, "Latinos and the 'New Immigration': Responses from the Mexican American Community," p. 51.

28. Richard D. Lamm and Gary Imhoff, *The Immigration Time Bomb: The Fragmenting of America* (New York: Truman Talley Books, 1986).

29. Cited in Cockcroft, p. 130.

30. David E. Hayes-Bautista, Werner O. Schinek and Jorge Chapa, "Young Latinos in an Aging American Society," *Social Policy*, Vol. 15, no. 1 (1984): 49-52.

31. Ibid., p. 135.

32. "A Surging New Spirit," *Time Magazine*, July 11, 1988, pp. 46-76.

33. Quoted in Shirley and Shirley, p. 88.

34. Carl Shirley and Paula Shirley, Understanding Chicano Literature (Columbia: University of South Carolina Press, 1988), pp. 41-48. This book has a fine bibliography of surveys and original works in Chicano literature.

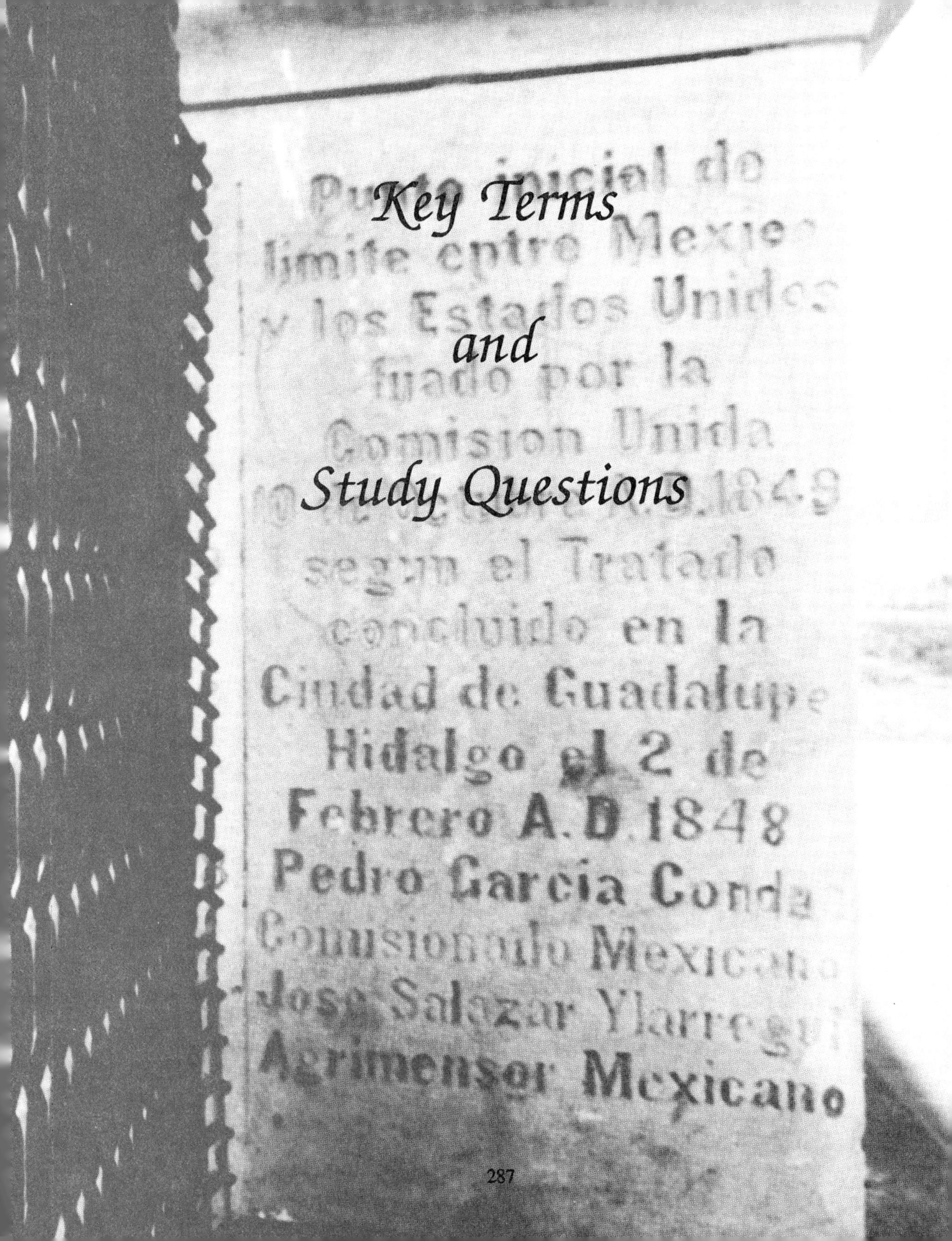

Key Terms and Study Questions

The Treaty of Guadalupe Hidalgo

Discussion Questions

1. Discuss the significance of Article V.

2. What does Article VIII assert with regard to the citizenship of Mexicans who remained in the acquired territories?

3. What were the important historical precedents established by Article VIII with regard to citizenship rights for Chicanos?

4. What does Article X (prior to its omission) assert in terms of ownership of Spanish and Mexican land grants?

The Protocol of Querétaro

Discussion Questions

1. Why was the Statement of Protocol necessary?

2. What does the Protocol assert with regard to the legal ownership of Spanish and Mexican land grants?

The United States Courts and the Treaty
Richard Griswold del Castillo

Key Terms

Mintern v. Bower et al.
Asociación de Reclamantes
United States v. Moreno
Botiller v. Dominguez
Cessna v. United States et al.
Article X

Palmer v. United States
Reies López Tijerina
McKinney v. Saviego
Tenorio v. Tenorio
Texas Mexican Rail Road v. Locke

Discussion Questions

1. In what ways did the courts interpret the treaty liberally during the 1848-1889 period?

2. In what ways was the conservative interpretation of the treaty evident during the 1889-1930 period?

3. What was the significance of the *Botiller v. Dominguez* Supreme Court decision?

4. How did Reies López Tijerina use the treaty?

The Lost Land
John R. Chávez

Key Terms

californios

El Clamor Público

Francisco P. Ramírez

Foreign Miners' Tax Law of 1850

Tiburcio Vásquez

Land Law of 1851

El bejareño

nuevomexicanos

El Horizonte

Juan N. Cortina

Miguel Antonio Otero I

Miguel A. Otero II

Casimiro Barela

Francisco Perea

Discussion Questions

1. What were the various impacts of the California gold rush on the *californios*?

2. What was the Land Law of 1851? What impact did it have on the *californio* land base?

3. Why did numerous *nuevomexicanos* oppose statehood in 1889?

4. Why was Miguel A. Otero considered a progressive?

5. How did Casimiro Barela reflect the interests of the traditionalists?

Race, Labor, and the Frontier
David Montejano

Key Terms

patrón-peón

vaqueros

ex-*peón*

Catarino Garza

rancheros

hacendado

"race situation"

Discussion Questions

1. Why was southern Texas attractive to ex-*peónes* and black slaves during the middle of the 19th century?

2. Discuss the various methods utilized to secure stable Mexican labor.

3. What was the "race situation?"

4. How did landed Mexicans complicate the "race situation?"

5. How did the pattern of land acquisitions contradict American notions of "fair play" and egalitarianism?

6. How did the railroad accelerate Americanization of the region?

Race and Class in a Southwestern City:
The Mexican Community of Tucson, 1854-1941
Thomas E. Sheridan

Key Terms

Alianza Hispano-Americana
Tucsonenses
"institutionalized subordination"
"geographic dualization"

Ramón Soto
Lingua franca
mutualistas
La Liga Protectora Latina

Discussion Questions

1. Discuss the Mexican contribution to the early settlement and development of southern Arizona.

2. How did the arrival of the railroad in 1880 alter the southern Arizona economy?

3. How did the Tucson occupational structure reveal the subordination of the Mexican working class?

4. What does Sheridan mean by "institutionalized subordination?"

5. How did residence patterns reveal subordination?

6. Discuss the various methods utilized by Mexicans to resist subordination.

El Partido del Pueblo Unido

Robert J. Rosenbaum

Key Terms

Las Gorras Blancas
Juan José Herrera
Lorenzo López
Court of Private Land Claims
La Voz
El Sol de Mayo

"los hombres pobres"
Félix Martínez
Thomas Catron
"los extranjeros"
El Sol

Discussion Questions

1. In what ways was El Partido a coalition of diverse political interests?

2. Why did El Partido support creation of the Court of Private Land Claims?

3.How did the Billy Green incident contribute to the polarization of two political factions?

4. What are the various factors which account for the demise of El Partido?

An Essay on Understanding the Work Experience of Mexicans, 1900-1930

Douglas Monroy

Discussion Questions

1. What are the various factors which account for employment instability for Mexican workers during this time?

2. Why were urban industrial occupations more attractive to Mexican workers?

3. In what ways did urban industrial occupations disrupt the traditional Mexican family unit?

4. In what ways did urban industrial occupations often produce generational conflicts?

Responses to Mexican Immigration: 1910-1930
Ricardo Romo

Key Terms

1917 Immigration Act   *enganchadores*
Restriction League

Discussion Questions

1. Discuss the role played by Mexican labor in the growth of Southwestern agriculture and industry.

2. Why did Congress exclude Mexican immigration from provisions of the 1917 Immigration Act?

3. What measures did the Mexican government take in an attempt to stem the flow of immigration to the United States?

4. Why did organized labor generally oppose Mexican immigration at this time?

El Primer Congreso Mexicanista de 1911:
A Precursor to Contemporary Chicanismo
José E. Limón

Key Terms

Nicasio Idar

La Crónica

Liga Feminil Mexicanista

Orden Caballeros de Honor

Raza Unida Party

Discussion Questions

1. What were some of the oppressive social conditions facing Tejanos at this time?

2. How did *La Crónica* note oppressive conditions in Texas schools?

3. In what ways was the "nationalistic style" of the Congreso shown?

4. Compare and contrast the English-language press coverage and the Spanish-language press coverage.

5. List Congreso issues which are similar to Chicano movement ones.

Chicano Political Development:
Historical Considerations
Christine M. Sierra

Key Terms

Treaty of Guadalupe Hidalgo

League of United Latin American Citizens (LULAC)

El Partido Liberal Mexicano (PLM)

El Congreso de Pueblos que Hablan Español

La alianza Hispano Americana

Luisa Moreno

mutualistas

El Congreso Mexicanista

"reserve army of labor"

Discussion Questions

1. What is meant by "people of conquest?"

2. In what ways was Mexican immigration distinct from that of other ethnic groups?

3. Why does sociologist Rodolfo Alvarez regard the first massive population movements from Mexico as "migrants?"

4. What does Sierra mean by "reserve army of labor?"

5. What was "strategic" about the importation of Mexican labor?

6. Why were *mutualistas* necessary for Mexicans?

The Urbanization of Southwestern Chicanos in the Early Twentieth Century

Ricardo Romo

Key Terms

"structural urbanization"
vecindad
Orden Hijos de America
Club Ortiz Politico Social
"behavioral urbanization"

"internal spacial structure"
colonia
Alianza Hispano Americana
corridos

Discussion Questions

1. Name the characteristics of southwestern urban centers that attracted Chicano settlement at this time.

2. What specific factors encouraged southwestern economic development during the early decades of the twentieth century?

3. What specific factors compelled Chicanos to migrate to urban centers at this time?

4. What factors contributed to the construction of the internal spacial structure of most southwestern cities?

5. How does Romo define "behavioral urbanization?" List examples.

6. In what ways did increased urbanization impact on Chicanas/Mexicanas in the work force?

Closing America's Back Door
Abraham Hoffman

Key Terms

Repatriation
1917 Immigration Act
repatriados

Quota Act of 1924
"LPC"

Discussion Questions

1. Why did some U.S. interests favor the restriction of Mexican immigration?

2. Which interest groups opposed the restriction of Mexican immigration? Why?

3. What methods were utilized to encourage Mexicans to voluntarily return to Mexico?

4. How did the Mexican government attempt to accommodate the *repatriados*?

Mexican American Labor and the Left:
The Asociación Nacional México Americana, 1949-1954
Mario García

Key Terms

Progreso   Alfredo C. Montoya
McCarren Act   McCarthyism

Discussion Questions

1. How did ANMA's version of Mexican American history differ from LULAC's?

2. How did ANMA analyze race and class issues?

3. How did ANMA encourage internationalism?

4. In what ways did ANMA promote the preservation of Mexican culture?

5. In what ways was ANMA the target of harassment and political persecution?

The Militant Challenge:
The Chicano Generation
Carlos Muñoz Jr.

Key Terms

Ernesto Galarza

Mexican American Political Association (MAPA)

National Farm Worker Association (NFWA)

Rodolfo "Corky" González

César Chávez

Mexican American Youth Organization (MAYO)

United Mexican American Students (UMAS)

Mexican American Student Confederation (MASC)

Luis Valdez

Ralph Guzmán

José Angel Gutiérrez

Reies López Tijerina

Sal Castro

TWLF

I Am Joaquín

Discussion Questions

1. In what ways did the Mexican American generation promote assimilation and political accommodation?

2. How did the Valdez/Rubalcava manifesto of 1964 represent a radical departure from Mexican American thought?

3. In what ways did *I Am Joaquín* represent the newly emerging Chicano thought?

4. Why was the 1968 student strike significant?

5. What were the various issues addressed by Chicano youth at this time?

Latinos and the "New Immigrants" Since 1975
Richard Griswold del Castillo

Key Terms

Southwest Voter Registration Project (SWVRP)   Latino
Mexican American Legal Defense and Education Fund (MALDEF)   Chicano
National Association of Latino Elected and Appointed Officials (NALEO)
San Antonio School District v. Rodríguez   U. S. English
Gloria Molina   Henry Cisneros   *Doe v. Plyler*
Xavier Suárez   Federico Peña   Bob Martínez
Toney Anaya   *Lau v. Nichols*
Simpson-Mazzoli bill   Immigration Reform and Control Act (IRCA)

Discussion Questions

1. What variables impacted on the way resident Chicanos responded to the new immigration?

2. In what ways were Latinos viewed as a market for commercial products?

3. Name and discuss two impediments to Latino electoral progress?

4. In what ways have Latinos influenced the direction of modern American popular culture?

Contributors

John R. Chávez is an associate professor of history at Southern Methodist University. He did his undergraduate work at California State University, Los Angeles and received his Ph.D from the University of Michigan. He has written several articles and a book, *The Lost Land: The Chicano Image of the Southwest*, that was nominated for a Pulitzer Prize. A second book, *Eastside Landmark: A History of the East Los Angeles Community Union* is forthcoming.

Mario T. García is professor of History and Chicano Studies at the University of California, Santa Barbara. He received his Ph.D. from the University of California, San Diego. His publications include *Desert Immigrants: The Mexicans of El Paso, 1880-1929* (Yale University Press, 1981); *Mexican Americans: Leadership, Ideology, and Identity, 1930-1960* (Yale University Press, 1989); and *Memories of Chicano History: The Life and Narrative of Bert Corona* (forthcoming, 1994, The University of California Press). His awards include a Guggenheim fellowship in 1992-93.

Richard Griswold del Castillo is a Professor of Mexican American Studies at San Diego State University. He received his Ph.D. in History, with an emphasis on Chicano and U.S. history, from the University of California, Los Angeles. He has served as a consultant for a variety of film and publication projects and is active in promoting the inclusion of Chicano history within the school curriculum. He is the author of three major books: *The Los Angeles Barrio* (UC Press, 1980), *La Familia: Chicano Urban Families in the Southwest* (Notre Dame, 1984) and *The Treaty of Guadalupe Hidalgo* (University of Oklahoma Press, 1990). Currently he is collaborating on a biography of Cesar Chavez as well as a college level textbook history of Chicanos.

Abraham Hoffman is author of *Unwanted Mexican Americans in the Great Depression*.

José E. Limón is Professor of English and Anthropology at the University of Texas at Austin. He received his Ph.D. in Anthropology from the same institution. He has held post-doctoral research fellowships at UCLA, UC Berkeley and Stanford University. He is also the author of two books: *Mexican Ballads, Chicano Poems: History and Influence in Mexican American Social Poetry*, (University of California Press, 1992) and *Dancing with the Devil: Society and Cultural Poetics in Mexican American South Texas* (University of Wisconsin Press, 1994).

Douglas Monroy is Associate Professor of History and W.M. Keck Foundation Director of the Hulbert Center for Southwest Studies at The Colorado College. A native of Los Angeles and a graduate of UCLA he presently lives in Colorado Springs with his two children. Author of *Thrown among Strangers: The Making of Mexican Culture in*

Frontier California (University of California Press, 1990), an Organization of American Historians prize winner, he is presently at work on a book about twentieth century Mexican Southern California.

David Montejano is Associate Professor of History and Sociology at the University of Texas at Austin. Montejano received his Ph.D. at Yale University. He he has received numerous awards and honors including the prestigious Frederick Jackson Turner Award in American History for his work, *Anglos and Mexicans in the Making of Texas, 1836-1986*. He has also received Post-Doctoral Fellowships from the National Endowment for the Humanities and the Rockefeller Foundation. He is currently working on a book entitled, *Chicano Politics and Society*.

Carlos Muñoz Jr. is currently a Professor in the Department of Ethnic Studies at the University of California, Berkeley. He received his Ph.D. from the Claremont Graduate School. He is author of *Youth, Identity, Power: The Chicano Movement*, winner of the Gustavus Myers award.

Ricardo Romo is currently Professor of History at the University of Texas at Austin. He received his Ph.D. in History from the University of California, San Diego and is author of *East Los Angeles: History of a Barrio*.

Robert J. Rosenbaum received his Ph.D. in American History from the University of Texas at Austin. He is now a Special Assistant to the Commissioner of the Texas General Land Office. He is author of *Mexican Americans in Texas* and *Mexicano Resistance in the Southwest: "The Sacred Right of Self-Preservation."*

Thomas E. Sheridan is Associate Curator of Ethnohistory at the Arizona State Museum in Tucson. Dr. Sheridan received his Ph.D. in anthropology from the University of Arizona. His books include *Los Tucsonenses: The Mexican Community in Tucson, 1854-1941* and *Where the Dove Calls: The Political Ecology of a Peasant Corporate Community in Northwestern Mexico*. He is past director of the Mexican Heritage Project at the Arizona Historical Society and is currently completing a history of Arizona.

Christine M. Sierra received her Ph.D. from Stanford University in Political Science and is currently Associate Professor of Political Science at the University of New Mexico, Albuquerque. She has received numerous fellowships including the Ford Foundation Fellowship for Minorities and numerous awards and research grants.

The Editor

Michael R. Ornelas received his B.A. and M.A. degrees in History from the University of California, Santa Barbara. He is Professor of Chicano Studies at San Diego Mesa College, San Diego, California. He also studied Southwestern History as a fellow of the National Endowment for the Humanities at the University of Arizona, Tucson. He is also editor of *Between the Conquests: Readings in Early Chicano History.*